Azure for Architect

Second Edition

Implementing cloud design, DevOps, containers, IoT, and serverless solutions on your public cloud

Ritesh Modi

BIRMINGHAM - MUMBAI

Azure for Architects
Second Edition

Copyright © 2019 Packt Publishing

Commissioning Editor: Vijin Boricha
Acquisition Editor: Shrilekha Inani
Content Development Editor: Abhishek Jadhav
Technical Editor: Aditya Khadye
Copy Editor: Safis Editing
Project Coordinator: Jagdish Prabhu
Proofreader: Safis Editing
Indexer: Priyanka Dhadke
Graphics: Tom Scaria
Production Coordinator: Shraddha Falebhai

First published: October 2017
Second edition: January 2019

Production reference: 1310119

Published by Packt Publishing Ltd.
Livery Place
35 Livery Street
Birmingham
B3 2PB, UK.

ISBN 978-1-78961-450-3

www.packtpub.com

`mapt.io`

Mapt is an online digital library that gives you full access to over 5,000 books and videos, as well as industry leading tools to help you plan your personal development and advance your career. For more information, please visit our website.

Why subscribe?

- Spend less time learning and more time coding with practical eBooks and videos from over 4,000 industry professionals

- Improve your learning with Skill Plans built especially for you

- Get a free eBook or video every month

- Mapt is fully searchable

- Copy and paste, print, and bookmark content

Packt.com

Did you know that Packt offers eBook versions of every book published, with PDF and ePub files available? You can upgrade to the eBook version at `www.packt.com` and, as a print book customer, you are entitled to a discount on the eBook copy. Get in touch with us at `customercare@packtpub.com` for more details.

At `www.packt.com`, you can also read a collection of free technical articles, sign up for a range of free newsletters, and receive exclusive discounts and offers on Packt books and eBooks.

Contributors

About the author

Ritesh Modi is an ex-Microsoft Senior Technology Evangelist. He is Microsoft Regional Director as well as Regional lead for Microsoft Certified Trainers.

He is an architect, a senior evangelist, cloud architect, published author, speaker, and a known leader for his contributions towards blockchain, Ethereum, data centers, Azure, bots, cognitive services, DevOps, artificial intelligence, and automation. He is the author of five books.

He has spoken at more than 15 conferences including TechEd and PowerShell Asia, and is a published author for MSDN magazine. He has more than a decade of experience in building and deploying enterprise solutions for customers. He has more than 25 technical certifications.

I have personally grown into a person who has more patience, perseverance, and tenacity while writing this book. I must thank the people who mean the world to me. I am talking about my mother, Bimla Modi, my wife, Sangeeta Modi, and my daughter, Avni Modi. I also thank the Packt team for their support.

About the reviewers

Kasam Shaikh, a Microsoft Azure enthusiast, is a seasoned professional with a can-do attitude and 10 years of industry experience working as a cloud architect with one of the leading IT companies in Mumbai, India. He is a certified Azure architect, recognized as an MVP by a leading online community, as well as a global AI speaker, and has authored books on Azure Cognitive, Azure Bots, and Microsoft Bot frameworks. He is head of the Azure India (az-INDIA) community, the fastest growing online community for learning Azure.

Alexey Bokov is experienced cloud architect, worked for Microsoft as Azure Technical Evangelist and Senior Engineer since 2011 helping software developers all around the world to develop applications based on Azure platform. Main area of interests is security in cloud and especially security and data protection for containerized applications.

Packt is searching for authors like you

If you're interested in becoming an author for Packt, please visit authors.packtpub.com and apply today. We have worked with thousands of developers and tech professionals, just like you, to help them share their insight with the global tech community. You can make a general application, apply for a specific hot topic that we are recruiting an author for, or submit your own idea.

Table of Contents

Preface

Over the years, Azure cloud services have grown quickly, and the number of organizations adopting Azure for their cloud services has also been on the increase. Leading industry giants are discovering that Azure fulfills their extensive cloud requirements.

This book starts with an extensive introduction to all the categories of designs available with Azure. These design patterns focus on different aspects of the cloud, including high availability and data management. Gradually, we move on to various other aspects, such as building your cloud deployment and architecture. Every architect should have a good grasp of some of the important architectural concerns related to any application. These relate to high availability, security, scalability, and monitoring. They become all the more important because the entire premise of the cloud is dependent on these important concerns. This book will provide architects with all the important options related to scalability, availability, security, and the monitoring of **Infrastructure of a Service (IaaS)** as well as **Platform as a Service (PaaS)** deployments. Data has become one of the most important aspects of cloud applications. This book covers the architecture and design considerations for deploying **Online Transaction Processing (OLTP)** applications on Azure. Big data and related data activities, including data cleaning, filtering, formatting, and using **Extract-Transform-Load** (ETL) services are provided by the Azure Data Factory service. Finally, serverless technologies are gaining a lot of traction with their orchestration using Azure Logic Apps. This will also be covered comprehensively in this book.

By the end of this book, you will be able to develop a fully-fledged Azure cloud instance.

Who this book is for

If you are a cloud architect, DevOps engineer, or developer who wants to learn about key architectural aspects of the Azure cloud platform, then this book is for you.

Prior basic knowledge of the Azure cloud platform is good to have.

What this book covers

Chapter 1, *Getting Started*, introduces the Azure cloud platform. It provides details regarding IaaS and PaaS and provides an introduction to some of the important features that help in designing solutions.

Chapter 2, *Azure Solution Availability and Scalability*, takes you through an architect's perspective for deploying highly available and scalable applications on Azure.

Chapter 3, *Security and Monitoring*, helps you to understand how security is undoubtedly the most important non-functional requirement for architects to implement.

Chapter 4, *Cross-Subscription Deployments Using ARM Templates*, explains how ARM templates are the preferred mechanism for provisioning resources.

Chapter 5, *ARM Templates – Modular Design and Implementation*, focuses on writing modular, maintainable, and extensible Azure Resource Manager (ARM) templates.

Chapter 6, *Designing and Implementing Serverless Solutions*, focuses on providing an explanation of the serverless paradigm, Azure Functions, and their capabilities.

Chapter 7, *Azure Integration Solutions*, is a continuation of the previous chapter, continuing the discussion on Serverless technologies, covering Azure Event Grid as part of serverless events, and Azure Logic Apps as part of Serverless workflows.

Chapter 8, *Cost Management*, focuses on calculating the cost of deployment on Azure using the Azure cost calculator. It also demonstrates how changing the location, size, and type of resources affects the cost of solutions and provides best practices for reducing the overall cost of Azure deployments.

Chapter 9, *Designing Policies, Locks, and Tags*, helps you to understand the best practices for implementing policies and locks, and how both can work together to provide complete control over Azure resources.

Chapter 10, *Azure Solutions Using Azure Container Services*, sheds some light on numerous services, including Azure Container Services, Azure Container Registry, and Azure Container Instances for hosting containers, as well managing them using orchestration services such as Kubernetes.

Chapter 11, *Azure DevOps*, is about adopting and implementing practices that reduce risk considerably and ensure that high-quality software can be delivered to the customer.

Chapter 12, *Azure OLTP Solutions Using Azure SQL Sharding, Pools, and Hybrid*, focuses on various aspects of using the transaction data store, such as Azure SQL, and other open source databases typically used in OLTP applications.

Chapter 13, *Azure Big Data Solutions Using Azure Data Lake Storage and Data Factory*, focuses on big data solutions on Azure. We will study Data Lake Storage, Data Lake Analytics, and Data Factory.

Chapter 14, *Azure Stream Analytics and Event Hubs*, concerns the creation of solutions for these events. It focuses on reading these events, storing and processing them, and then making sense of them.

Chapter 15, *Designing IoT Solutions*, covers topics related to IoT Hub, Stream Analytics, Event Hubs, registering devices, device-to-platform conversion, and logging and routing data to appropriate destinations.

To get the most out of this book

This book assumes a basic level of knowledge of cloud computing and Azure. To use this book, all you need is a valid Azure subscription and internet connectivity. A Windows 10 OS with 4 GB of RAM is sufficient for using PowerShell and executing ARM templates.

Download the example code files

You can download the example code files for this book from your account at www.packt.com. If you purchased this book elsewhere, you can visit www.packt.com/support and register to have the files emailed directly to you.

You can download the code files by following these steps:

1. Log in or register at www.packt.com.
2. Select the **SUPPORT** tab.
3. Click on **Code Downloads & Errata**.
4. Enter the name of the book in the **Search** box and follow the onscreen instructions.

Once the file is downloaded, please make sure that you unzip or extract the folder using the latest version of:

- WinRAR/7-Zip for Windows
- Zipeg/iZip/UnRarX for Mac
- 7-Zip/PeaZip for Linux

The code bundle for the book is also hosted on GitHub at https://github.com/PacktPublishing/Azure-for-Architect-Second-Edition. In case there's an update to the code, it will be updated on the existing GitHub repository.

We also have other code bundles from our rich catalog of books and videos available at https://github.com/PacktPublishing/. Check them out!

Conventions used

There are a number of text conventions used throughout this book.

`CodeInText`: Indicates code words in text, database table names, folder names, filenames, file extensions, pathnames, dummy URLs, user input, and Twitter handles. Here is an example: "Browse to the extracted `*.ova` file for Kali Linux and click **Open**."

A block of code is set as follows:

```
html, body, #map {
  height: 100%;
  margin: 0;
  padding: 0
}
```

When we wish to draw your attention to a particular part of a code block, the relevant lines or items are set in bold:

```
[default]
exten => s,1,Dial(Zap/1|30)
exten => s,2,Voicemail(u100)
exten => s,102,Voicemail(b100)
exten => i,1,Voicemail(s0)
```

Any command-line input or output is written as follows:

```
$ mkdir css
$ cd css
```

Bold: Indicates a new term, an important word, or words that you see on screen. For example, words in menus or dialog boxes appear in the text like this. Here is an example: "Select **System info** from the **Administration** panel."

Warnings or important notes appear like this.

Tips and tricks appear like this.

Get in touch

Feedback from our readers is always welcome.

General feedback: If you have questions about any aspect of this book, mention the book title in the subject of your message and email us at customercare@packtpub.com.

Errata: Although we have taken every care to ensure the accuracy of our content, mistakes do happen. If you have found a mistake in this book, we would be grateful if you would report this to us. Please visit www.packt.com/submit-errata, selecting your book, clicking on the Errata Submission Form link, and entering the details.

Piracy: If you come across any illegal copies of our works in any form on the internet, we would be grateful if you would provide us with the location address or website name. Please contact us at copyright@packt.com with a link to the material.

If you are interested in becoming an author: If there is a topic that you have expertise in, and you are interested in either writing or contributing to a book, please visit authors.packtpub.com.

Reviews

Please leave a review. Once you have read and used this book, why not leave a review on the site that you purchased it from? Potential readers can then see and use your unbiased opinion to make purchase decisions, we at Packt can understand what you think about our products, and our authors can see your feedback on their book. Thank you!

For more information about Packt, please visit packt.com.

1
Getting Started

Every few years, there are technological innovations that change the entire landscape and ecosystem around them. If we go back in time, the 70s and 80s were the time of mainframes. They were huge, occupying large rooms, and almost all computing work was carried out by them. It was difficult to procure one and it was also time-consuming. Enterprises used to order months in advance, before they could have an operational mainframe set up.

The first part of the 90s was the era of personal computing and the internet. Computers became much smaller in size and were comparatively easier to procure. Continuous innovation on the personal computing and internet fronts changed the entire computer industry. People had a desktop through which they could run multiple programs and could connect to the internet. The rise of the internet also propagated the rise of client-server deployments. Now, there could be centralized servers hosting applications and services that could be reached by anyone who had a connection to the internet anywhere on the globe. This was also when server technology gained a lot of prominence. Windows NT was released during this time and was followed by Windows 2000 and Windows 2003 at the turn of the century.

The most remarkable innovation of the 2000s was the rise and adoption of portable devices, especially smartphones, and with them came a plethora of apps. Apps could connect to centralized servers on the internet and could carry out business as normal. Users were no longer dependent on browsers to make this work. All servers were typically either self-hosted or hosted with a service provider, such as an **Internet Service Provider (ISP)**.

Users did not have much control over their servers. Multiple customers and their deployments were part of the same server, even without customers knowing about it.

However, there was something else happening toward the middle and later parts of the first decade of the 2000s. This was the rise of cloud computing, and it again rewrote the entire landscape of the IT industry. Initially, adoption was slow and people approached it with caution, either because the cloud was in its infancy and yet had to mature, or because people had various negative notions about what it was.

We will cover the following topics in the chapter:

- Cloud computing
- IaaS, PaaS, and SaaS
- Understanding Azure
- Azure Resource Manager
- Virtualization, Containers, and Docker
- Interacting with the intelligent cloud

Cloud computing

Today, cloud computing is one of the most promising upcoming technologies and enterprise—no matter how big or small, almost every companies and organization has adopted it as a part of their IT strategy. It is difficult these days to have any meaningful conversation about an IT strategy without including cloud computing in the overall solution discussions.

Cloud computing, or simply the cloud in layman terms, refers to the availability of resources on the internet. These resources are made available to users on the internet as services. For example, storage is available on demand through the internet to users for them to store their files, documents, and so on. Here, storage is a service provided by a cloud provider.

A cloud provider is an enterprise or consortium of companies that provide cloud services to other enterprises and consumers. They host and manage the services on behalf of the user. They are responsible for enabling and maintaining the health of services. Typically, there are large data centers across the globe opened by cloud providers to cater to IT demands from users.

Cloud resources consist of hosting services on on-demand infrastructure, such as compute, network, and storage facilities. This flavor of the cloud is known as **Infrastructure as a Service**.

Advantages of cloud computing

Cloud adoption is at an all-time high and is further growing because of the advantages it provides. Some of these advantages are mentioned here:

- **Pay-as-you-go**: Customers do not need to purchase hardware and software for cloud resources. There is no capital expenditure for using cloud resource. Customers just pay for the resource for the time they are used.
- **Global access**: Cloud resources are available globally via the internet. Customers can access their resources on demand from any where.
- **Unlimited resources**: The scale of the cloud is unlimited. Customers can provision as many resources as they want, without any constraints. This is also known as unlimited scalability.
- **Managed Services**: The cloud provides numerous services that are managed by the cloud provider for customers. This takes away the technical and financial burdens from customers.

Deployment Patterns in Azure

There are three different deployment patterns available on Azure. They are

- Infrastructure as a Service (also popularly known as IaaS)
- Platform as a Service (also popularly known as PaaS)
- Software as a Service (also popularly known as SaaS)

The difference between these three deployment patterns is the level of control exercised by customer viz-a-viz Azure. The next image shows different levels of control within each of these deployment patterns.

Iaas	Paas	Saas
Applications	Applications	Applications
Data	Data	Data
Runtime	Runtime	Runtime
Middleware	Middleware	Middleware
OS	OS	OS
Virtualization	Virtualization	Virtualization
Servers	Servers	Servers
Storage	Storage	Storage
Networking	Networking	Networking

Managed by Consumer
Managed by Vendor

Cloud services- IaaS, PaaS, SaaS

It is clear from the previous image that customers have more control using IaaS deployments and it keeps reducing from PaaS to SaaS deployments.

Infrastructure as a Service

IaaS is a deployment types in which customer provision their own infrastructure on Azure. Azure provides infrastructure resources and customers can provision them on demand. Customer are responsible for maintaining and governing their infrastructure. Azure will ensure to maintain the physical infrastructure on which these virtual infrastructure resources are hosted. Under this approach, customers needs active management and operations on the Azure environment.

Platform as a Service

PaaS takes away infrastructure deployments and control from customer. This is a higher level abstraction compared to infrastructure as service. In this approach, customers bring their application, code and data and deploy them on Azure provided platform. These platform are managed and governed by Azure and customer are responsible solely for their application. Customers perform activities related to their applications deployment only. This model provides faster and easier options for deployment of applications compared to infrastructure as a service.

Software as a Service

SaaS is a level higher abstraction compared to PaaS. In this approach, software and its services are available for end user consumption. Customer bring only their data into these services. Customers do not have any control over these services.

Understanding Azure

Azure provides all the benefits of the cloud, while being open and flexible. Azure supports a variety of operating systems, languages, tools, platforms, utilities, and frameworks. It supports both Linux and Windows, SQL Server, MySQL, PostgreSQL and more, as well as C#, Python, Java, Node.js, Bash, and other languages; MongoDB and DocumentDB NoSQL databases, and Jenkins to VSTS as continuous integration tools. The whole idea behind this ecosystem is to enable users to have their choice and freedom of language, their choice of platform and operating system, their choice of database, their choice of storage, and their choice of tools and utilities. Users should not be constrained from the technology perspective; instead, they should be able to build and focus on their business solution, and Azure provides them with a world-class technology stack. Azure is compatible with the user's choice of technology stack.

For example, Azure supports all popular (open source or commercial) database environments. Azure provides Azure SQL, MySQL, and Postgres PaaS services. It provides a Hadoop ecosystem and offers HDInsight, a 100% Apache Hadoop-based PaaS. It also provides a Hadoop on Linux virtual machine implementation for customers who prefer the IaaS approach. Azure also provides a Redis cache service and supports other popular database environments, such as MongoDB, Couchbase, Oracle, and many others as an IaaS implementation.

The number of services is increasing by the day, and the following diagram displays the rich set of services provided by Azure. Not all services are shown here, and the list keeps on growing. The most updated list of services can be found at `https://azure.microsoft.com/en-in/services/`.

Azure also provides a unique cloud computing paradigm—the hybrid cloud. The hybrid cloud refers to a deployment strategy in which a subset of services are deployed on a public cloud, while other services are deployed in an on-premise private cloud or data center. There is a **Virtual Private Network (VPN)** connection between both the public and private cloud. Azure provides users the flexibility to divide and deploy their workload on both the public cloud and an on-premise data center.

Azure has data centers across the globe. Azure combines these data centers into regions. Each region has multiple data centers to ensure that recovery from disasters is quick and efficient. At the time of writing, there are 38 regions across the globe. This provides users the flexibility to deploy their services at their choice of location and region. They can also combine these regions to deploy a solution that is disaster-resistant and deployed near their customer base.

 In China and Germany, the Azure cloud is separate for general use and for governmental use. This means that the cloud services are maintained in separate data centers.

Azure as an intelligent cloud

Azure provides infrastructure and services to ingest millions and billions of transactions with hyper-scale processing. It provides multi-petabytes of storage for data. It provides a host of inter-connected services that can pass data between themselves. With such capabilities in place, data can be processed to generate meaningful knowledge and insights. There are multiple types of insights that can be generated through data analysis, which are as follows:

- **Descriptive**: This kind of analysis provides details about what is happening or has happened in the past.
- **Predictive**: This kind of analysis provides details about what is going to happen in the near-future or the future.

- **Prescriptive**: This kind of analysis provides details about what should be done to either enhance or prevent the current or future events happening.
- **Cognitive**: This actually executes the actions determined by prescriptive analytics in an automated manner.

While deriving insights from data is good, it is equally important to act on them. Azure provides a rich platform to ingest large volume of data, process and transform it, eventually store and generate insights from them, and display them on real-time dashboards. It is also possible to take action on the insights automatically. These services are available to every user of Azure and provide a rich ecosystem on which to create solutions. Enterprises are creating applications and services that are completely disrupting industries because of the easy availability of these intelligent services from Azure that are easily combined to create meaningful value to end customers. Azure ensures that services that are commercially unviable to implement by small and medium companies can now be readily consumed and deployed in a few minutes.

Azure Resource Manager

Azure Resource Manager (**ARM**) is the technology platform and orchestration service from Microsoft that ties up all components discussed earlier. It brings Azure resource providers, resources, and resource groups together to form a cohesive cloud platform. It helps in the registration of resource providers to subscriptions and regions; it makes the resource types available to resource groups; it makes the resource and resource APIs accessible to the portal and other clients; and it authenticates access to resources. It also enables features such as tagging, authentication, **Role-Based Access Control** (**RBAC**), resource locking, and policy enforcement for subscriptions and its resource groups. It provides the same deployment and management experience, whether through a portal or client-based tools such as PowerShell or a command-line interface.

The ARM architecture

The architecture of ARM and its components are as shown in the following diagram. As we can see in the following figure, **Azure Subscription** comprises multiple resource groups. Each resource group contains resource instances that are created from resource types available in the resource provider:

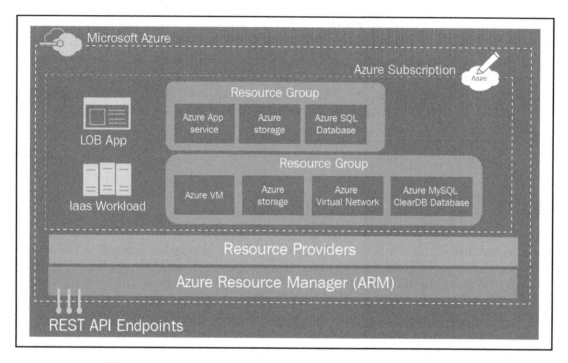

Azure Resource Manager architecture

Limitations of Azure Service Manager (ASM)

ASM has inherent constraints, and some of the major ones are discussed here: ASM deployments are slow and blocking. Operations are blocked if an earlier operation is already in progress. Some of the limitations to ASM are mentioned here:

- **Parallelism**: Parallelism is a challenge in ASM. It is not possible to execute multiple transactions successfully in parallel. The operations in ASM are linear and executed one after another. Either there are parallel operation errors or they will get blocked.
- **Resources**: Resources in ASM are provisioned and managed in isolation from each other; there is no relation between ASM resources. Grouping services and resources or configuring them together is not possible.
- **Cloud services**: Cloud services are the unit of deployment in ASM. They are reliant on affinity groups and not scalable due to their design and architecture.

Granular and discreet roles and permissions cannot be assigned to resources in ASM. Users are either service administrators or co-administrators in the subscription. They either get full control over resources or do not have access to them at all. ASM provides no deployment support. Deployments are either manual or you will need to resort to writing procedural scripts in PowerShell or .NET. ASM APIs are not consistent between resources.

ARM advantages

ARM provides distinct advantages and benefits over ASM, which are as follows:

- **Grouping**: ARM allows grouping of resources together in a logical container. These resources can be managed together and go through a common life cycle as a group. This makes it easier to identify related and dependent resources.
- **Common life cycle**: Resources in a group have the same life cycle. These resources can evolve and be managed together as a unit.
- **Role-Based Access Control**: Granular roles and permissions can be assigned to resources providing discreet access to users. Users can also have only those rights that are assigned to them.
- **Deployment support**: ARM provides deployment support in terms of templates enabling DevOps and **Infrastructure as Code (IAC)**. The deployments are faster, consistent, and predictable.

- **Superior technology**: Cost and billing of resources can be managed as a unit. Each resource group can provide their usage and cost information.
- **Manageability**: ARM provides advanced features, such as security, monitoring, auditing, and tagging, for better manageability of resources. Resources can be queried based on tags. Tags also provide cost and billing information for resources tagged similarly.
- **Migration**: Easier migration and updating of resources within and across resource groups.

ARM concepts

With ARM, everything in Azure is a resource. Examples of resources are virtual machines, network interfaces, public IP addresses, storage accounts, and virtual networks. ARM is based on concepts related to resource providers and resource consumers. Azure provides resources and services through multiple resource providers that are consumed and deployed in groups.

Resource providers

These are services that are responsible for providing resource types through ARM. The top-level concept in ARM is resource providers. These providers are containers for resource types. Resource types are grouped into resource providers. They are responsible for deploying and managing the resources. For example, a virtual machine resource type is provided by a resource provider called **Microsoft.Compute Namespace**. The REST API operations are versioned to distinguish between them. The version naming is based on the dates on which they are released by Microsoft. It is necessary that a related resource provider is available to a subscription to deploy a resource. Not all resource providers are available to a subscription out of the box. If a resource is not available in the subscription, you need to check whether the required resource provider is available in each region. If it is available, the user can explicitly register in the subscription.

Resource types

These are an actual resource specification defining their public API interface and implementation. They implement the working and operations supported by the resource. Similar to resource providers, resource types also evolve over time with regard to their internal implementation and have multiple versions of their schema and public API interface. The version names are based on the dates that they are released by Microsoft as a preview or **General Availability (GA)**. The resource types become available to a subscription after a resource provider is registered to it. Also, not every resource type is available in every Azure region. The availability of a resource is dependent on the availability and registration of a resource provider in an Azure region and must support the API version needed for provisioning it.

Resource groups

Resource groups are a unit of deployment in ARM. They are containers grouping multiple resource instances in a security and management boundary. A resource group is uniquely named in a subscription. Resources can be provisioned on different Azure regions and yet belong to the same resource group. Resource groups provide additional services to all the resources within it. Resource groups provide metadata services, such as tagging, which enables the categorization of resources, policy-based management of resources, RBAC, protection of resources from accidental deletion or updates, and more. As mentioned before, they have a security boundary, and users that don't have access to a resource group cannot access resources contained within it. Every resource instance needs to be part of a resource group or else it cannot be deployed.

Resource and resource instances

Resources are created from resource types and should be unique within a resource group. The uniqueness is defined by the name of the resource and its type together. In OOP parlance, resource instances can be referred to as objects, while resource types can be referred to as a class. The services are consumed through the operations supported and implemented by resource instances. They define properties that should be configured before usage. Some are mandatory properties, while others are optional. They inherit the security and access configuration from its parent resource group. These inherited permissions and role assignments can be overridden for each resource. A resource can be locked in such a way that some of its operations can be blocked and not made available to roles, users, and groups even though they have access to it. They can be tagged for easy discoverability and manageability.

ARM features

The following are some of the major features provided by ARM:

- **Role-Based Access Control**: **Azure Active Directory** (**AAD**) authenticates users to provide access to subscriptions, resource groups, and resources. ARM implements OAuth and RBAC within the platform, enabling authorization and access control for resources, resource groups, and subscriptions based on roles assigned to a user or group. A permission defines access to operations on a resource. These permissions could allow or deny access to the resource. A role definition is a collection of these permissions. Roles map AAD users and groups to the permissions. Roles are subsequently assigned to a scope, which can be an individual, collection of resources, resource group, or subscription. The AAD identities (users, groups, and service principles) added to a role gain access to the resource according to permissions defined in the role. ARM provides multiple out-of-the-box roles. It provides system roles, such as **owner**, **contributor**, and **reader**. It also provides resource-based roles, such as SQL DB contributor and virtual machine contributor. ARM allows the creation of custom roles.

- **Tags**: Tags are name-value pairs that add additional information and metadata to resources. Both resources and resource groups can be tagged with multiple tags. Tags help in the categorization of resources for better discoverability and manageability. Resources can be quickly searched and identified easily. Billing and cost information can be fetched for resources that have the same tags. While this feature is provided by ARM, an IT administrator defines its usage and taxonomy with regard to resources and resource groups. Taxonomy and tags, for example, can relate to departments, resource usage, location, projects, or any other criteria deemed fit from a cost, usage, billing, or search perspective. These tags can then be applied to resources. Tags defined at the resource group level are not inherited by its resources.

- **Policies**: Another security feature provided by ARM is policies. Custom policies can be created to control access to resources. Policies are defined conventions and rules and must be adhered to while interacting with resources and resource groups. The policy definition contains an explicit denial of actions on resources or access to resources. By default, every access is allowed if it is not mentioned in the policy definition. These policy definitions are assigned to resource, resource group, and subscriptions scope. It is important to note that these policies are not replacements or substitutes for RBAC. In fact, they complement and work together with RBAC. Policies are evaluated after a user is authenticated by AAD and authorized by the RBAC service. ARM provides a JSON-based policy definition language for defining policies. Some examples of policy definition are that it must tag every provisioned resource, and resources can only be provisioned to specific Azure regions.
- **Locks**: Subscriptions, resource groups, and resources can be locked to prevent accidental deletion and updates by an authenticated user. Locks applied at higher-levels flow downstream of child resources. Locks applied at the subscription level lock every resource group and the resources within it.
- **Multi-region**: Azure provides multiple regions for provisioning and hosting resources. ARM allows resources to be provisioned at different locations and yet reside within the same resource group. A resource group can contain resources from different regions.
- **Idempotent**: This feature ensures predictability, standardization, and consistency in resource deployment by ensuring that every deployment will result in the same state of resources and configuration, no matter the number of times it is executed.
- **Extensible**: ARM architecture provides an extensible architecture to allow the creating and plugging of new resource providers and resource types into the platform.

Virtualization

Virtualization was a breakthrough innovation that completely changed the way physical servers were looked at. It refers to the abstraction of a physical object into a logical object.

The virtualization of physical servers led to virtual servers known as virtual machines. These virtual machines consume and share the same physical CPU, memory, storage, and other hardware with the physical server on which they are hosted. This enabled faster and easier provisioning of application environments on demand, providing high availability and scalability with reduced cost. One physical server was enough to host multiple virtual machines, each virtual machine containing its own operating system and hosting services on it.

There was no longer any need to buy additional physical servers for deploying new applications and services. The existing physical servers were sufficient to host more virtual machines. Furthermore, as part of rationalization, many physical servers were consolidated into a few with the help of virtualization.

Each virtual machine contains the entire operating system, and each virtual machine is completely isolated from other virtual machines, including the physical hosts. Although a virtual machine uses the hardware provided by the host physical server, it has full control over its assigned resources and its environment. These virtual machines can be hosted on a network such as a physical server with its own identity.

Azure can create Linux and Windows virtual machines in a few minutes. Microsoft provides its own images, along with images from partners and the community. Users can provide their own images. Virtual machines are created using these images.

Containers

Containers are also a virtualization technology; however, they do not virtualize a physical server. Instead, a container is an operating system-level virtualization. What this means is that containers share the operating system kernel, provided by the host, among themselves along with the host. Multiple containers running on a host (physical or virtual) share the host operating system kernel. Containers ensure that they reuse the host kernel instead of each having a dedicated kernel to themselves.

Containers are also completely isolated from the host and other containers, such as a virtual machine. Containers use Windows storage filter drivers and session isolation to isolate operating system services such as the filesystem, registry, processes, and networks. Each container gets its own copy of operating system resources.

The container has the perception that it has a completely new and untouched operating system and resources. This arrangement provides lots of benefits, as follows:

- Containers are fast to provision. They do not need to provide the operating system and its kernel services. They are available from the host operating system.
- Containers are lightweight and require fewer computing resources than virtual machines. The operating system resource overhead is no longer required in containers.
- Containers are much smaller than virtual machines.
- Containers help solve problems related to managing multiple application dependencies in an intuitive, automated, and simple manner.
- Containers provide infrastructure to define all application dependencies in a single place.

Containers are an inherent part and feature of Windows Server 2016 and Windows 10; however, they are managed and accessed using a Docker client and a Docker daemon. Containers can be created on Azure with Windows Server 2016 SKU as an image. Each container has a single main process that must be running for the container to exist. A container will stop when this process ends. Also, a container can either run in interactive mode or in a detached mode like a service.

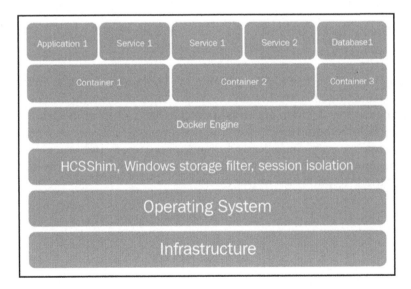

Container architecture

The preceding diagram shows all the technical layers that enable containers. The bottom-most layer provides the core infrastructure in terms of network, storage, load balancers, and network cards. At the top of the infrastructure is the compute layer, consisting of either a physical server, or both physical and virtual servers on top of a physical server. This layer contains the operating system with the ability to host containers. The operating system provides the execution driver that the layers above use to call kernel code and objects to execute containers. Microsoft has created **Host Container System Shim (HCSShim)** for managing and creating containers and uses Windows storage filter drivers for image and file management.

The container environment isolation ability is provided to the Windows session. Windows Server 2016 and Nano Server provide the operating system, enable the container features, and execute the user-level Docker client and Docker engine. The Docker engine uses the services of HCSShim, storage filter drivers, and sessions to spawn multiple containers on the server, each containing a service, application, or database.

Docker

Docker provides management features to Windows containers. It comprises of the following two executables:

- The Docker daemon
- The Docker client

The Docker daemon is the workhorse for managing containers. It is a Windows service responsible for managing all activities on the host related to containers. The Docker client interacts with the Docker daemon and is responsible for capturing inputs and sending them across to the Docker daemon. The Docker daemon provides the runtime, libraries, graph drivers, and engine to create, manage, and monitor containers and images on the host server. It also has the ability to create custom images that are used for building and shipping applications to multiple environments.

Interacting with the intelligent cloud

Azure provides multiple ways to connect, automate, and interact with the intelligent cloud. All methods require users to be authenticated with valid credentials before they can be used. The different ways to connect to Azure are the following:

- Azure Portal
- PowerShell
- Azure **Command-Line Interface (CLI)**
- Azure REST API

Azure Portal

Azure Portal is a great place to get started. With Azure Portal, users can log in and start creating and managing Azure resources manually. The Portal provides an intuitive and user-friendly user interface through the browser. The Azure Portal provides an easy way to navigate to resources using **blades**. The blades display all the properties of a resource, logs, cost, its relationship with other resources, tags, security options, and more. The entire cloud deployment can be managed through the Portal.

PowerShell

PowerShell is an object-based command-line shell and scripting language used for the administration, configuration, and management of infrastructure and environments. It is built on top of the .NET framework and provides automation capabilities. PowerShell has truly become a first-class citizen among IT administrators and automation developers for managing and controlling the Windows environment. Today, almost every Windows and many Linux environments can be managed by PowerShell. In fact, almost every aspect of Azure can also be managed by PowerShell. Azure provides rich support for PowerShell. It provides a PowerShell module for each resource provider containing hundreds of cmdlets. Users can use these cmdlets in their scripts to automate interaction with Azure. The Azure PowerShell module is available through the web platform installer on as well as through the **PowerShell Gallery**. Windows Server 2016 and Windows 10 provide package management and `PowerShellGet` modules for quick and easy downloading, and installation of PowerShell modules from the PowerShell gallery. The `PowerShellGet` module provides the `Install-Module` cmdlet for downloading and installing modules on the system.

Installing a module is a simple act of copying the module files at well-defined module locations that can be done as follows:

```
Import-module PowerShellGet
Install-Module -Name AzureRM -verbose
```

Azure Command-Line Interface (CLI)

Azure also provides Azure CLI 2.0, which can be deployed on Linux, Windows, and Mac operating systems. Azure CLI 2.0 is Azure's new command-line utility for managing Azure resources. Azure CLI 2.0 is optimized for managing and administering Azure resources from the command line, and for building automation scripts that work against the ARM. The CLI can be used to execute commands using Bash Shell or Windows command line. Azure CLI is a very famous among non-Windows users as it allows us to talk to Azure on Linux and Mac. Steps for installing Azure CLI 2 are available at https://docs.microsoft.com/en-us/cli/azure/install-azure-cli?view=azure-cli-latest.

Azure REST API

All Azure resources are exposed to users through REST endpoints. **Representational State Transfer (REST)** APIs are service endpoints that implement HTTP operations (methods), providing **create, retrieve, update,** or **delete (CRUD)** access to the service's resources. Users can consume these APIs to create and manage resources. In fact, the CLI and PowerShell mechanism uses these REST APIs internally to interact with resources on Azure.

ARM templates

In an earlier section, we witnessed deployment features, such as multi-service, multi-region, extensible, and idempotent, provided by ARM. ARM templates are the primary means of provisioning resources in ARM. ARM templates provide implementation support for ARM deployment features.

ARM templates provide a declarative model through which resources, their configuration, scripts, and extensions are specified. ARM templates are based on **JavaScript Object Notation (JSON)** format. They use the JSON syntax and conventions to declare and configure resources. JSON files are text-based, human-friendly, and easily readable files.

They can be stored in a source code repository and have version control. They are also a means to represent IAC that can be used to provision resources in an Azure resource group again and again, predictably, consistently, and uniformly. A template needs a resource group for deployment. It can only be deployed to a resource group and the resource group should exist before executing a template deployment. A template is not capable of creating a resource group.

Templates provide the flexibility to be generic and modular in their design and implementation. Templates provide the ability to accept parameters from users, declare internal variables, define dependencies between resources, link resources within same or different resource groups, and execute other templates. They also provide scripting language type expressions and functions that make them dynamic and customizable at runtime.

Deployments

PowerShell allows the following two modes of deployment of templates:

- **Incremental:** Incremental deployment adds resources declared in the template that don't exist in a resource group, leaves resources unchanged in a resource group that is not part of a template definition, and leaves resources unchanged in a resource group that exists in both the template and resource group with the same configuration state.
- **Complete:** Complete deployment, on the other hand, adds resources declared in a template to the resource group, deletes resources that do not exist in the template from the resource group, and leaves resources unchanged that exist in both the resource group and template with the same configuration state.

Summary

The cloud is not more than 10 years old. It is a new paradigm and still in its nascent stage. There will be a lot of innovation and capabilities added over time. Azure is one of the top cloud providers today and it provides rich capabilities through IaaS, PaaS, SaaS, and hybrid deployments. In fact, the Azure stack, which is an implementation of the private cloud from Microsoft, will be released soon. This will have the same features available on a private cloud as on the public cloud. They both will, in fact, connect and work seamlessly and transparently together.

It is very easy to get started with Azure, but developers and architects can also fall into a trap if they do not design and architect their solutions appropriately. This book is an attempt to provide guidance and directions toward architecting solutions the right way, using appropriate services and resources. Every service on Azure is a resource. It is important to understand how these resources are organized and managed in Azure. This chapter provided context around ARM and groups—the core framework that provides building blocks for resources. It provides a set of services to resources that help provide uniformity, standardization, and consistency in managing them. The services, such as RBAC, tags, policies, and locks, are available to every resource provider and resource. Azure also provides rich automation features to automate and interact with resources. Tools such as PowerShell, ARM templates, and Azure CLI can be incorporated as part of release pipelines and continuous deployment and delivery. Users can connect to Azure from heterogeneous environments using these automation tools.

The next chapter will discuss some of the important architectural concerns that help solve common cloud-based deployment problems and ensure the application is secure, available, scalable, and maintainable in the long run.

Azure Solution Availability and Scalability

2

Architectural concerns, such as high availability and scalability, are some of the highest-priority items for any architect. This is common across many projects and solutions. However, this becomes even more important when deploying applications on the cloud because of the complexity involved. Most of the time, the complexity does not come from the application, but because of the choices available in terms of similar resources on the cloud. The other complex issue that arises from the cloud is the constant availability of newer features. These new features can almost make an architect's architectural decisions completely redundant in hindsight.

In this chapter, we will go through an architect's perspective for deploying highly available, scalable applications on Azure.

Azure is a mature platform providing multiple options for implementing high availability and scalability at multiple levels. It is incumbent on an architect to know them, the differences between them, and the costs involved, and finally choose an appropriate solution that meets the best solution requirements. There is no one solution, but a good one for each project.

Running applications and systems that are available to users for consumption whenever they need them is one of the topmost priorities for CIOs. They want their applications to be operational and functional, and to continue to be available to their customers even when some untoward event happens. This is the theme for this chapter—high availability. *Keeping the lights on* is the common metaphor used for high availability. Achieving high availability for applications is not an easy task, and organizations have to spend considerable time, energy, resources, and money to achieve this. And even when using them, there is still the risk that their implementation will not produce the desired results. Azure provides a lot of high-availability features for virtual machines (**VMs**) and **Platform as a Service (PaaS)** services. In this chapter, we will go through the architectural and design features provided by Azure for ensuring high availability for applications and services.

In this chapter, we will cover the following topics:

- High availability
- Azure high availability
- Architectural considerations for high availability
- Scalability
- Upgrades and maintenance

High availability

High availability is one of the major architectural concerns for any architect. It forms one of the core non-functional technical requirements for any serious service and its deployment. High availability refers to the feature of a service or application that keeps it operational on a continuous basis, meeting or surpassing its promised defined **service level agreement (SLA)**. Users are promised a certain SLA based on service type. The service should be available for consumption based on its SLA. For example, an SLA can have 99% availability for an application for the entire year. This means it should be available for consumption by users for 361.35 days. If it becomes less than this, this constitutes a breach of the SLA. Most mission-critical applications define their high-availability SLA with five nines for a year. This means the application should be up, running, and available throughout the year, but it can only be down and unavailable for 5.2 hours.

It is important to note here that high availability is defined in terms of time—that is, yearly, monthly, weekly, and so on, and it could even be a combination of these.

A service or application is made up of multiple components and these components are deployed on separate tiers and layers. Moreover, it is deployed on an operating system and hosted on a physical machine or VM. It consumes network and storage services for various purposes. It might even be dependent on external systems. For these services or applications to be highly available, it is important that networks, storage, operating systems, VMs or physical machines, and each component of the application is designed with the SLA and high availability in mind. A definite application life cycle process used to ensure high availability should be baked from the start of application planning until its introduction to operations. This also involves introducing redundancy. Redundant resources should be included in the overall application and deployment architecture to ensure that if one goes down, the other takes over and serves the requests of the customer.

SLA

SLA is defined as a service-level agreement. This is an agreement between two or more parties, where one is the customer, and the others are service providers. Particular aspects of the service - quality, availability, and responsibilities - are agreed between the service provider and the service user. The most common component of the SLA is that the services should be provided to the customer as agreed upon in the contract.

Factors affecting high availability

Planned maintenance, unplanned maintenance, and application deployment architecture are the major factors affecting the high availability of an application. We will be looking into each of these factors in the following sections.

Planned maintenance

Planned maintenance refers to the process of keeping the application and its surrounding ecosystem—comprising platforms, frameworks, software, the operating system, and host and guest drivers—up to date with the latest stable releases. It is important to patch software, drivers, and operating systems with the latest updates, since this helps in keeping the environment healthy from a security, performance, and future-ready perspective. Not upgrading an environment is not an option and is a fact of life. Even applications should be upgraded with enhanced functionality, bugs, and hot fixes. Every organization plans for environment and application upgrades, and typically these involve shutting down and restarting the application and operating system. It might also involve starting the physical host operating system, which, in turn, will reboot all guest VMs running on top of it. In Microsoft Azure, you can manage, get notifications and view planned maintenance windows for VMs – please refer to `https://docs.microsoft.com/en-us/azure/virtual-machines/windows/maintenance-notifications` for more detailed information

Unplanned maintenance

As the name suggests, unplanned maintenance refers to maintenance that cannot be planned and is ad hoc in nature. It refers to hardware failures such as storage corruption, network or router failure, power loss, and a host of other failures, due to hardware and software. Bugs in the underlying platform that bring the application down are also part of unplanned maintenance.

Application deployment architecture

Application architecture plays a crucial role in ensuring the high availability of an application. An application whose components are deployed on a single machine is not highly available. When the machine reboots, the application is not available to its users. Similarly, depending on a single instance of a resource can become a single point of failure from a high-availability point of view. Each component of an application should be designed so that it can be deployed on multiple machines, and redundancy should not be a bottleneck. Some software provides features related to high availability and is not dependent on host operating systems or other third-party tools. SQL server availability groups is an example of such features.

High availability versus scalability

High availability is different to scalability, although both are serious architectural concerns. Scalability refers to the flexibility and elasticity to add more resources or reduce resources to existing deployment to accommodate more users than normal without comprising application performance. Scalability indirectly helps in making an application highly available. However, it does not mean scalability eventually leads to high availability. High availability is an architectural concern that is not dependent on the number of users, while scalability rules are determined by a number of users consuming the service. High availability could be a requirement even if there were very few users. High availability is about services being present and operational as and when users demand its consumption. It is a function of consumption based on the SLA.

High availability versus disaster recovery

High availability is again different from disaster recovery; however, the difference can be very subtle. High availability is a function of the application being in a consumable state as and when the user asks for it. So, it is designed for operations that come before a disaster, while disaster recovery is a function that comes into the picture after a disaster. Disaster recovery refers to the architecture implementation through which services are up and running after a disaster, while high availability takes care of availability prior to a disaster. Disaster recovery includes data backup and archived and dormant servers across continents, while high availability consists of load balancers, distribution of load, and active-passive and active-active redundancy.

Azure high availability

Achieving high availability and meeting high SLA requirements is tough. Azure provides lots of features that enable high availability for applications, from the host and guest operating system to applications using its PaaS. Architects can use these features to get high availability in their applications using configuration instead of building these features from scratch or being dependent on third-party tools.

In this section, we will look at the features and capabilities provided by Azure to make applications highly available. Before we get into the architectural and configuration details, it is important to understand Azure's high-availability, related concepts.

Concepts

The fundamental concepts provided by Azure to attain high availability are listed here:

- Availability sets
- Fault domain
- Update domain
- Availability zones

Availability sets

High availability in Azure is primarily achieved through **redundancy**. Redundancy means that there is more than one resource instance, such that in the event of a failure of a resource, the other takes over. But just having more similar resources does not make them highly available. For example, having more than one VM does not make these VMs highly available. Azure provides a resource known as an availability set, and any VM that is associated with it becomes highly available. All VMs in the availability set become highly available because they are placed on separate physical racks in the Azure data center and each VM is updated one at a time, instead of all at the same time. Availability sets provide a fault domain and updates domain to achieve this and this is discussed in the next section. In short, availability sets provide redundancy at a data center level, similar to locally redundant storage.

It is important to note that availability sets provide high availability within a data center. If the entire data center is down, then the availability of the application will be impacted. To ensure that applications are still available even when a data center goes down, Azure introduced a new feature known as **availability zones**, which we will understand in a little while.

Fault domain

When a VM is provisioned and assigned to an availability set, it is assigned a fault domain. With **Azure Resource Manager** (**ARM**), each availability set has two or three fault domains by default, depending on the Azure regions. Some provide two, while others provide three, fault domains in an availability set. Fault domains are non-configurable by users. When multiple VMs are created, they are placed on separate fault domains. If more than five VMs are provisioned on an availability set, they are placed in a round-robin fashion on five fault domains. Fault domains are related to physical racks in the Azure data center. Fault domains provide high availability from unplanned maintenance due to hardware, power, and network failure. Since a single VM is only placed on a rack, other VMs continue running in case the rack in consideration snaps off.

Update domain

A fault domain takes care of unplanned maintenance and an update domain handles planned maintenance. Each VM is also assigned an update domain. There can be as many as 20 update domains in a single availability set. Update domains are non-configurable by users. When multiple VMs are created, they are placed on separate update domains. If more than 20 VMs are provisioned on an availability set, they are placed in a round-robin fashion on these update domains. Update domains take care of planned maintenance.

Availability zones

This is a relatively new concept introduced in Azure and is very similar to zone redundancy for storage accounts. Availability zones provide high availability within a region by placing VM instances on separate data centers within a region. Availability Zones are applicable to VMs, managed disks, VM scale sets, and load balancers. This constituted a gap in Azure for a long time and it was removed recently, from a computing high-availability perspective, which was removed recently.

Each Azure region comprises multiple data centers. Some regions have more data centers, while some could have less; however, there are at least two data centers in every region. These data centers are known as zones. Deploying VMs in an availability zone ensures that those VMs are in different data centers and obviously are on different racks and networks, and so on. These data centers in a region relate to high-speed networks and there is no lag in communication between these VMs.

More information about Availability Zones is available
at `https://docs.microsoft.com/en-us/azure/availability-zones/az-o`
`verview.higher.`

If an application needs higher availability and wants to ensure that it is available even if an entire Azure region is down, the next rung of the ladder for availability is the traffic manager feature, which will be discussed later in this chapter.

Load balancing

Load balancing, as the name suggests, refers to the process of balancing the load among VMs and applications. With one VM, there is no need for the load balancer because the entire load is on a single VM and there is no other VM to share the load. However, with multiple VMs containing the same application and service, it is possible to distribute the load among them through load balancing. Azure provides a couple of resources for enabling load balancing, which are as follows:

- **Load balancers**: The Azure load balancer helps in designing solutions with high availability. Within the TCP stack, it is a layer 4 transport-level load balancer. It is a layer 4 load balancer that distributes incoming traffic among healthy instances of services defined in a load-balanced set. Level 4 load balancers work at a transport level and have network-level information, such as an IP address and port, to decide the target for the incoming request. Load balancers are discussed in detail later in this chapter.

- **Application gateways**: Azure application gateway delivers high availability to your applications. They are a layer 7 load balancer that distribute the incoming traffic among healthy instances of services. Level 7 load balancers can work at the application level and have application-level information such as cookies, HTTP, HTTPS, and sessions for the incoming request. Application gateways are discussed in detail later in this chapter. Application gateways are also used when deploying Azure Kubernetes services specifically for scenarios in which ingress traffic from internet should be routed to Kubernetes services in cluster.

VM high availability

VMs provide compute capabilities. They provide processing power and hosting for applications and services. If the application is deployed on a single VM and that machine is down, then even the application is not available. If the application is composed of multiple tiers and each tier is deployed in its own single instance of a VM, even downtime in a single VM can render the application non-available. Although Azure tries to make even single VM deployments highly available by placing them on different racks as soon as it can, Azure does not ensure or guarantee any SLA. Azure provides an SLA for those VMs that are grouped together in an availability set. It provides a five nines (99.999%) SLA for the availability of VMs if they are part of an availability set and more than two VMs are on that availability set.

Compute high availability

Applications demanding high availability should be deployed on multiple VMs on the same availability set. If applications are composed of multiple tiers, then each tier should have a group of VMs on their dedicated availability set. In short, if there are three tiers of an application, there should be three availability sets and a minimum of six VMs (two in each availability set) to make the entire application highly available.

How does Azure provide an SLA and high availability to VMs in an availability set with multiple VMs in each availability set? This is the question that might be coming to mind.

Here, the use of concepts that we considered before comes into play—fault and update domains. When Azure sees multiple VMs in an availability set, it places those VMs on a separate fault domain. In other words, these VMs are placed on separate physical racks instead of the same rack. This ensures that at least one VM continues to be available even if there is a power, hardware, or rack failure. There are two or three fault domains in an availability set and, depending on the number of VMs in an availability set, the VMs are placed on separate fault domains or repeated in a round-robin fashion. This ensures that high availability is not impacted because of the failure of the rack.

Azure also places these VMs on a separate update domain. In other words, Azure tags these VMs internally in such a way that these VMs are patched and updated one after another, such that any reboot in an update domain does not affect the availability of the application. This ensures that high availability is not impacted because of the VM and host maintenance.

With the placement of VMs in separate fault and update domains, Azure ensures that not all of them are down at the same time and are alive and available for serving requests, even though they might be undergoing maintenance or facing physical downtime challenges:

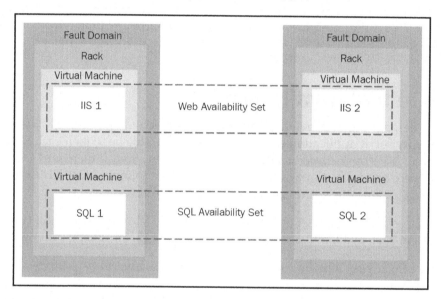

The preceding diagram shows four VMs (two are IIS and two are SQL-related). Both IIS and SQL VMs are part of their availability set. The IIS and SQL VMs are on a separate fault domain and different racks in the data center. They would also be on separate upgrade domains.

The following diagram shows the relationship of fault and update domains.

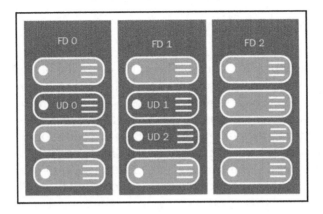

Storage high availability

VMs are backed up by storage accounts by storing their VHD files on them. While availability sets provide high availability to compute instances, they do not ensure the high availability of VHD files for VMs stored in storage accounts. The VHD files for all VMs might be placed on the same storage cluster, and any cluster failure can render all VMs non-available or less available than required. In short, it is not only computed services that need to be highly available, but even storage accounts storing VHD files should be placed on separate clusters such that in the event of failure, at least one or some VMs continue to be available, both from a computer and storage perspective.

Azure provides managed disks and disk management facilities. Managed disks provide better reliability for availability sets by ensuring that the disks of VMs in an availability set are sufficiently isolated from each other to avoid single points of failure. It does this by automatically placing the disks in different storage clusters. If a storage cluster fails due to hardware or software failure, only the VM instances with disks on those stamps fail. Each VM VHD in an availability set should be placed in a separate storage account, although, VMs from different availability sets can be placed in a storage account.

PaaS high availability

Azure provides app services and cloud services for hosting managed platforms. Services and applications can be deployed on top of them. They provide flexibility, elasticity, and economies to create and deploy applications. These platforms are managed by Azure, and users do not interact with the base infrastructure on which they are deployed. They bring in a higher level of abstraction compared to IaaS by letting developers concentrate on their business problem and using the platform to fast-track their development and deployment process. This alleviates them to manage, operate, and monitor the base infrastructure. When an application is deployed in app services or cloud services, Azure provisions VMs that are not visible to users. The applications are deployed on these VMs and the Azure fabric controller is responsible for provisioning, managing, and monitoring them. The fabric controller monitors the status of the hardware and software of the host and guest machine instances. When it detects a failure, it maintains SLAs by automatically relocating the VM instances. When multiple cloud service role instances are deployed, Azure deploys these instances to different fault and update domains:

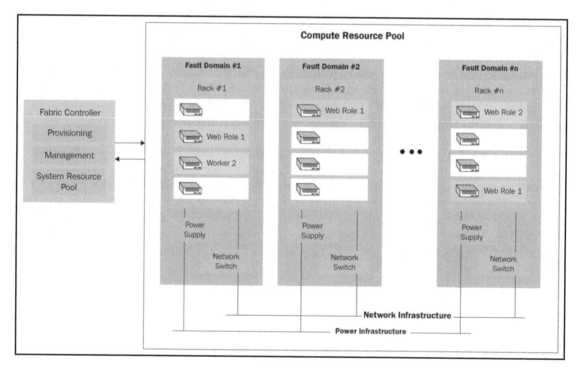

The previous diagram shows PaaS services with multiple VM instances deploying these web and worker roles on separate fault domains. Deploying on separate fault domains means deploying on separate racks within a data center. It also means that these services have separate network switches and power supplies, ensuring that even if one of the racks undergoes maintenance, or there is a disruption in the power supply to the rack or failure of the network switch, there are other instances available to serve customers requests.

High-availability platforms

Azure has introduced a lot of new features in recent times with regard to high availability for PaaS. One of them is related to containers and the ecosystem surrounding them. Azure has introduced the following services:

- Containers in app services
- Azure container instance groups
- Azure Kubernetes services
- Other container orchestrators, such as DC/OS and Swarm

The other important platform that brings high availability is **Service Fabric**. Both Service Fabric and container orchestrators that include Kubernetes ensure that a desired number of application instances are always up and running in an environment. What this means is that even if one of the instances goes down in the environment, the orchestrator will know about it by means of active monitoring and will spin up a new instance on a different node, thereby maintaining the ideal and desired number of instances. It does this without any manual or automated interference from the administrator.

While Service Fabric allows any type of application to become highly available, orchestrators such as Kubernetes, DC/OS, and Swarm are specific to containers. Also, it is important to understand that these platforms provide features that help in rolling updates, rather than a big bank update that might effect the availability of the application.

Data high availability

While VMs, app services, and containers provide high availability to compute, and managed disks provide high availability for storage, we also need to ensure that our data platforms and data is highly available.

Azure provides the following resources that make data highly available.

Azure CosmosDB

Azure CosmosDB is a truly global, highly available geo-replicated NoSQL data store. CosmosDB is available in almost all Azure regions, and it is also possible to configure geo-replication between all of these regions. CosmosDB allows for creating collections that are replicated across multiple regions asynchronously. It also provides flexibility in determining the consistency level, while configuring the replication strategy for high availability. These consistency levels help an architect to determine the criticality of the availability of data in other regions. These consistency levels are as follows:

- **Strong**: This ensures that every replicated region gets its data before returning to the user.
- **Bounded staleness**: This ensures that data is not stale in read regions beyond a point—either a fixed number of writes or a time span.
- **Sessions**: This ensures that data is consistent in a session.
- **Ordered prefixes**: This is when the writes will come to replicated regions in a similar order as they were written in the write region.
- **Eventual**: It is possible to have dirty reads here, and there is no SLA for determining the availability of data. It follows the principle of eventual consistency.

Azure SQL replication

Azure SQL provides the replication of the database to other regions to make them highly available. Replication can be done to any region. However, an architect should choose a peer region for replication. These peer regions are a minimum of 300 miles apart and are still connected with high-speed networks. These peer regions are also patched one at a time, and so there is no risk that the patch will happen in parallel to these regions.

The data in the replicated site can be made read-available to the applications.

Azure table storage

Azure provides table storage, which is a key value data storage in an Azure storage account. Azure maintains three copies of the data and makes them available in times of need. The data is stored in partitions with each partition, identified using a partition key and each row is assigned a RowId. Both the RowID and PartitionID are part of data payload. It provides storage for data without a schema, similar to NoSQL data stores. In fact, NoSQL data can be stored in Azure Tables easily.

A storage account can have multiple tables, and each table stores entities identified using partition and row identifiers.

Application high availability

High availability can be built-in within the software used for applications, or it can be built from the ground up within applications. One example of the high-availability feature provided by software is SQL server always-on availability groups. They help in keeping databases highly available.

Azure services also have a built-in, high-availability mechanism. In Azure SQL, data is replicated synchronously within the region. Active geo-replication allows up to four additional database copies in the same region or different regions. Azure storage has its own mechanism to make data available by replicating it to multiple data centers and regions.

Load balancing

Azure provides two constructs to provision load balancers. It provides a level 4 load balancer that works at the transport layer within the TCP OSI stack, and a level 7 load balancer that works at the application and session level.

Although both application gateways and load balancers provide the basic features of balancing the load, they serve different purposes. There are use cases in which it makes more sense to deploy the application gateway compared to the load balancer.

The application gateway provides the following features that are not available in the Azure load balancers:

- **Web application firewall**: This is an additional firewall on top of the operating system firewall and has the capability to peek into incoming messages. This helps in identifying and preventing common web-based attacks such, as SQL injection, cross-site scripting attacks, and session hijacks.
- **Cookie-based session affinity**: Load balancers distribute incoming traffic to service instances that are healthy and relatively free. A request can be served by any service instance. There are applications that need advance features in which all subsequent requests following the first request should be processed by the same service instance. This is known as cookie-based session affinity. The application gateway provides cookie-based session affinity to keep a user session on the same service instance using cookies.

- **Secure Sockets Layer (SSL) offload**: The encryption and decryption of request and response data is performed by SSL and is generally a costly operation. Web servers should ideally be spending resources on processing and serving requests, rather than encryption and decryption of traffic. SSL offload helps in transferring this cryptography process from the web server to the load balancer, thereby providing more resources to web servers serving users. The request from the user is encrypted, but gets decrypted at the application gateway instead of the web server. The request from the application gateway to the web server is unencrypted.

- **End-to-end SSL**: While SSL offload is a nice feature for a certain application, there are certain mission-critical secure applications that need complete SSL encryption and decryption even if traffic passes through load balancers. An application gateway can be configured for an end-to-end SSL cryptography as well.

- **URL-based content routing**: Application gateways are also useful for redirecting the traffic to different servers based on the URL content of incoming requests. This helps in hosting multiple services alongside other applications.

Azure load balancers

The Azure load balancer distributes incoming traffic based on transport level information available to it. It relies on the following:

- An originating IP address
- A target IP address
- An originating port number
- A target port number
- A type of protocol—TCP or HTTP

Public load balancing

In this configuration, load balancers are assigned a public IP address. Assigning a public IP address ensures that the load balancer can accept requests coming in from the internet. Without a public IP address, it is not possible to access the resource from the internet. The load balancer can be configured with load-balancing rules. Load-balancing rules work at the port level. It accepts a source and destination ports map them together such that whenever a load balancer receives a request for the source port, the request is forwarded to a VM from a group of VMs attached to the load balancer on the destination port. This is shown in the following diagram:

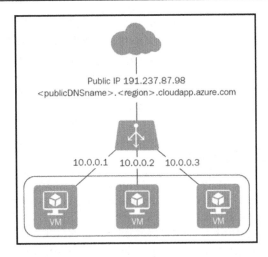

But how does this entire thing work? How is a public IP address assigned to a load balancer? What does the load balancer contain? How is it configured with load balancer rules? How does the load balancer send requests to the VMs? How does the VM know that it is attached to the load balancer? The answers to all these questions are visible in the following diagram:

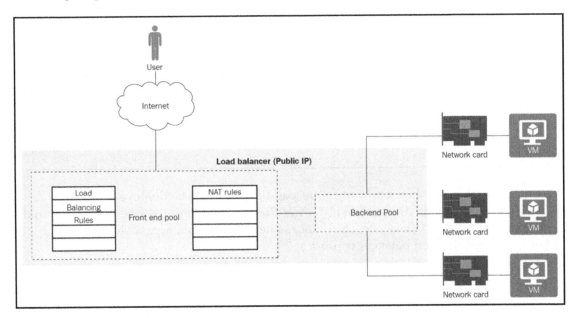

In this configuration, the load balancer is assigned a public IP address. The load balancer is accessible from the internet and can accept client requests. The load balancer can be configured with load-balancing and NAT rules. Both NAT and load-balancing rules are part of the frontend configuration. The frontend configuration sends client requests to one of the IP addresses available in the backend pool. These IP addresses are associated with the network interface card, which, in turn, is attached to VMs.

Internal load balancing

The following diagram shows the workings of an internal load balancer. You can see that the request comes from resources from Azure itself, since it is not accessible on the internet. In this configuration, the load balancer is assigned a private IP address. The load balancer is only accessible within the virtual network to which it is attached. It cannot be accessed through the internet. The remainder of its configuration is similar to a public load balancer. The load balancer can be configured with load-balancing and NAT rules:

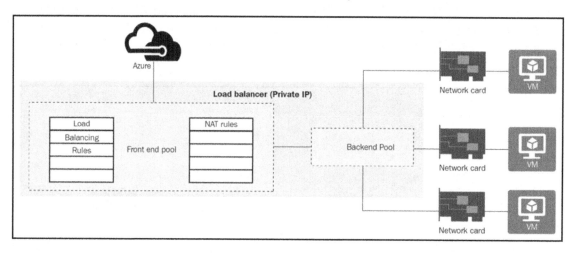

The following diagram shows how multiple load balancers can be deployed to create solutions. In this, there is a public load balancer that accepts client requests and an internal load balancer for the database tier. The database-tier VMs are not accessible on the internet, but only through the load balancer on port `1433`:

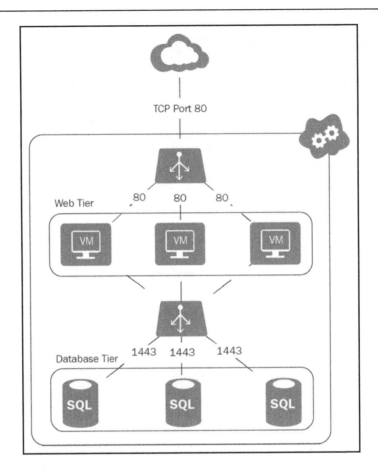

Port forwarding

At times, there is a need for a request to always redirect to a VM. The Azure load balancer helps us achieve this with the NAT rules. NAT rules are evaluated after load-balancing rules are evaluated and none of these rules are satisfied. NAT rules are evaluated for each incoming request and, once it finds them, it forwards the request to that VM through a backend pool. It is to be noted that a VM cannot register the same port for both port forwarding using NAT and load-balancing rules.

Azure application gateway

The Azure load balancer helps us to enable solutions at the infrastructure level. However, there are times when advanced services and features are required from the load balancer itself. These advance services include SSL termination, sticky sessions, advanced security, and more. Azure application gateway are built on top of Azure load balancers to provide these additional features. The Azure application gateway is a level 7 load balancer that works with the application and session payload in a TCP OSI stack.

Application gateways have more information compared to the Azure load balancer to make decisions on request routing and load balancing between servers. Application gateways are managed by Azure and are highly available.

An application gateway sits in between the users and VMs, as shown in the following diagram:

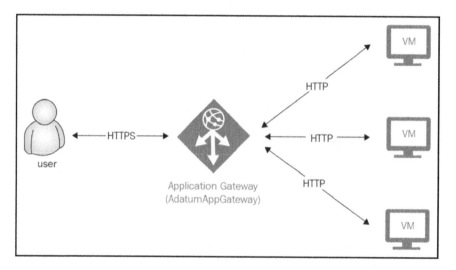

Application gateways are internally implemented using VMs. The **internet information service (IIS)** is installed and configured with **Application Request Routing (ARR)** on these VMs. These gateways can be installed on multiple VMs, providing high availability for the gateways themselves. Although not visible, Azure load balancers distribute loads among multiple application gateway servers. Creating an application gateway requires an internal or public IP address and that is used by users to send requests to it. This public IP or internal IP is provided by the Azure load balancer working at the transport level (TCP/UDP) and having all incoming network traffic being load balanced to the application gateway worker instances. The application gateway then routes the HTTP/HTTPS traffic based on its configuration, whether it's a VM, cloud service, or internal or external IP address.

An application gateway is similar to an Azure load balancer from a configuration perspective, with additional constructs and features. It provides a frontend IP, protocol, certificate, and port configuration, backend pool, port, session affinity, and protocol configuration.

Azure Traffic Manager

After gaining a good understanding of both the Azure load balancer and the application gateway, it's time to get into the details of Traffic Manager. Azure load balancers and application gateways are much-needed resources for high availability within a data center and region; however, to achieve high availability across regions and data centers, there is a need for another resource, and that is Traffic Manager.

Traffic Manager helps us to create highly available solutions that span multiple geographies, regions, and data centers. Traffic Manager is not similar to load balancers. It uses DNS to redirect requests to an appropriate endpoint determined by their health and configuration. Traffic Manager is not a proxy or a gateway. Traffic Manager does not see the traffic passing between the client and the service. It simply redirects the request based on the most appropriate endpoints.

Azure Traffic Manager enables you to control the distribution of traffic across your application endpoints. An endpoint is any internet-facing service hosted inside or outside of Azure.

Endpoints are internet-facing, reachable public URLs. Applications are provisioned within multiple geographies and Azure regions. Applications deployed to each region have a unique endpoint referred by **DNS CNAME**. These endpoints are mapped to the Traffic Manager endpoint. When a Traffic Manager is provisioned, it gets an endpoint by default with a `.trafficmanager.net` URL extension.

When a request arrives at the Traffic Manager URL, it finds the most appropriate endpoint out of its list and redirects the request to it. In short, Traffic Manager acts as a global DNS to identify the region that will serve the request.

However, how does Traffic Manager know which endpoints to use and redirect the client request to? There are two aspects that the Traffic Manager implements to determine the most appropriate endpoint and region.

First, Traffic Manager actively monitors the health of all endpoints. It can monitor the health of VMs, cloud services, and app services. If it determines that the health of an application deployed to a region is not suitable for redirecting traffic, it redirects the requests to a healthy endpoint.

Second, the Traffic Manager can be configured with routing information. There are four traffic routing methods available in Traffic Manager, which are as follows:

- **Priority**: Should be used when all traffic should go to a default endpoint, and backups are available in case the primary endpoints are unavailable.
- **Weighted**: Should be used to distribute traffic across endpoints evenly, or according to defined weights.
- **Performance**: Should be used for endpoints in different regions, and users should be redirected to the closest endpoint based on their location. This has a direct impact on network latency.
- **Geographic**: This should be used to redirect users from a specific geography to an endpoint (Azure, external, or nested) available in that geography or nearest to that geography. Examples include complying with data sovereignty mandates, localization of content and user experience, and measuring traffic from different regions.
- **Subnet**: This is a new routing method added and it helps in providing clients different endpoints based on their IP addresses. In this method, a range of IP addresses are assigned to each endpoint. These IP address ranges are mapped to the client IP address to determine an appropriate returning endpoint. Using this routing method, it is possible to provide different content to different people based on their originating IP address.
- **Multivalue**: This is also a new method added in Azure. In this method, multiple endpoints are returned back to the client and any of them can be used. This ensures that if one endpoint is unhealthy, other endpoints can be used. This helps in increasing the overall availability of the solution.

It should be noted that after the Traffic Manager determines a valid healthy endpoint, clients connect directly to the application.

Architectural considerations for high availability

Azure provides High availability to various means and at various levels. High availability could be at data center level, it could be at a region level, or across Azure. In this section, we will go through some of the architectures for high availability.

High availability within Azure regions

The architecture shown next shows high-availability deployment within a single Azure region. High availability is designed at the individual resource level. In this architecture, as shown in the following diagram, there are multiple VMs at each tier connected through either an application gateway or load balancer, and they are part of an availability set. Each tier is associated with an availability set. These VMs are placed on separate fault and update domains. While the web servers are connected to application gateways, the rest of the tiers, such as application and database tiers, have internal load balancers:

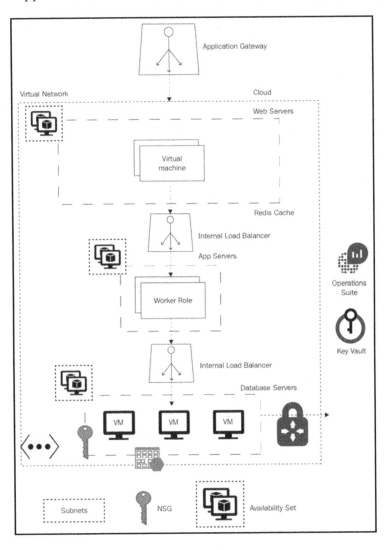

High availability across Azure regions

The architecture shown next shows similar deployments on two different Azure regions. As shown in the diagram, both the regions have the same resources deployed. High availability is designed at the individual resource level within these regions. There are multiple VMs at each tier, connected through the load balancer, and they are part of the availability set. These VMs are placed on separate fault and update domains. While the web servers are connected to external load balancers, the rest of the tiers, such as application and database tiers, have internal load balancers. It should be noted that application load balancers can be used for web servers and application tiers instead of Azure load balancers if there is a need for advanced services, such as session affinity, SSL termination, advance security using WAF, and path-based routing. Databases in both the regions are connected to each other using VNET peering and gateways. This is helpful in configuring log shipping, SQL Server AlwaysOn, and other data synchronization techniques.

The endpoints of load balancers from both the regions are used to configure Traffic Manager endpoints, and traffic is routed based on the priority load balancing method. Traffic Manager helps in routing all requests to the East US region and, after failover, to West Europe in the case of the non-availability of the first region:

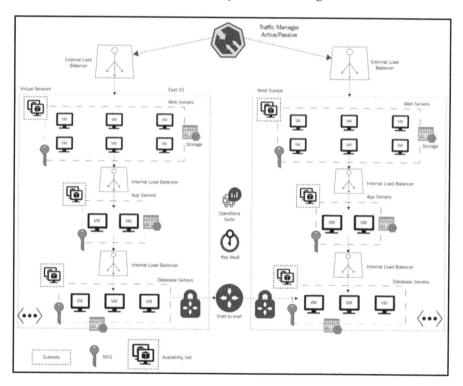

Best practices

This section describes high-availability best practices. They have been categorized into application, deployment, data management, and monitoring.

Application high availability

An application should be built with high availability as one of the most important architectural concerns. Some of the important application-related, high-availability practices are mentioned next:

- An application should implement appropriate exception handling to gracefully recover and inform stakeholders about the issue
- An application should try to perform the same operation again for a fixed interval and a certain number of times before exiting in the event of an error or exception
- An application should have the built-in timeout capability to decide that an exception cannot be recovered from
- Maintaining logs and writing logs for all errors, exceptions, and execution should be adopted within the application
- Applications should be profiled to find their actual resource requirements in terms of compute, memory, and network bandwidth for a different number of users

 Please refer to https://docs.microsoft.com/en-us/azure/ architecture/checklist/availability to learn more about applications and other high-availability best practices.

Deployment

A deployment strategy, to a large extent, affects the availability of the application and overall environment. Here are the few following things you should do:

- Deploy multiple instances of Azure resources, including multiple instances for VMs, cloud services, and other resources.
- Deploy VMs on availability sets or availability zones. They cannot be used together.

- Deploy multiple instances of VMs across multiple regions.
- Create multiple environments and keep at least one of them in standby mode.

Data management

Some of the important data-related best practices for high availability include the following:

- If possible, store data on Azure-provided services, such as Azure SQL, Cosmos DB, and table storage
- Use storage accounts that are based on the geo-redundant type
- Ensure that data is replicated to multiple regions and not only within a zone or data center
- Take periodic backups and conduct restore tests frequently
- If storing data in VMs, ensure that there are multiple VMs and that they are either on availability sets or availability zones
- Use keys and secrets to data stored in the Azure key vault

Monitoring

Some of the important monitoring-related best practices for high availability are as follows:

- Use OMS (log analytics) to monitor the environment and enable log auditing
- Use application insights to capture telemetry information from the custom application and environment related to compute, storage and networks, and other log information
- Ensure alerts are configured on OMS for issues related to the availability of the environment and application
- Visit the Azure monitor frequently to gather recommendations related to high availability

Scalability

Running applications and systems that are available to users for consumption is important for architects of any serious application. However, there is another equally important application feature that is one of the top priorities for architects, and this is the scalability of the application.

Imagine a situation in which an application is deployed and obtains great performance and availability with a few users, but both availability and performance degrades as the number of users start begins to increase. There are times when an application under normal load performs well, but degrades in performance with the increase in the number of users. This can happen if there is a sudden increase in the number of users and the environment is not built for such a large number of users.

To accommodate such spikes in the number of users, you might provision the hardware and bandwidth for handling spikes. The challenge with this is that the additional capacity is not used for a majority of the year and does not provide any return on investment. It is provisioned for use only during the holiday season or sales. I hope you are getting to know the problems architects are trying to solve. All these problems are related to capacity sizing and the scalability of an application. The focus of this chapter is to understand scalability as an architectural concern and to check out services provided by Azure for implementing scalability.

Capacity planning and sizing are a few of the top priorities for architects for their applications and services. Architects must find a balance between buying and provisioning too many resources versus fewer resources. Having fewer resources can lead to not being able to serve all users, turning them to the competition, while having more resources can hurt your budget and return on investment because most of the resources remain unused most of the time. Moreover, the problem is amplified with a varied level of demand during different times. It is almost impossible to predict the number of users for the application round the clock and year. However, it is possible to find an approximate number using past information and continuous monitoring.

Scalability refers to:

> *"Scalability is the capability of a system, network, or process to handle a growing amount of work, or its potential to be enlarged to accommodate that growth. For example, a system is considered scalable if it is capable of increasing its total output under an increased load when resources (typically hardware) are added."*

Scalability refers to the ability to handle a growing number of users and provide them with the same level of performance when there are fewer users in application deployment, processes, and technology. Scalability might refer to serving more requests without degradation of performance, or it might refer to handling larger and more time-consuming work without any loss of performance in both cases.

Capacity planning and sizing exercises should be undertaken by architects at the very beginning of the project during the planning phase to provide scalability to applications.

Some applications have stable demand patterns, while it is difficult to predict others. Scalability requirements are known for stable demand applications, while it is a more involved process for variable demand applications. Auto scaling, a concept we will review in the next section, should be used for such applications whose demands cannot be predicted.

Scalability versus performance

It is quite easy to get confused between scalability and performance architectural concerns , because scalability is all about ensuring that, no matter the number of users consuming the application, all get the same pre-determined level of performance.

Performance relates to application features that ensure that the application caters to predefined response times and throughput. Scalability refers to having provisions for more resources when needed, to accommodate more users without sacrificing performance.

It is better to understand this using an analogy. The speed of a train refers to the performance of railway systems. However, accommodating more trains to run in parallel at the same or a higher speed will be referred to the scalability of the railway network.

Azure scalability

In this section, we will look at the features and capabilities provided by Azure to make applications highly available. Before we get into the architecture and configuration details, it is important to understand Azure's high-availability concepts.

Concepts

The fundamental constructs provided by Azure to attain high availability are as follows:

- Scaling
- Scaling up and down
- Scaling out and in
- Auto scaling
- Rolling updates

Scaling

Scaling refers to the transformation that either increases or decreases the units of resources used to serve requests from users. Scaling can be automatic or manual. Manual scaling requires an administrator to manually initiate the scaling process, while automatic scaling refers to an automatic increase or decrease in resources based on events available from the environment and ecosystem, such as memory and CPU availability. Scaling can be effected up or down, or out and in, which will be explained later in this section.

Scaling up

Scaling up a virtual machine or service refers to the adding of additional resources to existing servers, such as CPU, memory, and disks. Its aim is to increase the capacity of existing physical hardware and resources:

Scaling down

Scaling down a virtual machine or service refers to the removal of existing resources from existing servers, such as CPU, memory, and disks. Its aim is to decrease the capacity of existing physical and virtual hardware and resources.

Scaling out

Scaling out refers to the process of adding additional hardware in terms of additional servers and capacity. This typically involves adding new servers, assigning them IP addresses, deploying applications on them, and making them part of the existing load balancers such that traffic can be routed to them. Scaling out can be automatic or manual as well. However, for better results, automation should be used:

Scaling in

Scaling in refers to the process of removing the existing hardware in terms of existing servers and capacity. This typically involves removing existing servers, de-allocating their IP addresses, and removing them from the existing load balancer configuration such that traffic cannot be routed to them. In the same way as scaling out, scaling in can be automatic or manual.

Auto scaling

Auto scaling refers to the process of either scaling up/down or scaling out/in dynamically based on application demand, and it happens using automation. Auto scaling is helpful because it ensures that deployment always consists of a correct and ideal number of server instances. Auto scaling helps in building applications that are fault tolerant. It not only helps in scalability, but also makes applications highly available. Finally, it provides the best cost management. Auto scaling helps in having the optimal configuration for server instances based on demand. It helps in not over-provisioning servers that are underutilized and removes servers that are no longer required after scaling out.

PaaS scalability

Azure provides app services for hosting managed applications. App services is a PaaS offering from Azure. It provides the web and mobile platform. Behind the web and mobile platform is a managed infrastructure that is managed by Azure on behalf of its users. Users do not see or manage the infrastructure; however, they have the capability to extend the platform and deploy their applications on top of it. With this, architects and developers can concentrate on their business problems instead of worrying about the base platform and infrastructure provisioning, configuration, and troubleshooting. Developers have the flexibility to choose any language, operating system, and framework to develop their applications. App services provide multiple plans and, based on the plans chosen, capabilities of scalability are available. App services provide the following five plans:

- **Free**: This uses shared infrastructure. It means multiple applications will be deployed on the same infrastructure from the same or multiple tenants. It provides 1 GB of storage free of cost. No scaling facility is available in this plan.
- **Shared**: This also uses shared infrastructure and provides 1 GB of storage free of cost. Additionally, custom domains are also provided as an extra feature. No scaling facility is available in this plan.
- **Basic**: This has three different **stock keeping units** (**SKU**)—B1, B2, and B3. They have increasing units of resources available to them in terms of CPU and memory. In short, they provide improved configuration of the VMs backing these services. Additionally, they provide storage, custom domains, and SSL support. The basic plan provides basic features for manual scaling. There is no automatic scaling available in this plan. A maximum of three instances can be used for scaling out the application.
- **Standard**: This also has three different SKUs—S1, S2, and S3. They have increasing units of resources available to them in terms of CPU and memory. In short, they provide improved configuration of the VMs backing these services. Additionally, they provide storage, custom domains, and SSL support similar to the basic plan. This plan also provides a traffic manager, staging slots, and one daily backup as an additional feature on top of the basic plan. The standard plan provides features for automatic scaling. A maximum of 10 instances can be used for scaling out the application.

- **Premium**: This also has three different SKUs—P1, P2, and P3. They have increasing units of resources available to them in terms of CPU and memory. In short, they provide improved configuration of the VMs backing these services. Additionally, they provide storage, custom domains, and SSL support similar to the basic plan. This plan also provides a traffic manager, staging slots, and 50 daily backups as an additional feature on top of the basic plan. The standard plan provides features for automatic scaling. A maximum of 20 instances can be used for scaling out the application.

PaaS – Scaling up and down

Scaling up and down services hosted in app services is quite simple. The Azure app services menu items to scale up, which opens a new blade with all plans and their SKUs listed. Choosing a plan and SKU will scale the service up or down, as shown in the following screenshot:

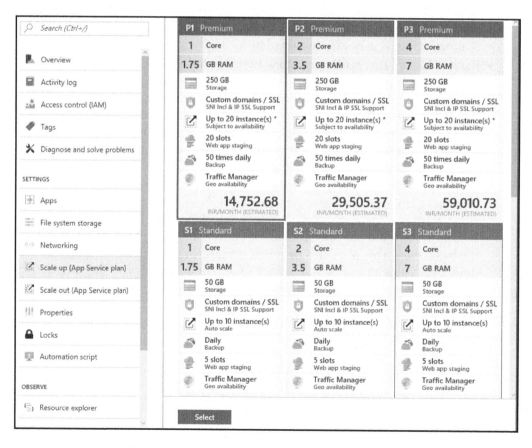

PaaS – Scaling out and in

Scaling out and in services hosted in app services is also quite simple. The Azure app services menu items to scale out, which opens a new blade with scaling configuration options.

By default, auto scaling is disabled for both premium and standard plans. It can be enabled using the **Scale Out** menu item and by clicking on the **Enable autoscale** button, as shown:

Manual scaling does not require configuration but auto scaling helps in configuring with the aid of the following properties:

- **Mode of scaling**: Based on some metric, such as CPU or memory usage or just scale to specify the number of instances.
- **When to scale**: Multiple rules can be added that determine when to scale out and in. Each rule can determine the criteria such as CPU or memory consumption, whether to increase or decrease instances, and how many instances to increase or decrease at a time. At least one rule for scale out and one rule for scale in should be configured. Threshold definitions help in defining the upper and lower limits that should trigger the auto scale—either increase or decrease the number of instances.

- **How to scale**: Specifies how many instances to create or remove in each scale out or in operation:

This is a quite to good feature to enable in any deployment. However readers should enable both scaling out and in together to ensure that the environment is back to normal capacity after scaling out.

IaaS scalability

There are users who want to have complete control over the base infrastructure, platform, and application. They prefer to consume IaaS solutions compared to PaaS solutions. For such customers, when they create VMs, they are also responsible for capacity sizing and scaling. There is no out-of-the-box configuring for manual or auto scaling VMs. These customers will have to write their own automation scripts, triggers, and rules to achieve auto scaling. With VMs comes the responsibility of maintaining them as well. Patching, updating, and the upgrading of VMs is the responsibility of owners. Architects should think about both planned as well as unplanned maintenance. How these VMs should be patched, the order, grouping, and other factors must be thought through to ensure that both the scalability and availability of an application is not compromised. To help alleviate such problems, Azure provides VM scale sets as a solution.

VM scale sets

VM scale sets (**VMSS**) are an Azure compute resource that you can use to deploy and manage a set of identical VMs. With all VMs configured in the same way, scale sets are designed to support true auto scaling, and no pre-provisioning of VMs is required. It helps in provisioning multiple identical VMs connected to each other through a virtual network and subnet.

VMSS consists of multiple VMs, but they are managed at VMSS level. All VMs are part of this unit and any changes made are applied to the unit, which, in turn, applies it to VMs using a pre-determined algorithm:

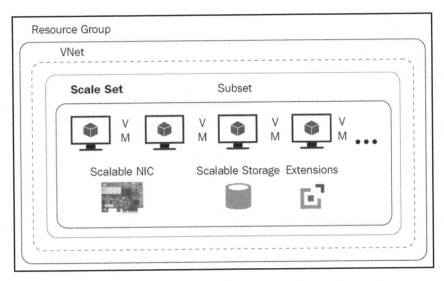

It allows these VMs to be load balanced using the Azure load balancer or application gateways. All the VMs could be either Windows or Linux operating systems. They can run automated scripts using a PowerShell extension and they can be managed centrally using desired state configuration. They can be monitored as a unit and individually using log analytics as well.

VMSS can be provisioned from the Azure portal, Azure command-line interface, Azure resource manager templates, REST APIs, and PowerShell cmdlets. It is possible to invoke REST APIs and Azure CLI from any platform, environment, and operating system, and in any language.

Already, a lot of Azure services use VMSS as its underlying architecture. Among them are Azure Batch, Azure Service Fabric, and Azure container services. Azure container services, in turn, provision Kubernetes and DC/OS on these VM scale sets.

VMSS architecture

VMSS allows for the creation of up to 1,000 VMs in a scale set when using a platform images and 100 VMs if using a custom image. If the number of VMs is less than 100 in a scale set, they are placed in a single availability set; however, if they are greater than 100, multiple availability sets are created, known as placement groups, and VMs are distributed among these availability sets. We know from the last chapter that VMs in an availability set are placed on separate fault and update domains. Availability sets related to VMSS have five fault and update domains by default. VMSS provides a model that holds metadata information for the entire set. Changing this model and applying changes impacts all VM instances. This information includes maximum and minimum VM instances, the operating system SKU and version, the current number of VMs, fault and update domains, and more. This is demonstrated in the following diagram:

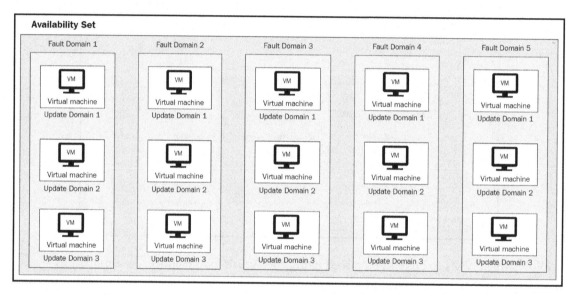

VMSS scaling

Scaling refers to an increase or decrease in compute and storage resources. VMSS is a feature-rich resource that makes scaling easy and efficient. It provides auto scaling, which helps in scaling up or down based on external events and data such as CPU and memory usage. Some of the VMSS scaling features are mentioned as follows.

Horizontal versus vertical scaling

Scaling can be horizontal or vertical, or both. Horizontal scaling is another name for scaling out and in, while vertical scaling is about scaling up and down.

Capacity

VMSS have a capacity property that determines the number of VMs in a scale set. VMSS can be deployed with zero as a value for this property. It will not create a single VM; however, if you provision VMSS by providing a number for the capacity property, that number of VMs are created.

Auto scaling

Automatic scaling of VMs in VMSS refers to the addition or removal of VM instances based on configured environments to meet the performance and scalability demands of an application. Generally, in the absence of VMSS, this is achieved using automation scripts and runbooks.

VMSS helps in this automation process with the help of configuration. Instead of writing scripts, VMSS can be configured for automated scaling up and down.

Auto scaling consists of multiple integrated components to achieve its end goal. Auto scaling continuously monitors the VMs and collects telemetry data from them. It stores this data combines it and then evaluates it against a set of rules to determine whether it should trigger the auto scale. The trigger could be to scale out or scale in. It could also be to scale up or down.

Auto scale uses diagnostic logs for collecting telemetry data from VMs. These logs are stored in storage accounts as diagnostic metrics. Auto scale also uses the insight monitoring service that reads these metrics, combines them together, and stores them in their own storage account.

Auto scale background jobs run continually to read the insights' storage data, evaluate them based on all the rules configured for auto scaling, and execute the process of auto scaling, should any of the rules or combination of rules return positive. The rules can take into consideration metrics from guest VMs as well as the host server.

The rules defined using the property descriptions are available at `https:/ /docs.microsoft.com/en-us/azure/virtual-machine-scale-sets/ virtual-machine-scale-sets-autoscale-overview`.

The auto scale architecture is shown in the following diagram:

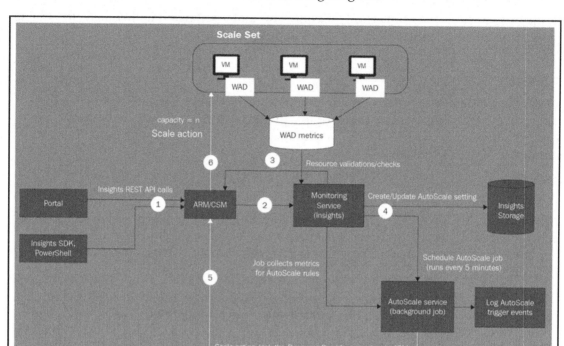

Auto scale can be configured for scenarios that are more complex than general metrics available from environments. For example, scaling could be based on any of the following:

- Scaling on a specific day
- Scaling on a recurring schedule such as weekends
- Scaling differently on weekdays and weekends
- Scaling during holidays, that is, one of the events
- Scaling on multiple resource metrics

These can be configured using the schedule property of insight resources that help in registering rules.

Architects should ensure that at least two actions—scale out and scale in—are configured together. Scaling in or scaling out configuration will not help in achieving the scaling benefits provided by VMSS.

Upgrades and maintenance

After VMSS and applications are deployed, they need to be actively maintained. Planned maintenance should be conducted periodically to ensure that both the environment and application is up to date with the latest features, and the environment is current from a security and resilience point of view.

Upgrades can be associated with applications, the guest VM instance, or the image itself. Upgrades can be quite complex because they should happen without affecting the availability, scalability, and performance of environments and applications. To ensure that updates can take place one instance at a time using rolling upgrade methods, it is important that VMSS supports and provides capabilities for these advanced scenarios.

There is a utility provided by the Azure team to manage updates for VMSS. It's a Python-based utility that can be downloaded from `https://github.com/gbowerman/vmssdashboard`. It makes REST API calls to Azure to manage scale sets. This utility can be used for starting, stopping, upgrading, and re-imaging VMs on a fault domain or group of VMs, as shown in the following screenshot:

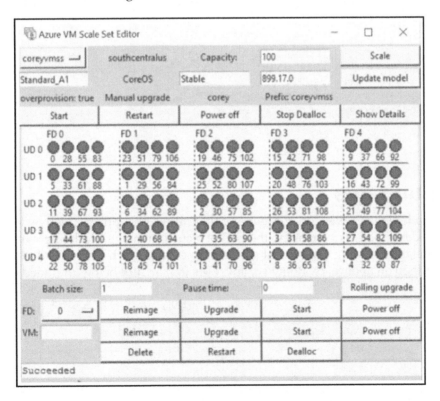

Application updates

Application updates in VMSS should not be executed manually. They must be executed as part of release management and pipelines using automation. Moreover, the update should happen one application instance at a time, not affecting the overall availability and scalability of the application. Configuration management tools, such as the desired state configuration, should be deployed to manage application updates. The DSC pull server can be configured with the latest version of the bits and they should be applied on a rolling basis to each instance.

Guest updates

Updates to VM are the responsibility of administrator. Azure is not responsible for patching guest VMs. Guest updates are in preview mode and users should control patching manually or using custom automation such as runbooks and scripts. However, rolling patch upgrades are in preview mode and can be configured in the ARM template using the upgrade policy, as shown here:

```
"upgradePolicy": {
"mode": "Rolling",
"automaticOSUpgrade": "true" or "false",
  "rollingUpgradePolicy": {
    "batchInstancePercent": 20,
    "maxUnhealthyUpgradedInstanceCount": 0,
    "pauseTimeBetweenBatches": "PT0S"
  }
}
```

Image updates

VMSS can update the OS version without any downtime. OS updates involve changing the version or SKU of the OS or changing the URI of a custom image. Updating without downtime means updating VMs one at a time or in groups (such as one fault domain at a time) rather than all at once. By doing so, any VMs that are not being upgraded can keep running.

Best practices of scaling provided by VMSS

In this section, we will go through some of the best practices that applications should implement to take advantage of the scalability capability provided by VMSS.

The preference for scaling out

Scaling out is a better scaling solution compared to scaling up. Scaling up or down means resizing VM instances. When a VM is resized, it generally needs to be restarted, which has its own disadvantages. First, there is downtime for the machine. Second, if there are active users connected to the application on that instance, they might face the unavailability of the application, or they might even have lost transactions. Scaling out does not impact existing VMs. It provisions newer machines and adds them to the group.

Bare-metal versus dormant instances

Scaling new instances can take two broad approaches: creating the new instance from scratch, which means to install applications, configure, and test, or start the dormant, sleeping instances when they are needed due to scalability pressure on other servers.

Configuring the maximum and minimum number of instances appropriately

Setting a value of two for both the minimum and maximum instance count, with the current instance count being two, means no scaling action can occur. There should be an adequate margin between the maximum and minimum instance counts, which are inclusive. Auto scale always scales between these limits.

Concurrency

Applications are designed for scalability to focus on concurrency. Applications should use asynchronous patterns to ensure that client requests do not wait indefinitely to acquire resources if resources are busy serving other requests. Implementing asynchronous patterns in code ensures that threads do not wait for resources and systems are exhausted of all available threads. Applications should implement the concept of timeouts if intermittent failures are expected.

Stateless

Applications and services should be designed to be stateless. Scalability can become a challenge to achieve with stateful services, and it is quite easy to scale stateless services. With states comes the requirement for additional components and implementations, such as replication, centralized or decentralized repository, maintenance, and sticky sessions. All these are impediments on the path to scalability. Imagine a service maintaining an active state on a local server. No matter the number of requests on the overall application or on the individual server, the subsequent requests must be served by the same server. Subsequent requests cannot be processed by other servers. This makes scalability implementation a challenge.

Caching and CDN

Applications and services should take advantage of caching. Caching helps eliminate multiple subsequent calls to either databases or filesystems. This helps in making resources available and free for more requests. The **Content Distribution Network (CDN)** is another mechanism for caching static files such as images and JavaScript libraries. They are available on servers across the globe. They also make resources available and free for additional client requests. This makes applications highly scalable.

N+1 design

N+1 design refers to building redundancy within the overall deployment for each component. It means to plan for some redundancy even when it is not required. It could mean additional VMs, storage, and network interface cards.

Summary

High availability and scalability are important and crucial architectural concerns. Almost every application and every architect tries to implement high availability. Azure is a mature platform that understands the need for these architectural concerns in applications and provides resources to implement them at multiple levels. These architectural concerns are not an afterthought, and should be part of the application life cycle development, starting from the planning phase itself.

3
Security and Monitoring

Security is undoubtedly the most important non-functional requirement for architects to implement. Enterprises prioritize and provide extreme focus on getting their security strategy implemented correctly. In fact, security is one of the top concerns for almost every stakeholder in an application's development, deployment, and management. It becomes all the more important when the same application is built for deployment to the cloud.

The following topics will be covered in this chapter:

- Security
- Monitoring
- Azure Monitoring
- Application Insights
- Log Analytics
- Executing Runbooks on Alerts
- Integrating PowerBI

Security

Running applications and systems that are available to users for consumption is an important consideration for architects of any serious application. However, there is another equally important application feature that is one of the top priorities for architects, and this is the scalability of applications. Imagine situations in which applications are deployed and obtain great performance and availability with a few users, but both availability and performance suffer as users start increasing. Another situation could be when the application is performant and available, with a large number of users, but there is a certain time of the day or week, or there are special events during which the number of users spikes, and you cannot gauge or predict the number of users. Extending the previous situation, you might have provisioned the hardware and bandwidth for handling users during these occasions when there are spikes, but most of the time, the additional hardware is not used and does not provide any return on investment. They are provisioned for use only during peak times. I hope you are realizing the problems architects are trying to solve. All these problems are related to the capacity, sizing, and scalability of an application. The focus of this chapter is on scalability as an architectural concern, and it details the features provided by Azure to address these concerns.

Securing an application means not allowing unknown and unauthorized entities to access it. It also means that communication with the application is secure and not tampered with. This includes the following:

- **Authentication**: Authentication refers to establishing the identity of a user and ensuring that the given identity can access the application or service. Authentication is performed in Azure using **OpenID Connect**.
- **Authorization**: Authorization refers to allowing and establishing permissions that an identity can perform within the application or service. Authorization is performed in Azure using OAuth.
- **Confidentiality**: Confidentiality refers to the communication between the user and the application being secure. The payload exchange between entities is encrypted so that it will make sense only to the sender and receiver, but not otherwise. Confidentiality of messages is performed using symmetric and asymmetric encryption. Certificates are used to implement cryptography; that is, the encryption and decryption of messages.

- **Integrity**: Integrity ensures that the payload and message exchange between sender and receiver is not tampered with. The receiver receives the same message that's sent by the sender. Digital signatures and hashes are the implementation mechanisms to check the integrity of incoming messages.

Security is a partnership between the service provider and the service consumer. Both parties have different levels of control over deployment stacks, and each should implement security best practices to ensure that all threats are identified and mitigated. We already know from Chapter 1, *Getting Started*, that the cloud broadly provides three paradigms—IaaS, PaaS, and SaaS—each having different levels of collaborative control over the deployment stack. Each party should implement security practices for components under its control and within its ambit. Failure to implement security at any layer in the stack or by any party would make the entire deployment and application vulnerable to attack.

Security life cycle

Security is generally regarded as a non-functional requirement for a solution. However, with the growing number of cyber-attacks, it is considered a functional requirement these days.

Every organization follows some sort of application life cycle management for their applications. When security is treated as a functional requirement, it should follow the same process of application development. Security should not be an afterthought; it should be part of the application from the beginning. Within the overall planning phase for an application, security should also be planned. Depending on the nature of the application, different kinds and categories of threats should be identified, and based on these identifications, they should be documented in terms of approach and scope to mitigate them. A threat modeling exercise should be undertaken to illustrate the threat each component could be subjected to. This will lead to designing security standards and policies for the application. This is typically the security design phase. The next phase is called the **threat mitigation** or **build** phase. In this phase, the implementation of security in terms of code and configuration is executed to mitigate the security threats and risks.

A system cannot be secure until it is tested. Appropriate penetration tests and other security tests should be performed to identify potential threat mitigation that has not been implemented, or has been overlooked. The bugs from testing are remediated and the cycle continues throughout the life of the application. This process of application life cycle management, as shown in the following diagram, should be followed for security:

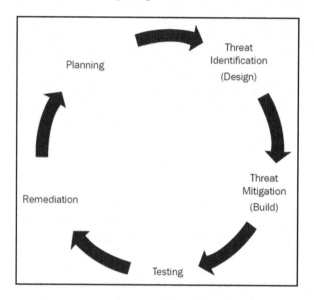

Threat modeling, identification, mitigation, testing, and remediation are iterative processes that continue even when an application or service is operational. There should be active monitoring of entire environments and applications to proactively identify threats and mitigate them. Monitoring should also enable alerts and audit logs to help in reactive diagnosis, troubleshooting, and the elimination of threats and vulnerabilities.

The security life cycle of any application starts with the planning phase, which eventually leads to the design phase. In the design phase, the application's architecture is decomposed into granular components with discrete communication and hosting boundaries. Based on their interaction with other components within and across hosting boundaries, threats are identified. Identified threats are mitigated by implementing appropriate security features within the overall architecture and testing to identify whether the identified vulnerability still exists. After the application is deployed to production and becomes operational, it is monitored for any security breaches and vulnerabilities, and either proactive or reactive remediation is conducted.

Microsoft provides complete guidance and information about the security life cycle, available at https://www.microsoft.com/en-us/securityengineering/sdl/practices.

Azure security

Azure provides all its services through data centers in multiple regions. These data centers are interconnected within regions, as well as across regions. Azure understands that it hosts mission-critical and important applications, services, and data for its customers. It must ensure that security is of the utmost importance for its data centers and regions. Customers deploy applications to the cloud based on their trust that Azure will protect their applications and data from vulnerabilities and breaches. Customers will not move to the cloud if this trust is broken, and hence, Azure implements security at all layers, as seen in next diagram, from the physical perimeter of data centers to logical software components. Each layer is protected, and even the Azure data center team does not have access to them.

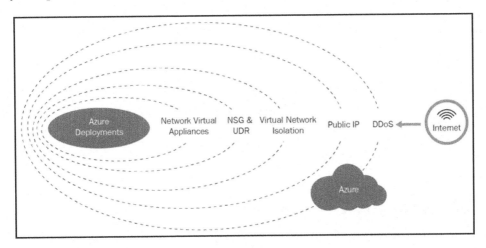

Security is of paramount importance to both Microsoft and Azure. Azure is a cloud platform hosted by Microsoft. Microsoft ensures that trust is built with its customers, and it does so by ensuring that its customer deployment, solutions, and data are completely secure, physically and virtually. People will not use any cloud platform if it is not physically and digitally secure. To ensure that customers have trust in Azure, each activity in the development of Azure is planned, documented, audited, and monitored from a security perspective. The physical Azure data centers are protected for any intrusion and unauthorized access. In fact, even Microsoft personnel and operations teams do not have access to customer solutions and data. Some of the out-of-the-box security features provided by Azure are listed here:

- **Secure user access**: A customer's deployment, solution, and data can only be accessed by the customer. Even Azure data center personnel do not have access to customer artifacts. Customers can allow access to other people; however, that is at the discretion of the customer.

- **Encryption at rest**: Azure encrypts all its management data so that it cannot be read by anyone. It also provides this functionality to its customers, as well as those who can encrypt their data at rest.
- **Encryption at transit**: Azure encrypts all data that flows from its network. It also ensures that its network backbone is protected from any unauthorized access.
- **Active monitoring and auditing**: Azure monitors all its data centers actively on an ongoing basis. It actively identifies any breach, threat, or risk, and mitigates them.

Azure meets country-specific, local, international, and industry-specific compliance standards. They can be found at `https://www.microsoft.com/en-us/trustcenter/compliance/complianceofferings`.

IaaS security

Azure is a mature platform for deploying IaaS solutions. There are lots of users of Azure who want complete control over their deployments, and they typically use IaaS for their solutions. It is important that these deployments and solutions are secure, by default and by design. Azure provides rich security features to secure IaaS solutions. In this section, some of the major features will be covered.

Network Security Groups

The bare minimum of IaaS deployment consists of virtual machines and virtual networks. The virtual machines might be exposed to the internet by applying a public IP to its network interface, or it might be available to internal resources only. The internal resources in turn might be exposed to the internet. In any case, virtual machines should be secured so that unauthorized requests should not even reach them. Virtual machines should be secured using facilities that can filter requests on the network itself, rather than the requests reaching a virtual machine and it having to take action on them, such as ring-fencing virtual machines. This fence can allow or deny requests depending on their protocol, origin IP, destination IP, originating port, and destination port. This feature is deployed using the Azure **Network Security Groups (NSGs)** resource. NSG is composed of rules that are evaluated for both incoming and outgoing requests. Depending on the execution and evaluation of these rules, it is determined whether the requests should be allowed or denied access.

NSGs are flexible and can be applied to a virtual network subnet or individual network interfaces. When applying to a subnet, the security rules are applied to any resource, that is, virtual machines or load balancers on this subnet, while applying them to a network interface affects the requests only for that network interface. It is also possible to apply NSGs to both network subnets and network interfaces simultaneously. Typically, this design should be used to apply common security rules at the network subnet level, and unique security rules at the network interface level. It helps with the design of modular security rules and applications.

The flow for evaluating NSG is shown in the following diagram:

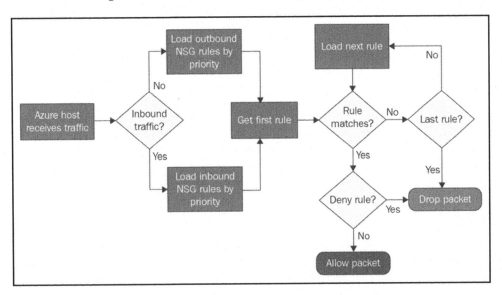

There are a few default rules provided by Azure out of the box. These are very important and come in handy when deployments want to use rules related to requests from/to the internet, virtual networks, and load balancers. Generally, IP addresses are constantly changing for these resources, and using these rules provides abstraction to use these IP addresses directly.

NSG design

The first step in designing is to ascertain the security requirements of the resource. The following questions should be answered:

- Is the resource accessible from the internet only?
- Is the resource accessible from both the internal resources and the internet?

- Is the resource accessible from the internal resource only?
- Determine the resources, load balancer, gateways, and virtual machines used.
- Configure a virtual network and its subnet.

Using the answers to these questions, an adequate NSG design should be created. Ideally, there should be multiple network subnets for each workload and type of resource. It is not recommended to deploy both load balancers and virtual machines on the same subnet.

Taking your requirements into account, rules should be determined that are common for different virtual machine workloads and subnets. For example, for a SharePoint deployment, the frontend application and SQL servers are deployed on separate subnets. Rules for each subnet should be determined.

After common subnet level rules are identified, rules for individual resources should be identified, and these should be applied to the network interface level. It is important to understand that if a rule allows an incoming request on a port, that port can also be used for outgoing requests without any configuration.

If resources are accessible from the internet, rules should be created with specific IP ranges and ports where possible. Careful functional and security testing should be executed to ensure that adequate and optimal NSG rules are opened and closed.

Firewalls

NSGs provides external security perimeters for requests. However, it does not mean that virtual machines should not implement additional security measures. It is always better to implement security both internally and externally. Virtual machines, whether in Linux or Windows, provide a mechanism to filter requests at the operating system level. This is known as a firewall in both Windows and Linux.

It is advisable to implement firewalls for operating systems. They help build a virtual security wall that allows only those requests that are considered trusted. Any untrusted requests are denied access. There are even physical firewall devices, but on the cloud, operating system firewalls are used. The following screenshot shows the firewall configuration in Windows operating system:

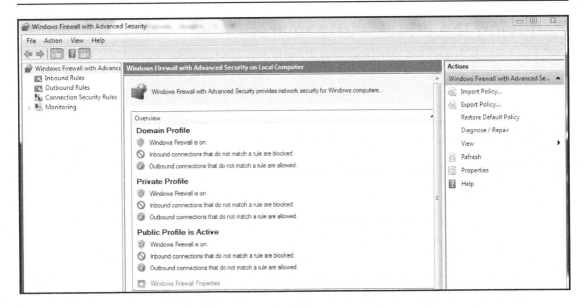

Firewalls filter network packets, and identify incoming ports and IP addresses. Using the information from these packets, the firewall evaluates the rules and decides whether it should allow or deny access.

Firewall design

As a best practice, firewalls should be evaluated for individual operating systems. Each virtual machine has a distinct responsibility within the overall deployment and solution. Rules for these individual responsibilities should be identified and firewalls should be opened and closed accordingly.

While evaluating firewall rules, it is important to keep network security group rules at both the subnet and individual network interface level into consideration. If it's not done properly, it is possible that rules are denied at the NSG level, but left open at the firewall level, and vice versa. If a request is allowed at the NSG level and denied at the firewall level, the application will not work as intended, while security risks increase if a request is denied at the NSG level and allowed at the firewall level.

A firewall helps you build multiple networks isolated by its security rules. Careful functional and security testing should be executed to ensure that adequate and optimal firewall rules are opened and closed.

Reducing the attack surface area

NSGs and firewalls help you to manage authorized requests to the environment. However, the environment should not be overtly exposed to security attacks. The surface area of the system should be optimally enabled to achieve its functionality, but disabled enough that attackers cannot find loopholes and access areas that are opened without any intended use, or opened but not adequately secured. Security should be adequately hardened, making it difficult for any attacker to break into the system.

Some of the areas that should be configured include the following:

- Remove all unnecessary users and groups from the operating system.
- Identify group membership for all users.
- Implement group policies using directory services.
- Block script execution unless it is signed by trusted authorities.
- Log and audit all activities.
- Install malware and anti-virus software, schedule scans, and update definitions frequently.
- Disable or shut down services that are not required.
- Lock down the filesystem so only authorized access is allowed.
- Lock down changes to the registry.
- A firewall must be configured according to the requirements.
- PowerShell script execution should be set to restricted or **RemoteSigned**.
- Enable enhanced protection through Internet Explorer.
- Restrict the ability to create new users and groups.
- Remove internet access and implement jump servers for RDP.
- Prohibit logging into servers using RDP through the internet. Instead, use site-to-site VPN, point-to-site VPN, or express route to RDP into remote machines from within the network.
- Regularly deploy all security updates.
- Run the security compliance manager tool on the environment and implement all of its recommendations.
- Actively monitor the environment using the Security Center and Operations Management suite.
- Deploy virtual network appliances to route traffic to internal proxies and reverse proxies.
- All sensitive data, such as configuration, connection strings, and credentials, should be encrypted.

Implementing jump servers

It is a good idea to remove internet access from virtual machines. It is also a good practice to limit remote desktop services' accessibility from the internet, but then how do you access the virtual machines at all? One good way is to only allow internal resources to RDP into virtual machines using Azure VPN options. However, there is also another way—using **jump servers**.

Jump servers are servers that are deployed in the **Demilitarized Zone (DMZ)**. This means it is not on the network hosting the core solutions and applications. Instead, it is on a separate network or subnet. The primary purpose of the jump server is to accept RDP requests from users and help them log in to it. From this jump server, users can further navigate to other virtual machines using RDP. It has access to two or more networks: one that has connectivity to the outside world, and another internal to the solution. The jump server implements all the security restrictions and provides a secure client to connect to other servers. Normally, access to emails and the internet is disabled on jump servers.

An example of deploying a jump server with the VMSS is available at `https://azure.` `microsoft.com/en-in/resources/templates/201-vmss-windows-jumpbox/` using Azure Resource Manager templates.

PaaS security

Azure provides numerous PaaS services, each with their own security features. In general, PaaS services can be accessed using credentials, certificates, and tokens. PaaS services allow the generation of short-lived security access tokens. Client applications can send this security access token to represent trusted users. In this section, we will cover some of the most important PaaS services that are used in almost every solution.

Operations Management Suite (OMS)

Microsoft OMS, also known as Log Analytics, is a new platform for managing cloud deployments, on-premise data centers, and hybrid solutions.

OMS provides multiple modular solutions—a specific functionality that helps to implement a feature. For example, security and audit solutions help to ascertain a complete view of security for an organization's deployment. Similarly, there are many more solutions, such as automation and change tracking, that should be implemented from a security perspective.

The OMS security and audit provides information in the following five categories:

- **Security domains**: These provide the ability to view security records, malware assessments, update assessments, network security, identity and access information, and computers with security events. Access is also provided to the Azure Security Center dashboard.

- **Antimalware assessment**: This helps identify servers that are not protected against malware and have security issues. It provides an overall exposure to potential security problems and assesses their criticality. Users can take proactive actions based on these recommendations. Azure Security Center sub-categories provide information collected by Azure Security Center.

- **Notable issues**: This quickly identifies active issues and grades their severity.

- **Detections**: This category is in preview mode. It enables the identification of attack patterns by visualizing security alerts.

- **Threat intelligence**: This helps identify attack patterns by visualizing the total number of servers with outbound malicious IP traffic, the malicious threat type, and a map that shows where these IPs are coming from.

The preceding details, when viewed from the portal, are shown in the following screenshot:

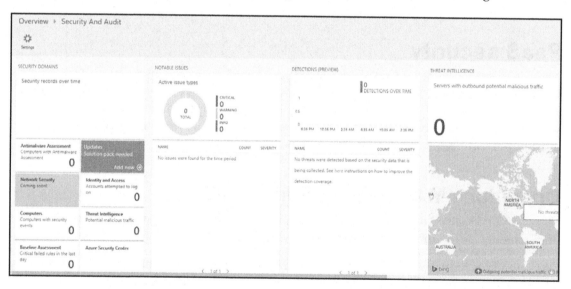

Storage

Storage accounts play an important part in the overall solution architecture. Storage accounts can store important information, such as user PII data, business transactions, data, and more. It is of utmost importance that storage accounts are secure and only allow access to authorized users. The data stored is encrypted and transmitted using secure channels. The storage, as well as the users and client applications consuming the storage account and its data, play a crucial role in the overall security of the data. They should also keep data encrypted at all times. This also includes credentials and connection strings connecting to data stores.

Azure provides Role Based Access Control (RBAC) to govern who can manage Azure storage accounts. These RBAC permissions are allowed to users and groups in Azure **Active Directory** (**AD**). However, when an application to be deployed on Azure is created, it will have users and customers that are not available in Azure AD. To allow users to access the storage account, Azure Storage provides storage access keys. There are two types of access keys at the storage account level—primary and secondary. Users possessing these keys can connect to the storage account. These storage access keys are used in the authentication step when accessing the storage account. Applications can access storage accounts using either primary or secondary keys. Two keys are provided so that if the primary key is compromised, applications can be updated to use the secondary key, while the primary key is regenerated. This helps minimize application downtime. Moreover, it provides and enhances security by removing the compromised key without impacting applications. The Storage key details, as seen on the Azure Portal, as shown in the following screenshot:

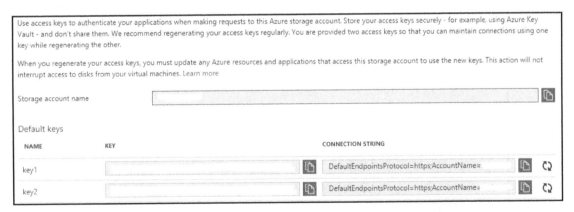

Azure Storage provides four services—blob, files, queues, and tables—in an account. Each of these services also provides infrastructure for securing themselves using secure access tokens. A **shared access signature (SAS)** is a URI that grants restricted access rights to Azure storage services: blob, files, queues, and tables. These SAS token can be shared with clients who should not be trusted with the entire storage account key to constrain access to certain storage account resources. By distributing a SAS URI to these clients, access to resources is granted for a specified period.

SAS tokens exist at both the storage account and the individual blob, file, table, and queue levels. A storage account-level signature is more powerful and has the right to allow and deny permissions at the individual service level. It can also be used instead of individual resource service levels:

Generating and sharing SAS tokens is preferable to sharing storage account keys. SAS tokens provide granular access to resources and can be combined together as well. These tokens include **read**, **write**, **delete**, **list**, **add**, **create**, **update**, and **process**. Moreover, even access to resources can be determined while generating SAS tokens. It could be for blobs, tables, queues, and files individually, or a combination of them. Storage account keys are for the entire account and cannot be constrained for individual services. Neither can they be constrained from the permissions perspective. It is much easier to create and revoke SAS tokens than it is for storage access keys. SAS tokens can be created for use for a certain period of time, after which they become invalid automatically.

It is to be noted that if storage account keys are regenerated, then the SAS token based on them will become invalid and a newer SAS token should be created and shared with clients.

Cookie stealing, script injection, and denial of service attacks are common means used by attackers to disrupt an environment and steal data. Browsers and the HTTP protocol implement a built-in mechanism that ensures that these malicious activities cannot be performed. Generally, anything that is cross-domain is not allowed by either HTTP or browsers. A script running in one domain cannot ask for resources from another domain. However, there are valid use cases where such requests should be allowed. The HTTP protocol implements **Cross Origin Resource Sharing (CORS)**. With the help of CORS, it is possible to access resources across domains and make them work. Azure Storage configures CORS rules for blobs, file, queue, and table resources. Azure Storage allows the creation of rules that are evaluated for each authenticated request. If the rules are satisfied, the request is allowed to access the resource.

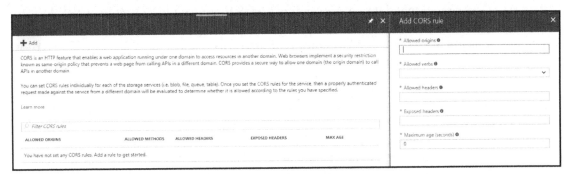

Data must not only be protected while in transit; it should also be protected while at rest as well. If data at rest is not encrypted, anybody who has access to the physical drive in the data center can read the data. Although the possibility is negligible, customers still should encrypt their data. Storage service encryption also helps protect data at rest. This service works transparently and injects itself without users knowing about it. It encrypts data when the data is saved in a storage account, and decrypts it automatically when it is read. This entire process happens without users performing any additional activity.

Azure account keys must be rotated periodically. This will ensure that an attacker is not able to breach access to storage accounts.

It is also a good idea to regenerate the keys; however, this must be evaluated in regard to its usage in existing applications. If it breaks the existing application, these applications should be prioritized for change management, and changes should be applied gradually.

As much as possible, individual service-level SAS tokens with a limited timeframe should be generated and provided to users who should access the resources. Permissions must be evaluated and optimum permissions must be provided.

SAS keys and storage account keys should be stored in an Azure Key Vault. This provides security storage and access to them. These keys can be read at runtime by applications from the key vault, instead of storing them in configuration files.

Azure SQL

SQL Server stores relational data on Azure. It is a SaaS that provides a highly available, scalable, performance-centric, and secure platform for storing data. It is accessible from anywhere, with any programming language and platform. Clients need a connection string comprising the server, database, and security information to connect to it.

SQL Server provides firewall settings that prevent access to anyone by default. IP addresses and ranges should be whitelisted to access SQL Server. Only IP addresses that architects are confident belong to customers or partners should be whitelisted. There are deployments in Azure for which either there are a lot of IP addresses or the IP addresses are not known, such as applications deployed in Azure Functions or Logic Apps. For such applications to access Azure SQL, Azure SQL allows whitelisting of all IP addresses to Azure services across subscriptions.

It is to be noted that firewall configuration is at the server level and not the database level. This means any changes here affect all databases within a server.

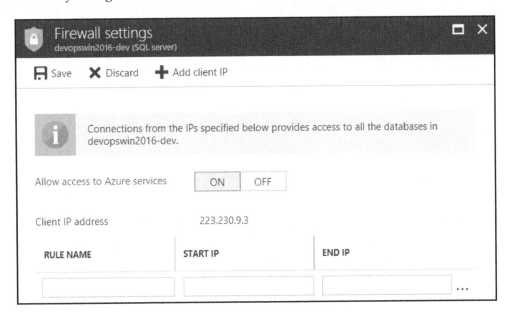

Azure SQL also provides enhanced security by encrypting data at rest. This ensures that nobody, including the Azure data center administrators, can view the data stored in SQL Server. The technology used by SQL Server for encrypting data at rest is known as **Transparent Data Encryption (TDE)**. There are no changes required at the application level to implement TDE. SQL Server encrypts and decrypts data transparently when the user saves and reads data. This feature is available at the database level.

SQL Server also provides **Dynamic Data Masking (DDM)**, which is especially useful for masking certain types of data, such as credit cards or user PII data. Masking is not the same as encryption. Masking does not encrypt data, but only masks, which ensures that data is not in human-readable format. Users should mask and encrypt sensitive data in the Azure SQL server.

SQL Server also provides an **Auditing & Threat Detection** service for all servers. There are advanced data collection and intelligence services running on top of these databases to discover threats and vulnerabilities and alert users to them. Audit logs are maintained by Azure in storage accounts and can be viewed by administrators for action. Threads such as SQL injection and anonymous client logins can generate alerts that administrators can be informed about over email.

Data can be masked in Azure SQL. This helps us store data in a format that does not make sense:

Azure SQL also provides **Transparent data encryption** to encrypt data at rest, as shown in the following screenshot:

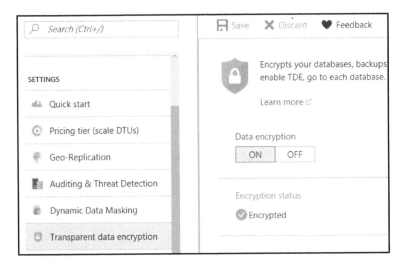

Azure Key Vaults

Securing resources using passwords, keys, credentials, certificates, and unique identifiers are an important element for any environment and application. They are important elements from the security perspective. They need to be protected, and to ensure that these resources remain secure and do not get compromised is an important pillar of security architecture. Management and operations that keep the secrets and keys secure, while making them available when needed, is an important aspect that cannot be ignored. Typically, these secrets are used all over the place—within the source code, configuration file, pieces of paper, and in other digital formats. To overcome these challenges and store all secrets uniformly in a centralized secure storage, Azure Key Vaults should be created.

Azure Key Vault is well integrated with other Azure services. For example, using a certificate stored in Azure Key Vault and deploying it on Azure virtual machines certificate store can be easily performed. All kinds of keys, including storage keys, IoT and event keys, and connection strings, can be stored as secrets in Azure Key Vault. They can be retrieved and used transparently without anyone viewing them or storing them temporarily anywhere. Credentials for SQL Server and other services can also be stored in Azure Key Vault.

Azure Key Vault works on a per-region basis. What this means is that an Azure Key Vault resource should be provisioned at the same region where the application and service is deployed. If a deployment consists of more than one region and needs services from Azure Key Vault, multiple Azure Key Vault instances should be provisioned.

An important feature of Azure Key Vault is that the secrets, keys, and certificates are not stored on general storage. This sensitive data is backed up by the Hardware security module. This means that this data are stored in separate hardware on Azure that can only be unlocked by keys owned by users.

Security monitoring and auditing

Azure provides the following two important security resources to manage all security aspects of the Azure subscription, resource groups, and resources:

- Azure Monitor
- Azure Security Center

Azure Monitor

Azure Monitor is a one-stop place for monitoring Azure resources. It provides information about Azure resources and their state. It provides a rich query interface, using which information can be sliced and diced using data at the levels of subscription, resource group, individual resource, resource type.

Azure Monitor can be used through Azure Portal, PowerShell, CLI, and REST API.

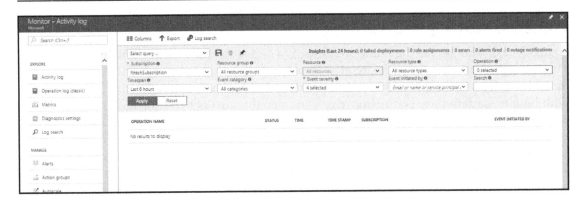

The following logs are those provided by Azure Monitor:

- **Activity log**: This provides all management-level operations performed on resources. It provides details about the creation time, creator, resource type, and status.
- **Operation log (classic)**: This provides details of all operations performed on resources within a resource group and subscription.
- **Metrics**: This gets performance information for individual resources and sets alerts on them.
- **Diagnostic settings**: This helps us configure the effects logs by setting up Azure Storage for storing logs, streaming logs in real time to Azure Event Hubs, and sending them to Log Analytics.
- **Log search**: This helps integrate Logs Analytics with Azure Monitor.

Azure Monitor can help identify security-related incidents and take appropriate actions. It is important that only authorized individuals should be allowed to access Azure Monitor, since it might contain sensitive information.

Azure Security Center

Azure Security Center, as the name suggests, is a one-stop place for all security needs. There are generally two activities related to security—implementing security and monitoring for any threats and breaches. Security Center has been built primarily to help with both these activities. Azure Security Center enables users to define their security policies and get them implemented on Azure resources. Based on the current state of Azure resources, Azure Security Center provides security recommendations to harden the solution and individual Azure resources. The recommendations include almost all Azure security best practices, including the encryption of data and disks, network protection, endpoint protection, access control lists, whitelisting of incoming requests, and blocking of unauthorized requests. The resources range from infrastructure components such as load balancers, network security groups, and virtual networks, to PaaS resources such as Azure SQL and Storage.

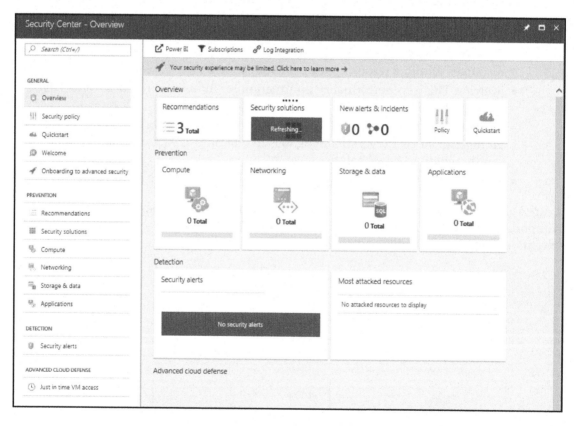

Azure Security Center is a rich platform, and provides recommendations for multiple services, as shown in the following screenshot:

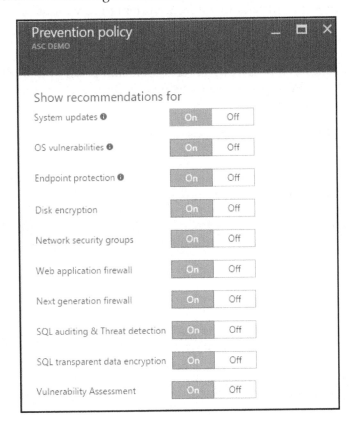

Monitoring

Monitoring is an important architectural concern that should be part of any solution, big or small, mission-critical or not, cloud or not. It should not be avoided at any cost.

Monitoring refers to the act of keeping track of solutions and capturing various telemetry information, processing it, identifying the information that qualifies for alerts based on rules, and raising them. Generally, an agent is deployed within the environment and monitors it, sending telemetry information to a centralized server, where the rest of the processing of generating alerts and notifying stakeholders happens.

Monitoring takes both proactive and reactive actions and measures on the solution. It is also the first step towards the auditability of the solution. Without the availability of monitoring log records, it is difficult to audit the system from various perspectives, such as security, performance, and availability.

Monitoring helps us identify availability, performance, and scalability issues before they happen. Hardware failure, software misconfiguration, and patch update challenges can be discovered well before they impact users by using monitoring. Performance degradation can be fixed before it happens.

Reactively, logs pinpoint areas and locations that are causing issues, identify the issues, and enable faster and better repairing.

Teams can identify patterns of issues using monitoring telemetry information and eliminate them by innovating new solutions and features.

Azure is a rich cloud environment that provides multiple rich monitoring features and resources to monitor not only cloud-based deployment, but also on-premise deployment.

Azure monitoring

The first question that should be answered is, *what must we monitor?* This question becomes more important for solutions that are deployed on the cloud because of the constrained control over it.

There are some important components that should be monitored. They include the following:

- Custom applications
- Azure resources
- Guest operating systems (virtual machines)
- Host operating systems (Azure physical servers)
- Azure infrastructure

There are different Azure logs and monitoring for these components.

Azure activity logs

Previously known as audit logs and operational logs, these are control plane events in the Azure platform. They provide information and telemetry information at the subscription level, instead of the individual resource level. They track information about all changes that happen at the subscription level, such as creating, deleting, and updating resources using **Azure Resource Manager (ARM)**. They help us discover the identity (such as service principal, users or groups) and perform an action (such as write or update) on resources (for example, storage, virtual machines, SQL) at any given point of time. They provide information about resources that are modified in their configuration, but not their inner workings and execution.

Azure diagnostic logs

The information originating within the inner workings of Azure resources is captured in what are known as **diagnostic logs**. They provide telemetry information about the operations of resources that are inherent to the resource. Not every resource provides diagnostic logs, and resources that provide logs on their own content are completely different from other resources. Diagnostic logs are configured individually for each resource. Examples of diagnostic logs include storing a file in a container in a blob service in a storage account.

Azure application logs

The application logs can be captured by Application Insights resources and can be managed centrally. They get information about the inner workings of custom applications, such as their performance metrics and availability, and users can get insights from them in order to manage them better.

Guest and host operating system logs

Both guest and host operating system logs are surfaced to users using Azure Monitor. They provide information about the status of host and guest operating systems.

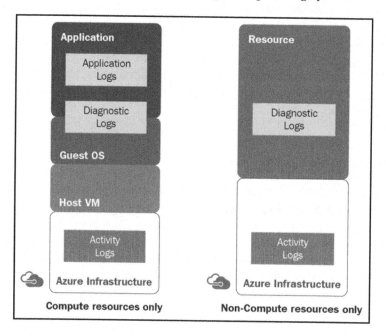

The important resources from Azure related to monitoring are as follows:

- Azure Monitor
- Azure Application Insights
- Log Analytics, previously known as **Operational Insights**

There are other tools, such as **System Center Operations Manager (SCOM)**, that are not part of the cloud feature but can be deployed on IaaS-based virtual machines to monitor any workload on Azure or an on-premise data center.

Azure Monitor

Azure Monitor is a central tool and resource that provides complete management features that allow you to monitor an Azure subscription. It provides management features for activity logs, diagnostic logs, metrics, Application Insights, and Log Analytics. It should be treated as a dashboard and management resource for all other monitoring capabilities.

Azure Application Insights

Azure Application Insights provides centralized, Azure-scale monitoring, logs, and metrics capabilities to custom applications. Custom applications can start sending metrics, logs, and other telemetry information to Azure Application Insights. It also provides rich reporting, dashboarding, and analytics capabilities to get insights from incoming data and act on them.

Azure Log Analytics

Azure Log Analytics provides centralized processing of logs and generates insights and alerts from them. Activity logs, diagnostic logs, application logs, event logs, and even custom logs can send information to Log Analytics, which can further provide rich reporting, dashboarding, and analytics capabilities to get insights from incoming data and act on them.

Application Insights

As the name suggests, Azure Application Insights provides insights into the workings of an application. The insights relevant for a web application include the number of incoming requests per second, requests failed per second, hardware usage in terms of CPU utilization, and memory availability. Application Insights provides a dashboard, reports, and charts to view various metrics related to the application. This allows us to view and better understand the trends in terms of usage of the application, its availability, number of requests, and more, to take both precautionary and reactive actions on the application. Trend information can be used to find out things that are not working in favor of the application and things that are working fine over a specific period.

The first step in working with Application Insights is to provision this service on Azure in a resource group that has all general and management services consumed by all applications. If you remember, we created a similar resource group named `Win2016devOps` that houses all common services, such as Azure Key Vault, Application Insights, Operational Insights, and Storage, to hold scripts and templates used across environments and applications.

Provisioning

As mentioned before, the first step in consuming an Application Insights service is to provision it on Azure.

Application Insights can be provisioned manually using the Azure Portal, Azure REST APIs, PowerShell, and ARM templates. Here we will use the Azure Portal:

1. Log in to the Azure Portal using your credentials and navigate to an existing resource group, or create a new resource group. Click on the **Add** button:

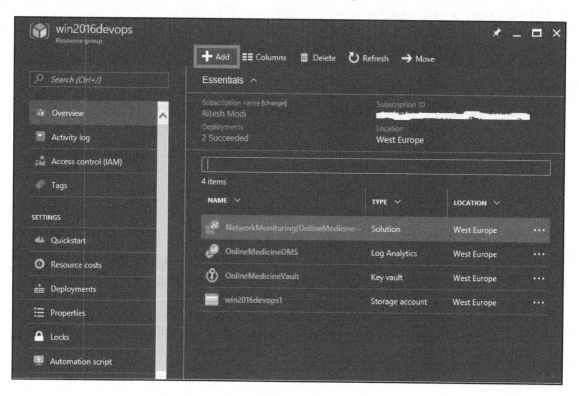

2. Type `Application Insights` in the search box in the next blade. The first link should refer to Application Insights. Click on it to create a new Application Insights service instance. Click on the **Create** button to get started:

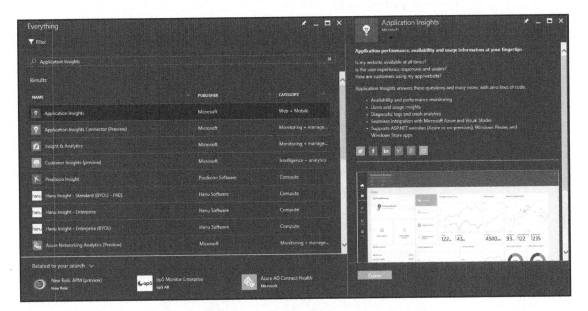

3. The next blade will ask for the Application Insights service instance name, the type of application, the subscription name, the resource group name, and the location of the service. Provide the appropriate details and click on the **Create** button. This will provision the service:

4. Now navigate to the service that shows the essential properties, such as its **Instrumentation Key** highlighted in the following screenshot. The key will be different in every instance, and generally copied and used in Visual Studio. Please note that some of the information has been blacked out for security reasons:

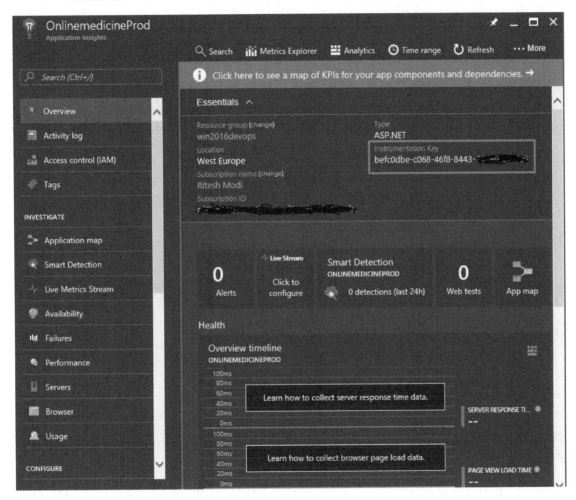

Log Analytics

Log Analytics service helps in providing information about these environments using its rich log storage and analytic features. Application Insights is used for monitoring applications. However, it is equally important to monitor the environment on which an application is hosted and running. This involves the infrastructure, such as virtual machines, Docker containers, and related components.

Provisioning

Log Analytics, also known as the **Operational Management Suite (OMS)**, must be provisioned on Azure before it can be used to monitor virtual machines and containers. Again, similar to Application Insights, Operational Insights can be provisioned through the Azure Portal, PowerShell, REST APIs, and resource group manager templates. An Operational Insights workspace is a security boundary that can be accessed by certain users. Multiple workspaces should be created to isolate users and their corresponding access to environment telemetry data.

The JSON script used to provision an Operational Insights workspace is shown here:

```
{
    "apiVersion": "2015-11-01-preview",
    "type": "Microsoft.OperationalInsights/workspaces",
    "name": "[parameters('workspaceName')]",
    "location": "[parameters('deployLocation')]",
    "properties": {
      "sku": {
        "Name": "[parameters('serviceTier')]"
      }
    }
}
```

The `name`, `location`, and `sku` information is needed to provision a workspace, and their values are provided using parameters.

The workspace after provisioning is shown in the following screenshot:

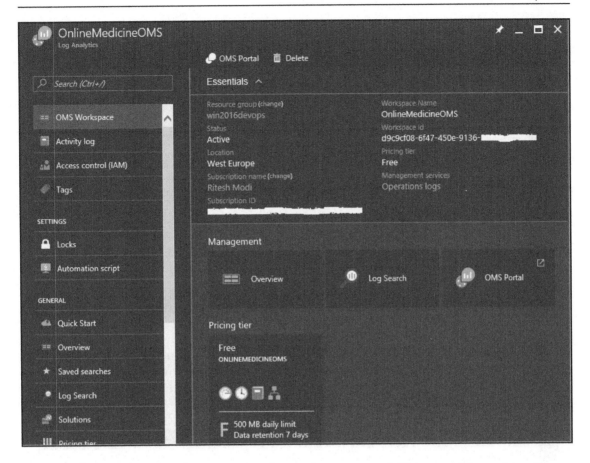

Click on the OMS portal section to open the workspace portal. This portal is used to view all telemetry information captured by Operational Insights, configure Operational Insights, and provide dashboard features and functionality.

The home screen of Operational Insights is shown here:

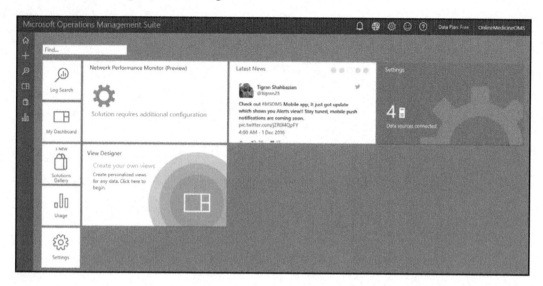

The **Settings** section shows that four data sources are connected. These are four virtual machines connected to the OMS workspace from the test and production environments. A different strategy of having a separate workspace for each environment can be adopted, and it is left to readers to decide what's best for their applications and solutions. Operational Insights can be configured using the **Settings** tile:

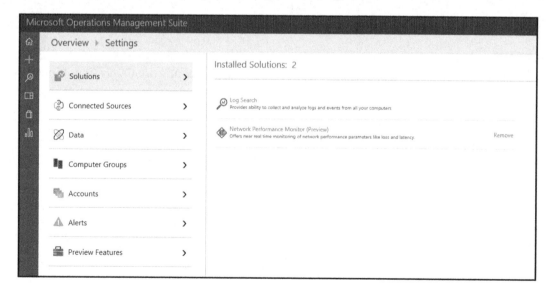

OMS agents

You may have noticed, no assembly or code changes are made to the application to consume Operational Insights. Operational Insights depends on the installation of an agent on virtual machines. These agents keep collecting telemetry data from these hosts and send them to the Operational Insights workspace, where they are stored for a specified period of time depending upon the `sku` chosen. These agents can be installed manually on virtual machines. ARM virtual machine extensions install agents automatically, immediately after provisioning the virtual machines. The JSON code for provisioning of an agent on a virtual machine is shown here:

```
{
        "apiVersion": "2015-06-15",
        "type": "Microsoft.Compute/virtualMachines/extensions",
        "name": "[concat(variables('vmName'),copyIndex(1),'/omsscript')]",
        "location": "[resourceGroup().location]",
        "dependsOn": [
    "[concat('Microsoft.Compute/virtualMachines/',variables('vmName'),copyIndex
(1))]",
            "[resourceId('Microsoft.Compute/virtualMachines/extensions',
concat(variables('vmName'),copyIndex(1)),'powershellscript')]"
        ],
        "copy": {
          "count": "[parameters('countVMs')]",
          "name": "omsloop"
        },
        "properties": {
          "publisher": "Microsoft.EnterpriseCloud.Monitoring",
          "type": "MicrosoftMonitoringAgent",
          "typeHandlerVersion": "1.0",
          "settings": {
            "workspaceId": "[parameters('WorkspaceID')]"
          },
          "protectedSettings": {
            "workspaceKey": "[listKeys(variables('accountid'),'2015-11-01-
preview').primarySharedKey]"
          }
        }
      }
```

The `workspaceId` and `accountid` are available from the **Settings** tile of the OMS workspace, and the `copy` element is used to deploy it to multiple virtual machines. This resource is a child resource of the virtual machine resource, ensuring that this extension is executed whenever a virtual machine is provisioned or updated.

The configuration related to workspace ID and account ID is shown next. The primary key is used as an account ID for configuring the agents using ARM templates.

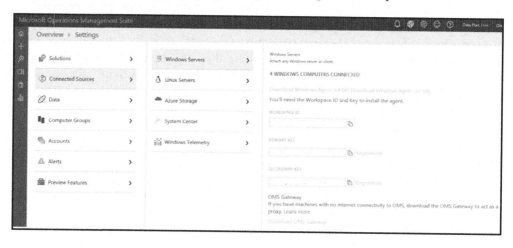

Search

The OMS workspace provides search capabilities to search for specific log entries, export all telemetry data to Excel and/or PowerBI, and search language specific to OMS.

The **Log Search** screen is shown here:

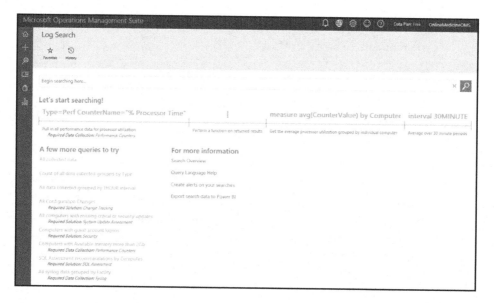

Solutions

Solutions in OMS are additional capabilities that can be added to the workspace, capturing additional telemetry data that is not captured by default. When these solutions are added to the workspace, appropriate management packs are sent to all the agents connected to the workspace in the context of configuring themselves for capturing solution-specific data from virtual machines and containers, and then start sending it to the OMS workspace.

The following screenshot shows the solution gallery and capacity and performance solution on the OMS workspace. Clicking on any solution and subsequently clicking on the **Add** button adds the solution to the workspace, as shown below:

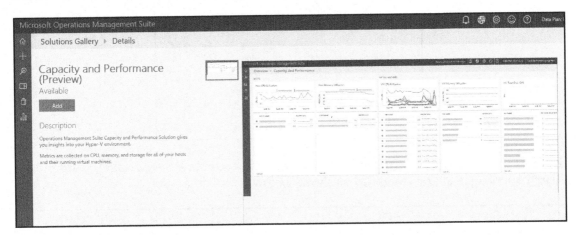

Azure provides lots of OMS solutions for tracking and monitoring different aspects of environments and applications. At a minimum, a set of solutions that are generic and applicable to almost any environment should be added to the workspace:

- Capacity and performance
- Agent health
- Change tracking
- Containers
- Security and audit
- Update management
- Network performance monitoring

Alerts

Log Analytics allows us to generate alerts on the ingested data. It does so by running a pre-defined query composed of conditions on the incoming data. If it finds any records that fall within the ambit of the query, it generates an alert. Log Analytics provides a highly configurable environment for determining the conditions for generating alerts, time windows in which the query should return the records, time windows in which the query should be executed, and actions to be taken when the query returns results as alerts.

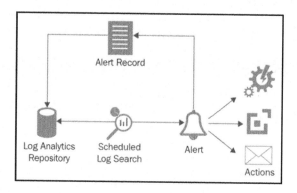

The first step in configuring an alert is to create a saved search. A saved search is simply a search query against Log Analytics, as shown below:

Save the query by providing a name for it. After saving the query, click on the **Alert** button from the **Log Search** menu. It provides the user an interface for defining and adding a new alert rule:

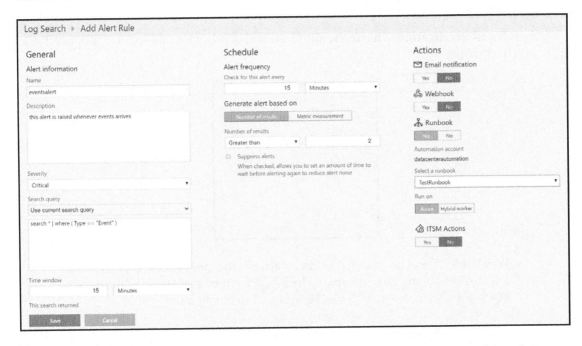

Within this single screen, all configurations related to an alert rule can be performed. You need to provide a name, description, severity, and the query to be executed as part of the rule evaluation within their respective fields.

The time window specifies the data interval in which the query should be executed. In the screenshot, whenever the rule is executed, it processes data from the last 15 minutes.

The schedule section helps you configure the frequency of rule execution. It answers the question, *How frequently should the query run?* In the previous screenshot, the rule is executed every 15 minutes. The time window should be more than the alert frequency. The alerts can be further configured based on the number of results found. It need not be that an alert is generated for every instance of data found based on the query. It can further be quantified to accumulate a certain quantity of results before raising the requests. The alerts can also be generated based on metric measurements. Additional configuration to suppress alerts can be done. You can create a time interval that should elapse before the action is executed. In this case, alerts are generated but the action is executed only after the configured interval has elapsed.

The **Actions** section allows us to configure things that should follow an alert. Generally, there should be a remedial and/or notification action. Log Analytics provides four different ways to create a new action. They can be combined in any way. An alert will execute any and all the following configured actions:

- **Email notification**: This is the simplest, and sends an email to the configured recipients:

- **Webhook**: A webhook executes an arbitrary external process using a HTTP POST mechanism. For example, a REST API can be executed, or the Service Manager/ServiceNow APIs can be invoked to create a ticket:

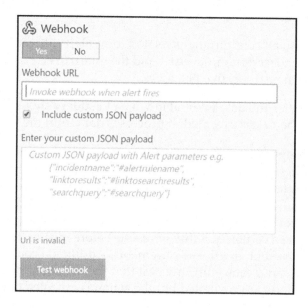

- **Runbooks**: This action executes Azure Automation runbooks. In the next section, we will see the entire process of executing an Azure Automation runbook.
- **ITSM actions**: ITSM solutions should be provisioned before using this option. It helps with connecting and sending information to ITSM systems.

Executing runbooks on Alerts

One of the actions provided by a Log Analytics alert is to execute the Azure Automation runbook. This facility of executing runbooks on an alert provides the opportunity to act on the alert to remediate it and inform the relevant stakeholders using notifications.

1. The first step in executing a runbook in response to an alert is to create an Azure Automation Account:

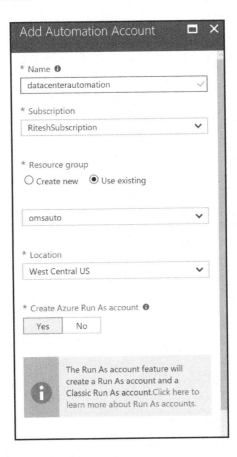

2. After the account is provisioned, create a runbook, as shown in the following screenshot, to prove that it can be executed as part of the alert generation. In this case, the runbook sends an email as part of the notification. It uses Azure Automation credentials to send an email using the O365 SMTP server. Users should have a valid O365 account before sending an email using Azure Automation.

3. It has to be noted that this is just a demonstration. The runbook can also accept parameters and Log Analytics alerts and send a single `object` parameter. This parameter contains all the data pertaining to the source of the alert, details about the alert, and information that is available with Log Analytics:

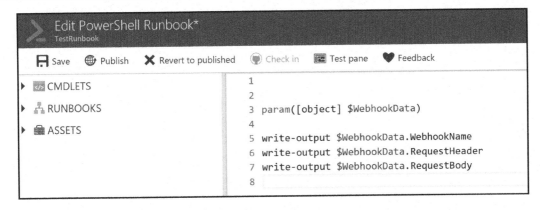

4. The data is in JSON format and a `ConvertFrom-JSON` cmdlet can be used to create PowerShell objects.
5. The next step is to configure a Log Analytics configuration so that it can connect to the Azure Automation account. For this, an **Automation & Control** solution needs to be enabled and deployed.
6. Clicking on this tile will navigate to the **Solutions Gallery** configuration window. Click on **Configure Workspace** to deploy it:

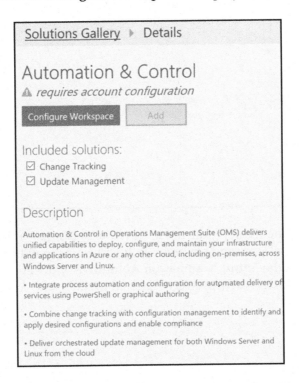

7. Select the newly-created Azure **Automation Account** as part of the deployment of the solution:

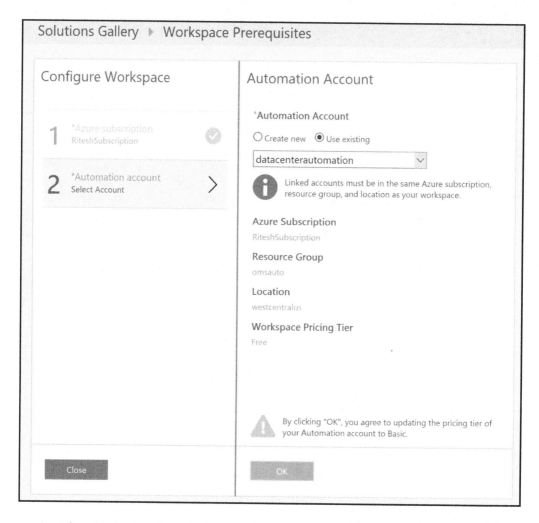

8. After deploying the solution, navigate to the **Settings** window within the Log Analytics workspace and ensure that the Azure Automation settings shows details about the Azure **Automation Account** as shown below. This ensures that the Log Analytics workspace is connected to the Azure **Automation Account**:

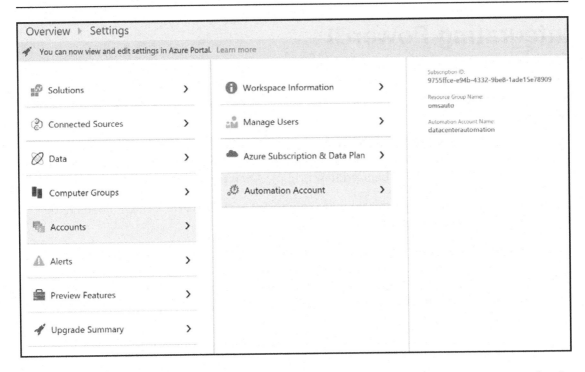

9. Now the runbook should be available while configuring the alert action runbook, as shown in the following screenshot:

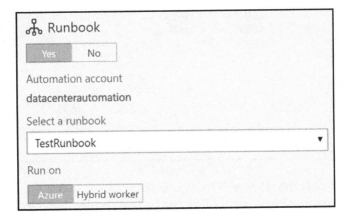

Integrating PowerBI

Gathering data and storing it in a central repository is an important aspect. However, there should be tools and utilities to process the data and generate insights out of it. PowerBI is a Microsoft-provided service specifically meant for visualizing and generating insights from raw data.

PowerBI can be enabled using the **Settings** menu, just like the configuration for Azure Automation. The connection to PowerBI should be made from the **Settings** menu. Once, this connection is made, it can be used to send Log Analytics data to PowerBI.

Log Analytics provides two different ways to interact with PowerBI. First, it needs to be enabled from the **Settings** menu.

Like alerts, the PowerBI menu option is available from the top-level log search menu. Clicking on it allows us to configure the PowerBI connectivity. A scheduler runs periodically to execute search queries and send the resulting data to PowerBI. The data is stored as datasets in PowerBI and can be used to generate charts, reports, and dashboards as shown in the following diagram:

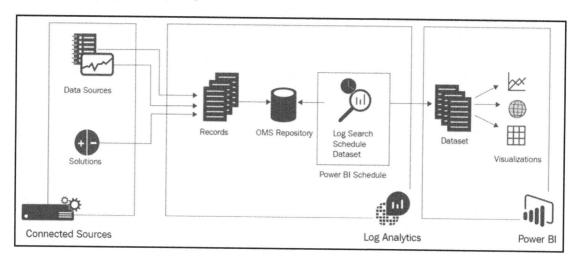

The other way to get data into PowerBI from Log Analytics is to use the **Power Query** language within PowerBI. This is scaffolding the code provided by Log Analytics.

The exported **Power Query Formula Language** (**M Language**) can be used with Power Query in Microsoft Excel and PowerBI Desktop.

For using PowerBI desktop, follow the next instructions to download and generate reports using queries:

1. Download PowerBI Desktop from
   `https://powerbi.microsoft.com/en-us/desktop/`.

2. In the PowerBI Desktop, select **Get Data | Blank Query | Advanced Query Editor**.

3. Paste the following M Language script into the **Advanced Query Editor** and select **Done**. This will result in the execution of the query and bring the OMS data into PowerBI. Provide a name and add a new dataset by clicking on the **Apply and Close** button in the PowerBI query editor:

```
let AnalyticsQuery =
let Source =
Json.Document(Web.Contents("https://management.azure.com/subscripti
ons/9755ffce-
e94b-4332-9be8-1ade15e78909/resourceGroups/omsauto/providers/Micros
oft.OperationalInsights/workspaces/data
centermonitoring/api/query?api-version=2017-01-01-preview",
[Query=[#"query"="search * | where ( Type == ""Event"" ) ",#"x-ms-
app"="OmsAnalyticsPBI",#"timespan"="PT24H",#"prefer"="ai.response-
thinning=true"],Timeout=#duration(0,0,4,0)])),
TypeMap = #table(
{ "AnalyticsTypes", "Type" },
{
{ "string",   Text.Type },
{ "int",      Int32.Type },
{ "long",     Int64.Type },
{ "real",     Double.Type },
{ "timespan", Duration.Type },
{ "datetime", DateTimeZone.Type },
{ "bool",     Logical.Type },
{ "guid",     Text.Type }
}),
DataTable = Source[tables]{0},
Columns = Table.FromRecords(DataTable[columns]),
ColumnsWithType = Table.Join(Columns, {"type"}, TypeMap ,
{"AnalyticsTypes"}),
Rows = Table.FromRows(DataTable[rows], Columns[name]),
Table = Table.TransformColumnTypes(Rows,
Table.ToList(ColumnsWithType, (c) => { c{0}, c{3}}))
in
Table
in AnalyticsQuery
```

Summary

Security is always an important aspect for any deployment and solution. It has become much more important and relevant because of deployment onto the cloud. Moreover, there is the increasing threat of cyber attacks. In these circumstances, security has become a focal point for organizations. No matter the type of deployment or solution—whether it's IaaS, PaaS, or SaaS—security is needed across all of them. Azure data centers are completely secure and they have a dozen international security certifications. They are secure by default. They provide IaaS security resources such as NSGs, network address translation, secure endpoints, certificates, key vaults, storage, and virtual machine encryption, and PaaS security features for individual PaaS resources. Security has a complete life cycle of its own and it should be properly planned, designed, implemented, and tested, just like any other application functionality.

Monitoring is an important architectural aspect for any solution. It is also the first step towards auditability. It enables operations to manage a solution, both reactively and proactively. It provides the necessary records for troubleshooting and fixing the issues that might arise from platforms and applications. There are many resources in Azure that are specific to implementing monitoring for Azure, other clouds, and on-premise data centers. Application Insights, OMS, and Log Analytics are some of the most important resources in this regard. Needless to say, it is a must for making your solutions and products better by innovating based on insights from monitoring data.

4
Cross-Subscription Deployments Using ARM Templates

ARM templates are the preferred mechanism for provisioning resources and configuring them on Azure.

ARM templates help to implement a relatively new paradigm known as **Infrastructure as Code (IaC)**. ARM templates convert the infrastructure and its configuration into code. Converting infrastructure into code has numerous advantages. IaC brings high level of consistency and predictability in deployments across environments. It also ensures that environments can be tested before going to production and finally it gives high level of confidence in deployment process, maintenance, and governance.

The following topics will be covered in this chapter:

- ARM templates
- Deploying resource groups with ARM templates
- Deploying resources across subscriptions and resource groups
- Deploying cross-subscription and resource-group deployments using linked templates

ARM templates

Some of the prominent advantages of IaC is that it can be version-controlled. It can be reused across environments, which provides a high degree of consistency and predictability in deployments. It also ensures that the impact and result of deploying an ARM template is the same no matter the number of times the template is deployed. This feature is known as **idempotent template**.

ARM templates debuted with the introduction of the ARM specification and have been getting richer in features and more mature since then. It's important to understand that there's generally a feature gap of a few weeks to a couple of months between the actual resource configuration and the availability of this configuration in ARM templates.

The resource has its own configuration. This configuration can be affected in a multitude of ways, including using Azure PowerShell, Azure CLI, Azure SDKs, REST API, and ARM templates.

Each of these ways has their own development and release life cycle, which is different from the actual resource development. Let's try to understand this with the help of an example.

The Azure databricks resource has its own cadence and development life cycle. The consumers of this resource have their own development life cycle, which is different from the actual resource development. If databricks gets its first release on December 31st, the Azure PowerShell cmdlets for it might not be available on the same date and they might get released January 31st of the next year; similarly, the availability of these features in the REST API and ARM templates might be around January 15th.

ARM templates are JSON-based documents that, when executed, invoke REST API on the Azure management plane and submit the entire document to it. The REST API has its own development life cycle, and the JSON schema for the resource has its own life cycle.

It means Azure development of a feature within a resource should happen in at least three different components before they can be consumed from ARM templates. These include the following:

- The resource itself
- The REST API for the resource
- The ARM template resource schema

Each resource in the ARM template has the `apiVersion` property. This property helps to decide the REST API version that should be used to provision and deploy the resource. The next diagram shows the flow of requests from the ARM template to resource APIs that are responsible for the creation, updation, and deletion of resources:

A resource configuration, such as a storage account in ARM template, looks as follows:

```
{
  "type": "Microsoft.Storage/storageAccounts",
   "apiVersion": "2017-06-01",
    "name": "[variables('storage2')]",
    "location": "[resourceGroup().location]",
    "kind": "Storage",
    "sku": {
                "name": "Standard_LRS"
            }
}
```

In this code listing, the availability of this schema for defining sku is based in the development of the ARM template schema. The availability of the REST API and its version number is determined by the apiVersion, which happens to be 2017-06-01. The actual resource is determined by the type property, which has the following two parts:

- **Resource-provider namespace**: Resources in Azure are hosted within namespaces and related resources are hosted within the same namespace.
- **Resource type**: Resources are referenced using their type name.

In this case, the resource is identified by its provider name and type, which happens to be Microsoft.Storage/storageaccounts.

Until recently, ARM templates expected resource groups to be available prior to their deployment. They were also limited to deploying to a single resource group within a single subscription.

This means that, until recently, an ARM template could deploy all resources within a single resource group. This was the practice for years, until recently Azure announced that a single ARM template could be used for deploying resources to multiple resource groups within the same subscription of multiple subscriptions simultaneously. It's now possible to create resource groups as part of ARM templates, which means it's now possible to deploy resources to multiple regions into different resource groups.

Why would we need to create resource groups from within ARM templates, and why would we need cross-subscription and resource-group deployments simultaneously?

To appreciate the value of creating resource group and cross-subscription deployments, we need to understand how deployments were carried out prior to these features being available.

To deploy an ARM template, a resource group is a prerequisite. Resource groups should be created prior to the deployment of a template. Developers use PowerShell, the Azure CLI, or the REST API to create resource groups and then initiate the deployment of ARM templates. This means that any end-to-end deployment consists of multiple steps. The first step is the provision of the resource group and the next step is deployment of the ARM template to newly created resource group. These steps could be executed using a single PowerShell script or individual steps from the PowerShell command line. The PowerShell script should implement exception handling, compensating code, rollback at a minimum until it's enterprise ready. It is important to note that resource groups can be deleted from Azure and the next time the script runs they might be expected to be available. It would fail because it might assume that the resource group exists. In short, the deployment of the ARM template to a resource group should be an atomic step rather than multiple steps.

Compare this with the ability to create resource groups and its constituent resources together within the same ARM templates. Whenever you deploy the template, it ensures that the resource groups are created if they don't yet exist, and continues to deploy resources to them after creation.

Let's also understand how these new features can help to remove some of the technical constraints related to disaster-recovery sites.

Prior to these features, if you had to deploy a solution that was designed with disaster recovery in mind, there were two separate deployments: one deployment for the primary region and another deployment for the secondary region. For example, if you were deploying an ASP.NET MVC application using App Services, you would create an app service and configure it for the primary region, and then you would conduct another deployment with the same template to another region with the same configuration.

With the availability of cross-subscription and resource-group deployment, it's possible to create the disaster-recovery site at the same time as the primary site. This eliminates two deployments and ensures that the same configuration can be used on multiple sites.

Deploying resource groups with ARM templates

In this section, an ARM template will be authored and deployed, which will create a couple of resource groups within the same subscription.

To use PowerShell to deploy templates that contain resource groups and cross-subscription resources, the latest version of PowerShell should be used. At the time of writing, Azure module version 6.6.0 was used:

```
PS C:\Users\rites> Get-Module azurerm.resources

ModuleType Version    Name                    ExportedCommands

Script     6.6.0      AzureRM.Resources       {Add-AzureRmADGroupMember,
```

If the latest Azure module is not installed, it can be installed using the command as follows:

```
install-module -Name Azurerm -Force
```

Now, it's time to create an ARM template that will create multiple Resource groups within same subscription. The code for ARM template is shown next:

```
{
  "$schema":
"https://schema.management.azure.com/schemas/2015-01-01/deploymentTemplate.
json#",
  "contentVersion": "1.0.0.0",
  "parameters": {
    "resourceGroupInfo": {
      "type": "array"    },
    "multiLocation": {
      "type": "array"
    }
  },
  "resources": [
    {
      "type": "Microsoft.Resources/resourceGroups",
      "location": "[parameters('multiLocation')[copyIndex()]]",
      "name": "[parameters('resourceGroupInfo')[copyIndex()]]",
      "apiVersion": "2018-05-01",
      "copy": {
        "name": "allResourceGroups",
        "count": "[length(parameters('resourceGroupInfo'))]"
      },
      "properties": {}
    }
  ],
  "outputs": {}
}
```

The first section of the code listing is about parameters that the ARM templates expect. These are mandatory parameters, and anybody deploying these templates should provide values for them. Array values must be provided for both the parameters.

The second major section is the `resources` JSON array, which can contain multiple resources. In this example, we are creating resource groups, so it is declared within the `resources` section. Resource groups are getting provisioned in a loop because of the use of the `copy` element. The `copy` element ensures that the resource is run for a specified number of times and creates a new resource in every iteration. If we send two values for the `resourceGroupInfo` array parameter, the length of the array would be two and the `copy` element will ensure that the `resourceGroup` resource is executed twice.

All resource names within a template should be unique for a resource type, so the `copyIndex` function is used to provide a current iteration number and assigned to the name to make it unique. Also, we want the resource groups to be created in different regions using distinct regions names sent as parameter. The assignment of name and location for each resource group is done using the `copyIndex` function.

The code for the `parameters` file is shown next. This code is pretty straightforward and provides array values to the two parameters expected by the previous template. The values in this file should be changed for all parameters according to readers environment.

```
{
  "$schema":
"https://schema.management.azure.com/schemas/2015-01-01/deploymentParameter
s.json#",
  "contentVersion": "1.0.0.0",
  "parameters": {
    "resourceGroupInfo": {
      "value": [ "firstResourceGroup", "SeocndResourceGroup" ]
    },
    "multiLocation": {
      "value": [
        "West Europe",
        "East US"
      ]
    }
  }
}
```

To deploy this template using PowerShell, log into Azure with valid credentials using the following command:

```
Login-AzureRmAccount
```

The valid credentials could be a user account or a service principal. Then use a newly-released `New-AzureRmDeployment` cmdlet to deploy the template. The deployment script is available in file `multipleResourceGroups.ps1`:

```
New-AzureRmDeployment  -Location "West Europe"  -TemplateFile
"c:\users\rites\source\repos\CrossSubscription\CrossSubscription\multipleRe
sourceGroups.json" -TemplateParameterFile
"c:\users\rites\source\repos\CrossSubscription\CrossSubscription\multipleRe
sourceGroups.parameters.json"  -Verbose
```

It's important to understand that `New-AzureRMResourceGroupDeployment` cmdlet can't be used here. It can't be used because the scope of `New-AzureRMResourceGroupDeployment` cmdlet is a resource group and it expects a resource group to be available as a prerequisite. For deploying resources at subscription level, Azure had released a new cmdlet that can work above the resource group scope. The new cmdlet, `new-AzureRmDeployment`, works at the subscription level.

The same template can also be deployed using the Azure CLI. Here are the steps to deploy it using the Azure CLI:

1. Use the latest version of the Azure CLI to create resource groups using ARM template. At the time of writing, version 2.0.43 was used for deployment, as shown here:

```
C:\Users\rites>az --version
azure-cli (2.0.43)
```

2. Log into Azure using the following command and select the right subscription for usage:

```
C:\Users\rites>az login
```

3. In case, the login has access to multiple subscriptions; select an appropriate subscription using command shown next:

```
C:\Users\rites>az account set --subscription xxxxxxxx-xxxx-xxxx-xxxx-xxxxxxxxxxxx
```

4. Execute the deployment using the following command and the deployment script is available in file `multipleResourceGroupsCLI.txt`:

```
C:\Users\rites>az deployment create  --location WestUS --template-file "c:\users\rites\source\r
epos\CrossSubscription\CrossSubscription\azuredeploy.json"  --parameters @"c:\users\rites\sourc
e\repos\CrossSubscription\CrossSubscription\azuredeploy.parameters.json"  --verbose
```

Deploying resources across subscriptions and resource groups

In the last section, resource groups were created as part of ARM templates and this is a relatively new Azure feature. Another new Azure feature is provisioning of resources into multiple subscriptions simultaneously from a single deployment using a single arm template. In this section, we will provision a new storage account into two different subscriptions and resource groups. The person deploying the ARM template would select one of the subscriptions as base subscription using which they would initiate the deployment and provision the storage account into the current and another subscription. The prerequisite for deploying this template is that the person doing the deployment should have access to at least two subscriptions and that they have contributor rights on these subscriptions. The code listing is shown here and available in `CrossSubscriptionStorageAccount.json` file within the accompanied code.

```
{
    "$schema":
"https://schema.management.azure.com/schemas/2015-01-01/deploymentTemplate.
json#",
    "contentVersion": "1.0.0.0",
    "parameters": {
      "storagePrefix1": {
        "type": "string",
        "defaultValue": "st01"
    ...
        "type": "string",
        "defaultValue": "rg01"
      },
      "remoteSub": {
        "type": "string",
        "defaultValue": "xxxxxxxx-xxxx-xxxx-xxxx-xxxxxxxxxxxx"
      }
    ...
```

```
                    }
                }
            ],
            "outputs": {}
        }
    }
}
],
"outputs": {}
}
```

It is important to note that the names of the resource group used within code should already be available in respective subscriptions. The code will throw error in case the resource groups are not available. Moreover, the names of the resource group should exactly match in arm template.

The code for deploying this template is shown next. In this case, we use New-AzureRmResourceGroupDeployment because the scope of deployment is a resource group. The deployment script is available in CrossSubscriptionStorageAccount.ps1 file:

```
New-AzureRmResourceGroupDeployment  -TemplateFile "<< path to your
CrossSubscriptionStorageAccount.json file >>" -ResourceGroupName "<<provide
your base subscription resource group name>>" -storagePrefix1 <<provide
prefix for first storage account>> -storagePrefix2 <<provide prefix for
first storage account>> -verbose
```

Another example of cross-subscription and resource-group deployments

In this section, we create two storage accounts in two different subscriptions, resource groups, and regions from one ARM template and a single deployment. It uses the nested templates approach along with the copy element to provide different names and locations to these resource groups in different subscriptions.

However, before we can execute the next set of ARM templates, an Azure Key Vault should be provisioned as a pre-requisites and a secret should be added to it. This is because the names of the stroage accounts are retrieved from Azure Key Vault as passed as parameters to ARM templates for provisioning the storage account.

To provision an Azure Key Vault using Azure PowerShell, the next set of commands can be executed. The code for commands shown next is available in `CreateKeyVaultandSetSecret.ps1` file with accompanied code.

```
New-AzureRmResourceGroup -Location <<replace with location of your key
vault>> -Name <<replace with name of your resource group for key vault>> -
verbose
New-AzureRmKeyVault -Name <<replace with name of your key vault>> -
ResourceGroupName <<replace with name of your resource group for key
vault>>  -Location <<replace with location of your key vault>> -
EnabledForDeployment -EnabledForTemplateDeployment -
EnabledForDiskEncryption -EnableSoftDelete -EnablePurgeProtection -Sku
Standard -Verbose
```

Readers should note the `ResourceID` value should be noted from the result of `New-AzureRmKeyVault` cmdlet. This value will be needed to replace in `parameters` file. See next image for details.

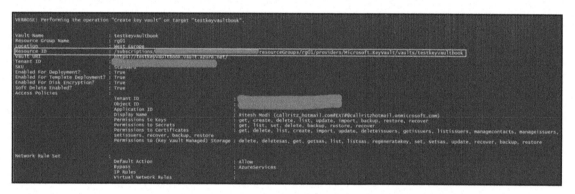

Execute the command shown next to add a new secret to the newly created Azure Key Vault.

```
Set-AzureKeyVaultSecret -VaultName <<replace with name of your key vault>>
-Name <<replace with name of yoursecret>> -SecretValue $(ConvertTo-
SecureString -String <<replace with value of your secret>> -AsPlainText -
Force ) -Verbose
```

The code listing is available in file `CrossSubscriptionNestedStorageAccount.json` from within the accompanied code:

```
{
  "$schema":
"https://schema.management.azure.com/schemas/2015-01-01/deploymentTemplate.
json#",
  "contentVersion": "1.0.0.0",
```

```
  "parameters": {
    "hostingPlanNames": {
      "type": "array",
      "minLength": 1
    },
  ...
      "type": "Microsoft.Resources/deployments",
      "name": "deployment01",
      "apiVersion": "2017-05-10",
      "subscriptionId": "[parameters('subscriptions')[copyIndex()]]",
      "resourceGroup": "[parameters('resourceGroups')[copyIndex()]]",
      "copy": {
        "count": "[length(parameters('hostingPlanNames'))]",
        "name": "mywebsites",          "mode": "Parallel"
      },
      ...
              "kind": "Storage",
              "properties": {
              }
          }
      }
    ]
...
```

Here's the code for the `parameters` file. It is available in file `CrossSubscriptionNestedStorageAccount.parameters.json`.

```
{
  "$schema":
"https://schema.management.azure.com/schemas/2015-01-01/deploymentParameter
s.json#",
  "contentVersion": "1.0.0.0",
  "parameters": {
    "hostingPlanNames": {
    ...
    "storageKey": {
      "reference": {
        "keyVault": { "id": "<<replace it with the value of Key vault
ResourceId noted before>>" },
        "secretName": "<<replace with the name of the secret available in
Key vault>>"
      }
    }
  }
}
```

Here's the PowerShell code for deploying the previous template. The deployment script is available in file `CrossSubscriptionNestedStorageAccount.ps1`:

```
New-AzureRmResourceGroupDeployment  -TemplateFile
"c:\users\rites\source\repos\CrossSubscription\CrossSubscription\CrossSubsc
riptionNestedStorageAccount.json" -ResourceGroupName rg01 -
TemplateParameterFile
"c:\users\rites\source\repos\CrossSubscription\CrossSubscription\CrossSubsc
riptionNestedStorageAccount.parameters.json" -Verbose
```

Deploying cross-subscription and resource-group deployments using linked templates

The previous example used nested templates to deploy to multiple subscriptions and resource groups. In the next example, we'll deploy multiple app service plans in separate subscriptions and resource groups using linked templates. The linked templates are stored in Azure Blob Storage that is protected using policies. This means that only the holder of the storage account key or a valid shared access signature can access this template. The access key is stored in the Azure Key Vault and is accessed from the `parameters` file using references under the `storageKey` element. Readers should upload the `website.json` file within a container of Azure Blob Storage. `website.json` file is a linked template responsible for provisioning an App Service plan and an App Service. The file is protected using **Private (no anonymous access)** policy as shown in the next screenshot. Privacy policy ensures that anonymous access is not allowed. I have created a container named `armtemplates` and set it with a private policy.

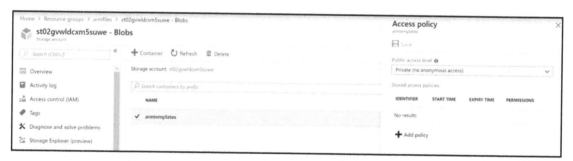

This file can only be accessed using the SAS keys. The SAS keys can be generated from Azure portal for a storage account using the **Shared access signature** on left menu as shown next. Readers should click on **Generate SAS and connection string** button to generate the SAS token. It is to be noted that SAS token is displayed once and not stored with Azure. So, copy it and store it somewhere such that it can be uploaded to Azure Key Vault. The next screenshot should the generation of SAS token.

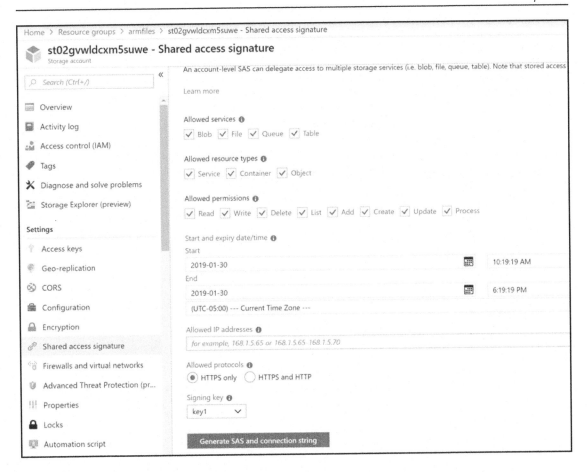

We will use the same key vault that was created in the previous section. We just have to ensure that there are two secrets available within the key vault. The first secret is the `StorageName` and the other one is `StorageKey`. The commands to create these secrets on key vault is shown next:

```
Set-AzureKeyVaultSecret -VaultName "testkeyvaultbook" -Name "storageName" -
SecretValue $(ConvertTo-SecureString -String "uniquename" -AsPlainText -
Force ) -Verbose

Set-AzureKeyVaultSecret -VaultName "testkeyvaultbook" -Name "storageKey" -
SecretValue $(ConvertTo-SecureString -String
"?sv=2018-03-28&ss=bfqt&srt=sco&sp=rwdlacup&se=2019-03-29T21:51:03Z&st=2019
-01-30T14:51:03Z&spr=https&sig=gTynGhj20er6pD17Ab%2Bpc29WO3%2BJhvi%2BfF%2F6
rHYWp4g%3D" -AsPlainText -Force ) -Verbose
```

Readers are advised to change the names of key vault and the secret key value based on their storage account.

After ensuring that key vault has the necessary secrets, the ARM template file code can be used for deploying the nested template across subscriptions and resource groups.

The ARM template code is available in file `CrossSubscriptionLinkedStorageAccount.json` and the same has been shown here. Readers are advised also to change the value of variable `templateUrl` within this file. It should be updated with a valid Azure Blob Storage file location.

```
{
  "$schema":
"https://schema.management.azure.com/schemas/2015-01-01/deploymentTemplate.
json#",
  "contentVersion": "1.0.0.0",
  "parameters": {
    "hostingPlanNames": {
      "type": "array",
      "minLength": 1
  ...
      "type": "Microsoft.Resources/deployments",
      "name": "fsdfsdf",
      "apiVersion": "2017-05-10",
      "subscriptionId": "[parameters('subscriptions')[copyIndex()]]",
      "resourceGroup": "[parameters('resourceGroups')[copyIndex()]]",
      "copy": {
        "count": "[length(parameters('hostingPlanNames'))]",
        "name": "mywebsites",
        "mode": "Parallel"
    ...
    ]
  }
}
```

Here's the code for the `parameters` file is shown next. Readers are advised to change the values of the parameters including the `resourceid` of key vault and the secret name. The names of APP Services should be unique otherwise the template will fail to deploy. The code for parameters file is available in code file `CrossSubscriptionLinkedStorageAccount.parameters.json`:

```
{
  "$schema":
"https://schema.management.azure.com/schemas/2015-01-01/deploymentParameter
s.json#",
  "contentVersion": "1.0.0.0",
  "parameters": {
```

```
    "hostingPlanNames": {
      "value": [ "firstappservice", "secondappservice" ]
  ...
    "storageKey": {
      "reference": {
        "keyVault": { "id": "/subscriptions/xxxxxxxx-xxxx-xxxx-xxxx-
xxxxxxxxxxxx/resourceGroups/keyvaluedemo/providers/Microsoft.KeyVault/vault
s/forsqlvault1" },
        "secretName": "storageKey"
      }
    }
  }
}
```

Here's the command to deploy the template. The deployment script is available in file `CrossSubscriptionLinkedStorageAccount.ps1`:

```
New-AzureRmResourceGroupDeployment  -TemplateFile
"c:\users\rites\source\repos\CrossSubscription\CrossSubscription\CrossSubsc
riptionLinkedStorageAccount.json" -ResourceGroupName <<replace with the
base subscription resource group name >> -TemplateParameterFile
"c:\users\rites\source\repos\CrossSubscription\CrossSubscription\CrossSubsc
riptionLinkedStorageAccount.parameters.json" -Verbose
```

Summary

The ability to deploy resources using a single deployment to multiple subscriptions, resource groups, and regions provides better ability to deploy, reduce bugs in deployment, and provide advanced benefits, such as creating disaster-recovery sites and high availability.

In the next chapter, we will focus on creating modular ARM templates, an essential skill for architecture that really wants to take their ARM templates to the next level. The next chapter will show various ways to design ARM templates and create reusable and modular ARM templates.

5
ARM Templates - Modular Design and Implementation

We know that there are multiple ways to author an ARM template. It is quite easy to author one that provisions all of the needed resources in Azure using Visual Studio and Visual Studio Code. A single ARM template can consist of all the required resources for a solution on Azure. This single ARM template could be as small as a few resources, or it could be a larger one consisting of many resources.

While authoring a single template consisting of all resources is quite tempting, it is advisable to plan an ARM template implementation divided into multiple smaller ARM templates beforehand so that future troubles related to them can be avoided.

In this chapter, we will look at how to write ARM templates in a modular way so that they can evolve over a period of time with minimal involvement in terms of changes and effort in testing and deployment.

However, before writing modular templates, it is best to understand the problems solved by writing them in a modular fashion.

The following topics will be covered in this chapter:

- Problems with a single template
- Understanding nested and linked deployment
- Linked templates
- Nested templates
- Free-flow configurations
- Known configurations

Problems with the single template

On the surface, it might not sound like a single large template consisting of all resources will have problems, but there are issues that could arise in the future. Let's understand the issues that might come up with single large templates.

Reduces flexibility in changing templates

Using a single large template with all resources makes it difficult to change it in future. With all dependencies, parameters, and variables in a single template, changing the template can take a considerable amount of time compared to smaller templates. The change could have an impact on other sections of the template, which might go unnoticed, as well as introducing bugs.

Troubleshooting large templates

Large templates are difficult to troubleshoot. This is a known fact. The larger the number of resources in a template, the more difficult it is to troubleshoot the template. A template deploys all resources in it, and finding a bug involves deploying the template quite often. Developers would have reduced productivity while waiting for the completion of template deployment.

Also, deploying a single template is more time-consuming than smaller templates. Developers have to wait for resources containing errors to be deployed before taking any action.

Dependency abuse

The dependencies between resources also tend to become more complex in larger templates. It is quite easy to abuse the usage of the `dependsOn` feature in ARM templates because of the way they work. Every resource in a template can refer to all its prior resources rather than building a tree of dependencies. ARM templates do not complain if a single resource is dependent on all other resources in the ARM template, even though those other resources might inter-dependencies within themselves. This makes changing ARM templates bug prone and also, at times, it is not possible to even change them.

Reduced agility

Generally, there are multiple features teams in a project, with each owning their own resources in Azure. These teams will find it difficult to work with a single ARM template because a single developer should be updating them. Updating a single temple with multiple teams might induce conflict and difficult-to-solve merges. Having multiple smaller templates can enable each team to author their own piece of an ARM template.

No reusability

If you have a single template, then that's what you have, and using this template means deploying all resources. There is no possibility, out of the box, to select individual resources without some maneuvering, such as adding conditional resources. A single large template loses reusability since you take all the resources or none.

Knowing that single large templates have so many issues, it is a good practice to author modular templates so that we get the benefits of the following:

- Multiple teams can work on their templates in isolation
- Templates can be reused across projects and solutions
- Templates are easy to debug and troubleshoot

Understanding the Single Responsibility Principle

The **Single Responsibility Principle** is one of the core principles of SOLID. It states that a class or code segment should be responsible for a single functionality and that it should own that functionality completely. The code should change or evolve only if there is a functional change or bug in the current functionality and not otherwise. This code should not change because of changes in some other component or code that is not part of the current component.

Applying the same principle to ARM templates helps to create templates that have the sole responsibility of deploying a single resource or functionality instead of deploying all resources and a complete solution.

Using this principle will help you create multiple templates, each responsible for a single resource or a smaller group of resources rather than all resources.

Faster troubleshooting and debugging

Each template deployment is considered a separate deployment and has separate logs for them. When multiple templates are deployed for deploying a solution, each template deployment will have separate logs for its input and output descriptions. It is far easy to isolate bugs and troubleshoot issues in smaller templates compared to a single large template.

Modular templates

When a single large template is decomposed into multiple templates in which each smaller template takes care of the resources in it, and those resources are solely owned, maintained, and the responsibility of the template containing it, we can say we have modular templates. Each template within these templates follows the Single Responsibility Principle.

Before understanding how to divide a large template into multiple smaller reusable templates, it is important to understand the technology behind creating smaller templates and how to compose them to build complete applications.

Deployments resources

Azure provides a facility to link templates. Although we have already gone through linked templates in detail, I mention it here again to help you understand how linking templates helps in achieving modularity, composition, and decomposition.

ARM templates provide specialized resources known as **deployments** available within the `Microsoft.Resources` namespace. A deployments resource in an ARM templates looks very similar to the code segment shown as follows:

```
"resources": [
  {
      "apiVersion": "2017-05-10",
      "name": "linkedTemplate",
      "type": "Microsoft.Resources/deployments",
      "properties": {
          "mode": "Incremental",
          <nested-template-or-external-template>
      }
  }
]
```

This template is self-explanatory, and the two most important configurations in this resource are the type and the properties. The type here is deployments rather than any specific Azure resource (storage, VM, and so on) and the properties decide whether the deployment is a linked template deployment or a nested template deployment. The property values change accordingly.

However, what does the deployments resource do? The job of a deployments resource is to deploy another template. Another template could be an external template in a separate ARM template file, or it could be a nested template. It means it is possible to invoke other templates from a template, just like a function call.

There can be nested levels of deployments in ARM templates. What this means is that a single template can call another template, and the called template can further call another template, and this can go on for five levels of nested calling. In the next diagram, there is a master template that internally calls two other templates using two distinct deployments resources, and those two deployment resources further call a template that deploys multiple resources. This parent-child relationship can go five levels deep:

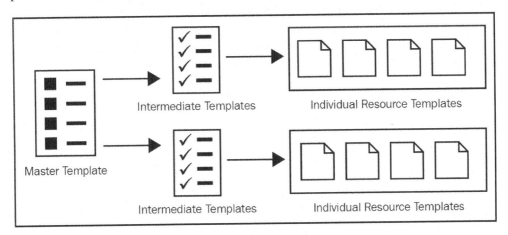

Linked templates

Linked templates are templates that invoke external templates. External templates are stored in different ARM template files. An example of linked templates is shown next.

```
"resources": [
    {
        "apiVersion": "2017-05-10",
        "name": "linkedTemplate",
        "type": "Microsoft.Resources/deployments",
```

```
          "properties": {
            "mode": "Incremental",
            "templateLink": {
    "uri":"https://mystorageaccount.blob.core.windows.net/AzureTemplates/newSto
    rageAccount.json",
              "contentVersion":"1.0.0.0"
            },
            "parametersLink": {
    "uri":"https://mystorageaccount.blob.core.windows.net/AzureTemplates/newSto
    rageAccount.parameters.json",
              "contentVersion":"1.0.0.0"
            }
          }
        }
      ]
```

Important additional properties in this template compared to the previous template are `templateLink` and `parametersLink`. `templateLink` refers to the actual URL of the location of the external template file, and `parametersLink` is the URL location for the corresponding parameters file. It is important to note that the caller template should have access rights to the location of the called template. For example, if the external templates are stored in Azure Blob Storage, which is protected by keys, then the appropriate SAS keys must be available to the caller template to be able to access the linked templates.

It is also possible to provide explicit inline parameters instead of the `parametersLink` value, as shown here:

```
    "resources": [
      {
        "apiVersion": "2017-05-10",
        "name": "linkedTemplate",
        "type": "Microsoft.Resources/deployments",
        "properties": {
          "mode": "Incremental",
          "templateLink": {
    "uri":"https://mystorageaccount.blob.core.windows.net/AzureTemplates/newSto
    rageAccount.json",
              "contentVersion":"1.0.0.0"
          },
          "parameters": {
            "StorageAccountName":{"value": "
                              [parameters('StorageAccountName')]"}
          }
        }
      }
    ]
```

Nested templates

Nested templates are a relatively new feature in ARM templates compared to external linked templates.

Nested templates do not define resources in external files. The resources are defined within the caller template itself and within the deployments resource, as shown here:

```
"resources": [
  {
    "apiVersion": "2017-05-10",
    "name": "nestedTemplate",
    "type": "Microsoft.Resources/deployments",
    "properties": {
      "mode": "Incremental",
      "template": {
        "$schema": "https://schema.management.azure.com/schemas/2015-
            01-01/deploymentTemplate.json#",
        "contentVersion": "1.0.0.0",
        "resources": [
          {
            "type": "Microsoft.Storage/storageAccounts",
            "name": "[variables('storageName')]",
            "apiVersion": "2015-06-15",
            "location": "West US",
            "properties": {
              "accountType": "Standard_LRS"
            }
          }
        ]
      }
    }
  }
]
```

In this code segment, we can see that the storage account resource is nested within the original template as part of the deployments resource. Instead of using the `templateLink` and `parametersLink` attributes, a resources array is used to create multiple resources as part of a single deployment. The advantage of using a nested deployment is that resources within a parent can be used to reconfigure them by using their names. Usually, a resource with a name can exist only once within a template. Nested templates allow us to use them within the same template. Nested templates ensure that all templates are self-sufficient rather than storing them separately, and they might or might not be accessible to those external files.

Now that we understand the technology behind modular arm templates, however, how should we divide a large template into smaller templates?

There are multiple ways a large template can be decomposed into smaller templates. Microsoft recommends the following pattern for the decomposition of ARM templates:

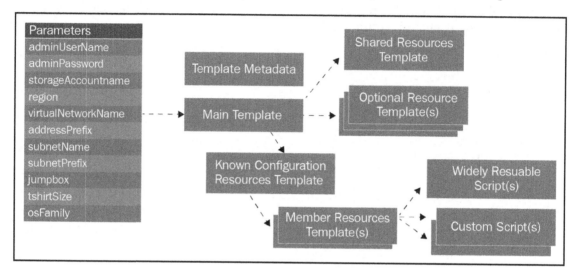

When we decompose a large template into smaller templates, there is always a main template that is used for deploying the solution. This main or master template internally invokes other nested or linked templates and they, in turn, invoke other templates, and finally the templates containing Azure resources are deployed.

The main template can invoke a known configuration resource template, which in turn will invoke templates comprising Azure resources. The known configuration resource template is specific to a project or solution and they do not have much of reusable factor associated with them. The Member Resources templates are reusable templates invoked by the known configuration resources template.

Optionally, the master template can invoke shared resource templates and other resource templates if they exist.

It is important to understand known configurations. Templates can be authored as known configurations or as free-flow configurations.

Free-flow configurations

ARM templates can be authored as generic templates where most of the values assigned to variables, if not all, are obtained as parameters. This allows the person using the template to pass any value they deem necessary to deploy resources in Azure. For example, the person deploying the template could choose a virtual machine of any size, any number of virtual machines, and any configuration for its storage and networks. This is known as free-flow configuration, where most of the configuration is allowed and the templates indeed come from the user instead of being declared within the template.

There are challenges with this kind of configuration. The biggest one is that not all configurations are supported on every Azure region and data center in Azure. The templates will fail to create resources if those resources are not allowed to be created in a specific locations or regions. Another issue with free-flow configuration is that users can provide any value they deem necessary and a template will honor them, thereby increasing both the cost and deployment footprint even though they are not completely required.

Known configurations

Known configurations, on the other hand, are specific pre-determined configurations for deploying an environment using ARM templates. These pre-determined configurations are known as **T-shirt sizing configuration**. The T-shirt sizing acts as an analogy. Similar to the way a T-shirt is available in a pre-determined configuration such as small, medium, and large, ARM templates can be pre-configured to deploy a small, medium, or large environment depending on the need. This means users cannot determine any custom size for the environment, but they can choose from various options, and ARM templates execution during runtime will ensure that an appropriate configuration of the environment is provisioned.

So the first step in creating a modular ARM template is deciding on the known configurations for an environment.

As an example, here is the configuration of a data center deployment on Azure:

T-shirt size	ARM template configuration
Small	4 virtual machines with 7 GB of memory along with 4 CPU cores
Medium	8 virtual machines with 14 GB of memory along with 8 CPU cores
Large	16 virtual machines with 28 GB of memory along with 8 CPU cores

Now that we know the configurations, we can create modular ARM templates.

There are two ways to write modular ARM templates:

- **Composed templates**: Composed templates link to other templates. Examples of composed templates are master and intermediate templates.
- **Leaf-level templates**: Leaf-level templates are templates that contains a single Azure resource.

ARM templates can be divided into modular templates based on the following:

- Technology
- Functionality

An ideal way to decide on the modular method to author an ARM template is as follows:

- Define resource or leaf-level templates consisting of single resources. In the upcoming diagram, the extreme right templates are leaf-level templates. Within the diagram, virtual machines, virtual network, storage and others in the same column represent leaf-level templates.
- Compose environment specific templates using the leaf-level templates. These environment specific templates provisions an Azure environment such as an SQL Server environment, an app service environment, or a data center environment. Let's drill down a bit more into this topic. Let's take the example of an Azure SQL environment. To create an Azure SQL environment, multiple resources are needed. At a bare minimum, a logical SQL Server, an SQL database, and a few SQL firewall resources should be provisioned. All these resources are defined in individual templates at leaf level. These resources can be composed together in a single template that has capability to create an Azure SQL environment. Anybody wanting to create an SQL environment can use this composed template. The image shown next has Data center, messaging and App Services as environment specific templates.
- Create templates with higher abstraction composing multiple environment specific templates into solutions. These templates are composed of environment specific templates that were created in previous step. For example, to create an e-commerce inventory solution that needs an app service environment and a SQL environment, two environment templates -APP Service environment and an SQL Server environment template can be composed together. The image shown next has functional 1 and functional 2 as solution specific templates.
- Finally, a master template should be created, which should be composed of multiple templates where each template is capable of deploying a solution.

The preceding steps for creating a modular designed template can be easily be understood by means of an diagram, as shown next:

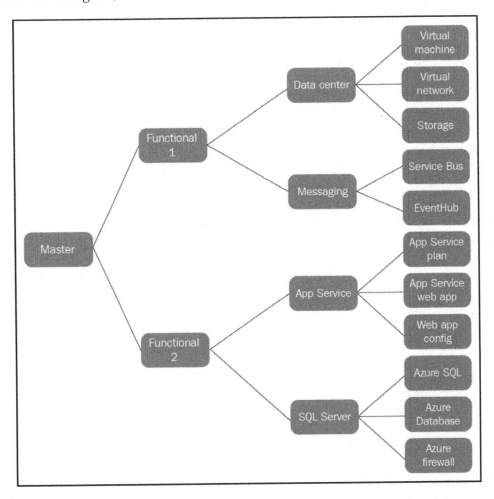

Now, let's implement a part of the functionality shown in the previous diagram. In this implementation, we will provision a virtual machine with a script extension using a modular approach. The custom script extension deploys Docker binaries and prepares a container environment on Windows Server 2016 virtual machine.

Now, we are going to create a solution using ARM templates using a modular approach. As mentioned before, the first step is to create individual resource templates. These individual resource templates will be used to compose additional templates capable of creating an environment. These templates would be needed to create a virtual machine. All arm templates shown here are available in accompanied chapter code. The names and code of these templates are shown next:

- `Storage.json`
- `virtualNetwork.json`
- `PublicIPAddress.json`
- `NIC.json`
- `VirtualMachine.json`
- `CustomScriptExtension.json`

First, let's look at the code for the `Storage.json` template. This template provisions a storage account that every virtual machine needs for storing its OS and data disk files:

```json
{
    "$schema": "https://schema.management.azure.com/schemas/2015-01-
01/deploymentTemplate.json#",
    "contentVersion": "1.0.0.0",
  "parameters": {
    "storageAccountName": {
      "type": "string",
      "minLength": 1
    },
    "storageType": {
      "type": "string",
      "minLength": 1
    },
    ...
  "outputs": {
    "resourceDetails": {
      "type": "object",
      "value": "[reference(parameters('storageAccountName'))]"
    }
  }
}
```

Next, let's look at the code for the public IP address template. A virtual machine that should be accessible over the internet needs a public IP address resource assigned to its network interface card. Although exposing a virtual machine to the internet is optional, this resource optionally might get used for creating a virtual machine. The code shown next is available in `PublicIPAddress.json` file:

```
{
    "$schema": "https://schema.management.azure.com/schemas/2015-01-
01/deploymentTemplate.json#",
    "contentVersion": "1.0.0.0",
  "parameters": {
    "publicIPAddressName": {
      "type": "string",
      "minLength": 1
    },
    "publicIPAddressType": {
      "type": "string",
      "minLength": 1
  . . .
      }
    }
  ],
  "outputs": {
    "resourceDetails": {
      "type": "object",
      "value": "[reference(parameters('publicIPAddressName'))]"
    }
  }
}
```

Next, let's look at the code for the virtual network. Virtual machines on Azure need a virtual network for communication. This template will be used to create a virtual network on Azure with pre-defined address range and subnets. The code shown next is available in `virtualNetwork.json` file:

```
{
    "$schema": "https://schema.management.azure.com/schemas/2015-01-
01/deploymentTemplate.json#",
    "contentVersion": "1.0.0.0",
  "parameters": {
    "virtualNetworkName": {
      "type": "string",
      "minLength": 1
  . . .
    },
    "subnetPrefix": {
      "type": "string",
```

```
                "minLength": 1
            },
            "resourceLocation": {
              "type": "string",
              "minLength": 1
            }
      ...
                "subnets": [
                  {
                    "name": "[parameters('subnetName')]",
                    "properties": {
                      "addressPrefix": "[parameters('subnetPrefix')]"
                    }
                  }
                ]
              }
            }
      ],
      "outputs": {
        "resourceDetails": {
          "type": "object",
          "value": "[reference(parameters('virtualNetworkName'))]"
        }
      }
    }
```

Next, let's look at the code for the Network Interface Card. A virtual network card is needed by virtual machine to connected to a virtual network and to accept and send requests from and to the internet. The code shown next is available in NIC.json file:

```
{
    "$schema": "https://schema.management.azure.com/schemas/2015-01-
01/deploymentTemplate.json#",
    "contentVersion": "1.0.0.0",
  "parameters": {
    "nicName": {
      "type": "string",
      "minLength": 1
    },
    "publicIpReference": {
      "type": "string",
      "minLength": 1
  ...
[resourceId(subscription().subscriptionId, resourceGroup().name,
'Microsoft.Network/publicIPAddresses', parameters('publicIpReference'))]",
    "vnetRef":
"[resourceId(subscription().subscriptionId, resourceGroup().name,
'Microsoft.Network/virtualNetworks',
```

```
    parameters('virtualNetworkReference'))]",
      "subnet1Ref": "[concat(variables('vnetRef'),'/subnets/',
  parameters('subnetReference'))]"
    },
  ...
                    "id": "[variables('subnet1Ref')]"
                }
            }
        }
    ]
  }
}
],
    "outputs": {
      "resourceDetails": {
        "type": "object",
        "value": "[reference(parameters('nicName'))]"
      }
    }
  }
}
```

Next, let's look at the code for creating a virtual machine. Each virtual machine is a resource in Azure, and note that this template has no reference to storage, network, public IP address, or other resources created earlier. This reference and composition will happen later in this section using another template. The code shown next is available in `VirtualMachine.json` file:

```
{
  "$schema": "https://schema.management.azure.com/schemas/2015-01-
01/deploymentTemplate.json#",
  "contentVersion": "1.0.0.0",
  "parameters": {
    "vmName": {
      "type": "string",
      "minLength": 1
  ...
    },
    "imageOffer": {
      "type": "string",
      "minLength": 1
    },
    "windowsOSVersion": {
      "type": "string",
      "minLength": 1
    },
    ...
    "outputs": {
```

```
    "resourceDetails": {
      "type": "object",
      "value": "[reference(parameters('vmName'))]"
    }
  }
    }
```

Next, let's look at the code for creating a custom script extension. This resource executes a PowerShell script on a virtual machine after it is provisioned. This resource provides an opportunity to execute post-provisioning tasks in Azure virtual machines. The code shown next is available in `CustomScriptExtension.json` file:

```
{
    "$schema":
"http://schema.management.azure.com/schemas/2015-01-01/deploymentTemplate.json#",
    "contentVersion": "1.0.0.0",
    "parameters": {
      "VMName": {
        "type": "string",
        "defaultValue": "sqldock",
        "metadata": {
...
            "commandToExecute": "[concat('powershell -ExecutionPolicy
Unrestricted -file docker.ps1')]"
          },
          "protectedSettings": {
          }
        }
      }
    ],
    "outputs": {
    }
}
```

Next, we'll look at the custom script extension PowerShell code that prepares the Docker environment. Please note that a virtual machine reboot might happen while executing the PowerShell script, depending on whether the containers Windows feature is already installed or not. The following script installs the NuGet package, the `DockerMsftProvider` provider, and Docker executable. `docker.ps1` file is available with the accompanied chapter code.

```
#
# docker.ps1
#
Install-PackageProvider -Name Nuget -Force -ForceBootstrap -Confirm:$false
Install-Module -Name DockerMsftProvider -Repository PSGallery -Force -
```

```
Confirm:$false -verbose
Install-Package -Name docker -ProviderName DockerMsftProvider -Force -
ForceBootstrap -Confirm:$false
```

All the linked templates shown before should be uploaded to a container within an Azure Blob Storage account. This container can have private access policy applied as we saw in the previous chapter however for this example, we will set the access policy as `container`. This means these linked templates can be accessed without the need of any SAS token.

Finally, let's focus on writing the master template. Within Master template, all the linked templates are composed together to create a solution—to deploy a virtual machine and execute a script within it. The same approach can be used for creating other solutions like provisioning a data center consisting of multiple inter-connected virtual machines. The code shown next is available in `Master.json` file.

```
{
    "$schema":
"https://schema.management.azure.com/schemas/2015-01-01/deploymentTemplate.
json#",
    "contentVersion": "1.0.0.0",
  "parameters": {
    "storageAccountName": {
      "type": "string",
      "minLength": 1
    ...
    },
    "subnetName": {
      "type": "string",
      "minLength": 1
    },
    "subnetPrefix": {
      "type": "string",
      "minLength": 1
    },
  ...
    "windowsOSVersion": {
      "type": "string",
      "minLength": 1
    },
    "vhdStorageName": {
      "type": "string",
      "minLength": 1
    },
    "vhdStorageContainerName": {
      "type": "string",
      "minLength": 1
...[concat('https://',parameters('storageAccountName'),'armtfiles.blob.core
.windows.net/',variables('containerName'),'/Storage.json')]",
```

```
        "contentVersion": "1.0.0.0"
      },
      "parameters": {
        "storageAccountName": {
          "value": "[parameters('storageAccountName')]"
        },
        "storageType": {
          "value": "[parameters('storageType')]"
        },
        "resourceLocation": {
          "value": "[resourceGroup().location]"
      ...
  "outputs": {
    "resourceDetails": {
      "type": "object",
      "value": "[reference('GetVM').outputs.resourceDetails.value]"
  }
  }
}
```

The master templates invoke the external templates and also co-ordinates inter-dependencies among them.

The external templates should be available at a well-known location so that the master template can access and invoke them. In this example, the external templates are stored in Azure Blob Storage container and this information was passed to ARM template by means of parameters.

The external templates in Azure Blob Storage could be access protected by setting up access policies. The command used to deploy the master template is shown next. It might look like a complex command but a majority of values are used as parameters. Readers are advised to change the value of these parameters before running it. The linked templates have been uploaded to a storage account named st02gvwldcxm5suwe within armtemplates container. The resource group should be created if it does not exists. The first command is used to create a new Resource Group in West Europe region:

```
New-AzureRmResourceGroup -Name "testvmrg" -Location "West Europe" -Verbose
```

Rest of the parameter values are needed for configuring each resource. The storage account name and dnsNameForPublicIP value should be unique within Azure:

```
New-AzureRmResourceGroupDeployment -Name "testdeploy1" -ResourceGroupName
testvmrg -Mode Incremental -TemplateFile "C:\chapter 05\Master.json" -
storageAccountName "st02gvwldcxm5suwe" -storageType "Standard_LRS" -
publicIPAddressName "uniipaddname" -publicIPAddressType "Dynamic" -
dnsNameForPublicIP "azureforarchitectsbook" -virtualNetworkName vnetwork01
```

```
-addressPrefix "10.0.1.0/16" -subnetName "subnet01" -subnetPrefix
"10.0.1.0/24" -nicName nic02 -vmSize "Standard_DS1" -adminUsername
"sysadmin" -adminPassword $(ConvertTo-SecureString -String sysadmin@123 -
AsPlainText -Force) -vhdStorageName oddnewuniqueacc -
vhdStorageContainerName vhds -OSDiskName mynewvm -vmName vm10 -
windowsOSVersion 2012-R2-Datacenter -imagePublisher MicrosoftWindowsServer
-imageOffer WindowsServer -containerName armtemplates -Verbose
```

Summary

ARM templates are the preferred means of provisioning resources in Azure. They are idempotent in nature, bringing consistency, predictability, and reusability to environment creation. In this chapter, we looked at how to create a modular ARM template. It is important for teams to spend quality time designing ARM templates in an appropriate way, so that multiple teams can work on them together. They are highly reusable and require minimal changes to evolve.

The next chapter will move on to a different very popular set of technology known as serverless within Azure. Azure functions is one of the major serverless resources on Azure, and that will be covered in complete depth, including durable functions.

6
Designing and Implementing Serverless Solutions

Serverless is one of the hottest buzzwords in technology these days, and everyone wants to ride this bandwagon. Serverless brings a lot of advantages in overall computing, software development processes, infrastructure, and technical implementation. There is a lot going on in the industry: at one end of the spectrum is **Infrastructure as a Service (IaaS)**, and at the other is serverless. In between are **Platform as a Service (PaaS)** and containers. I have met many developers and it seems to me that there exists some level of confusion among them about IaaS, PaaS, containers, and serverless computing. Also, there is much confusion about use cases, applicability, architecture, and implementation for the serverless paradigm. Serverless is a new paradigm that is changing not only technology but also culture and processes within organizations.

We will explore serverless by covering the following topics:

- Serverless
- Azure Functions
- Serverless events
- Azure Event Grid
- Serverless workflows
- Logic Apps
- Creating a complete solution using serverless integration

Serverless

Serverless refers to a deployment model in which users are responsible for only their application code and configuration. Customers of serverless do not have to bother about the underlying platform and infrastructure and can concentrate on solving their business problems by writing code.

Serverless does not mean there are no servers. Code and configuration will always need some server to run on. However, from the customer's perspective, an application can be practically serverless. Serverless means that the customer does not see the server at all. They do not care about the underlying platform and infrastructure. They do not need to manage or monitor anything. Serverless provides an environment that can scale up and down, out and in, automatically, without the customers even knowing about it. All operations related to platforms and infrastructures happen behind the scenes. Customers are provided with performance-related **service level agreements (SLAs)** and Azure ensures that it meets those SLAs irrespective of the server demands.

Customers are required to only bring in their only; the rest of the artifacts needed to run the code is the responsibility of the cloud provider.

The evolution of serverless

Before we understand serverless architecture and implementation, it is important to understand its history and how it has evolved. In the beginning, there were physical servers. Although users had complete control over physical servers, there were a lot of disadvantages, as follows:

- Long gestation periods between the ordering and the actual deployment of the server
- Capital-intensive in nature
- Waste of resources
- Lower return on investment
- Difficult to scale out and up

A natural evolution from physical servers was virtualization. Virtualization refers to the creation of virtual machines on top of physical servers and deploying applications within them. Virtual machines provide several advantages:

- No need to procure physical hardware
- Comparatively easier to create newer virtual machines
- Complete isolation of environments
- Lower costs compared to physical servers

However, virtualization had its own set of disadvantages:

- Still dependent on the physical procurement of a server for scaling out after a number of virtual machine instances
- Still costly because of human and hardware dependence
- Wastage of compute resources—each virtual machine runs a complete operating system within it
- High maintenance costs

The next evolution was IaaS from cloud providers. Instead of procuring and managing data centers and infrastructures, the strategy was to create virtual machines, storage, and networks in the cloud. The cloud provides software-defined infrastructure services and hides all the details related to physical servers, networks, and storage. This had some advantages:

- No capital expenditure, only operational expenses. Functions are charged based on consumption model instead of fixed cost (although there is an App Service model based on fixed cost).
- No gestation time to create new virtual machines—new virtual machines can be provisioned within minutes rather than hours.
- Flexible size of virtual machines.
- Easier scaling up and out of virtual machines.
- Completely secure.

Virtual machines in the cloud do have some disadvantages:

- Requires active monitoring and auditing
- Requires active maintenance of virtual machines
- Scalability, high-availability, and performance of virtual machines should be managed by users – any degradation and subsequent improvement is the user's responsibility
- A costly option because users pay for the entire machine whether it is used or not

The cloud also provides another pattern for deploying applications, popularly known as PaaS. PaaS provides abstraction from the underlying infrastructure in terms of virtual machines, virtual networks, and storage on the cloud. It provides a platform and an ecosystem where users do not need to know a thing about the infrastructure at all; they can simply their application on these platforms. There are definite advantages using PaaS compared to IaaS, but there are still better options. The main disadvantages of PaaS are the following:

- PaaS applications are deployed on virtual machines behind the scenes and the payment model is not granular; it is still at the deployment level.
- PaaS still demands monitoring for scaling out and in.
- Users still need to identify the requirements for their platform. There are limited options available for different types of platform. Azure exclusively provided a Windows-based environment until recently when it began to offer Linux as well. Moreover, the installation of packages, utilities, and software is the responsibility of its users.

Further, a new paradigm emerged known as containers, which is primarily made popular by Docker. Containers provide a lightweight, isolated, and secure environment that has all the benefits of virtual machines, minus their disadvantages. They do not have a dedicated operating system and instead rely on a base server operating system. Containers come in both IaaS and PaaS patterns. Containers provide many advantages:

- Faster provisioning of environments
- Consistent and predictable creation of environments
- Eases the creation of microservices architectures
- A rich ecosystem with advanced services from Kubernetes, Swarm, and DC/OS

Containers do have a few disadvantages, they are as follows:

- They require active monitoring and auditing.
- They require active maintenance.
- The scalability, high-availability, and performance of containers should be managed by orchestration tools like Kubernetes. These orchestration tools need extension deployments and skills to manage.

Serverless by definition is a deployment paradigm. It can be deployed on virtual machines as well as on containers. To get the best out of serverless, they should be deployed on to containers to take advantage of their faster creation and tear-down features. This will have a direct impact on scalability and high availability of serverless platform and also will be much faster, quicker compared to a virtual machine.

Principles of serverless technology

Serverless technology is based on the following principles:

- **Lower cost**: Cost is based on the actual consumption of computing resources and power. There is no cost if there is no consumption.
- **Unlimited scalability**: With serverless, there is no need to perform either manual or automatic scaling operations. All scaling up and down is handled directly by the Azure platform. The platform ensures that enough servers are provisioned to support the serverless deployment whether there are a few hundred users or millions of users; this scaling happens transiently without any interference or knowledge of the organization deploying the serverless components.
- **Event-driven**: Serverless functions should be able to execute based on certain events happening. The event should trigger the execution of the function. In other words, serverless should allow functions to decouple themselves from other functions and instead rely on the firing of certain events in which they are interested.
- **Single responsibility**: Serverless should implement a single functionality and responsibility and it should do that well. Multiple responsibilities should not be coded or implemented within a single function.
- **Execute quickly**: Serverless functions should not take a long time to complete a job. They should be able to execute quickly and return back.

Azure Functions advantages

Serverless computing is a relatively new paradigm and helps organizations convert large functionalities into smaller, discrete, on-demand functions that can be invoked and executed through automated triggers and scheduled jobs. They are also known as **Functions as a Service (FaaS)**, in which organizations can focus on their domain challenges instead of the underlying infrastructure and platform. FaaS also helps in devolving solution architectures into smaller, reusable functions, thereby increasing return on investments.

There is a plethora of serverless compute platforms available. Some of the important ones are listed here:

- Azure Functions
- AWS Lambda
- IBM OpenWhisk

- Iron.io
- Google Cloud Functions

In fact, every few days it feels like there is a new framework being introduced, and it is becoming increasingly difficult for enterprises to decide on the framework that works best for them. Azure provides a rich serverless environment known as Azure Functions, and I would like to point out a few features that it supports:

- Numerous ways to invoke a function—manual, on schedule, or based on an event
- Numerous types of binding support
- Ability to run function synchronously as well as asynchronously
- Execute functions based on multiple types of triggers
- Ability to run both long and short duration functions
- Ability to use proxy features to use different function architectures
- multiple usage models including consumption as well as App Service model
- Able to author functions using multiple languages such as JavaScript, Python, C#, and others
- Authorization based on oAuth
- Multiple authentication options including Azure AD, Facebook, Twitter, and other identity providers
- Easily configure inbound and outbound parameters
- Visual Studio integration for authoring of Azure Functions
- Massive parallelism

FaaS

Azure provides *Functions as a Service*. These are serverless implementations from Azure. With Azure Functions, code can be written in any language the user is comfortable with and an Azure Functions will provide a runtime to execute it. Based on the language chosen, an appropriate platform is provided for users to bring their own code. Functions are a unit of deployment and can automatically be scaled out and in. When dealing with Functions, users cannot view the underlying virtual machines and platform, but Azure Functions provides a small window to see them via the **Kudu** console.

There are two main components of Azure Functions:

- Azure Functions runtime
- Azure Functions binding and triggers

Azure Functions runtime

The core of Azure Functions is its Azure runtime. The precursor to Azure Functions was Azure WebJobs. The code for Azure WebJobs also forms the core for Azure Functions. There are additional features and extensions added to Azure WebJobs to create Azure Functions. The Functions runtime is the magic behind making Functions work. Azure Functions are hosted within Azure App Service. Azure App Service loads the Azure runtime and either waits for an external event to occurs or for any HTTP requests. On arrival of a request or the occurrence of a trigger, App Service loads the incoming payload, reads the Function's `function.json` file to find the Function's bindings and trigger, maps the incoming data to incoming parameters, and invokes the Function with parameter values. Once the Function completes its execution, the value is again passed back to the Azure Functions runtime by way of an outgoing parameter defined as a binding in the `function.json` file. The Function runtime returns the values to the caller. The Azure Functions runtime acts as the glue that enables the entire performance of Functions.

Azure Functions bindings and triggers

If the Azure Functions runtime is the brain of Azure Functions, then Function bindings and triggers are the heart. Azure Functions promote loose-coupling and high cohesion between services using triggers and bindings. The application implements code using imperative syntax for incoming and outgoing parameters and return values. This generally results in hardcoding the incoming parameters. Since Azure Functions should be capable of invoking any function defined, they implement a generic mechanism to invoke functions by means of triggers and bindings.

Binding refers to the process of creating a connection between the incoming data and the Azure Function, mapping the data types. The connection could be a single direction from the runtime to the Azure Functions, from the Azure Functions to runtime for return values, or could be multi-directional—the same binding can transmit data between the Azure runtime and Azure Functions. Azure Functions use a declarative way to define bindings.

Triggers are a special type of binding through which functions can be invoked based on external events. Apart from invoking the function, triggers also pass the incoming data, payload, and metadata to the function.

Bindings are defined in the `function.json` file:

```
{
   "bindings": [
     {
        "name": "checkOut",
        "type": "queueTrigger",
        "direction": "in",
        "queueName": "checkout-items",
        "connection": "AzureWebJobsDashboard"
     },
     {
        "name": "Orders",
        "type": "table",
        "direction": "out",
        "tableName": "OrderDetails",
        "connection": "<<Connection to table storage account>>"
     }
   ],
   "disabled": false
}
```

In this example, a trigger is declared that invokes the Function whenever there is a new item in the storage queue. The type is `queueTrigger`, the direction is inbound, `queueName` is `checkout-items`, and details about the target storage account connection and table name are also shown. All these values are important for the functioning of this binding. The `checkOut` name can be used within the Function's code as a variable.

Similarly, a binding for the return values is declared. Here the return value is named `Orders` and the data is the output from the Azure Functions. The binding writes the return data into Azure table storage using the connection string provided.

Both bindings and triggers can be modified and authored using the **Integrate** tab in Azure Functions. Behind the scenes, the `function.json` file is updated. The `checkOut` trigger is declared, as shown here:

The **Orders** output is shown next:

The authors of Azure Functions do not need to write any plumbing code to get data from multiple sources. They just decide the type of data expected from the Azure runtime. This is shown in the next code segment. Notice the checkout is available as a string to the Function. Functions provide multiple different types to be able to send to a function. For example, a queue binding can provide the following:

- **Plain old simple object (POCO)**
- String
- Byte[]
- CloudQueueMessage

The author of the Function can use any one of these datatypes, and the Azure Functions runtime will ensure that a proper object is sent to the Function as a parameter:

```
using System;
public static void Run(string checkOut, TraceWriter log)
{
    log.Info($"C# Queue trigger function processed: { checkOut }");
}
```

It is also important to know that in the previous screenshots, the storage account names are `AzureWebJobsStorage` and `AzureWebJobsDashboard`. These are keys that are defined within the Azure Functions **appSettings** setting.

> For more information on Azure bindings and triggers, refer to the following link: https://docs.microsoft.com/en-us/azure/azure-functions/functions-bindings-storage-queue.

Monitoring

Complete log information is provided for each request or trigger in the **Monitor** tab of Azure Functions. This helps in identifying issues and auditing any risks, bugs, or exceptions in Azure Functions:

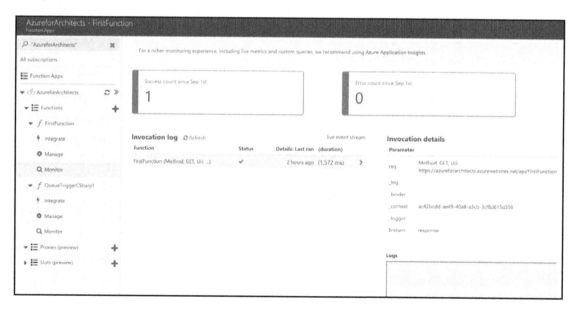

Authentication and authorization

Azure Functions rely on Azure App Service for their authentication needs. App Service has rich authentication features where clients can use OpenConnectID for authentication and OAuth for authentication. Users can be authenticated using Azure Active Directory, Facebook, Google, Twitter, or Microsoft accounts:

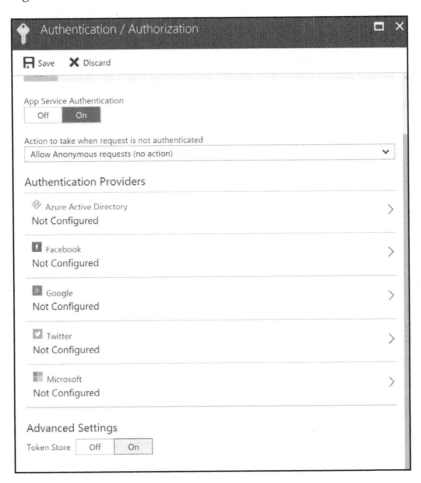

Azure Functions that are based on HTTP can also incorporate the use of keys, which should be sent along with HTTP requests:

The following keys are available from the **Manage** tab in Azure Functions:

- **Function keys**: Allows authorization to individual Functions. These keys should be sent as part of the HTTP request header.
- **Host keys**: Allows authorization to all Functions within a function app. These keys should be sent as part of the HTTP request header.
- **Default keys**: Used when using function and host keys. There is an additional host key named **_master** that helps in administrative access to the Azure Functions runtime API.

Azure Functions configuration

Azure Functions provide configuration options at multiple levels. They provide configuration for the following:

- The platform itself
- The Function app services

These settings affect every Function contained by them. More information about these settings are available at https://docs.microsoft.com/en-us/azure/azure-functions/functions-how-to-use-azure-function-app-settings.

Platform configuration

Azure Functions are hosted within Azure App Service, so they get all of its features. Diagnostic and monitoring logs can be configured easily using platform features. Furthermore, App Service provides options for assigning SSL certificates, using a custom domain, authentication, and authorization as part of it's networking features.

Although customers are not concerned about the infrastructure, operating system, filesystem, and platform on which the Functions actually execute, Azure Functions provides the necessary tooling to peek within the underlying system and make changes. The console and the Kudu console are the tools used for this purpose. They provide a rich editor to author Azure Functions and edit their configuration.

Azure Functions, just like App Service, allow the storage of configuration information within the `web.config` application setting section, which can be read on demand:

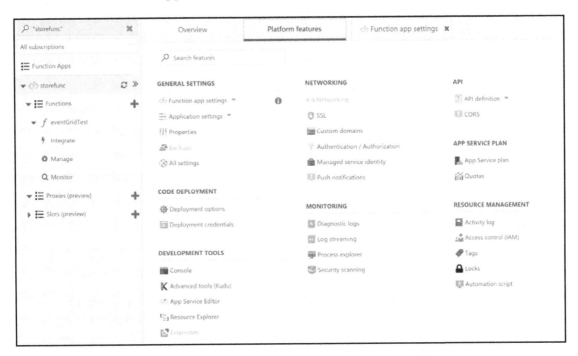

App Service Function settings

These settings affect all Functions. Application settings can be managed here. Azure Functions proxies can be enabled and disabled. We will discuss proxies later in this chapter. They also help in changing the edit mode of a function app and the deployment to slots:

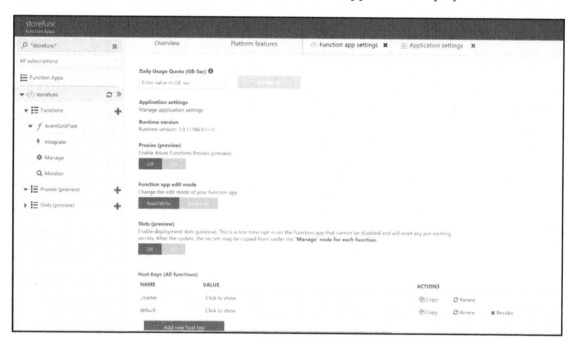

Azure Functions cost plans

Azure Functions are based on Azure App Service and provide a better costing model for users. There are two cost models:

- **Consumption plan**: This is based on the actual consumption and execution of Functions. This plan calculates the cost based on the compute usage during the actual consumption and execution of the Function. If a Function is not executed, there is no cost associated with it. However, it does not mean that performance is compromised in this plan. Azure Functions will automatically scale out and in based on demand to ensure basic minimum performance levels are maintained. A Function execution is allowed 10 minutes for its completion.

- **App service plan**: This plan provides complete dedicated virtual machines behind the scenes to Functions, and so the cost is directly proportional to the cost of the virtual machine and its size. There is a cost associated with this plan even if Functions are not executed at all. Function code can run for as long as necessary. There is no time limit. Within the App Service plan, the Function runtime goes idle if not used within a few minutes and can be awoken only using an HTTP trigger. There is an **Always On** setting that can be used for not letting the Function runtime go idle. Scaling is either manual or based on auto-scale settings.

Azure Functions use cases

There are many valid use cases for using and implementing Azure Functions:

- **Implementing microservices**: Azure Functions help in breaking down large applications into smaller, discreet functional code units. Each unit is treated independently of the other and evolves in its own life cycle. Each such code unit has its own compute, hardware, and monitoring requirements. Each Function can be connected to all other functions. These units are weaved together by orchestrators to build complete functionality. For example, in an e-commerce application, there can be individual Functions (code units), each responsible for listing catalogs, recommendations, categories, subcategories, shopping carts, checkouts, payment types, payment gateways, shipping addresses, billing addresses, taxes, shipping charges, cancellations, returns, emails, SMS, and so on. Some of these functions are brought together to create use cases for e-commerce applications, such as product browsing, checkout flow, and so on.
- **Integration between multiple endpoints**: Azure Functions can build overall application functionality by integrating multiple Functions. The integration can be based on the triggering of events or it could be on a push basis. This helps in decomposing large monolithic applications into small components.

- **Data processing**: Azure Functions can be used for processing incoming data in batches. They can help in processing data in multiple formats, such as XML, CSV, JSON, TXT, and so on. They can also run conversion, enrichment, cleaning, and filtering algorithms. In fact, multiple Functions can be used, each doing either conversion or enrichment, cleaning or filtering. Azure Functions can also be used to incorporate advanced cognitive services, such as **optical character recognition (OCR)**, computer vision, and image manipulation and conversion.
- **Integrating legacy applications**: Azure Functions can help in integrating legacy applications with newer protocols and modern applications. Legacy applications might not be using industry-standard protocols and formats. Azure Functions can act as a proxy for these legacy applications, accept requests from users or other applications, convert the data into a format understood by a legacy application, and talk to it on protocols it understands. This opens a world of opportunity for integrating and bringing old and legacy applications into the mainstream portfolio.
- **Scheduled jobs**: Azure Functions can be used to execute continuously or periodically for certain application Functions. These application Functions can perform tasks such as periodically taking backups, restoring, running batch jobs, exporting and importing data, and bulk emailing.
- **Communication gateways**: Azure Functions can be used in communication gateways when using notification hubs, SMS, and email, for instance.

Types of Azure Functions

Azure Functions can be categorized into three different types:

- **On-demand functions**: These are Functions that are executed when they are explicitly called or invoked. Examples of such Functions include HTTP-based Functions and webhooks.
- **Scheduled functions**: These Functions are like timer jobs and execute Functions on fixed intervals.
- **Event-based functions**: These Functions are executed based on external events. For example, uploading a new file to Azure blob storage generates an event that could start execution of the Azure Functions.

Creating your first Azure Functions

Azure Functions can be created using the Azure portal, PowerShell, Azure CLI, and REST APIs. The steps for for creating a Function using the ARM template are already detailed at `https://docs.microsoft.com/en-us/azure/azure-functions/functions-infrastructure-as-code`. In this section, Azure Functions will be provisioned using the portal.

Azure Functions are hosted within Azure App Service. Users create a new function app, which in turn creates an App Service plan and App Service. The App Service plan is configured based on the following:

1. After you have configured the App Service plan, filling in the details:
   - **Name**: The name of app service. The name should be unique within `.azurewebsites.net` domain.
   - **Location**: The location for hosting the Azure Functions App Service.
   - **Hosting plan**: This is also known as the pricing plan. Here, two options, as discussed previously, are available—the consumption plan and the App Service plan.
   - **Resource group name**: The name of the resource group containing both the App Service plan and App Service.
   - **Storage account**: Azure Functions need an Azure Storage account to store their internal data and logs.
   - **Enable application insights**: Enable this to capture telemetry information from Azure Functions.

Once the details are filled, click on **Create**:

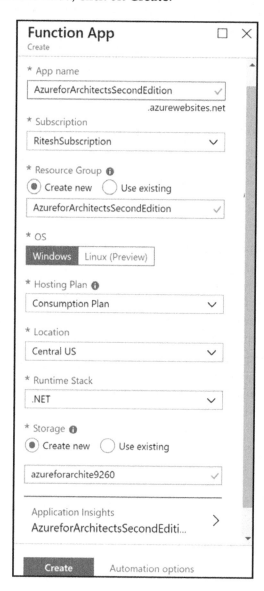

Creating an Azure function app will lead you to the following dashboard after provisioning:

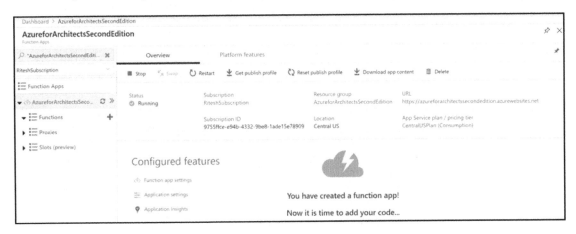

2. Clicking on the **+** button next to the **Functions** will show a wizard for creating a new function. This wizard shows the tools that can be used to create Azure Functions. Select **In-Portal** as an option and click on **Continue** button to navigate to next screen that displays multiple types of template like **WebHook + API**, **Timer**, and **More Templates....** Select **WebHook + API** and click on **Create** button. This would create the function with scaffolding code and structure for getting started. This scaffolding code is also generated for default bindings and triggers.

```csharp
run.csx          Save              ▶ Run        </> Get function URL

 1  #r "Newtonsoft.Json"
 2
 3  using System.Net;
 4  using Microsoft.AspNetCore.Mvc;
 5  using Microsoft.Extensions.Primitives;
 6  using Newtonsoft.Json;
 7
 8  public static async Task<IActionResult> Run(HttpRequest req, ILogger log)
 9  {
10      log.LogInformation("C# HTTP trigger function processed a request.");
11
12      string name = req.Query["name"];
13
14      string requestBody = await new StreamReader(req.Body).ReadToEndAsync();
15      dynamic data = JsonConvert.DeserializeObject(requestBody);
16      name = name ?? data?.name;
17
18      return name != null
19          ? (ActionResult)new OkObjectResult($"Hello, {name}")
20          : new BadRequestObjectResult("Please pass a name on the query string or in the request body");
21  }
22
```

3. Creating this Function provides a complete Function-authoring integrated environment, along with some code. This code gets the raw content from the incoming `req` parameter, which is filled up by the Azure runtime with incoming data (query string, form values, and so on). There could be multiple types of data within this incoming parameter,
   and in this function a single value is extracted out of it. The value is converted from JSON to .NET object and based on whether the name parameter is present or absent, appropriate response is returned back to user.

4. This Function can be invoked using an HTTP request from the browser. The URL for this Function is available from the environment and is composed of the function app name, along with the Function name. The format is `https://<<function app name>>.azurewebsites.net/api/<<function name>>`. In this case, the URL will be `https://azureforarchitects.azurewebsites.net/api/FirstFunction`.

5. To send parameters to this Function, additional query string parameters can be appended at the end of the URL. For example, to send `name` parameters to this Function, the `https://azureforarchitects.azurewebsites.net/api/FirstFunction?name=ritesh` URL can be used. The output of the Function is shown in the following screenshot:

6. For HTTP-based functions, the Azure Functions already provides triggers and binding within the `function.json` file, as shown here. This file is used for defining all Function-level triggers and bindings, and there is one associated with every Function:

```
function.json        Save            ▶ Run                                    </> Get function URL
 1  {
 2    "bindings": [
 3      {
 4        "name": "req",
 5        "type": "httpTrigger",
 6        "direction": "in",
 7        "authLevel": "anonymous"
 8      },
 9      {
10        "name": "res",
11        "type": "http",
12        "direction": "out"
13      }
14    ],
15    "disabled": false
16  }
```

The HTTP template creates a trigger for all incoming requests. The trigger invokes the Azure Functions and passes in the entire incoming data and payload as a parameter named as `req`. This parameter is available within the Azure Functions. The response from the Function is a binding that takes output from the `res` variable from the Azure Functions and sends it back to the HTTP channel as a response.

Creating an event-driven Function

In this example, an Azure Functions will be authored and connected to the Azure Storage account. The Storage account has a container for holding all blob files. The name of the storage account is `incomingfiles` and the container is `orders`, as shown in the following screenshot:

Create a new Azure Functions from the Azure portal.

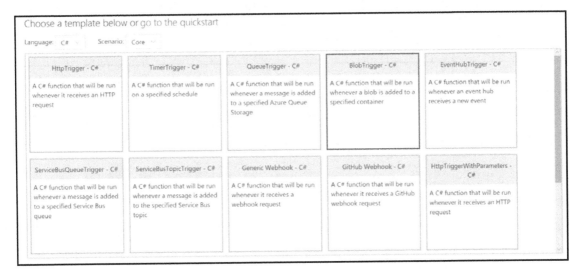

Right now, this Azure Functions does not have connectivity to the Storage account. Azure Functions need connection information for the Storage account, and that is available from the Access keys tab in the Storage account. The same information can be obtained using the Azure Functions editor environment. In fact, that environment allows for the creation of a new Storage account from the same editor environment.

This can be added using the new button beside the **Storage account connection** input type. It allows for the selection of an existing Storage account or the creation of a new Storage account. Since I already have a couple of Storage accounts, I am reusing them. You should create a separate Azure Storage account. Selecting a Storage account will update the settings in the **appsettings** section with the connection string added to it.

Ensure that a container already exists within the blob service of the target Azure Storage account. The path input refers to the path to the container. In this case, the **orders** container already exists within the Storage account. The **Create** button shown here will provision the new Function monitoring the Storage account container.

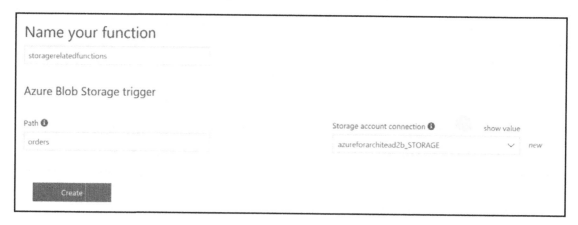

The code for the Azure Functions is as follows:

```
public static void Run(Stream myBlob, TraceWriter log)
{
    log.Info($"C# Blob trigger function Processed blob\n  \n Size
{myBlob.Length} Bytes");
}
```

The bindings are shown here:

```
{
  "bindings": [
    {
      "name": "myBlob",
      "type": "blobTrigger",
      "direction": "in",
      "path": "orders",
      "connection": "azureforarchitead2b_STORAGE"
    }
  ],
  "disabled": false
}
```

Now, uploading any blob file in the orders container should trigger the Function:

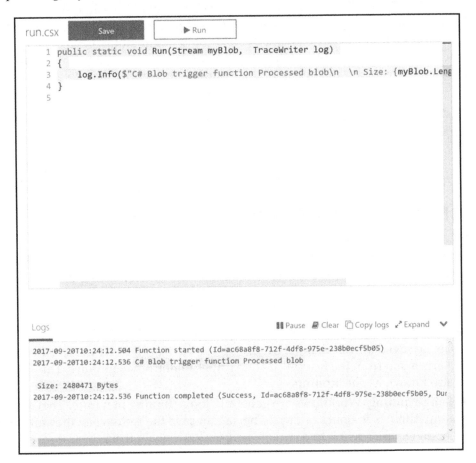

Function proxies

Azure Functions proxies are one of the latest additions to Azure Functions. After starting using Azure Functions, there will be a time when there might be lots of Function implementation and it will be difficult to integrate the Functions together in a workflow. Instead of letting clients weave these Functions together, Azure proxies can be used. Proxies help by providing clients with a single function URL and then invoking multiple Azure Functions behind the scenes to complete workflows.

It is important to understand that proxies are applicable in those cases where Functions accept requests on demand, instead of being driven by events. These internal Functions connected to proxies can be within a single function app or on multiple separate apps. Proxies get requests from clients, convert, override, and augment the payload, and send them to backend internal Functions. Once they get a response from these Functions, they can again convert, override, and augment the response and send it back to the client.

 More information about Azure Functions can be found at `https://docs.microsoft.com/en-us/azure/azure-functions/functions-proxies`.

Understanding workflows

A workflow is a series of steps or activities that are executed either in parallel or in sequence, or in a combination of the two. Since activities can be executed in parallel, they can perform jobs across multiple services at the same time without being blocked.

The following are the features of workflows:

- **Ability to recover from failure**: A workflow can be hydrated, meaning its state can be saved at well-defined points within the workflow. If the workflow fails, it starts again from the last saved state rather than from beginning. This feature is also known as **checkpoints**.
- **Long-running**: Workflows are generally long-running in nature. They can run from minutes to hours or days. They again save the state when they are waiting for an external action to complete and can start again from the last saved state once the external activity is complete.
- **Execute steps in parallel**: We've already discussed this point, but this is a major benefit of a workflow compared to sequence programming.
- **Maintaining state**: Workflows typically are stateful in nature. They maintain state such that in the event of failure or the restart of a workflow, the workflow does not start from beginning, but can continue from these checkpoints.

Azure Functions need to have finished executing within 5 minutes. This means they are short-lived, and composing workflows with them can really be difficult. There is the possibility of implementing multiple functions and ensuring they are coordinated to execute one after another. Even this endeavor has its limitations.

This is more of a hack and needs considerable effort, design, and operations. All the Functions will need to have inputs tied to the outputs of their previous Function, and each Function will still run for few minutes. Another drawback of implementing workflows this way is that it is extremely difficult to understand their connectivity, dependency, and sequence of execution at a glance. In short, Azure Functions are good for implementing a single responsibility that is short-lived. They are not well suited for implementing workflows.

Another important feature of Azure Functions is that they are stateless. This means that the Functions are fleeting, available only at the time they are being executed. One Function instance execution has no relation to the previous or consequent running instance. This means there is no possibility of storing state with Azure Functions.

Azure Functions can run on any server behind the scenes, and that server might not be the same as in subsequent executions. This means Functions cannot store their state in the server they are executed on.

The only way to save state in Azure Functions is to store state externally in data stores such as Cosmos DB, SQL databases, or Azure Storage. But this design will have significant performance issues, since every time the Function executes, it would need to connect to a data store, retrieve, and eventually write to it. Now that we have looked into understanding workflows, we will proceed with Durable Functions.

Durable Functions

Durable Functions are one of the latest additions to Azure Functions and they really fill a gap that existed for a while:

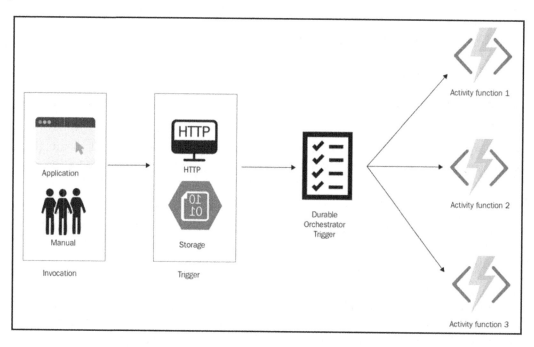

Azure Durable Functions can be invoked by any trigger provided by Azure Functions. These triggers include HTTP, blob storage, table storage, Service Bus queues, and more. They can be triggered manually by someone with access to them, or by an application. The preceding diagram shows a couple of triggers as an example. These are also known as starter Durable Functions. The starter Durable Functions invokes the **Durable Orchestrator Trigger**, which contains the main logic for orchestration, and orchestrates the invocation of activity functions. These activity functions can be called with or without a retry mechanism. Durable Functions help solve many challenges and provide features to write Functions that can do the following:

- Execute long-running Functions
- Maintain state
- Execute child Functions in parallel or sequence
- Recover from failure easily
- Orchestrate execution of Functions in a workflow

Steps for creating a Durable Functions

Here are the following steps to create a Durable Functions:

1. Navigate to the Azure portal and click on **Resource groups** in the left menu.
2. Click on the **+Add** button in the top menu to create a new resource group.
3. Provide the resource group information on the resultant form and click on the **Create** button, as shown here:

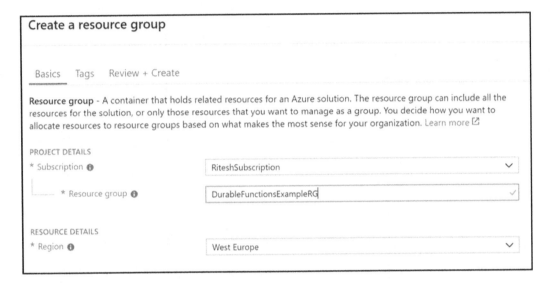

4. Navigate to the newly created resource group and add a new function app by clicking on the **+Add** button in the top menu and search for `function app` in the resultant search box.

5. Select Function App and click on the **Create** button. Fill the resultant function app form and click on the **Create** button as shown here:

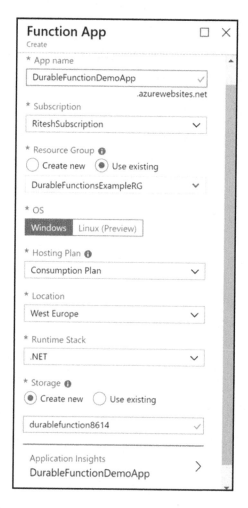

6. Once the function app is provisioned, click on the **Functions +** button in the left menu to create a new Function. Select **In-Portal** | **Continue** | **More templates...** | **Finish and view templates**.

7. In the resultant search box, search for `Durable Functions activity` and select the **Durable Functions activity** template. If the `Microsoft.Azure.WebJobs.Extensions.DurableTask` extension is not already installed within the function app, it will ask you to install it.

8. Click on the **Install** button to install the extension:

9. Durable Functions activities are functions that are invoked by the main orchestrator function. There is generally one main orchestrator function and multiple Durable Functions activities. Once the extension is installed, provide a name for the function and write code that does something useful, such as sending an email or an SMS, connecting to external systems and executing logic, executing services using their endpoints such as Cognitive Services, and so on.

There should be one Durable Functions activity for each distinct job within the workflow.

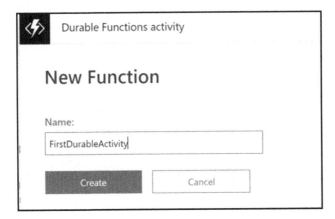

10. The generated code should be modified to reflect the code as shown in the following screenshot:

```
#r "Microsoft.Azure.WebJobs.Extensions.DurableTask"

public static async Task< string> Run(string name)
{
    await Task.Delay(10000);
    return $"Hello {name}!";
}
```

The only change is addition of a single line of code that makes the function wait for 10 seconds.

Similarly create another activity function with same code within it and name it differently for example `SecondDurableActivity`.

Create a new orchestrator function called `OrchestratorFlow` as shown in the following screenshot:

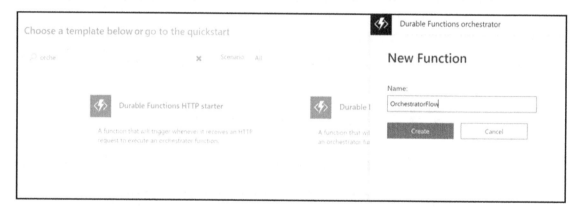

Change the generated code with the code listing shown here:

```
#r "Microsoft.Azure.WebJobs.Extensions.DurableTask"
public static async Task<List<string>> Run(DurableOrchestrationContext
context)
{
 var outputs = new List<string>();
 // Replace "Hello" with the name of your Durable Activity Function.
 outputs.Add(await
context.CallActivityAsync<string>("FirstDurableActivity", "Tokyo"));
 outputs.Add(await
```

```
context.CallActivityAsync<string>("SecondDurableActivity", "Seattle"));
// returns ["Hello Tokyo!", "Hello Seattle!", "Hello London!"]
   return outputs;
   }
```

Next, create an orchestrator trigger function. There is a HTTP Starter Durable Function provided out-of-the-box however it is possible to create a start Durable Function that is based on external triggers like a file getting added to Azure blob storage container. Here we are creating a simple function that simply starts the orchestrator workflow by calling the `OrchestratorFlow` orchestrator durable function. We can start the workflow by invoking it using a browser or tools like Postman:

The code for this is listed here:

```
#r "Microsoft.Azure.WebJobs.Extensions.DurableTask"
#r "Newtonsoft.Json"
using System.Net;
public static async Task<HttpResponseMessage> Run(
    HttpRequestMessage req,
    DurableOrchestrationClient starter,
    ILogger log)
{
    // Function input comes from the request content.
    dynamic eventData = await req.Content.ReadAsAsync<object>();
    // Pass the function name as part of the route
    string instanceId = await starter.StartNewAsync("OrchestratorFlow",
eventData);
    log.LogInformation($"Started orchestration with ID = '{instanceId}'.");
    return starter.CreateCheckStatusResponse(req, instanceId);
}
```

The `function.json` file containing the declaration of triggers and bindings is modified and the resultant code is shown next:

```json
{
  "bindings": [
    {
      "authLevel": "function",
      "name": "req",
      "type": "httpTrigger",
      "direction": "in",
      "route": "orchestrators",
      "methods": [
        "post",
        "get"
      ]
    },
    {
      "name": "$return",
      "direction": "out"
    },
    {
      "name": "starter",
      "type": "orchestrationClient",
      "direction": "in"
    }
  ],
  "disabled": false
}
```

Click on **Get Function URL** link from the UI and copy the resultant URL.

We are going to invoke this URL using a tool known as **Postman** (can be downloaded from `https://www.getpostman.com/`). This activity is shown in the following screenshot:

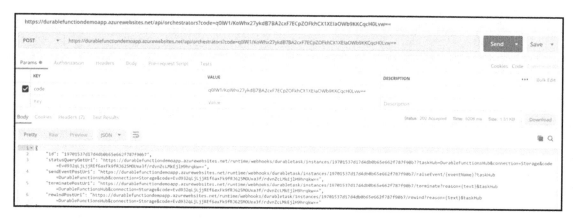

Notice that four URLs are generated when you start an orchestrator.

- `statusQueryGetUri` URL is used to find the current status of the orchestrator. Clicking this URL on Postman opens a new tab and shows the status of the workflow:

- `terminatePostUri` URL is used for stopping an already running orchestrator function.
- `sendEventPostUri` URL is used to post an event to a suspended durable function. Durable Functions can be suspended if they are waiting for an external event. This URL is used in those cases.
- `rewindPostUri` URL is used to post a message to rewind an orchestrator function.

Creating a connected architecture with Functions

A connected architecture with Functions refers to creating multiple Functions, whereby the output of one Function triggers another Function and provides data for the next Function to execute its logic. In this section, we will continue with the previous scenario of the Storage account. In this case, the output of the Function being triggered using Azure Storage blob files will write the size of the file to Azure Cosmos DB.

The configuration of Cosmos DB is shown next. By default, there are no collections created in Cosmos DB.

A collection will automatically be created when creating a function that will be triggered when Cosmos DB gets any data.

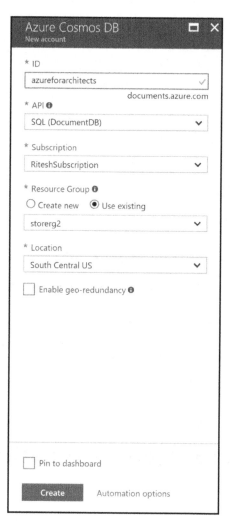

Create a new database, `testdb`, within Cosmos DB, and create a new collection named `testcollection` within it. You need both the database and collection name when configuring Azure Functions.

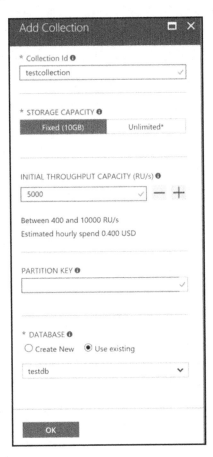

It's time to revisit the `storagerelatedfunctions` function and change its binding to return the size of the data for the uploaded file. This returned value will be written to Cosmos DB. This will require a change to the bindings as well, with an additional one responsible for capturing output values. This binding will eventually write to the Cosmos DB collection. Navigate to the **Integrate** tab and click on the **New Output** button below the **Outputs** label and select **Azure Cosmos DB**.

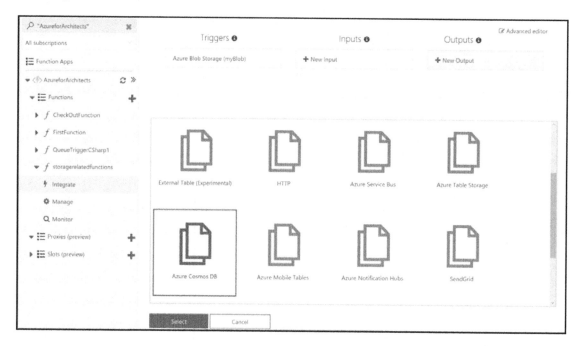

Provide the appropriate names for the database and collection (check the checkbox to create the collection if it does not exist), click on the **New** button to select our newly created Azure Cosmos DB, and leave the parameter name as `outputDocument`.

Modify the function as shown in the following screenshot:

```
1  public static void Run(string  myBlob, out object outputDocument, TraceWriter log)
2  {
3          log.Info($"C# blob trigger function processed: {myBlob.Length}");
4          log.Info($"C# blob trigger function processed: {myBlob}");
5      outputDocument = new {
6          id = myBlob.Length.ToString(),
7          len = myBlob.Length,
8          data = myBlob
9      };
10
11 }
12
```

Now uploading a new file to the orders collection in the Azure Storage account will execute a Function that will write to the Azure Cosmos DB collection. Another Function can be written with the newly created Azure Cosmos DB account as a trigger binding. It will provide the size of files and the Function can act on it. This is shown next:

Summary

The evolution of functions from traditional methods has led to the design of the loosely coupled, independently evolving, self-reliant serverless architecture that was only a concept in earlier days. Functions are a unit of deployment and provide an environment where users do not need to manage the environment at all. All they have to care about is the code written for the functionality. Azure provides a mature platform for hosting functions and integrating them seamlessly, based on events or on demand. Nearly every resource in Azure can participate in an architecture composed of Azure Functions. The future is functions, as more and more organizations want to stay away from managing infrastructures and platforms. They want to offload this to cloud providers. Azure Functions is an essential feature to master for every architect dealing with Azure.

The next chapter will build on what we learned in this chapter as it will explore other serverless technologies such as Azure Logic Apps and Event Grids. It will also show a complete end-to-end solution using all of these technologies.

Azure Integration Solutions

7

This chapter is a continuation of the previous chapter. In the last chapter, we discussed serverless compute Azure Functions, and in this chapter, we will continue our discussion of serverless technologies and cover Azure Event Grids as part of serverless events and Azure Logic Apps as part of serverless workflows. A complete end-to-end solution will also be created using multiple Azure services, such as Automation, Logic Apps, Functions, Event Grid, SendGrid, Twilio, PowerShell, **Active Directory (AD)**, and Key Vaults.

The following topics will be covered in this chapter:

- Azure Event Grid
- Azure Logic Apps
- Creating an end-to-end solution using serverless technologies

Azure Event Grid

Azure Event Grid is a relatively new service. It has also been referred to as a serverless eventing platform. It helps with the creation of applications based on events (also known as **event-driven design**). It is important to understand what events are and how we dealt with them prior to Event Grid. An event is *something that happened*—an activity that changed the state of a subject. When a subject undergoes a change in its state, it generally raises an event.

Events typically follow the publish/subscribe pattern (also popularly known as the **pub/sub pattern**), in which a subject raises an event due to its state change, and that event can then be subscribed to by multiple interested parties, also known as **subscribers**. The job of the event is to notify the subscribers of such changes and also provide them with data as part of its context. The subscribers can take whatever action they deem necessary, which varies from subscriber to subscriber.

Prior to Event Grid, there was no service that could be described as a real-time event platform. There were separate services, and each provided its own mechanism for handling events.

For example, Log Analytics, also known as **Operations Management Suite (OMS)**, provides an infrastructure for capturing environment logs and telemetry on which alerts can be generated. These alerts can be used to execute a runbook, a webhook, or a function. This is near real-time, but not completely real-time. Moreover, it was quite cumbersome to trap individual logs and act on them. Similarly, there is Application Insights, which provides similar features to Log Analytics but for applications.

There are other logs, such as activity logs and diagnostic logs, but again, they rely on similar principles as other log-related features. Solutions are deployed on multiple resource groups in multiple regions, and events raised from any of these should be available to resources deployed elsewhere.

Event Grid removes all barriers, and now events can be generated by most resources (they are increasingly becoming available), and even custom events can be generated. These events can then be subscribed to by any resource, in any region, in any resource group within the subscription.

Event Grid is already laid down as part of the Azure infrastructure, along with data centers and networks. Events raised in one region can easily be subscribed to by resources in other regions, and since these networks are connected, it is super-efficient for the delivery of events to subscribers.

Event Grid architecture

The Event Grid architecture is based on service bus topics. Service bus topics, as we already know, are based on the publish/subscribe mechanism. There are publishers of events and there are consumers of events; however, there can be multiple subscribers for the same event.

The publisher of an event can be an Azure resource, such as Blob storage, IoT hubs, and many others. These publishers are also known as **event sources**. These publishers use out-of-the-box Azure topics to send their events to Event Grid. There is no need to configure either the resource or the topic. The events raised by Azure resources are already internally using topics to send their events to Event Grid. Once the event reaches the grid, it can be consumed by the subscribers.

The subscribers, or consumers, are resources who are interested in events and want to execute an action based on these events. These subscribers provide an event handler when they subscribe to the topic. The event handlers can be Azure functions, custom web hooks, logic apps, or other resources. Both the event sources and subscribers that execute event handlers are shown in the following diagram:

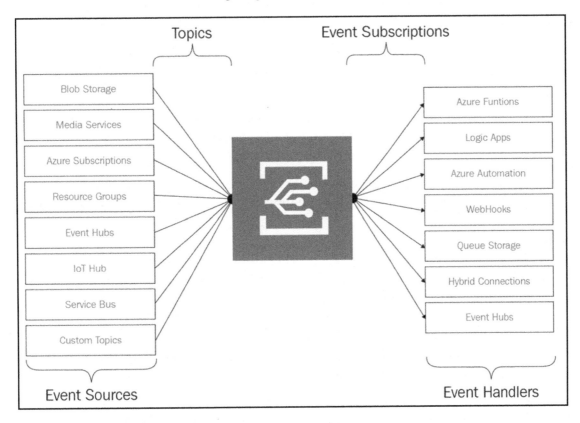

When an event reaches a topic, multiple event handlers can be executed simultaneously, each taking its own action.

It is also possible to raise a custom event and send a custom topic to Event Grid. Event Grid provides features for creating custom topics, and these topics are automatically attached to Event Grid. These topics know the storage for Event Grid and automatically send their messages to it. Custom topics have two important properties, which are as follows:

- **An endpoint**: This is the endpoint of the topic. Publishers and event sources use this endpoint to send and publish their events to Event Grid. In other words, topics are recognized using their endpoints.
- **Keys:** Custom topics provide a couple of keys. These keys enable security for the consumption of the endpoint. Only publishers with these keys can send and publish their messages to Event Grid.

Each event has an event type and it is recognized by it. For example, blob storage provides event types, such as `blobAdded` and `blobDeleted`. Custom topics can be used to send a custom-defined event, such as a custom event of the type `KeyVaultSecretExpired`.

On the other hand, subscribers have the ability to accept all messages or only get events based on filters. These filters can be based on the event type or other properties within the event payload.

Each event has at least the following five properties:

- `id`: This is the unique identifier for the event.
- `eventType`: This is the event type.
- `eventTime`: This is the date and time when the event was raised.
- `subject`: This is a short description of the event.
- `data`: This is a dictionary object and contains either resource-specific data or any custom data (for custom topics).

Currently, Event Grid's functionalities are not available with all resources. Azure is continually adding more and more resources with Event Grid functionality.

 To find out more about resources that can raise events related to Event Grid and handlers that can handle these events, please go to `https://docs.microsoft.com/en-us/azure/event-grid/overview`.

Resource events

In this section, steps are provided to create a solution in which events raised by Blob storage are published to Event Grid and ultimately routed to an Azure function:

1. Log in to the Azure portal using appropriate credentials and create a new storage account in an existing or a new resource group. The storage account should be either StorageV2 or blob storage. As shown in the following screenshot, Event Grid will not work with StorageV1:

Create storage account

Basics   Advanced   Tags   Review + create

Azure Storage is a Microsoft-managed service providing cloud storage that is highly available, secure, durable, scalable, and redundant. Azure Storage includes Azure Blobs (objects), Azure Data Lake Storage Gen2, Azure Files, Azure Queues, and Azure Tables. The cost of your storage account depends on the usage and the options you choose below. Learn more

PROJECT DETAILS

Select the subscription to manage deployed resources and costs. Use resource groups like folders to organize and manage all your resources.

* Subscription	RiteshSubscription ⌄
* Resource group	azureclitest ⌄
	Create new

INSTANCE DETAILS

The default deployment model is Resource Manager, which supports the latest Azure features. You may choose to deploy using the classic deployment model instead. Choose classic deployment model

* Storage account name ❶	storageforeventgrid ✓
* Location	West Europe ⌄
Performance ❶	⦿ Standard ○ Premium
Account kind ❶	StorageV2 (general purpose v2) ⌄
Replication ❶	Read-access geo-redundant storage (RA-GRS) ⌄
Access tier (default) ❶	○ Cool ⦿ Hot

Review + create   Previous   Next : Advanced >

2. Create a new function app or reuse an existing function app to create an Azure function. The Azure function will be hosted within the function app.

3. Create a new function using **Azure Event Grid trigger** template. Install the `Microsoft.Azure.WebJobs.Extensions.EventGrid` extension if it's not already installed, as shown in the following screenshot:

4. Name the function `StorageEventHandler` and create it. The following default generated code will be used as the event handler:

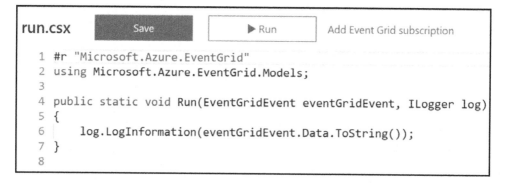

```
1 #r "Microsoft.Azure.EventGrid"
2 using Microsoft.Azure.EventGrid.Models;
3
4 public static void Run(EventGridEvent eventGridEvent, ILogger log)
5 {
6     log.LogInformation(eventGridEvent.Data.ToString());
7 }
8
```

The subscription to storage events can be configured either from the Azure Functions user interface by clicking on **Add Event Grid subscription**, or from the storage account itself.

5. Click on the **Add Event Grid subscription** link in the Azure Functions UI to add subscription to events raised by the storage account created in the previous step. Provide a name for the subscription, and then choose **Event Schema** followed by **Event Grid Schema**. Set **Topic Types** as **Storage Accounts**, set an appropriate **Subscription**, and the resource group containing the storage account:

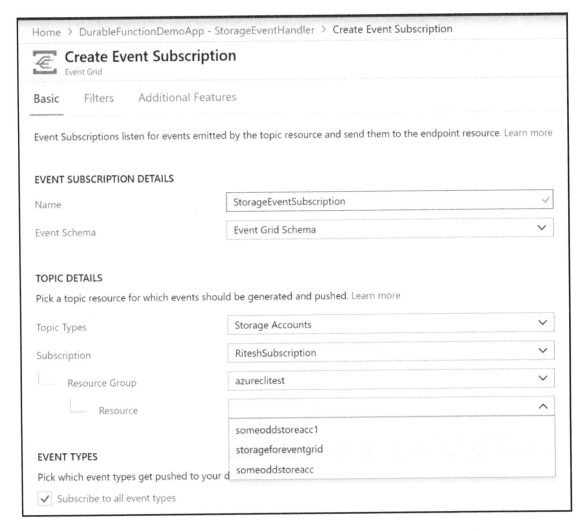

Ensure that the **Subscribe to all event types** checkbox is checked and click on the **Create** button (it should be enabled as soon as a storage account is selected).

6. If we now navigate to the storage account in Azure portal and click on **Events** link in the left-hand menu, the subscription for the storage account should be visible:

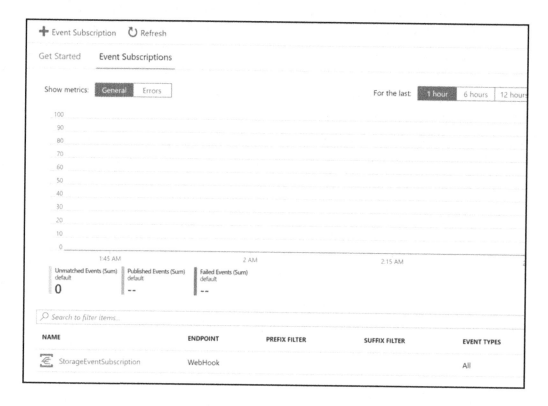

7. Upload a file to the blob storage after creating a container, and the Azure function should be executed. The upload action will trigger a new event of `blobAdded` type and send it to the Event Grid topic for storage accounts. As shown in the following screenshot, the subscription is already set to get all events from this topic, and the function gets executed as part of the event handler:

Custom events

In this example, instead of using out-of-the-box resources to generate events, custom events will be used. We will use PowerShell to create this solution and reuse the same Azure function that was created in last exercise as the handler:

1. Log in and connect to your Azure subscription of choice using `Login-AzureRMAccount` and `Set-AzureRmContext` cmdlet.

2. The next step is to create a new Event Grid topic in Azure in a resource group. The `New-AzureRmEventGridTopic` cmdlet is used to create a new topic:

```
New-AzureRmEventGridTopic -ResourceGroupName CustomEventGridDemo -
Name "KeyVaultAssetsExpiry" -Location "West Europe"
```

3. Once the topic is created, its endpoint URL and key should be retrieved as they are needed to send and publish the event to it. `Get-AzureRmEventGridTopic` and `Get-AzureRmEventGridTopicKey` cmdlets are used to retrieve these values. Note that `Key1` is retrieved to connect to the endpoint:

```
$topicEndpoint = (Get-AzureRmEventGridTopic -ResourceGroupName
containers -Name KeyVaultAssetsExpiry).Endpoint

$keys = (Get-AzureRmEventGridTopicKey -ResourceGroupName containers
-Name KeyVaultAssetsExpiry).Key1
```

4. A new hash table is created with all five important Event Grid event properties. A new `guid` is generated for the ID, the `subject` is set to `Key vault Asset Expiry`, `eventType` is set to `Certificate Expiry`, `eventTime` is set to current time, and `data` contains information regarding the certificate:

```
$eventgridDataMessage = @{
id = [System.guid]::NewGuid()
subject = "Key Vault Asset Expiry"
eventType = "Certificate Expiry"
eventTime = [System.DateTime]::UtcNow
data = @{
CertificateThumbprint = "sdfervdserwetsgfhgdg"
ExpiryDate = "1/1/2019"
Createdon = "1/1/2018"
}
}
```

5. Since Event Grid data should be published in the form of a JSON array, the payload is converted in the JSON array. The `"[","]"` square brackets represents a JSON array:

```
$finalBody = "[" + $(ConvertTo-Json $eventgridDataMessage) + "]"
```

6. The event will be published using the HTTP protocol, and appropriate header information has to be added to the request. The request is sent using the application/JSON content type and the key belonging to the topic is assigned to the `aeg-sas-key` header. It is mandatory to name the header with key set to `aeg-sas-key`:

```
$header = @{
"contentType" = "application/json"
"aeg-sas-key" = $keys}
```

7. A new subscription is created to the custom topic with a name, the resource group containing the topic, the topic name, the webhook endpoint, and the actual endpoint that acts as the event handler. The event handler in this case is the Azure function:

```
New-AzureRmEventGridSubscription -TopicName KeyVaultAssetsExpiry -
EventSubscriptionName "customtopicsubscriptionautocar" -
ResourceGroupName CustomEventGridDemo -EndpointType webhook `
-Endpoint
"https://durablefunctiondemoapp.azurewebsites.net/runtime/webhooks/
EventGrid?functionName=StorageEventHandler&code=0aSw6sxvtFmafXHvt7i
Ow/Dsb8o1M9RKKagzVchTUkwe9EIkz14mCg==`
-Verbose
```

The URL of the Azure function is available from the **Integrate** tab, as shown in the following screenshot:

8. By now, both the subscriber (event handler) and the publisher have been configured. The next step is to send and publish an event to the custom topic. The event data was already created in the previous step and, by using the `Invoke-WebRequest` cmdlet, the request is sent to the endpoint along with the body and the header:

```
Invoke-WebRequest -Uri $topicEndpoint -Body $finalBody -Headers
$header -Method Post
```

Azure Logic Apps

Logic Apps is the serverless workflow offering from Azure. It has all the features of serverless technologies, such as consumption-based costing and unlimited scalability. Logic Apps helps us to build a workflow solution with ease using the Azure portal. It provides a drag and drop user interface to create and configure the workflow.

Using Logic Apps is the preferred way to integrate services and data, create business projects, and create a complete flow of logic. There are a number of important concepts that should be understood before building a logic app.

Activity

Activity refers to performing a single unit of work. Examples of activities include converting XML to JSON, reading blobs from Azure storage, and writing to a Cosmos DB document collection. Logic Apps is a workflow consisting of multiple co-related activities in a sequence. There are two types of activity in Logic Apps:

- **Trigger:** Triggers refers to the *initiation of an activity*. All logic apps have a single trigger that forms the first activity. It is the trigger that creates an instance of the logic app and starts the execution. Examples of triggers are the arrival of Event Grid messages, the arrival of an email, an HTTP request, and a schedule.
- **Actions**: Any activity that is not a trigger is a step activity, and they each perform one responsibility. Steps are connected to each other in a workflow.

Connectors

Connectors are Azure resources that help connect a logic app to external services. These services could be in the cloud or on premises. For example, there is a connector for connecting Logic Apps to Event Grid. Similarly, there is another connector to connect to Ofifice 365 Exchange. Almost all types of connector are available in Logic Apps, and they can be used to connect to services. Connectors contain connection information and logic to connect to external services using the connection information.

 The whole list of connectors is available at `https://docs.microsoft.com/en-us/connectors/`.

Working on a logic app

Let's create a Logic Apps workflow that gets triggered when one of the email accounts receives an email. It replies to the sender with a default email and performs sentiment analysis on the content of the email. For sentiment analysis, the Text Analytics resource from Cognitive Services should be provisioned before creating the logic app:

1. Navigate to the Azure portal, log in, and create a **Text Analytics** resource in a resource group, as shown in the following screenshot:

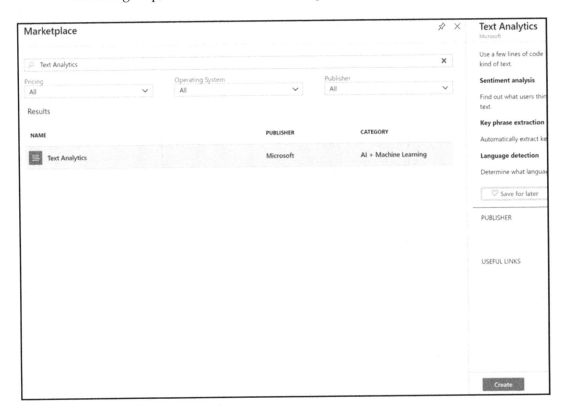

2. Provide a **Name**, **Location**, **Subscription** name, **Resource group** name, and **Pricing tier**:

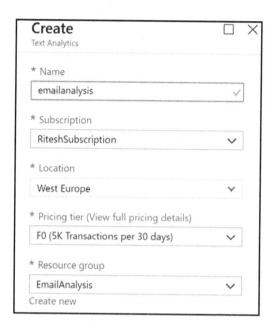

3. Once the resource is provisioned, navigate to the **Overview** page and copy the endpoint URL. Store it in a temporary location. This value will be required when configuring the logic app:

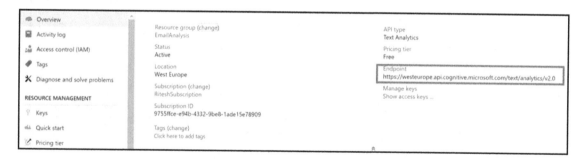

4. Navigate to the **Keys** page and copy the value from **Key 1** and store it in a temporary location. This value will be needed when configuring the logic app.

5. The next step is to create a logic app. To create a logic app, navigate to the resource group in the Azure portal in which the logic app should be created. Search for `Logic App` and create it by providing a name, location, resource group name, and subscription name:

6. After the logic app has been created, navigate to the resource, click on **Log app designer** in the left-hand menu, and select the **When a new email is received in Outlook.com** template to create a new workflow. The template provides a jump-start by adding boilerplate triggers and activities. This will add an Office 365 Outlook trigger automatically to the workflow, as shown in the following screenshot:

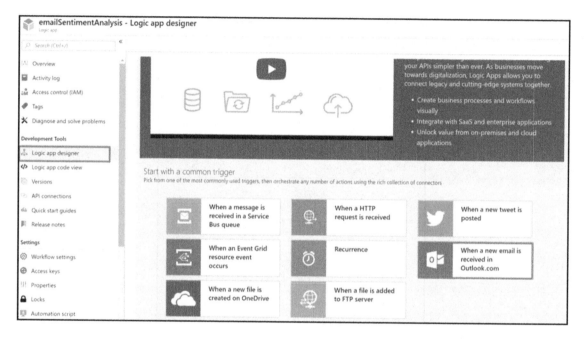

7. Click on the **Sign in** button on the trigger. It will open a new Internet Explorer window. Sign in to your account. After successfully connecting, a new Office 365 mail connector will be created, containing the connection information to the account.

8. Click on the **Continue** button and configure the trigger with a 3-minute poll frequency, as shown in the following screenshot:

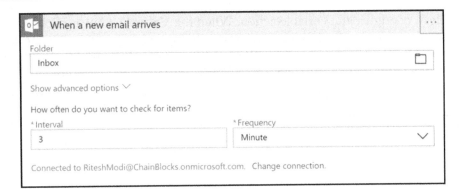

9. Click on the next step to add another action and type `variables` in it. Select the **Initialize variable** action:

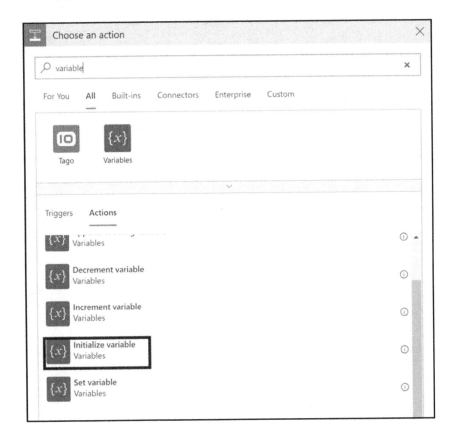

10. Next, configure the variable action. When the **Value** text box is clicked, a pop-up window appears that shows **Dynamic content** and **Expression**. Dynamic content refers to properties available to the current action, which are filled with runtime values from previous actions and triggers. Variables help in keeping the workflows generic. From this window, select **Body** from **Dynamic content**:

11. Add another action by clicking on **Add step**, typing outlook, and selecting the **Reply to email** action:

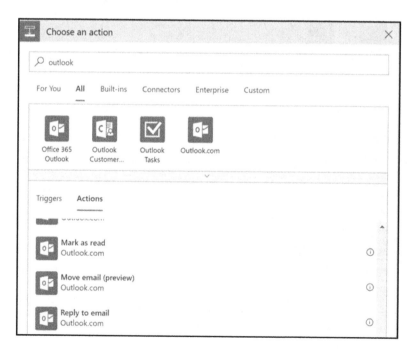

12. Configure the new action. Ensure that **Message Id** is set with dynamic content **Message Id** and type the reply you'd like to send in the **Comment** box:

13. Add another action, type `text analytics`, and select **Detect Sentiment (preview)**:

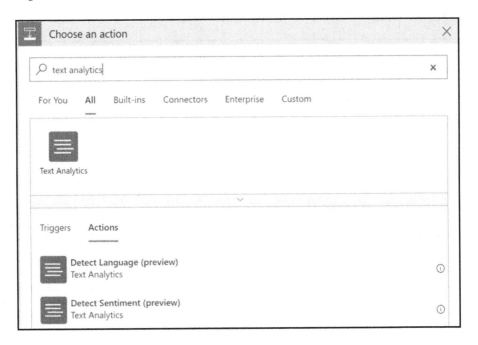

14. Configure the sentiment action, as shown in the following screenshot. Both the endpoint and key values should be used here. Click on the **Create** button:

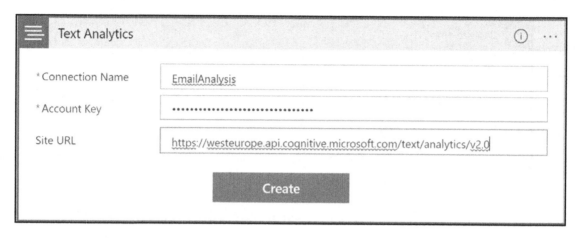

15. Provide the text to the action by adding dynamic content and selecting the previously created variable, `emailContent`. Also, click on **Show advanced options** and select **en** for language:

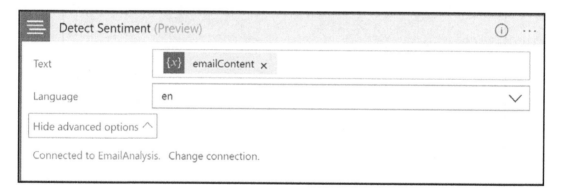

16. Add a new action, select Outlook, and select **Send an email**. This action sends the original recipient the email content with the sentiment score in its subject. It should be configured as shown in the following screenshot. If the score is not visible in the dynamic contents window, click on the **See more** link beside it:

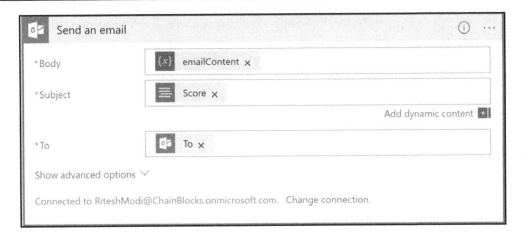

17. Save the logic app, navigate back to the overview page, and click **Run trigger**. The trigger will check for new emails every 3 minutes, reply to the senders, perform sentiment analysis, and send an email to the original recipient. A sample email with negative connotations is sent to the given email ID:

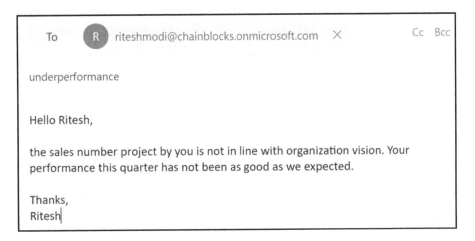

18. After a few seconds, the logic app executes, and the sender gets the following reply:

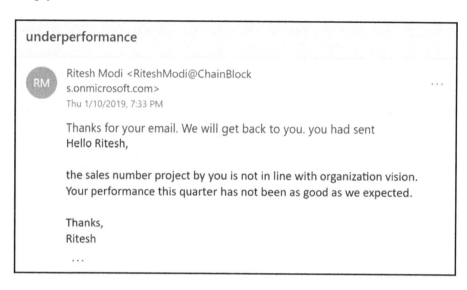

19. The original recipient gets an email with the sentiment score and the original email text, as shown in the following screenshot:

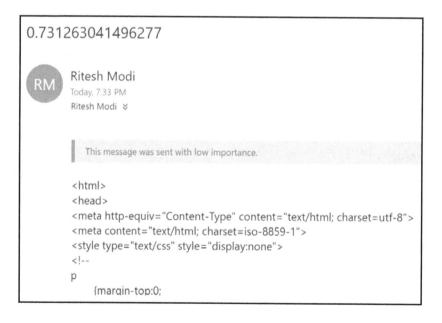

Creating an end-to-end solution using Serverless technologies

In this section, we will create an end-t-end solution comprising serverless technologies that we discussed in previous sections.

Problem statement

The problem we are going to solve here is that users and organizations are not notified regarding the expiration of any secret in their key vault, and applications stop working when they expire. Users are complaining that Azure does not provide the infrastructure to monitor key vault secrets, keys, and certificates.

Vision

Azure Key Vault is an Azure service that provides secure storage and access to credentials, keys, secrets, and certificates. It provides a vault that is backed up by hardware devices known as **Hardware Security Modules (HSM)**, and it forms the highest form of secure storage for secrets and keys.

Azure Key Vault allows storage of these keys, secrets, and credentials, and they have an expiry date. For example, a certificate uploaded to the Azure Key Vault will expire in one year, or a secret will expire in two years. While it is one of the Azure security best practices to store sensitive information in Key Vault, Key Vault does not provide any infrastructure to monitor these secrets and notify users that these secrets are expiring in advance. In such situations, if the user is not monitoring their Key Vault secrets actively, applications that rely on these secrets (such as connection strings, and usernames) will stop working, and reactive measures would need to be undertaken to fix the application by renewing the secret in Key Vault.

The vision is to create a complete end-to-end solution using Azure services so that users are notified well in advance that Key Vault secrets are going to expire soon and that they need to take action to renew them.

Solution

The solution to this problem is to combine multiple Azure services and integrate them so that users can be proactively notified of the expiration of secrets. The solution will send notifications using two channels—email and SMS.

The Azure services used to create this solution include the following:

- Azure Key Vault
- Azure **Active Directory** (**AD**)
- Azure Event Grid
- Azure Automation
- Logic Apps
- Azure Functions
- SendGrid
- Twilio SMS

Architecture

The architecture of the solution comprises multiple services, as shown in the following diagram:

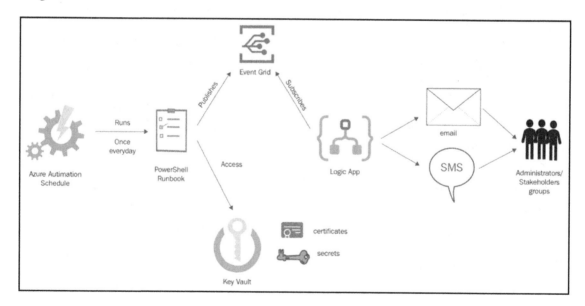

Let's go through each of these services and understand their roles and the functionality they provide in the overall solution.

Azure Automation

Azure Automation provides runbooks, and these runbooks can be executed to run logic using PowerShell, Python, and other scripting languages. The runbook can be executed either on-premises or in the cloud, and provides rich infrastructure and facilities to create scripts. These scripts are known as **runbooks**. Typically, runbooks implement a scenario such as stopping or starting a virtual machine, or creating and configuring storage accounts. It is quite easy to connect to the Azure environment from runbooks with the help of assets such as variables, certificates, and connections.

In the current solution, we want to connect to Azure Key Vault, read all the secrets and keys stored within it, and fetch their expiry dates. These expiry dates should be compared with today's date, and if the expiry date is within a month, the runbook should raise a custom event on Event Grid using an Event Grid custom topic.

An Azure Automation runbook using a PowerShell script will be implemented to achieve this. Along with the runbook, a scheduler will also be created that will execute the runbook once a day at 12.00 AM. The process of configuring the Azure Automation account is shown in the next section.

Custom Azure Event Grid topic

Once the runbook identifies that a secret or key is going to expire within a month, it will raise a new custom event and publish it to the custom topic created specifically for this purpose. Again, we will go into the details of the implementation in the next section.

Azure Logic Apps

A logic app is a serverless service that provides workflow capabilities. Our logic app will be configured to be triggered as and when an event is published on the custom Event Grid topic. After it is triggered, it will invoke the workflow and execute all the activities in it one after the another. Generally, there are multiple activities, but for the purpose of this example, we will invoke one Azure function that will send both email and SMS messages. In a full-blown implementation, these notification functions should be implemented separately in separate Azure functions.

Azure Functions

Azure Functions is used to notify users and stakeholders about the expiration of secrets and keys using email and SMS. SendGrid is used to send emails, and Twilio is used to send SMS from Azure Functions.

Prerequisites

You will need an Azure subscription with at least contributor rights.

Implementation

An Azure Key Vault should already exist. If not, it should be created.

This step should be performed if a new Azure Key Vault needs to be provisioned. Azure provides multiple ways to provision resources in Azure. Prominent among them is Azure PowerShell and Azure CLI. Azure CLI is a command-line interface that works across platforms. The first task would be to provision a key vault in Azure. Azure PowerShell is used to provision the Azure Key Vault.

Before Azure PowerShell can be used to create a key vault, it is important to log in to Azure so that subsequent commands can be executed successfully and create a key vault.

Step 1

The first step is to prepare the environment for the sample. This involves logging in to Azure portal, selecting an appropriate subscription, and then creating a new Azure Resource Group and a new Azure Key Vault resource.

1. Execute the `Login-AzureRmAccount` command to log in to Azure. It will prompt for credentials in a new window.
2. After a successful login, if there are multiple subscriptions available for the login ID provided , they will all be listed. It is important to select an appropriate subscription. This can be done by executing the `Set-AzureRmContent` cmdlet:

```
Set-AzureRmContext -Subscription xxxxxxxx-xxxx-xxxx-xxxx-
xxxxxxxxxxx
```

3. Create a new resource group in your preferred location. In this case, the name of the resource group is `IntegrationDemo` and it is created in the `West Europe` region:

```
New-AzureRmResourceGroup -Name IntegrationDemo -Location "West
Europe" -Verbose
```

4. Create a new Azure Key Vault. The name of the vault in this case is `keyvaultbook`, and it is enabled for deployment, template deployment, disk encryption, soft delete, and purge protection:

```
New-AzureRmKeyVault -Name keyvaultbook -ResourceGroupName
IntegrationDemo -Location "West Europe" -EnabledForDeployment -
EnabledForTemplateDeployment -EnabledForDiskEncryption -
EnableSoftDelete -EnablePurgeProtection -Sku Standard -Verbose
```

The preceding command, when executed successfully, will create a new Azure Key Vault. The next step is to provide access to a service principal on the key vault.

Step 2

Instead of using an individual account to connect to Azure, Azure provides service principals, which are, in essence, service accounts that can be used to connect to Azure Resource Manager and execute activities. Adding a user to Azure tenant makes them available everywhere, including in all resource groups and resources, due to the nature of security inheritance in Azure. Access has to be explicitly revoked from resource groups for users if they are not allowed to access it. Service principals help by assigning granular access and control to resource groups, resources, and, if required, can be given access to the subscription scope. They can also be assigned granular permissions, such as reader, contributor, or owner.

In short, service principals should be the preferred mechanism to consume Azure services. They can be configured either with a password or with a certificate key. The process of provisioning a service principal with a password using PowerShell is as follows:

1. Create a service application using `new-AzurermAdApplication` by passing values for display name, identified URIs, home page, and password. The password should be a secure string.

2. A secure string can be generated using the `ConvertTo-SecureString` cmdlet, as shown in the following code:

```
ConvertTo-SecureString -String sysadminpassword -AsPlainText -Force
```

3. The service application can be created, as shown next. The return value from the command is stored in a variable so that it can be used in the next command:

```
$app = New-AzureRmADApplication -DisplayName
"https://keyvault.book.com" -IdentifierUris
"https://keyvault.book.com" -HomePage "https://keyvault.book.com" -
Password (ConvertTo-SecureString -String sysadminpassword -
AsPlainText -Force) -Verbose
```

4. After the service application has been created, a service principal based on service application should be created. The application acts like a blueprint, and the principal acts like an instance of the application. We can create multiple principals using the same application in different tenants. The command to create a service principal is as follows:

```
New-AzureRmADServicePrincipal -ApplicationId $app.ApplicationId -
DisplayName "https://keyvault.book.com" -Password (ConvertTo-
SecureString -String sysadminpassword -AsPlainText -Force) -Scope
"/subscriptions/xxxxxxxx-xxxx-xxxx-xxxx-xxxxxxxxxxxx" -Role Owner -
StartDate ([datetime]::Now) -EndDate $([datetime]::now.AddYears(1))
-Verbose
```

5. The `ApplicationId` from the previous command is used in this command by means of the `$app` variable. A `StartDate` and `EndDate` is added for the service principal.

6. The important configuration values are the scope and role. The scope determines the access area for the service application. It is currently shown at the subscription level. Valid values for scope are as follows:

```
/subscriptions/{subscriptionId}
/subscriptions/{subscriptionId}/resourceGroups/{resourceGroupName}
/subscriptions/{subscriptionId}/resourcegroups/{resourceGroupName}/
providers/{resourceProviderNamespace}/{resourceType}/{resourceName}
/subscriptions/{subscriptionId}/resourcegroups/{resourceGroupName}/
providers/{resourceProviderNamespace}/{parentResourcePath}/{resourc
eType}/{resourceName}
```

The role provides permissions at the assigned scope. Valid values are as follows:

- Owner
- Contributor
- Reader
- Resource-specific permissions

In the previous command, owner permissions have been provided to the newly created service principal.

Step 3

To create a service principal using certificates, the following steps should be executed:

1. **Create a self-signed certificate or purchase a certificate**: A self-signed certificate is used to create this example end-to-end application. For real-life deployments, a valid certificate should be purchased from a certificate authority.

   To create a self-signed certificate, the following command can be executed. The self-signed certificate is exportable and stored in a personal folder on the local machine. It also has an expiry date:

   ```
   $currentDate = Get-Date
   $expiryDate = $currentDate.AddYears(1)
   $finalDate = $expiryDate.AddYears(1)
   $servicePrincipalName = "https://automation.book.com"
   $automationCertificate = New-SelfSignedCertificate -DnsName
   $servicePrincipalName -KeyExportPolicy Exportable -Provider
   "Microsoft Enhanced RSA and AES Cryptographic Provider" -NotAfter
   $finalDate -CertStoreLocation "Cert:\LocalMachine\My"
   ```

2. **Export the newly created certificate:** The new certificate must be exported to the filesystem so that later, it can be uploaded to other destinations, such as Azure AD, to create a service principal.

   The commands used to export the certificate to the local filesystem are shown next. Please note that this certificate has both public and private keys, and so while it is exported, it must be protected using a password, and the password must be a secure string:

   ```
   $securepfxpwd = ConvertTo-SecureString -String 'password' -
   AsPlainText -Force # Password for the private key PFX certificate
   $cert1 = Get-Item -Path
   Cert:\LocalMachine\My\$($automationCertificate.Thumbprint)
   Export-PfxCertificate -Password $securepfxpwd -FilePath
   "C:\book\azureautomation.pfx" -Cert $cert1
   ```

The Get-Item cmdlet reads the certificate from the certificate store and stores it in the $cert1 variable. The Export-PfxCertificate actually exports the certificate in the certificate store to the filesystem. In this case, it is in the C:\book folder.

3. **Read the content from the newly generated PFX file:** An object of X509Certificate is created to hold the certificate in memory, and the data is converted to a Base64 string using the System.Convert function:

```
$newCert = New-Object
System.Security.Cryptography.X509Certificates.X509Certificate -
ArgumentList "C:\book\azureautomation.pfx", $securepfxpwd
$newcertdata =
[System.Convert]::ToBase64String($newCert.GetRawCertData())
```

Create an instance of the PSADKeyCredential class and fill in the values of its data structure. This data structure is then used when creating the service principal. This class is available in the Microsoft.Azure.Graph.RBAC.Version1_6.ActiveDirectory namespace. A new Guid is also generated to assign it to the keyid property of this object. The Base64-encoded cert value is assigned to the CertValue property, and both the start date and the end date are assigned as well. When the service principal is created using this object, it will configure it according to the values provided here:

```
$keyid = [Guid]::NewGuid()
$keyCredential = New-Object -TypeName
Microsoft.Azure.Graph.RBAC.Version1_6.ActiveDirectory.PSADKeyCreden
tial
$keyCredential.StartDate = [datetime]::Now
$keyCredential.KeyId = $keyid
$keyCredential.CertValue = $newcertdata
$keyCredential.EndDate = [datetime]::Now.AddYears(1)
```

4. **Create the service application and service principal in Azure:** We have already executed these commands once when creating the service principal with a password. This time, the key difference is that instead of a password, the keyCredential property is used. Finally, a service principal is created with owner rights.

We will be using this same principal to connect to Azure from the Azure Automation account. It is important that the application ID, tenant ID, subscription ID, and certificate thumbprint values are stored in a temporary location so that they can be used to configure subsequent resources:

```
$adAppName = http://automationcertcred2
$adApp =New-AzureRmADApplication -DisplayName $adAppName -HomePage
$adAppName -IdentifierUris $adAppName -KeyCredentials
$keyCredential -Verbose
New-AzureRmADServicePrincipal -ApplicationId
$adApp.ApplicationId.Guid -Role owner
```

Step 4

At this stage, we have created the service principal and the key vault. However, the service principal still does not have access to the key vault. This service principal will be used to query and list all secrets, keys, and certificates from the key vault, and it should have the necessary permissions to do so.

To provide the newly created service principal permission to access the key vault, we will go back to the Azure PowerShell console and execute the following command:

```
Set-AzureRmKeyVaultAccessPolicy -VaultName keyvaultbook -ResourceGroupName
IntegrationDemo -ObjectId "ea36bc00-6eff-4236-8c43-65c0c2e7e4cb" -
PermissionsToKeys get,list,create -PermissionsToCertificates
get,list,import -PermissionsToSecrets get,list -Verbose
```

Referring to the previous command block, please have a look at the following points:

- `Set-AzureRmKeyVaultAccessPolicy` provides access permissions to users, groups, and service principals. It accepts the key vault name and the service principal object ID. This object is different from the application ID. The output of `New-AzureRmAdServicePrincipal` contains an `Id` property. The value of `ObjectId` is this value:

```
ServicePrincipalNames :
ApplicationId         :
DisplayName           :              Id
Id                    : 2e           -4c2f          c52a3aad9983
AdfsId                :
Type                  : ServicePrincipal
```

- `PermissionsToKeys` provides access to keys in the key vault, and `get`, `list`, and `create` permissions are provided to this service principal. There is no write or update permission provided to this principal.
- `PermissionsToSecrets` provides access to secrets in the key vault, and `get` and `list` permissions are provided to this service principal. There is no write or update permission provided to this principal.
- `PermissionsToCertificates` provides access to secrets in the key vault, and get, import, and list permissions are provided to this service principal. There is no write or update permission provided to this principal.

Step 5

Just like before, we will be using Azure PowerShell to create a new Azure Automation account within a resource group. Before creating a resource group and an automation account, a connection to Azure should be established. However, this time, the credentials used should not be the credentials used earlier. Instead, use the service application created in the previous step:

1. The command to connect to Azure using the service application is as follows:

   ```
   Login-AzureRmAccount -ServicePrincipal -CertificateThumbprint
   "003B0D26705C792DB60823DA5804A0897160C306" -ApplicationId
   "xxxxxxxx-xxxx-xxxx-xxxx-xxxxxxxxxxxx" -Tenant "xxxxxxxx-xxxx-xxxx-
   xxxx-xxxxxxxxxxxx"
   ```

2. Here, the `applicationId` is available after executing the `New-AzureRmADApplication` cmdlet, and the tenant ID and the subscription ID can be retrieved using the command shown next. The subscription ID will be needed in subsequent commands:

   ```
   Get-AzureRmcontext
   ```

3. After connecting to Azure, a new resource containing resources for the solution and a new Azure Automation account should be created, as shown next. We are naming the resource group `VaultMonitoring`, and creating it in the `West Europe` region. We will be creating the remainder of the resources in this resource group as well:

   ```
   $IntegrationResourceGroup = "VaultMonitoring"
   $rgLocation = "West Europe"
   $automationAccountName = "MonitoringKeyVault"
   New-AzureRmResourceGroup -name $IntegrationResourceGroup -Location
   $rgLocation
   ```

```
New-AzureRmAutomationAccount -Name $automationAccountName -
ResourceGroupName $IntegrationResourceGroup -Location $rgLocation -
Plan Free
```

4. Create three automation variables, as shown next. The values for these, that is, subscription ID, tenant ID, and application ID, should already be available using previous steps:

```
New-AzureRmAutomationVariable -Name "azuresubscriptionid" -
AutomationAccountName $automationAccountName -ResourceGroupName
$IntegrationResourceGroup -Value " xxxxxxxx-xxxx-xxxx-xxxx-
xxxxxxxxxxxx " -Encrypted $true

New-AzureRmAutomationVariable -Name "azuretenantid" -
AutomationAccountName $automationAccountName -ResourceGroupName
$IntegrationResourceGroup -Value " xxxxxxxx-xxxx-xxxx-xxxx-
xxxxxxxxxxxx " -Encrypted $true

New-AzureRmAutomationVariable -Name "azureappid" -
AutomationAccountName $automationAccountName -ResourceGroupName
$IntegrationResourceGroup -Value " xxxxxxxx-xxxx-xxxx-xxxx-
xxxxxxxxxxxx " -Encrypted $true
```

5. Now it's time to upload a certificate that will be used to connect to Azure from Azure Automation:

```
$securepfxpwd = ConvertTo-SecureString -String 'password' -
AsPlainText -Force # Password for the private key PFX certificate
New-AzureRmAutomationCertificate -Name
"RitestSubscriptionCertificate" -Path "C:\book\azureautomation.pfx"
-Password $securepfxpwd -AutomationAccountName
$automationAccountName -ResourceGroupName $IntegrationResourceGroup
```

6. The next step is to install PowerShell modules related to Key Vault and Event Grid in the Azure Automation account, as these modules are not installed by default.

7. From the Azure portal, navigate to the already-created `VaultMonitoring` resource group by clicking on the **Resource Groups** icon in the left-hand menu.

8. Click on the already provisioned Azure Automation account, **MonitoringKeyVault**, and click on **Modules** in the left-hand menu, as shown in the following screenshot:

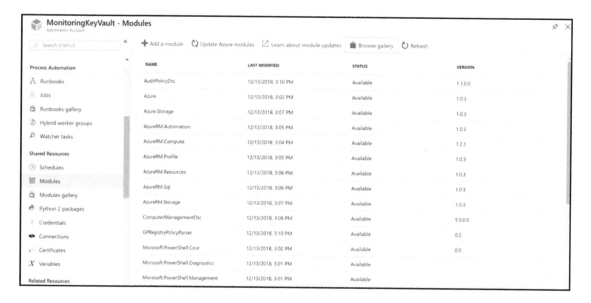

The Event Grid module is dependent on the `AzureRm.profile` module, and so we have to install it before the Event Grid module.

9. Click on **Browse Gallery** in the top menu and type `Azurerm.profile` in the search box, as shown in the following screenshot:

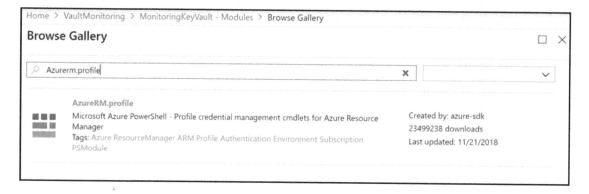

10. From the search results, select `AzureRM.profile` and click on the **Import** button in the top menu. Finally, click on the **OK** button. This step takes a few seconds to complete. After a few seconds, the module should be installed as shown in the following screenshot:

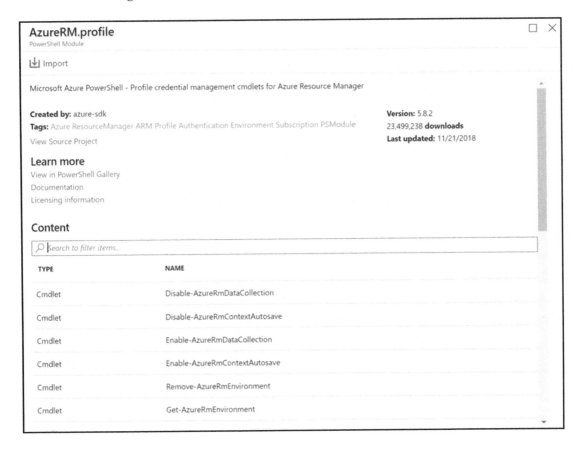

11. The status of the installation can be checked from the **Module** menu item. The following screenshot shows how we can import a module:

NAME	LAST MODIFIED	STATUS	VERSION
AuditPolicyDsc	12/13/2018, 3:10 PM	Available	1.1.0.0
Azure	12/13/2018, 3:02 PM	Available	1.0.3
Azure.Storage	12/13/2018, 3:07 PM	Available	1.0.3
AzureRM.Automation	12/13/2018, 3:05 PM	Available	1.0.3
AzureRM.Compute	12/13/2018, 3:04 PM	Available	1.2.1
AzureRM.profile	1/7/2019, 2:55 AM	Importing	
AzureRM.Resources	12/13/2018, 3:06 PM	Available	1.0.3
AzureRM.Sql	12/13/2018, 3:06 PM	Available	1.0.3
AzureRM.Storage	12/13/2018, 3:07 PM	Available	1.0.3
ComputerManagementDsc	12/13/2018, 3:08 PM	Available	5.0.0.0
GPRegistryPolicyParser	12/13/2018, 3:10 PM	Available	0.2
Microsoft.PowerShell.Core	12/13/2018, 3:02 PM	Available	0.0

Toolbar: Add a module · Update Azure modules · Learn about module updates · Browse gallery · Refresh

12. Perform similar steps as shown in step 9, 10 and 11 before to import and install the `AzureRM.EventGrid` module:

13. Perform similar steps as shown in step 9, 10 and 11 before to import and install the `AzureRM.KeyVault` module:

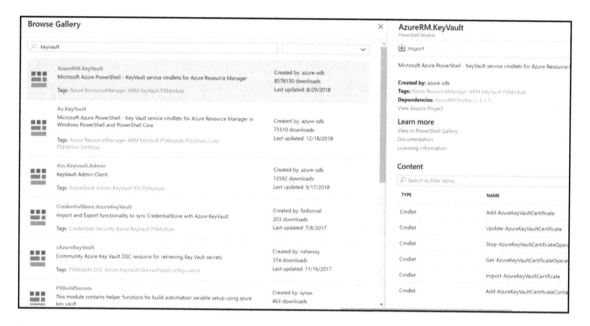

Step 6

The command that's used to create an Event Grid topic using PowerShell is as follows:

```
New-AzureRmEventGridTopic
```

The process of creating an Event Grid topic using the Azure portal are as follows:

1. From the Azure portal, navigate to the already created `Vaultmonitoring` resource group by clicking on the **Resource Groups** icon in the left-hand menu.
2. Next, click **+Add** and search for `Event Grid Topic` in the search box. Select it and click on the **Create** button:

3. Fill in the appropriate values in the resultant form by providing a name, selecting a subscription, the newly created resource group, the location, and the event schema:

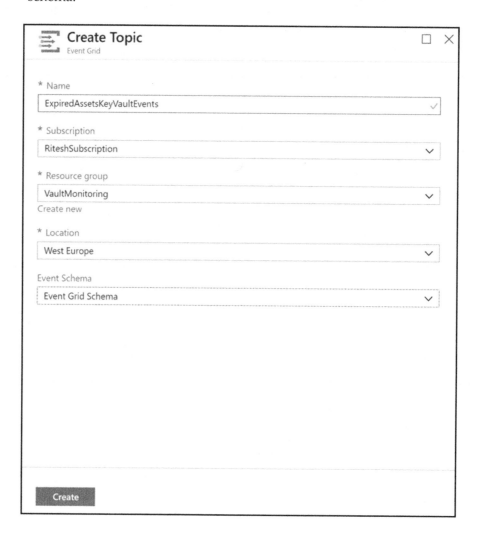

Step 7

1. **Create Azure Automation runbook**: From the Azure portal, navigate to the already created `Vaultmonitoring` resource group by clicking on the **Resource Groups** icon in the left-hand menu:
   1. Click on the already provisioned Azure Automation account, `MonitoringKeyVault`, click on **Runbooks** in the left-hand menu, and click on **+Add a Runbook** from the top menu.
   2. Click on **Create a new Runbook**. Provide a name. Let's call this runbook `CheckExpiredAssets`, and set the **Runbook type** as **PowerShell**:

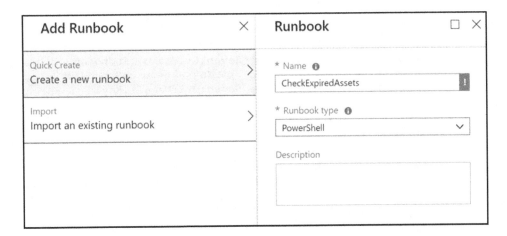

2. **Code the runbook:** Declare a few variables to hold subscription ID, tenant ID, application ID, and certificate thumbprint information. These values are already stored in Azure Automation variables, and the certificate is stored within the `RiteshSubscriptionCertificate` certificate store. The values are retrieved from the store and assigned to the variables as follows:

```
$subscriptionID = get-AutomationVariable "azuresubscriptionid"
$tenantID = get-AutomationVariable "azuretenantid"
$applicationId = get-AutomationVariable "azureappid"
$cert = get-AutomationCertificate "RitestSubscriptionCertificate"
$certThumbprint = ($cert.Thumbprint).ToString()
```

Log in to Azure using the service principal with pre-filled variables and select an appropriate subscription:

```
Login-AzureRmAccount -ServicePrincipal -CertificateThumbprint
$certThumbprint -ApplicationId $applicationId -Tenant $tenantID
Set-AzureRmContext -SubscriptionId $subscriptionID
```

Since Azure Event Grid was provisioned in the previous step, its endpoint and keys are retrieved using the Get-AzureRmEventGridTopic and Get-AzureRmEventGridTopicKey cmdlets.

Every Azure Event Grid generates two keys—primary and secondary—and so the first key reference is taken here.

```
$eventGridName = "ExpiredAssetsKeyVaultEvents"
$eventGridResourceGroup = "VaultMonitoring"
$topicEndpoint = (Get-AzureRmEventGridTopic -ResourceGroupName
$eventGridResourceGroup -Name $eventGridName).Endpoint
$keys = (Get-AzureRmEventGridTopicKey -ResourceGroupName
$eventGridResourceGroup -Name $eventGridName ).Key1
```

Next, all key vaults provisioned within the subscription are retrieved and looped over. While looping over the vault, all secrets are retrieved using the Get-AzureKeyVaultSecret cmdlet.

Even the secrets are looped, and within the loop, their expiry date is compared to today's date, and if it is less than a month away, then it generates an Event Grid event and publishes it using the invoke-webrequest command.

The same steps are executed for certificates stored within the key vault. The cmdlet used to retrieve all certificates is Get-AzureKeyVaultCertificate.

The event published to Event Grid should be in JSON format as an array, and so the message is converted to JSON using the ConvertTo-Json cmdlet and then converted into an array by adding [and] as a prefix and suffix.

To connect to Azure Event Grid and publish the event, the sender should supply the key in its header. The request will fail if this data is missing in the request payload:

```
$keyvaults = Get-AzureRmKeyVault
foreach($vault in $keyvaults) {
$secrets = Get-AzureKeyVaultSecret -VaultName $vault.VaultName
foreach($secret in $secrets) {
if( ![string]::IsNullOrEmpty($secret.Expires) ) {
if($secret.Expires.AddMonths(-1) -lt [datetime]::Now)
```

```
{
$secretDataMessage = @{
id = [System.guid]::NewGuid()
subject = "Secret Expiry happening soon !!"
eventType = "Secret Expiry"
eventTime = [System.DateTime]::UtcNow
data = @{
"ExpiryDate" = $secret.Expires
"SecretName" = $secret.Name.ToString()
"VaultName" = $secret.VaultName.ToString()
"SecretCreationDate" = $secret.Created.ToString()
"IsSecretEnabled" = $secret.Enabled.ToString()
"SecretId" = $secret.Id.ToString()
}
}
...
Invoke-WebRequest -Uri $topicEndpoint -Body $finalBody -Headers
$header -Method Post -UseBasicParsing
}
}
Start-Sleep -Seconds 5
}
}
```

Publish the runbook by clicking on the **Publish** button, as shown in the following screenshot:

3. **Scheduler**: Create an Azure Automation scheduler asset to execute this runbook once every day at 12.00 AM:
    1. Click on **Schedules** from the left-hand menu of Azure Automation and click on the **+Add a schedule** button in the top menu, as shown in the following screenshot:

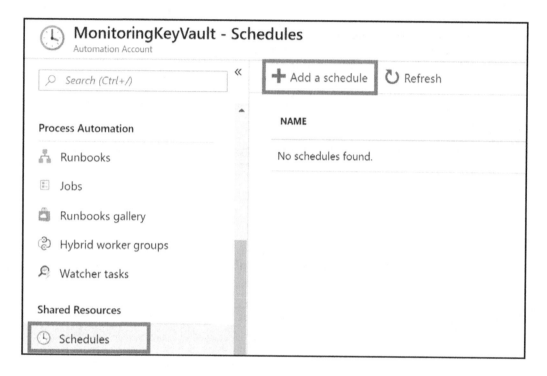

2. Provide scheduling information in the resulting form:

This should conclude the configuration of the Azure Automation account.

Step 8

Create a SendGrid resource: The SendGrid resource is used to send emails from the application without needing to install an SMTP server. It provides a REST API and a C# SDK, by means of which it is quite easy to send bulk emails. In the current solution, Azure Functions will be used to invoke SendGrid APIs to send emails, and so this resource needs to be provisioned. This resource has separate costing and is not covered as part of the Azure cost. There is a free tier available and can be used for sending emails:

1. A SendGrid resource is created just like any other Azure resource. Search for `sendgrid`, and we will get **SendGrid Email Delivery** in the results:

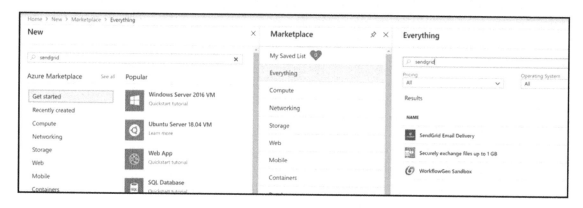

2. Select the resource and click on the **Create** button to open its configuration form:

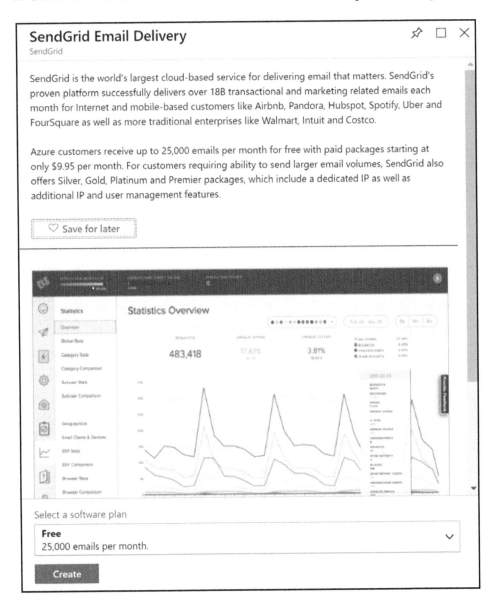

3. Select an appropriate pricing tier, as shown in the following screenshot:

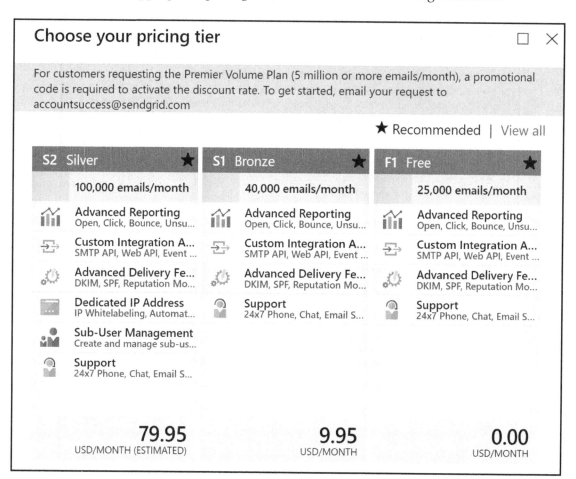

4. Provide appropriate contact details:

5. Accept the terms of use, as shown in the following screenshot:

Create   □ ✕

Offer details

SendGrid Email Delivery Free (monthly
subscription)   0.00 INR/month   ⚠
by SendGrid
Terms of use | privacy policy

⚠ **The highlighted Marketplace purchase(s) are not covered by your Azure credits, and will
be billed separately.**
You cannot use your Azure monetary commitment funds or subscription credits for these
purchases. You will be billed separately for marketplace purchases.

Terms of use

By clicking "Create", I (a) agree to the legal terms and privacy statement(s) associated with each
Marketplace offering above, (b) authorize Microsoft to charge or bill my current payment method for
the fees associated with my use of the offering(s), including applicable taxes, with the same billing
frequency as my Azure subscription, until I discontinue use of the offering(s), and (c) agree that
Microsoft may share my contact information and transaction details (including usage volume
associated with the offering) with the seller(s) of the offering(s). Microsoft does not provide rights for
third-party products or services. See the Azure Marketplace Terms for additional terms.

☐   I give Microsoft permission to use and share my contact information so that Microsoft or the
Provider can contact me regarding this product and related products.

Create

6. Complete the form and click on the **Create** button:

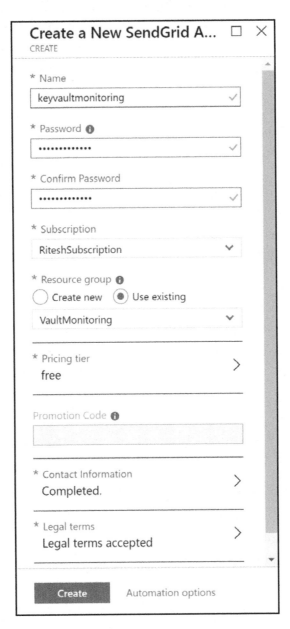

7. After the resource is provisioned, click on the **Manage** button in the top menu. This will open the SendGrid website. It may request email configuration. Select **API Keys** from the **Settings** section and click on the **Create API Key**:

8. From the resulting window, select **Full Access** and click on the **Create & View** button. This will create the keys for the SendGrid resource. Keep a note of this key, as it will be used with the Azure Function configuration for SendGrid:

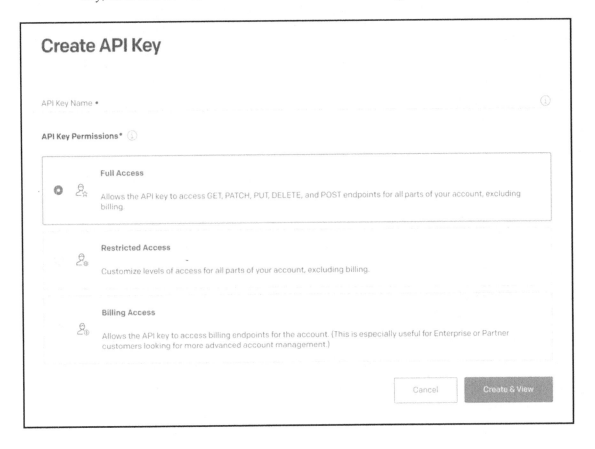

Step 9

Create a Twilio account: Twilio is used for sending bulk SMS messages. To create an account with Twilio, navigate to `twillio.com` and create a new account. After successfully creating an account, a mobile number is generated that can be used to send SMS messages to receivers:

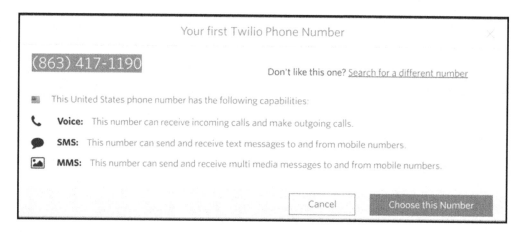

It also generated production and test keys. Copy the test key and token temporarily, as they will be used within Azure Functions:

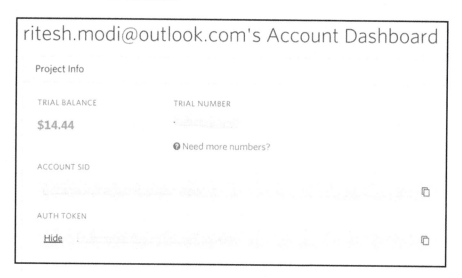

Step 10

Creating Azure function: In this section, a new function app and function will be created. The purpose of the Azure function within the solution is to send notification messages to users regarding the expiry of secrets in the key vault. A single function will be responsible for sending both emails and SMS messages. This could have been divided into two separate functions. The first step is to create a new function app and host a function within it:

1. As we have done before, navigate to your resource group, click on the **+Add** button in the top menu, and search for the `function app` resource. Click on the **Create** button to get the function app form:

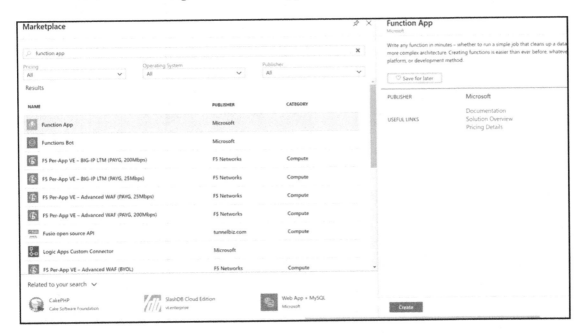

2. Fill up the function app form and click on the **Create** button. The name of the function app must be unique across Azure:

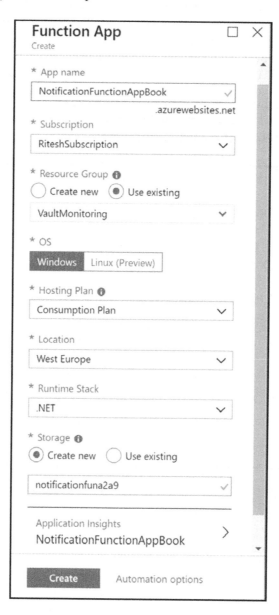

3. Once the function app is provisioned, create a new function called SMSandEMailFunction by clicking on the **+** button next to the **Functions** item in the left-hand menu, selecting **In-portal** from the central dashboard, and selecting more templates:

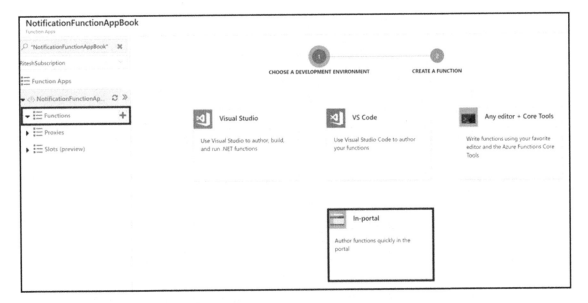

4. Select **HTTP trigger** and name it SMSandEMailFunction. Click on the **Create** button. The authorization level could be any value:

5. Remove the default code, replace it with the code shown in the following listing, and click on the **Save** button in the top menu:

```
#r "SendGrid"
#r "Newtonsoft.Json"
#r "Twilio.Api"
using System.Net;
using System;
using SendGrid.Helpers.Mail;
using Microsoft.Azure.WebJobs.Host;
using Newtonsoft.Json;
using Twilio;
using System.Configuration;
public static HttpResponseMessage Run(HttpRequestMessage req,
TraceWriter log, out Mail message,out SMSMessage sms)
{
log.Info("C# HTTP trigger function processed a request.");
string alldata =
req.Content.ReadAsStringAsync().GetAwaiter().GetResult();
message = new Mail();
var personalization = new Personalization();
personalization.AddBcc(new
Email(ConfigurationManager.AppSettings["bccStakeholdersEmail"]));
personalization.AddTo(new
Email(ConfigurationManager.AppSettings["toStakeholdersEmail"]));
var messageContent = new Content("text/html", alldata);
message.AddContent(messageContent);
message.AddPersonalization(personalization);
message.Subject = "Key Vault assets Expiring soon..";
message.From = new
Email(ConfigurationManager.AppSettings["serviceEmail"]);
string msg = alldata;
sms = new SMSMessage();
sms.Body = msg;
sms.To = ConfigurationManager.AppSettings["adminPhone"];
sms.From = ConfigurationManager.AppSettings["servicePhone"];
return req.CreateResponse(HttpStatusCode.OK, "Hello ");
}
```

6. Click on the function app name in the left-hand menu and click again on the **Application settings** link in the main window:

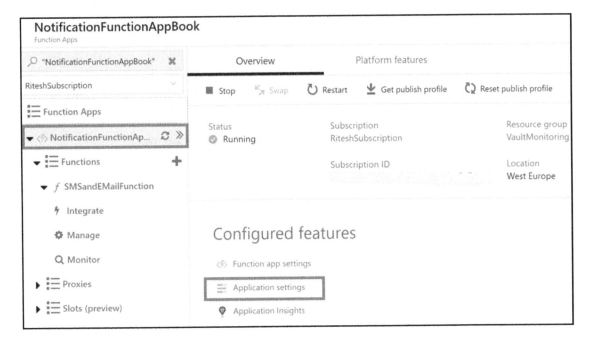

7. Navigate to the **Application settings** section as shown in the previous screenshot and add a few entries by clicking on **+ Add new setting** for each entry.

Note that the entries are in the form of key-value pairs, and the values should be actual real-time values. Both `adminPhone` and `servicePhone` should already be configured on the Twilio website. `servicePhone` is the phone number generated by Twilio used for sending SMS messages, and `adminPhone` is the phone number of the administrator to whom the SMS should be sent.

Also note that Twilio expects the destination phone number to be in a particular format depending on the country (for India, the format is +91 xxxxx xxxxx). Note the spaces and country code in the number.

We also need to add the keys for both SendGrid and Twilio within the application settings. These settings are mentioned in the following list. Readers may already have these values handy because of activities performed in the earlier steps:

- The value of `SendGridAPIKeyAsAppSetting` is the key for SendGrid.
- `TwilioAccountSid` is the system identifier for the Twilio account. This value was already copied and stored in a transient place in an earlier step.
- `TwilioAuthToken` is the token for the Twilio account. This value was already copied and stored in a temporary place in an earlier step.

8. Save the settings by clicking on the **Save** button in the top menu:

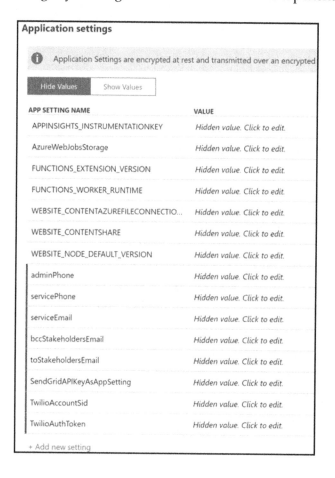

9. Click on the **Integrate** link in the left menu just below the name of the function, and click on **+ New Output**. This is to add an output for the SendGrid service:

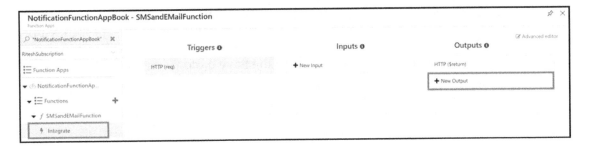

10. Select **SendGrid**. It might ask you to install the SendGrid extension. Install the extension, which will take a couple of minutes:

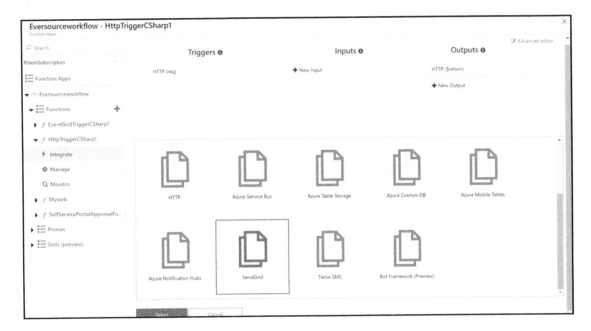

11. After installing the extension, the output configuration form appears. The important configuration items in this form are **Message parameter name** and **SendGridAPIKeyAppSetting**. Leave the default value for **Message parameter name** and click on the drop-down list to select **SendGridAPIKeyAsAppSetting** as the API app setting key. This was already configured in a previous step within the app settings configuration. The form should be configured as shown in the following screenshot, and then click on the **Save** button:

12. Click on **+ New Output** again. This is to add an output for the Twilio service.
13. Select **Twilio SMS**. It might ask you to install the Twilio SMS extension. Install the extension, which will take a couple of minutes.

14. After installing the extension, the output configuration form appears. The important configuration items in this form are **Message parameter name**, **Account SID setting**, and **Auth Token Setting**. Change the default value for the **Message parameter name** to `sms`. This is done because the `message` parameter is already used for the SendGrid service parameter. Ensure that the value of **Account SID setting** is `TwilioAccountSid` and the value of the **Auth Token Setting** is `TwilioAuthToken`. These values were already configured in a previous step within the app settings configuration. The form should be configured as shown in the following screenshot, and then click on **Save**:

Step 11

Create a Logic App workflow: We have authored an Azure Automation runbook that queries all the secrets in all key vaults and publishes an event in case it finds any of them expiring within a month. The logic app workflow acts as a subscriber to these events:

1. The first step within the logic app is to create a logic app workflow:

2. Fill up the resultant form after clicking on the **Create** button. We are provisioning the logic app in the same resource group as the other resources for this solution:

3. After the logic app is provisioned, it opens the designer window. Select **Blank Logic App** from the **Templates** section:

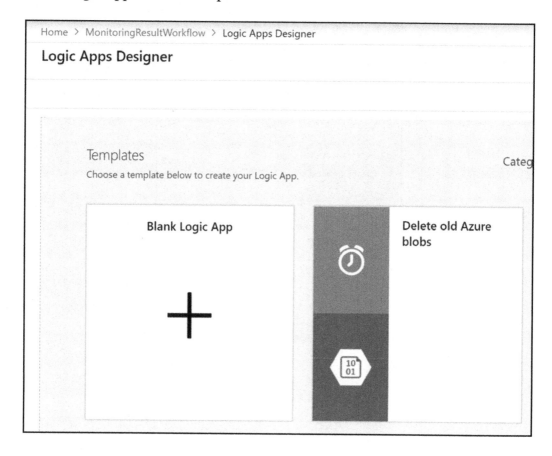

4. In the resultant window, add a trigger that can subscribe to Event Grid events. Logic Apps provides a trigger for Event Grid, and search for this to see whether it's available:

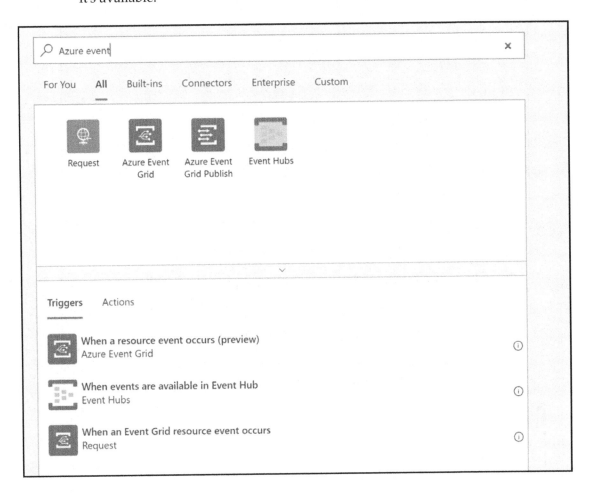

5. Select the **When a resource event occurs (preview)** trigger:

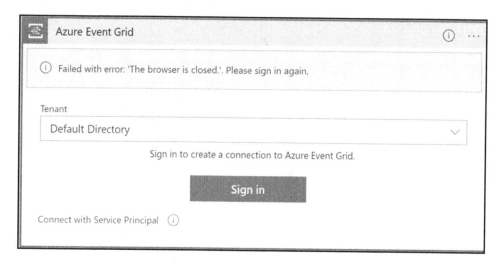

6. In the resultant window, select **Connect with Service Principal**.

Provide service principal details, including application ID (client ID), tenant ID, and password. This trigger does not accept a service principal that authenticates with certificate. It accepts a service principal only with a password. Create a new service principal at this stage that authenticates with a password (the steps for creating a Service Principal based on password authentication was covered earlier in this chapter) and use the details of the newly created application principal for Azure Event Grid configuration as shown next.

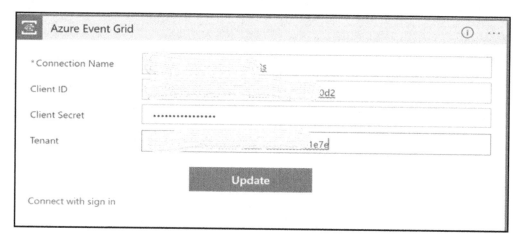

7. Select the subscription. Based on scope of service principal, this will get auto-filled. Select `Microsoft.EventGrid.Topics` as **Resource Type** and set the name of the custom topic as **ExpiredAssetsKeyVaultEvents**:

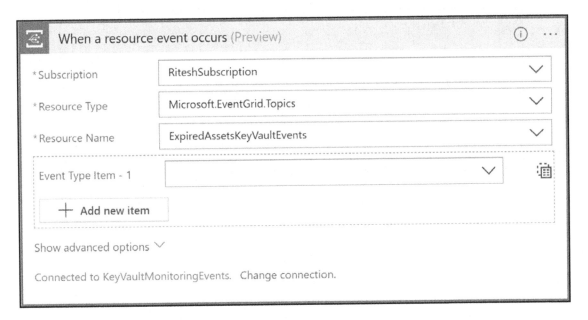

8. The previous step will create a connector, and the connection information can be changed be clicking on **Change connection**

9. The final configuration of Event Grid trigger should be similar to the following screenshot:

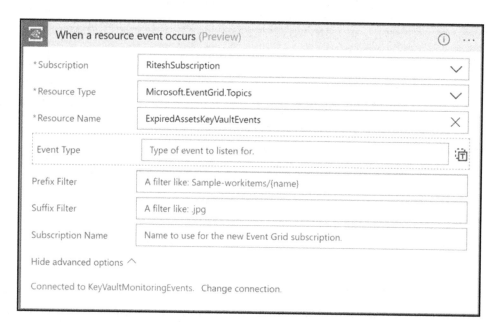

10. Add a new **Parse JSON** activity after the Event Grid trigger. This activity needs the JSON schema. Generally, the schema is not available, but this activity helps generate the schema if valid JSON is provided to it:

11. Click on **Use sample payload to generate schema** and provide data, as shown here:

```
{
"ExpiryDate": "",
"SecretName": "",
"VaultName": "",
"SecretCreationDate": "",
"IsSecretEnabled": "",
"SecretId": ""
}
```

A question might arise here regarding the sample payload. How do you know at this stage what the payload is that's generated by the Event Grid publisher? The answer to this lies in the fact that this sample payload is exactly the same as is used in the data element in the Azure Automation runbook. Let me show you that code snippet again:

```
data = @{
"ExpiryDate" = $certificate.Expires
"CertificateName" = $certificate.Name.ToString()
"VaultName" = $certificate.VaultName.ToString()
"CertificateCreationDate" = $certificate.Created.ToString()
"IsCertificateEnabled" = $certificate.Enabled.ToString()
"CertificateId" = $certificate.Id.ToString()
}
```

12. The **Content** text box should contain dynamic content coming out from the previous trigger:

13. Add another **Azure Functions** action after **Parse JSON** and select **Choose an Azure function**. Select the Azure function app called `NotificationFunctionAppBook` and `SMSAndEmailFunction`, which were created earlier:

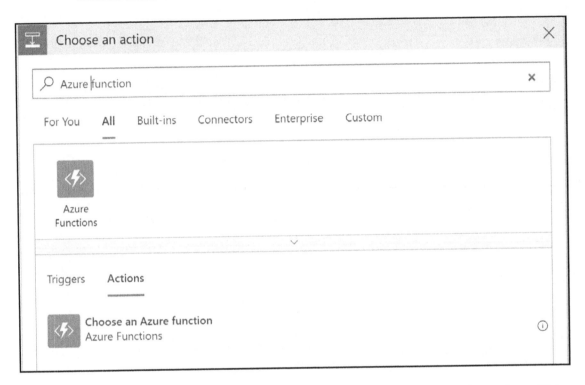

14. Click on the **Request Body** text area and fill it with code listing shown here. This is done to convert the data into JSON before sending it to the Azure function:

```
{
"alldata" :
}
```

15. Place the cursor after : in the preceding code and click on **Add dynamic content | Body** from the previous activity:

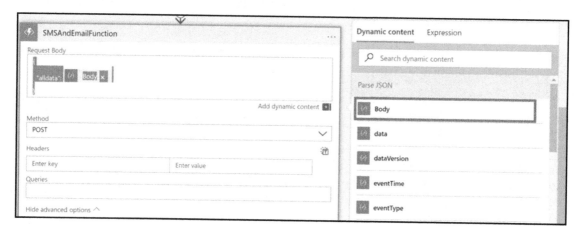

16. Save the entire logic app. The entire logic app should look like this:

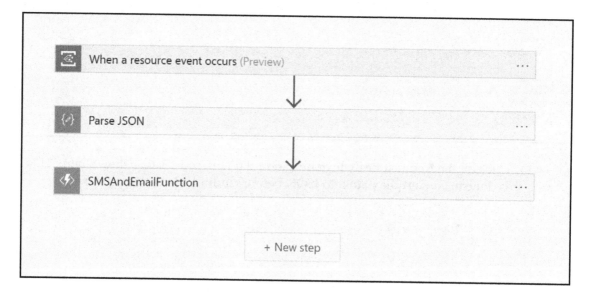

Testing

Upload some secrets and certificates that have expiry dates to Azure Key Vault and execute the Azure Automation runbook. The runbook is scheduled to run on a schedule. The runbook will publish events to Event Grid. The logic app should be enabled, and it will pick the event and finally invoke the Azure function to send email and SMS notifications.

The email should look like this:

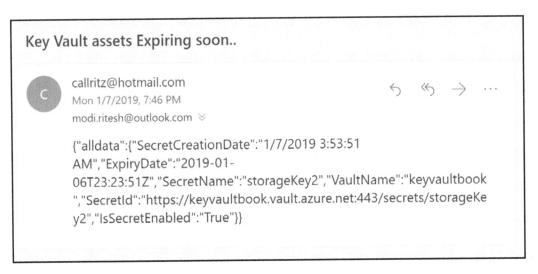

Summary

This was a big chapter. This chapter introduced Event Grid by providing a couple of end-to-end solutions using storage resources and custom topics. It also introduced Azure Logic Apps as automated serverless workflows. The chapter focused heavily on creating an architecture that integrated multiple Azure services to create an end-to-end solution. The services used in the solution were Azure Automation, Azure Logic Apps, Azure Event Grids, Azure Functions, SendGrid, and Twilio. These services were implemented using Azure portal and PowerShell using service principals as service accounts. It also showed a couple of ways to create service principals with passwords and certificates authentication.

The next chapter is an important chapter for Azure cost management perspective. It is quite easy to spin new resources on Azure without knowing the actual cost of running them. Next chapter will provide details about cost management.

8
Cost Management

The primary reason that corporations are moving to the cloud is to save costs. There is no upfront cost for having an Azure subscription. Azure provides a **pay-as-you-go** payment mechanism, meaning that payment is based on consumption; Azure measures usage and provides monthly invoices based on your consumption. There is no upper limit for how much you can consume—Azure provides unlimited resources, and anybody with access to Azure can create as many resources as they want. Of course, in such circumstances, it is important for companies to keep a close watch on their Azure consumption. Although they can create policies to set organizational standards and conventions, there is also a need to have Azure billing and consumption information readily available. Moreover, companies should look to employ best practices for consuming Azure resources such that the returns are maximized. For this, architects need to be fully aware of Azure resources and features, their corresponding costs, and to perform cost-benefit comparisons.

In this chapter, we will cover the following:

- Understanding Azure billing
- Invoicing
- Enterprise agreement customers
- Usage and Quotas
- Resource providers
- Usage and Billing APIs
- The Azure pricing models and calculator
- Best practices

Understanding billing

Azure is a service utility that offers the following benefits:

- No upfront costs
- No termination fees
- Billing on a per-minute basis
- Payment based on consumption

In such circumstances, it is very difficult to estimate the cost of consuming Azure resources. Every resource in Azure has its own cost model and charge based on storage, usage, and timespan. It is very important for the management, administration, and finance departments of a company to keep track of usage and costs. Azure provides the necessary usage and billing reports, such that an organization's management and administrators can generate cost and usage reports based on all sorts of criteria.

The Azure portal provides detailed billing and usage information through the **Billing** feature, which can be accessed from the master navigation blade:

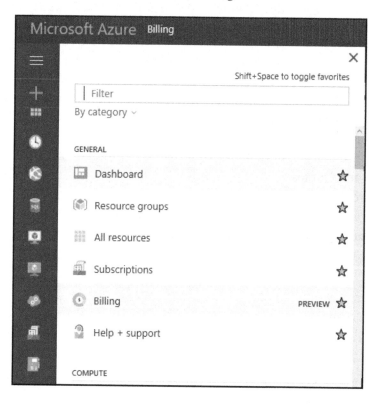

It provides a sub-menu for generating reports on both costs and billing:

Clicking on the **Subscriptions** menu on this blade provides a list of all the subscriptions that the user has access to for generating reports:

Clicking on the subscription name in this list will provide a dashboard through which the complete billing, invoice, usage, consumption, policies, resource groups, and resources information can be found. The chart in this **Overview** section provides a cost percentage by resource and also a burn rate:

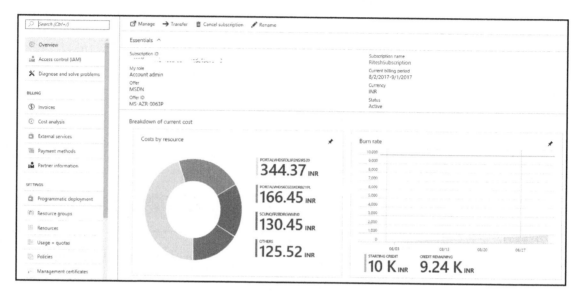

Clicking on the chart shows details of costs based on each resource. Here there are multiple Storage accounts provisioned on Azure, and the cost for each is displayed. Using this screen, many types of report can be generated by providing different criteria, such as any combination of the following:

- Resource types
- Resource group
- Timespan
- Tags

Tags are particularly interesting. Queries based on tags such as department, project, owner, cost center, or any other name-value pair can be used to display cost information. You can also download the cost report as a CSV file using the **Download** button:

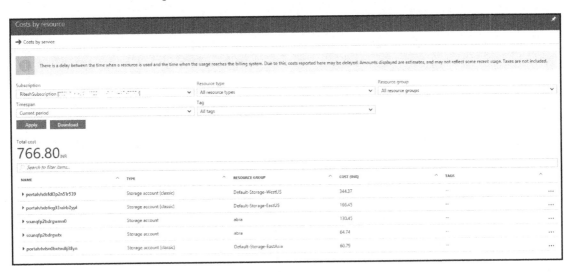

Clicking on an individual resource provides the daily cost consumption data for the resource:

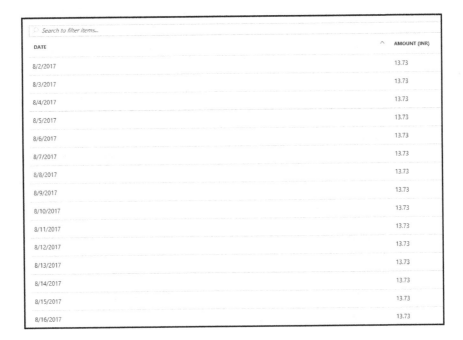

Invoicing

The Azure **Billing** feature also provides information about monthly invoices.

Clicking on the **Invoices** menu provides a list of all invoices generated:

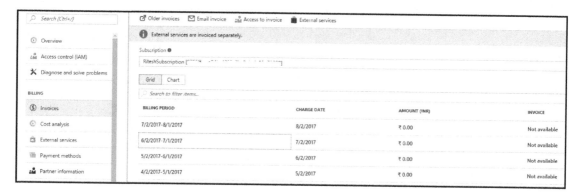

Clicking on any of the invoices provides details about that invoice:

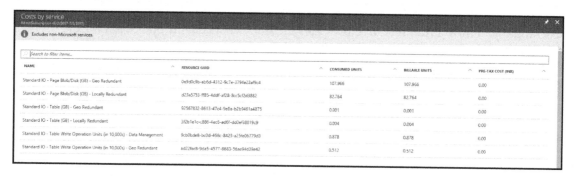

There is also an alternative way to download invoice details. The invoice details are available by logging into `https://account.azure.com` and downloading the invoice details:

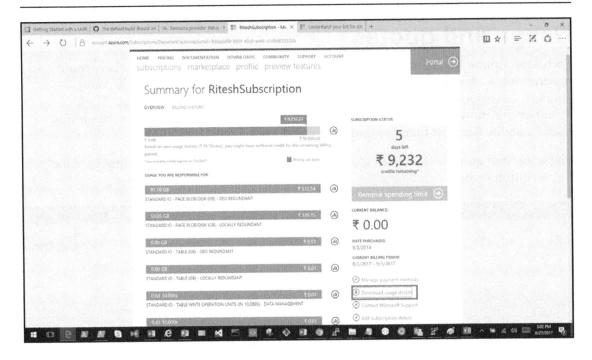

Enterprise agreement customers

Enterprise customers that have an enterprise agreement can utilize `https://ea.azure.com` to download their usage and billing reports. Also, a new Power BI content pack was released recently that can be utilized to view Azure usage and costs through reports and a dashboard in Power BI.

 More information about Enterprise agreements usage and costs is available at `https://azure.microsoft.com/en-us/blog/new-power-bi-content-pack -for-azure-enterprise-users/`.

Usage and quotas

Each subscription has a limited quota for each resource type. For example, there could be a maximum of 60 public IP addresses provisioned with an MSDN Microsoft account. Similarly, all resources have a maximum default limit for each resource type. These resource type numbers for a subscription can be increased by contacting Azure support or clicking on the **Request Increase** button.

The usage and quota information is available from the **Usage + quotas** sub-menu of the **Subscription** menu:

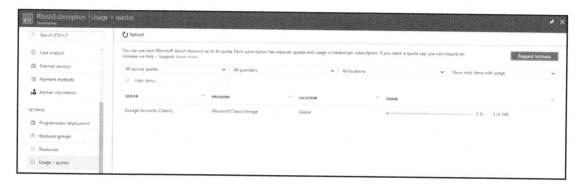

This blade shows all resource types provisioned in a subscription, along with their locations and counts. Here the quota for classic Storage accounts is 100, and currently, three classic Storage accounts have been consumed.

You can filter by location, provider, usage, and quota. Custom reports based on these filter criteria can be generated.

Resource providers

Resources are based on resource types and are available from resource providers. There are numerous providers available in Azure, which provide the resource types needed by users to create their instances. For example, the **Microsoft.Compute** resource provider provides virtual machine resource types. Using virtual machine resource types, instances of virtual machines can be created.

Resource providers are required to be registered with Azure subscriptions. Resource types will not be available in a subscription if resource providers are not registered. To get a list of the providers that are available, or to see the ones that are registered and the ones that aren't, or even to register non-registered providers, this dashboard can be used:

The usage and billing APIs

Although the portal is a great way to find usage, billing, and invoice information manually, Azure also provides the following:

- **The Invoice Download API**: Use this API to download invoices.
- **The Resource Usage API**: Use this API to get estimated Azure resource consumption data.
- **The RateCard API**: Use the RateCard API to get a list of available Azure resources and estimated pricing information for each of them.

These APIs can be used to programmatically retrieve details and create customized dashboards and reports. Any programming or scripting language can use these APIs and create a complete billing solution.

Azure pricing models

Azure has multiple pricing models. It has a model for every type of customer. From free accounts for students and pay-as-you-go accounts for developers to enterprise agreements and cloud solution provider partner models. Apart from these account types, there are add-on pricing and discounts, such as reserved virtual machine instances and the Azure Hybrid Benefit.

Azure Hybrid Benefit

When a virtual machine is provisioned on Azure, there are two types of cost are involved. These two costs are the resource cost for running the virtual machine and the operating system license cost. Although Enterprise Agreement customers get some discounts compared to other accounts, Azure provides another offer for them: the Azure Hybrid Benefit. In this scheme, existing Enterprise Agreement customers can use their on-premises operating system licenses to create their virtual machines on Azure and Azure will not charge the cost of the license. The cost savings can be as high as 40 percent or original cost using this scheme. Enterprise Agreement customers should also have software assurance to enjoy this benefit, which is applicable for both Windows Standard and Datacenter editions. Each 2-processor license or each set of 16-core licenses is entitled to two instances of up to 8 cores or 1 instance of up to 16 cores. The Azure Hybrid Benefit for Standard edition licenses can only be used in one instance, whether on-premises or in Azure. The Datacenter edition allows simultaneous usage both on-premises and in Azure.

Azure reserved virtual machine instances

Customers can reserve a fixed number of virtual machines in advance, for one year to three years for both the Windows and Linux operating systems. Azure provides up to a 72 percent discount on these virtual machines based on a pay-as-you-go pricing model. Although there is an upfront commitment, there is no obligation to use the instances. These reserved instances can be canceled at any point in time. This offering can even be clubbed with the Azure Hybrid Benefit scheme to further reduce the cost of these virtual machines.

Pay-as-you-go accounts

These are general Azure accounts and are billed monthly to customers. Customers do not commit any usage and are free to use any resource based on their needs. Resource costs are calculated based on usage and uptime. However, each resource has its own cost model. There is also no upfront cost associated with these accounts. Generally, there are no discounts available in this scheme.

Enterprise Agreements

Customers who already have agreements with Microsoft can add their Azure tenants as part of Enterprise Agreements. Customers can enjoy great discounts if they are part of Enterprise Agreements. Customers just need to make an upfront annual monetary commitment and they can be added to this scheme. Customers are free to consume as they please. Please refer to https://azure.microsoft.com/en-in/pricing/enterprise-agreement/ for more information.

The cloud solution provider model

The **Cloud Solution Provider (CSP)** model is a model for Microsoft partners. CSP enables partners to have end-to-end ownership of the customer life cycle and relationship for Microsoft Azure. Partners can deploy their solutions to the cloud and charge customers using this scheme. Please refer to https://azure.microsoft.com/en-in/offers/ms-azr-0145p/ for more information.

The Azure pricing calculator

Azure provides a cost calculator for users and customers to estimate their cost and usage. This calculator is available at `https://azure.microsoft.com/en-in/pricing/calculator/`:

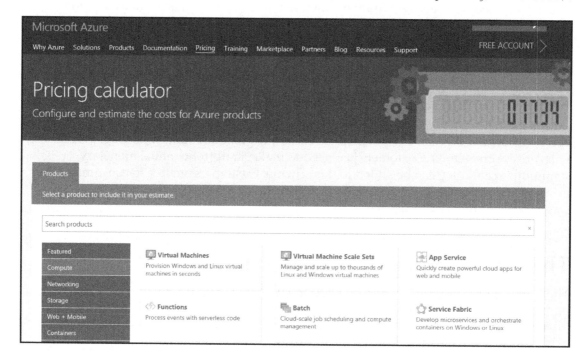

Users can select multiple resources from the left menu and they will be added to the calculator. In the following example, a virtual machine is added. Further configuration with regard to virtual machine region, operating system, type, tier, instance size, number of hours, and count can be done:

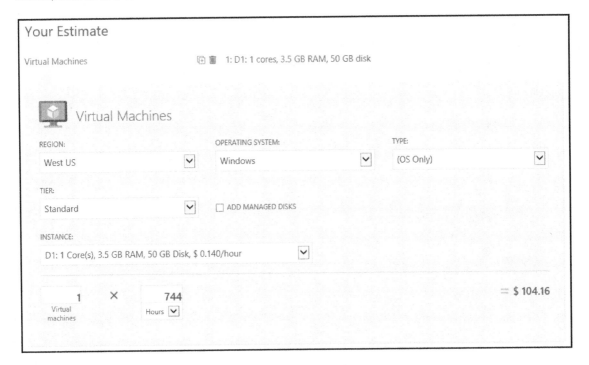

Similarly, the cost for Azure Functions in terms of virtual machine memory size, execution time, and execution per second is shown next:

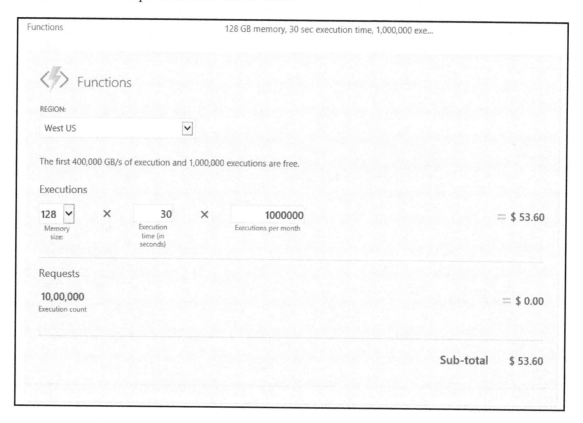

Azure provides different levels and plans of support, which are as follows:

- **Default support**: Free
- **Developer support**: $29 per month
- **Standard support**: $300 per month
- **Professional direct**: $1,000 per month

Finally, the overall estimated cost is displayed:

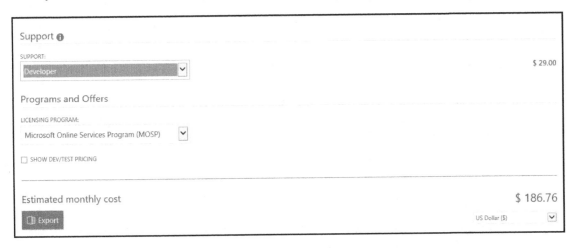

It is important that architects understand how each Azure feature is used in the overall architecture and solution. The accuracy of the Azure calculator depends on what resources are selected and what their configuration is. Any misrepresentation would lead to bias and incorrect estimates, which would be different to the actual billing.

Best practices

Architects need to put in additional effort to understand their architecture and the Azure components being utilized. Based on active monitoring, audits, and usage, they should be fully aware of the SKU, size, and features of the architecture. This section will detail some of the best practices to be adopted from a cost optimization perspective.

Compute best practices

Compute refers to services that help in the execution of services. Some of the best practices related to compute are as follows:

- Choose the best location for your compute services, such as virtual machines. Choose a location where all Azure features and resources are available together in the same region. This will avoid egress traffic.
- Choose the optimal size for your virtual machines. A bigger virtual machine costs more than a smaller one, and a bigger virtual machine might not be required at all.
- Resize virtual machines according to demand. Azure releases new virtual machine sizes frequently. If a new size becomes available that is better suited to your needs, then it should be used.
- Shut down compute services when they are not needed. This particularly applies to non-production environments.
- Deallocate virtual machines rather than shutting them down. This will release all resources and consumption will stop.
- Use development/testing labs for development and testing purposes. They provide policies and auto-shutdown and auto-start features.
- With virtual machine scale sets, provision few virtual machines and increase their count based on demand.
- Choose the correct size (whether small, medium, or large) for application gateways. They are backed up by virtual machines and can help reduce costs if sized optimally. Also, choose the basic tier application gateway if a web application firewall is not needed.
- Choose the correct tiers for virtual private network gateways (including a basic virtual private network, standard, high performance, and ultra performance).
- Minimize network traffic between Azure regions by collocating resources in the same region.
- Use a load balancer with a public IP to access multiple virtual machines rather than assigning a public IP to each virtual machine.
- Monitor virtual machines and their performance and usage metrics. Based on those metrics, determine whether you want to upscale or scale out the virtual machine. Consultation of the metrics could also result in downsizing the virtual machines.

Storage best practices

Here are some best practices for optimizing storage for cost:

- Choose the appropriate storage redundancy type (whether GRS, LRS, or RA-GRS). GRS is costlier than LRS, for instance.
- Archive storage data to cool or archive the access tier. Keep data that is frequently accessed in the hot tier.
- Remove blobs that are not required.
- Delete virtual machine operating system disks explicitly after deleting the virtual machine, if they are not needed.
- Storage accounts are metered based on their size, write, read, list, and container operations.
- Prefer standard disks over premium disks. Use premium disks only if business requirements demand it.
- Use the **Content Delivery Network** (**CDN**) and caching for static files instead of fetching them from storage every time.

Platform-as-a-Service (PaaS) best practices

Some of the best practices if PaaS is the preferred deployment model are listed here:

- Choose the appropriate Azure SQL tier (whether basic, standard, premium RS, or premium) and appropriate performance levels in terms of DTUs.
- Choose appropriately between single databases and elastic databases. If there are a lot of databases, it is more cost-efficient to use elastic databases compared to single databases.
- Ensure Azure SQL security - encrypt data at rest and in motion, data masking, threat protection are enabled.
- Ensure that backup strategy and data replication is set up according to business demands.
- Ensure there is redundancy for web apps with multi-region availability using traffic manager
- Use Redis cache and CDN for faster delivery of data and pages.

- Re-architect your solutions to use PaaS solutions (such as serverless solutions and microservices in containers) rather than **Infrastructure as a Service (IaaS)** solutions. These PaaS solutions remove maintenance costs and are available on the consumption-per-minute basis. If you do not consume these services, there is no cost, even though your code and services will still be available round the clock.

General best practices

Some of other general best practices are listed here:

- Resource costs differ across regions. Try using a region with lower costs.
- Enterprise agreements provide the best discounts. If you are not in an enterprise agreement, try to use one for the cost benefits.
- If Azure costs can be prepaid, then discounts for all kinds of subscription can be gained.
- Delete or remove unused resources. Figure out what resources are underutilized and reduce their SKU or size. If they are not needed, then delete them.
- Use Azure Advisor and take its recommendations seriously.

Summary

Cost management and administration is an important activity when dealing with the cloud. This is primarily because the monthly expense could be very low, but can be very high if proper attention is not given to it. Architects should design their applications in such a manner as to minimize cost as much as possible. They should use appropriate Azure resources, appropriate SKU, tier, and size, and should know when to start, stop, scale up, scale out, scale down, scale in, transfer data, and more. Proper cost management will ensure that actual expenses meet budgetary expenses.

The next chapter of this book deals with the monitoring and auditing capabilities of Azure.

Designing Policies, Locks, and Tags

9

Azure is a versatile cloud platform. Customers can not only create and deploy their applications; they can also actively manage and govern their environments. Clouds generally follow a pay-as-you-go paradigm, where a customer subscribes for a subscription and can deploy virtually anything to the cloud. It could be as small as a, basic virtual machine, or it could be thousands of virtual machines with higher SKUs. Azure will not stop any customer from provisioning the resources they want to provision. Within an organization, there could be a large number of people with access to the organization's Azure subscription. There needs to be a governance model in place such that only necessary resources are provisioned by people who have the right to create them. Azure provides resource management features, such as Azure **Role-Based Access Control (RBAC)**, policies, and locks, for managing and providing governance for resources.

Another major aspect of governance is cost, usage, and information management. An organization's management would always want to be kept updated about their cloud consumption and costs. They would like to identify what team, department, or unit is using what percentage of their total cost. In short, they want to have reports based on various dimensions about consumption and cost. Azure provides a tagging feature that can help provide this kind of information on the fly.

In this chapter, we will cover the following topics:

- Azure tags
- Azure policies
- Azure locks
- Azure RBAC
- Implementing Azure governance features

Azure tags

A tag is defined by the Oxford Dictionary (https://en.oxforddictionaries.com/definition/tag) as the following:

> *"a label attached to someone or something for the purpose of identification or to give other information."*

Azure allows the tagging of resource groups and resources with name-value pairs. Tagging helps in the logical organization and categorization of resources. Azure also allows the tagging of 15 name-value pairs for a resource group and its resources. Although a resource group is a container for resources, tagging a resource group does not mean the tagging of its constituent resources. Resource groups and resources should be tagged based on their usage, which will be explained later in this section. Tags work at a subscription level. Azure accepts any name-value pairs, and so it is important for an organization to define both the names and their possible values.

But why is tagging important? In other words, what problems can be solved using tagging? Tagging has the following benefits:

- **Categorization of resources**: An Azure subscription can be used by multiple departments within an organization. It is important for the management team to identify the owners of any resources. Tagging helps in assigning identifiers to resources that can be used to represent departments or roles.

- **Information management for Azure resources**: Again, Azure resources can be provisioned by anyone with access to the subscription. Organizations would like to have a proper categorization of resources in place to comply with information management policies. Such policies can be based on application life cycle management, such as management of the development, testing, and production environments. Such policies could be based on the usage, or based on any other priorities. Each organization has their own way of defining information categories, and Azure caters for this with tags.

- **Cost management**: Tagging in Azure can help in identifying resources based on their categorization. Queries can be executed against Azure to identify cost per category, for instance. For example, the cost of resources in Azure for the development of an environment for the finance department and the marketing department can be easily ascertained. Moreover, Azure also provides billing information based on tags. This helps in identifying the consumption rates of teams, departments, or groups.

Tags in Azure do have certain limitations, however:

- Azure allows a maximum of 15 tag name-value pairs to be associated with resource groups.
- Tags are non-inheritable. Tags applied to a resource group do not apply to the individual resources within it. However, it is quite easy to forget to tag resources when provisioning them. Azure policies are the mechanism to ensure that tags are tagged with the appropriate value during provision time. We will consider the details of such policies later in this chapter.

Tags can be assigned to resources and resource groups using PowerShell, Azure CLI 2.0, Azure Resource Manager templates, the Azure portal, and the Azure Resource Manager REST APIs.

An example of information management categorization using Azure tags is shown here. In this example, the **Department**, **Project**, **Environment**, **Owner**, **Approver**, **Maintainer**, **Start Date**, **Retire Date**, and **Patched Date** name-value pairs are used to tag resources. It is extremely easy to find all the resources for a particular tag or a combination of tags using PowerShell, the Azure CLI, or REST APIs:

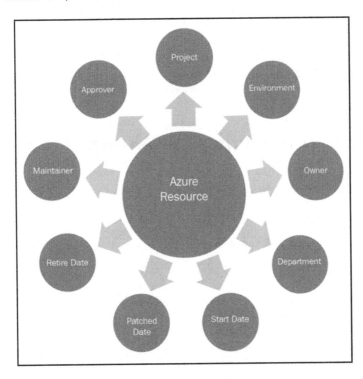

Tags with PowerShell

Tags can be managed using PowerShell, Azure Resource Manager templates, the Azure portal, and REST APIs. In this section, PowerShell will be used to create and apply tags. PowerShell provides a cmdlet for retrieving and attaching tags to resource groups and resources:

- To retrieve tags associated with a resource using PowerShell, the `Find-AzureRMResource` cmdlet can be used:

  ```
  (Find-AzureRmResource -TagName Dept -TagValue Finance).Name
  ```

- To retrieve tags associated with a resource group using PowerShell, the following command can be used:

  ```
  (Find-AzureRmResourceGroup -Tag @{ Dept="Finance" }).Name
  ```

- To set tags to a resource group, the `Set-AzureRmResourceGroup` cmdlet can be used:

  ```
  Set-AzureRmResourceGroup -Name examplegroup -Tag @{ Dept="IT";
  Environment="Test" }
  ```

- To set tags to a resource, the `Set-AzureRmResource` cmdlet can be used:

  ```
  Set-AzureRmResource -Tag @{ Dept="IT"; Environment="Test" } -
  ResourceName examplevnet -ResourceGroupName examplegroup
  ```

Tags with Azure Resource Manager templates

Azure Resource Manager templates also help in defining tags for each resource. They can be used to assign multiple tags to each resource, as follows:

```
{
    "$schema":
"https://schema.management.azure.com/schemas/2015-01-01/deploymentTemplate.
json#",
    "contentVersion": "1.0.0.0",
    "resources": [
    {
        "apiVersion": "2016-01-01",
        "type": "Microsoft.Storage/storageAccounts",
        "name": "[concat('storage', uniqueString(resourceGroup().id))]",
        "location": "[resourceGroup().location]",
        "tags": {
```

```
      "Dept": "Finance",
      "Environment": "Production"
    },
    "sku": {
      "name": "Standard_LRS"
    },
    "kind": "Storage",
    "properties": { }
  }
  ]
}
```

In the previous example, a couple of tags, `Dept` and `Environment`, are added to a Storage account resource using Azure Resource Manager templates.

Resource groups versus resources

It is a must for architects to decide the taxonomy and information architecture for Azure resources and resource groups. They should identify the categories by which resources will be classified based on the query requirements. However, they must also identify whether tags should be attached to individual resources or to resource groups.

If all resources within a resource group need the same tag, then it is better to tag the resource group, rather than tagging each resource. It is important to take the queries on tags into consideration before finalizing whether tags should be applied at the resource level or the resource group level. If the queries relate to individual resource types across a subscription and across resource groups, then assigning tags to individual resources makes more sense. However, if identifying resource groups is enough for your queries to be effective, then tags should be applied only to resource groups.

Azure policies

In the previous section, we talked about applying tags for Azure deployments. Tags are great for organizing resources; however, there is one more thing that was not discussed: how do organizations ensure that tags are applied for every deployment? There should be automated enforcement of Azure tags to resources and resource groups. There is no check from Azure to ensure that appropriate tags will be applied to resources and resource groups. Now, this is not just specific to tags—this applies to the configuration of any resource on Azure. For example, you may wish to restrict where your resources can be provisioned geographically (to only the US-East region, for instance).

You might have guessed by now that this section is all about formulating a governance model on Azure. Governance is an important element in Azure because it helps bring costs under control. It also ensures that everyone accessing the Azure environment is aware of organizational priorities and processes. It helps in defining organizational conventions for managing resources.

Each policy can be built using multiple rules, and multiple policies can be applied to a subscription or resource group. Based on whether the rules are satisfied, policies can execute various actions. An action could be to deny an on-going transaction, to audit a transaction (which means writing to logs and allowing it to finish), or to append metadata to a transaction if it's found to be missing.

Policies could be related to the naming convention of resources, the tagging of resources, the types of resources that can be provisioned, the location of resources, or any combination of these rules.

Built-in policies

Azure provides infrastructure for the creation of custom policies; however, it also provides some out-of-box policies that can be used for governance. These policies relate to allowed locations, allowed resource types, and tags. More information for these built-in policies can be found at
`https://docs.microsoft.com/en-us/azure/azure-resource-manager/resource-manager-policy`.

Policy language

Azure policies use JSON to define and describe policies.

There are two steps in policy adoption. The policy should be defined and then it should be applied and assigned. Policies have scope and can be applied at the subscription and resource group level.

Policies are defined using `if...then` blocks, similarly to in any popular programming language. The `if` block is executed to evaluate the conditions and based on the result of those conditions, the `then` block is executed:

```
{
  "if": {
    <condition> | <logical operator>
  },
```

```
  "then": {
    "effect": "deny | audit | append"
  }
}
```

Azure policies not only allow simple `if` conditions, but multiple `if` conditions can be joined together logically to create complex rules. These conditions can be joined using **AND, OR,** and **NOT** operators:

- The AND syntax requires all conditions to be true.
- The OR syntax requires one of the conditions to be true.
- The NOT syntax inverts the result of the condition.

The AND syntax is shown next. It is represented by the `allOf` keyword:

```
"if": {
  "allOf": [
    {
       "field": "tags",
        "containsKey": "application"
    },
    {
      "field": "type",
      "equals": "Microsoft.Storage/storageAccounts"
    }
  ]
},
```

The OR syntax is shown next. It is represented by the `anyOf` keyword:

```
"if": {
  "anyOf": [
    {
       "field": "tags",
        "containsKey": "application"
    },
    {
      "field": "type",
      "equals": "Microsoft.Storage/storageAccounts"
    }
  ]
},
```

The NOT syntax is shown next. It is represented by the `not` keyword:

```
"if": {
  "not": [
```

```
        {
            "field": "tags",
             "containsKey": "application"
        },
        {
            "field": "type",
            "equals": "Microsoft.Storage/storageAccounts"
        }
    ]
},
```

In fact, these logical operators can be combined together as follows:

```
"if": {
  "allOf": [
        {
          "not": {
             "field": "tags",
             "containsKey": "application"
          }
        },
        {
          "field": "type",
          "equals": "Microsoft.Storage/storageAccounts"
        }
    ]
},
```

This is very similar to the use of `if` conditions in popular programming languages such as C# and Node.js:

```
If ("type" == "Microsoft.Storage/storageAccounts") {
      Deny
}
```

It is important to note that there is no `allow` action, although there is a `Deny` action. This means that policy rules should be written with the possibility of denial in mind. Rules should evaluate the conditions and return `Deny` if they return true.

Allowed fields

The fields that are allowed in policies are as follows:

- Name
- Kind

- Type
- Location
- Tags
- Tags.*
- Property aliases

Azure locks

Locks are mechanisms for stopping certain activities on resources. RBAC provides rights to users, groups, and applications within a certain scope. There are out-of-the-box RBAC roles, such as owner, contributor, and reader. With the contributor role, it is possible to delete or modify a resource. How can such activities be prevented despite the user having a contributor role? Enter Azure locks.

Azure locks can help in two ways:

- They can lock resources such that they cannot be deleted, even if you have owner access.
- They can lock resources in such a way that it can be neither deleted nor have its configuration modified.

Locks are typically very helpful for resources in production environments that should not be modified or deleted accidentally.

Locks can be applied at the levels of subscription, resource group, and individual resource. Locks can be inherited between subscriptions, resource groups, and resources. Applying a lock at the parent level will ensure that those at the child level will also inherit it. Even resources you add later will inherit the lock from the parent. The most restrictive lock in the inheritance takes precedence. Applying a lock at the resource level will also not allow the deletion of the resource group containing the resource.

Locks are applied only to operations that help in managing the resource rather than operations that are within the resource. Users either need `Microsoft.Authorization/*` or `Microsoft.Authorization/locks/*` RBAC permissions to create and modify locks.

Locks can be created and applied through the Azure portal, Azure PowerShell, the Azure CLI, Azure Resource Manager templates, and REST APIs.

Creating a lock using an Azure Resource Manager template is done as follows:

```
{
  "$schema":
"https://schema.management.azure.com/schemas/2015-01-01/deploymentTemplate.
json#",
  "contentVersion": "1.0.0.0",
  "parameters": {
    "lockedResource": {
      "type": "string"
    }
  },
  "resources": [
    {
      "name": "[concat(parameters('lockedResource'),
'/Microsoft.Authorization/myLock')]",
      "type": "Microsoft.Storage/storageAccounts/providers/locks",
      "apiVersion": "2015-01-01",
      "properties": {
        "level": "CannotDelete"
      }
    }
  ]
}
```

Creating and applying a lock to a resource using PowerShell is done as follows:

```
New-AzureRmResourceLock -LockLevel CanNotDelete -LockName LockSite `
  -ResourceName examplesite -ResourceType Microsoft.Web/sites `
  -ResourceGroupName exampleresourcegroup
```

Creating and applying a lock to a resource group using PowerShell is done as follows:

```
New-AzureRmResourceLock -LockName LockGroup -LockLevel CanNotDelete `
  -ResourceGroupName exampleresourcegroup
```

Creating and applying a lock to a resource using the Azure CLI is done as follows:

```
az lock create --name LockSite --lock-type CanNotDelete \
  --resource-group exampleresourcegroup --resource-name examplesite \
  --resource-type Microsoft.Web/sites
```

Creating and applying a lock to a resource group using the Azure CLI is done as follows:

```
az lock create --name LockGroup --lock-type CanNotDelete \
  --resource-group exampleresourcegroup
```

Azure RBAC

Azure provides authentication using Azure Active Directory for its resources. Once an identity has been authenticated, the resources the identity should be allowed to access should be decided. This is known as authorization. Authorization evaluates the permissions that have been afforded to an identity. Anybody with access to an Azure subscription should be given just enough permissions so that their specific job can be performed, and nothing more.

Authorization is popularly also known as RBAC. RBAC in Azure refers to the assigning of permissions to identities within a scope. The scope could be a subscription, a resource group, or individual resources.

RBAC helps in the creation and assignment of different permissions to different identities. This helps in segregating duties within teams, rather than everyone having all permissions. RBAC helps in making people responsible for their job because others might not even have the necessary access to perform it. It should be noted that providing permissions at a greater scope automatically ensures that child resources inherit those permissions. For example, providing an identity with read access for a resource group means that the identity will have read access to all the resources within that group, too.

Azure provides three general-purpose built-in roles. They are as follows:

- The owner role, which has full access to all resources
- The contributor role, which has access to read/write resources
- The reader role, which has ready-only permissions to resources

There are more roles provided by Azure, but they are resource-specific, such as the network contributor and security manager roles.

To get all roles provided by Azure for all resources, execute the `Get-AzureRmRoleDefinition` command in the PowerShell console.

Each role definition has certain allowed and disallowed actions. For example, the owner role has all actions permitted and none of the actions are prohibited:

```
PS C:\Users\rimodi> Get-AzureRmRoleDefinition -Name "owner"
Name              : Owner
Id                : 8e3af657-a8ff-443c-a75c-2fe8c4bcb635
IsCustom          : False
Description       : Lets you manage everything, including access to
resources.
Actions           : {*}
NotActions        : {}
AssignableScopes  : {/}
```

Each role comprises multiple permissions. Each resource provides a list of operations. The operation supported by a resource can be obtained using the `Get-AzureRmProviderOperation` cmdlet. This cmdlet takes the name of the provider and resource to retrieve the operations:

```
Get-AzureRmProviderOperation -OperationSearchString "Microsoft.Insights/*"
```

This will result in the following output:

```
PS C:\Users\rimodi> get-AzureRmProviderOperation -OperationSearchString
"Microsoft.Insights/*" | select operation
Operation
---------
Microsoft.Insights/Register/Action
Microsoft.Insights/AlertRules/Write
Microsoft.Insights/AlertRules/Delete
Microsoft.Insights/AlertRules/Read
Microsoft.Insights/AlertRules/Activated/Action
Microsoft.Insights/AlertRules/Resolved/Action
Microsoft.Insights/AlertRules/Throttled/Action
Microsoft.Insights/AlertRules/Incidents/Read
Microsoft.Insights/MetricDefinitions/Read
Microsoft.Insights/eventtypes/values/Read
Microsoft.Insights/eventtypes/digestevents/Read
Microsoft.Insights/Metrics/Read
Microsoft.Insights/LogProfiles/Write
Microsoft.Insights/LogProfiles/Delete
Microsoft.Insights/LogProfiles/Read
Microsoft.Insights/Components/Write
Microsoft.Insights/Components/Delete
Microsoft.Insights/Components/Read
Microsoft.Insights/AutoscaleSettings/Write
Microsoft.Insights/AutoscaleSettings/Delete
Microsoft.Insights/AutoscaleSettings/Read
Microsoft.Insights/AutoscaleSettings/Scaleup/Action
```

```
Microsoft.Insights/AutoscaleSettings/Scaledown/Action
Microsoft.Insights/AutoscaleSettings/providers/Microsoft.Insights/MetricDef
initions/Read
Microsoft.Insights/ActivityLogAlerts/Activated/Action
Microsoft.Insights/DiagnosticSettings/Write
Microsoft.Insights/DiagnosticSettings/Delete
Microsoft.Insights/DiagnosticSettings/Read
Microsoft.Insights/LogDefinitions/Read
Microsoft.Insights/Webtests/Write
Microsoft.Insights/Webtests/Delete
Microsoft.Insights/Webtests/Read
Microsoft.Insights/ExtendedDiagnosticSettings/Write
Microsoft.Insights/ExtendedDiagnosticSettings/Delete
Microsoft.Insights/ExtendedDiagnosticSettings/Read
```

Custom Roles

Custom roles are created by combining multiple permissions. For example, a custom role can consist of operations from multiple resources, as follows:

```
$role = Get-AzureRmRoleDefinition "Virtual Machine Contributor"
$role.Id = $null
$role.Name = "Virtual Machine Operator"
$role.Description = "Can monitor and restart virtual machines."
$role.Actions.Clear()
$role.Actions.Add("Microsoft.Storage/*/read")
$role.Actions.Add("Microsoft.Network/*/read")
$role.Actions.Add("Microsoft.Compute/*/read")
$role.Actions.Add("Microsoft.Compute/virtualMachines/start/action")
    $role.Actions.Add("Microsoft.Compute/virtualMachines/restart/action")
$role.Actions.Add("Microsoft.Authorization/*/read")
$role.Actions.Add("Microsoft.Resources/subscriptions/resourceGroups/read")
$role.Actions.Add("Microsoft.Insights/alertRules/*")
$role.Actions.Add("Microsoft.Support/*")
$role.AssignableScopes.Clear()
$role.AssignableScopes.Add("/subscriptions/c276fc76-9cd4-44c9-99a7-4fd71546
436e")
$role.AssignableScopes.Add("/subscriptions/e91d47c4-76f3-4271-
a796-21b4ecfe3624")
New-AzureRmRoleDefinition -Role $role
```

How are locks different from RBAC?

Locks are not the same as RBAC. RBAC helps in allowing or denying permissions for resources. These permissions relate to performing operations such as read, write, and update operations on resources. Locks, on the other hand, relate to disallowing permissions to configure or delete resources.

An example of implementing Azure governance features

In this section, we will go through a sample architecture implementation for a fictitious organization that wants to implement Azure governance and cost management features.

Background

Company Inc is a worldwide company that is implementing a social media solution on an Azure IaaS platform. They use web servers and application servers deployed on Azure virtual machines and networks. Azure SQL Server acts as the backend database.

RBAC for Company Inc

The first task is to ensure that the appropriate teams and application owners can access their resources. It is recognized that each team has different requirements. For the sake of understanding, Azure SQL is deployed in a separate resource group to the Azure IaaS artifacts.

The administrator assigns the following roles for the subscription:

Role	Assigned to	Description
Owner	Administrator	Manages all resource groups and the subscription.
Security manager	Security administrators	This role allows users to look at Azure Security Center and the status of the resources.
Contributor	Infrastructure management	Managing virtual machines and other resources.

Reader	Developers	Can view resources, but cannot modify them. Developers are expected to work in their development/testing environments.

Azure policies

The company should implement Azure policies to ensure that its users always provisions according to the company guidelines.

Azure policies govern various aspects related to the deployment of resources. The policies will also govern the updates after initial deployment.

Some of the policies that should be implemented are given in the following section.

Deployments to certain location

Azure resources and deployments can only be executed for certain chosen locations. It would not be possible to deploy resources in regions out of the policy. For example, the regions that are allowed are West Europe and East US. It should be not possible to deploy resources in any other region.

Tags of resources and Resource Groups

Every resource in Azure including the resource groups will mandatorily have tags assigned to it. The tags will include details about the department, environment, creation data, and project name at minimum.

Diagnostic logs and Application Insights for all resources

Every resource deployed on Azure should have diagnostic logs and application logs enabled wherever possible.

Azure Locks

The company should implement Azure Locks to ensure that important and crucial resources not deleted accidentally.

Every resource that is crucial for the functioning of a solution needs to be locked down. It means even the administrators of the services running on Azure do not have the capability to delete these resources. The only way to delete the resource is to remove the lock first.

All production and pre-production environments apart from development and testing environment would be locked for deletion.

All development and testing environments that have single instances would also be locked for deletion.

All resources related to `https://www.eversource.com/content/` would be locked for deletion for all environments from development to production.

All shared resources will be locked for deletion irrespective of the environment.

Summary

Governance and cost management are among the top priorities for companies moving to the cloud. Having an Azure subscription with a pay-as-you-go scheme can harm the company budget because anyone with access to the subscription can provision as many resources as they like. Some resources are free but others are expensive. It is important for organizations to remain in control of their cloud costs. Tags help in generating billing reports. These reports could be based on departments, projects, owners, or any other criteria. While cost is important, governance is equally important. Azure provides locks, policies, and RBAC to implement proper governance. Policies ensure that resource operations can be denied or audited, locks ensure that resources cannot be modified or deleted, and RBAC ensures that employees have the right permissions to perform their jobs. With these four features, companies can have sound governance and cost control for their Azure deployments.

DevOps on Azure will be the focus of the next chapter, in which some of its important concepts and implementation techniques will be discussed.

10

Azure Solutions Using Azure Container Services

Containers are the most talked-about technologies these days. Corporations are talking about containers rather than virtual machines and want to see them in almost all their solutions. The solutions could be microservices, serverless functions, web applications, web APIs, or just about anything.

In this chapter, we will delve into most of the Azure features that are to do with containers, including the following:

- Azure Kubernetes Service
- Containers on virtual machines
- Azure Container Registry
- Azure Container Instance
- Web apps for containers
- Hosting images on Docker Hub

We will not go into the details and fundamentals of containers, and will concentrate more on Azure-specific container services.

Every container needs an image as a starting point. An image can be created using a Dockerfile or can be downloaded from a container registry. We will be using a single image for all our samples in this chapter, and this image will be created from a Dockerfile.

The content of the Dockerfile used for all examples in this chapter is listed here. The entire code and `samplewebapp` solution is available with the accompanying source code:

```
FROM microsoft/dotnet:2.1-aspnetcore-runtime-nanoserver-sac2016 AS base
WORKDIR /app
EXPOSE 80
FROM microsoft/dotnet:2.1-sdk-nanoserver-sac2016 AS build
WORKDIR /src
```

```
COPY ["samplewebapp/samplewebapp.csproj", "samplewebapp/"]
RUN dotnet restore "samplewebapp/samplewebapp.csproj"
COPY . .
WORKDIR "/src/samplewebapp"
RUN dotnet build "samplewebapp.csproj" -c Release -o /app
FROM build AS publish
RUN dotnet publish "samplewebapp.csproj" -c Release -o /app
FROM base AS final
WORKDIR /app
COPY --from=publish /app .
ENTRYPOINT ["dotnet", "samplewebapp.dll"]
```

Azure Container Registry

Prior to Azure Container Registry, Docker Hub was the most well-known registry service for Docker images.

Azure Container Registry is an alternative repository to Docker Hub. A registry is a location on the internet that provides listings of images, along with facilities to upload and download the images on demand. There are two types of registries:

- Public
- Private

A public repository, as the name suggests, is public in nature and images from it can be downloaded and used by anyone. However, the upload of images to a public repository is discretionary and, depending on the provider, may or may not allow the upload of images.

On the other hand, private repositories are meant only for people who have access to the repository. They need to authenticate before they can upload or download images.

Docker Hub provides the ability to create user accounts, and these accounts can have public as well as private repositories.

In fact, Microsoft has accounts on Docker Hub as well, where all well-known Windows images are available. You can find all Microsoft images by executing the `docker search Microsoft` command, as shown in the following screenshot:

```
C:\Users\citynextadmin>docker search Microsoft
NAME                                      DESCRIPTION                                        STARS
microsoft/dotnet                          Official images for .NET Core and ASP.NET Co…      1395
microsoft/mssql-server-linux              Official images for Microsoft SQL Server on …      1078
microsoft/aspnet                          Microsoft IIS images                               819
microsoft/windowsservercore               The official Windows Server Core base image        644
microsoft/aspnetcore                      Official images for running compiled ASP.NET…      582
microsoft/nanoserver                      The official Nano Server base image                473
microsoft/iis                             Microsoft IIS images                               356
microsoft/mssql-server-windows-developer  Official Microsoft SQL Server Developer Edit…      289
microsoft/mssql-server-windows-express    Official Microsoft SQL Server Express Editio…      281
microsoft/aspnetcore-build                Official images for building ASP.NET Core ap…      270
microsoft/azure-cli                       Official images for Microsoft Azure CLI            156
microsoft/powershell                      PowerShell for every system!                       145
microsoft/vsts-agent                      Official images for the Visual Studio Team S…      116
microsoft/dynamics-nav                    Official images for Microsoft Dynamics NAV o…      108
microsoft/dotnet-samples                  .NET Core Docker Samples                           70
microsoft/bcsandbox                       Business Central Sandbox                           53
microsoft/mssql-tools                     Official images for Microsoft SQL Server Com…      51
microsoft/oms                             Monitor your containers using the Operations…      41
microsoft/cntk                            CNTK images from github.com/Microsoft/CNTK-d…      38
microsoft/wcf                             Microsoft WCF images                               28
microsoft/dotnet-nightly                  Preview images for .NET Core and ASP.NET Cor…      23
microsoft/dotnet-framework-build          The .NET Framework build images have moved t…      17
microsoft/mmlspark                        Microsoft Machine Learning for Apache Spark        7
microsoft/aspnetcore-build-nightly        Images to build preview versions of ASP.NET …      4
microsoft/cntk-nightly                    CNTK nightly image from github.com/Microsoft…      2
```

As mentioned before, Microsoft also provides an alternate registry as an Azure service, known as **Azure Container Registry**. It provides similar functionality to that of Docker Hub.

One advantage of using Azure Container Registry over Docker Hub is that if you are using an image from Azure Container Registry that is in the same Azure location that is hosting containers based on the image, the image can be downloaded faster using the Microsoft backbone network instead of going through the internet. For example, hosting a container on Azure Kubernetes Service whose source image is within Azure Container Registry will be much faster than Docker Hub.

Azure Container Registry is a managed service that will take care of all operational needs concerning images, such as storage and availability. Users do not have to bother with providing access URLs and can instead manage these images as blobs. It is the responsibility of Azure to take care of these images and their layers.

The beauty of Azure Container Registry is that it works with the Azure CLI, PowerShell, and the Azure portal. And it does not stop there: it also has high fidelity with the Docker command line. You can use Docker commands to upload and download images from Azure Container Registry instead of Docker Hub.

Let's now focus on how to work with Azure Container Registry using the Azure CLI:

1. Obviously, the first task is to log into Azure using the `az login` command:

```
C:\Users\citynextadmin>az login
```

2. If you have multiple subscriptions associated with the same login, select an appropriate subscription for working with Azure Container Registry:

```
C:\Users\citynextadmin>az account set --subscription
```

3. Create a new resource group for hosting a new instance of Azure Container Registry:

```
C:\Users\citynextadmin>az group create --name rg03 --location "west europe" --verbose
{
  "id": "/subscriptions/                              /resourceGroups/rg03",
  "location": "westeurope",
  "managedBy": null,
  "name": "rg03",
  "properties": {
    "provisioningState": "Succeeded"
  },
  "tags": null
}
```

4. The Azure CLI provides `acr` commands. Create a new instance of Azure Container Registry using the command:

```
az acr create
```

5. You need to provide the SKU of Azure Container Registry, a name, and the name of a resource group. It can also optionally enable admin privileges.

6. The SKUs available for Azure Container Registry are as follows:
    - **Basic**: This is not recommended for production scenarios and is more suitable for dev/test work. This is because the amount of resources available for storage and bandwidth is constrained compared to higher SKUs.
    - **Standard**: This has all features of Basic along with higher configuration and availability of resources. This is suitable for production deployments.
    - **Premium**: This, again, has all the features of the Standard SKU along with higher resource availability. This has additional features such as geo-replication.
    - **Classic**: This is not a managed service and the images stored using this SKU are stored on user-provided storage accounts. Users need to actively manage these storage accounts in terms of security, administration, and governance.

7. The output from the following contains important information that is used quite frequently for uploading and downloading images. These include the `loginServer` and `name` properties. The username of Azure Container Registry is the same as its name:

```
C:\Users\citynextadmin>az acr create --sku basic --resource-group rg03 --name sampleappbookacr --verbose --admin-enabled
{
  "adminUserEnabled": true,
  "creationDate": "2018-12-31T07:15:48.719352+00:00",
  "id": "/subscriptions/                          /resourceGroups/rg03/providers/Microsoft.ContainerRegistry/registri
  "location": "westeurope",
  "loginServer": "sampleappbookacr.azurecr.io",
  "name": "sampleappbookacr",
  "provisioningState": "Succeeded",
  "resourceGroup": "rg03",
  "sku": {
    "name": "Basic",
    "tier": "Basic"
  },
  "status": null,
  "storageAccount": null,
  "tags": {},
  "type": "Microsoft.ContainerRegistry/registries"
}
```

8. The service on the portal is configured as shown in the following screenshot:

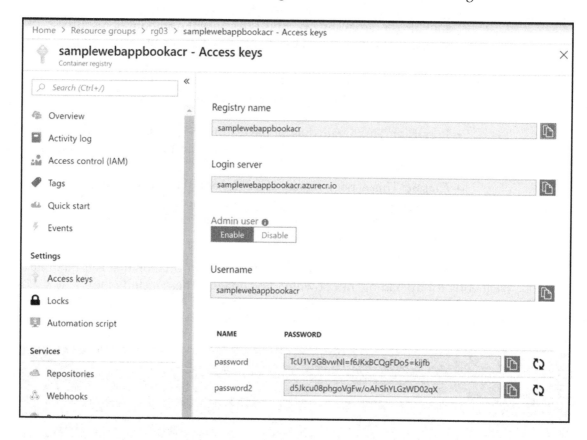

9. If admin is enabled, the credentials for the admin can be fetching using a command as shown in the following screenshot. There are two passwords generated, which can be used to swap when necessary. Login is needed for pushing images and is not required for pulling images from Azure Container Registry:

```
C:\Users\citynextadmin>az acr credential show --name sampleappbookacr --resource-group rg03 --verbose
{
  "passwords": [
    {
      "name": "password",
      "value": "igzgtUxlehYn2/92KvNk=+X4Utb1UQim"
    },
    {
      "name": "password2",
      "value": "XMbIrrHpl0H9DQmLu/ReXmYBietU8ht3"
    }
  ],
  "username": "sampleappbookacr"
}
```

10. Using the username and password data (which we have by now), it is possible to log into Azure Container Registry:

```
C:\Users\citynextadmin>az acr login --name sampleappbookacr --password "igzgtUxlehYn2/92KvNk=+X4Utb1UQim" --resource-group rg03 --username sampleappb
okacr
Login Succeeded
WARNING! Your password will be stored unencrypted in C:\Users\citynextadmin\.docker\config.json.
Configure a credential helper to remove this warning. See
https://docs.docker.com/engine/reference/commandline/login/#credentials-store
```

11. You will need to log into Azure Container Registry if it is protected by password. The next task is to prepare local images such that they can be uploaded to Azure Container Registry. This preparation needs to tag the local images with the server name of the registry.

12. The following screenshot shows a command in which a sample image named `samplewebapp` is tagged using the `tag` command to `sampleappbooacr.azurecr.io/samplewebapp:latest`.
Here, `sampleappbooacr.azurecr.io` refers to the server name that was created earlier as part of the creation of the registry. Note that Docker commands are used for tagging the images:

```
C:\Users\citynextadmin>docker tag samplewebapp:latest sampleappbookacr.azurecr.io/samplewebapp:latest
```

13. After tagging using the `docker push` command, the image can be pushed to Azure Container Registry:

```
C:\Users\citynextadmin>docker push sampleappbookacr.azurecr.io/samplewebapp:latest
The push refers to repository [sampleappbookacr.azurecr.io/samplewebapp]
036d27f25d59: Pushed
f6ac38202aab: Pushed
7605499be4ca: Pushed
1bd33b5316f6: Pushed
f3eff1ccb92a: Pushed
cbe35d8d94e0: Pushed
e36c5fabaebb: Pushed
8b28210b2d46: Pushed
cc80cb0b7044: Pushed
e4a9564a3ea3: Pushed
f5c673c58dcc: Skipped foreign layer
6c357baed9f5: Skipped foreign layer
latest: digest: sha256:da53d5ab40890824b24712e37129819f2d4b65d8eb1df5c5df8b2bc65786d1fd size: 3026
```

14. From now, it is possible to consume this image by anyone who has knowledge about the `sampleappbookacr` registry.

The registry on the portal is shown in the following screenshot:

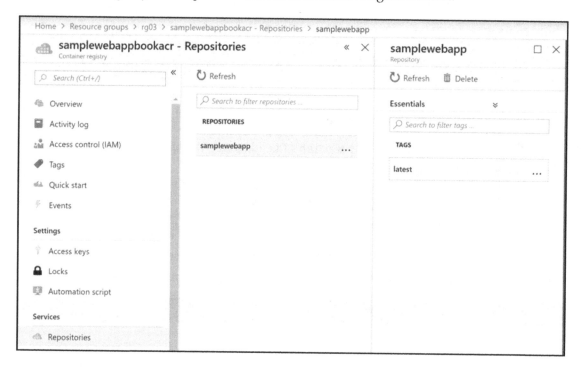

15. Create a container from the image that was just uploaded to Azure Container Registry. For this exercise, create a new virtual machine based on Windows Server 2016 or Windows 10 that has containers enabled, and execute the command, as shown in the following screenshot, to create a new container using the `samplewebapp` image from the `samplewebappbookacr` registry:

```
C:\Users\citynextadmin>docker run -it -p 80:80 samplewebappbookacr.azurecr.io/samplewebapp:latest powershell
```

16. It is important to note that even if the image is not locally available, the command will download the images while executing the command and then create a container out of it. The output from running the container is shown in the following screenshot:

```
Administrator: Command Prompt - docker run -it -p 80:80 samplewebapp:latest -d
Hosting environment: Production
Content root path: C:\app
Now listening on: http://[::]:80
Application started. Press Ctrl+C to shut down.
```

17. The result shown in the following screenshot displays that the web application is currently running:

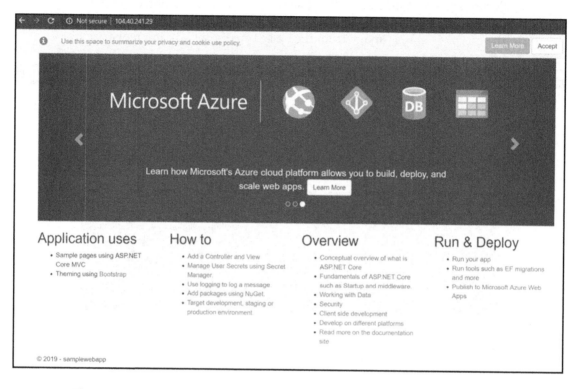

The Dockerfile, and solution file used to create the local image, are available as part of the source code. It is also possible to upload the same image to Docker Hub.

18. The first step is to have an account on Docker Hub. For this, a new account or an existing account can be used.

19. After creating the account, log into your account.

20. Create a new repository by selecting **Create a Repository**, as shown in the following screenshot:

Welcome to Docker Hub

Here are a few things to get you started.

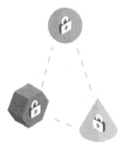

Create a Repository

Push container images to Docker Hub

Create an Organization

Manage Docker Hub repositories with your team

21. Provide a name and select a public repository:

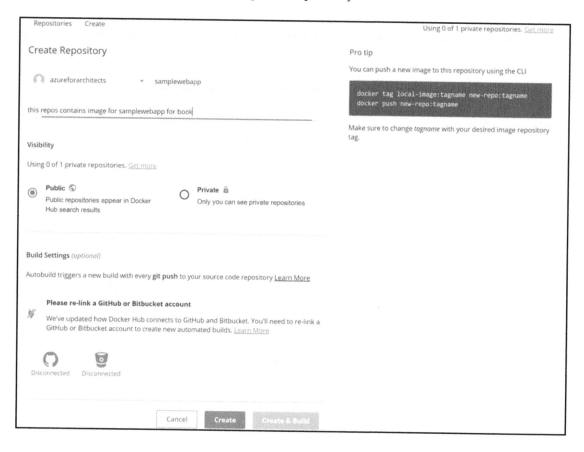

22. The next screenshot shows the command to be executed for pushing images to this repository:

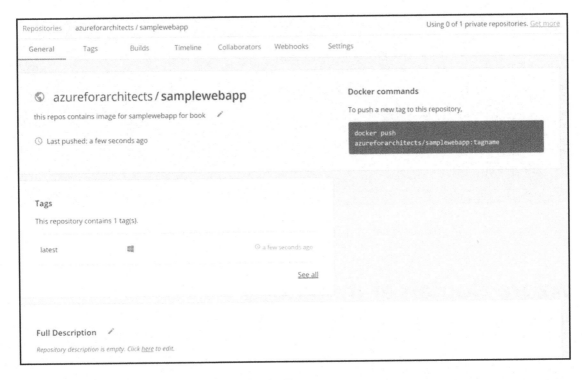

23. From your virtual machine containing the local image for `samplewebapp`, create a new tag. This is a similar exercise to that which we did for Azure Container Registry; however, this time, it is for Docker Hub:

```
C:\Users\citynextadmin>docker tag samplewebapp:latest azureforarchitects/samplewebapp:latest
```

24. Using the Docker CLI, log into the Docker Hub:

```
C:\Users\citynextadmin>docker login -u azureforarchitects -p Dsc123..
WARNING! Using --password via the CLI is insecure. Use --password-stdin.
WARNING! Your password will be stored unencrypted in C:\Users\citynextadmin\.docker\config.json.
Configure a credential helper to remove this warning. See
https://docs.docker.com/engine/reference/commandline/login/#credentials-store

Login Succeeded
```

25. Finally, push the newly tagged image to Docker Hub using the `docker push` command:

```
C:\Users\citynextadmin>docker push azureforarchitects/samplewebapp:latest
The push refers to repository [docker.io/azureforarchitects/samplewebapp]
036d27f25d59: Pushed
f6ac38202aab: Pushed
7605499be4ca: Pushed
1bd33b5316f6: Pushed
f3eff1ccb92a: Pushed
cbe35d8d94e0: Pushed
e36c5fabaebb: Pushed
8b28210b2d46: Pushed
cc80cb0b7044: Pushed
e4a9564a3ea3: Pushed
f5c673c58dcc: Skipped foreign layer
6c357baed9f5: Skipped foreign layer
latest: digest: sha256:da53d5ab40890824b24712e37129819f2d4b65d8eb1df5c5df8b2bc65786d1fd size: 3026
```

Now this new image can be used at different hosts, including Azure App Services.

Azure Container Instances

In last section, we created a container based on an Azure Container Registry image on a virtual machine. In this section, we will investigate Azure Container Instances. Azure Container Instances is a managed service provided by Azure to host containers. It is a service that helps in executing and running containers by providing a platform that is completely managed by Azure.

Using Azure Container Instances completely alleviates the need of any **Infrastructure as a Service (IaaS)** components, such as creating virtual machines to host containers. We will again use the Azure CLI to create Azure Container Instances as well.

If you have not yet logged into Azure using the CLI, log into Azure using the `az login` command and select an appropriate subscription.

The command for log in is as follows:

```
C:\Users\citynextadmin>az login
```

The command for setting up the subscription is as follows:

```
C:\Users\citynextadmin>az account set --subscription
```

Create a new resource group to host an Azure Container Instance using the following command:

```
C:\Users\citynextadmin>az group create --name rg04 --location "west europe" --verbose
```

Create an Azure Container Instance using the following command:

```
az container create
```

Pass the necessary information outlined in the following bullet points:

- The DNS name through which the container can be accessed.
- The number of CPUs allocated to the container.
- The fully qualified image name – this is the same name that we created in previous section (`samplewebappbookacr.azurecr.io/samplewebapp:latest`).
- The IP address type, whether public or private – a public IP address will ensure that the container is available to be consumed from the internet.
- The location of the container—in this case, it is same as the location of the container registry. This helps in the faster creation of containers.
- The memory in GB to be allocated to the container.
- The name of the container.
- The OS of the container using the `-os-type` option. It is Windows, in this case.
- The protocol and ports to be open. We open port 80 as our application will be hosted on that port.
- The restart policy is set to always. This will ensure that even if the host that is running the container restarts, the container will run automatically.
- Azure Container Registry information from where the image will be pulled, including the registry login server, password, and username:

```
C:\Users\citynextadmin>az container create --resource-group rg03 --cpu 4 --dns-name-label mysamplewebappcontainer --image sampleappbookacr.azurecr.io/samplewebapp:latest --ip-address Public --location "west europe" --memory 7 --name mysamplewebappcontainer --os-type Windows --protocol tcp --ports 8 --restart-policy Always --registry-login-server sampleappbookacr.azurecr.io --registry-password "1g2gtUxlehYn2/92KvNk++X4Utb1UQim" --registry-username
```

The command should run successfully to create a new container. This would create a new container on the Azure Container Instance. The portal configuration is as follows:

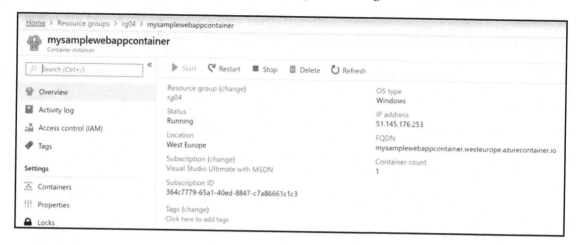

The container configuration is as follows:

The properties are the same as we provided when creating the container instance:

It is also possible to connect to the container using the **Connect** tab:

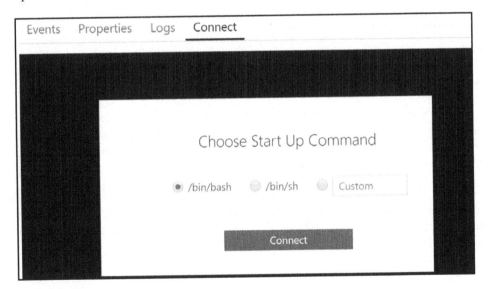

The final page output is shown in the following screenshot:

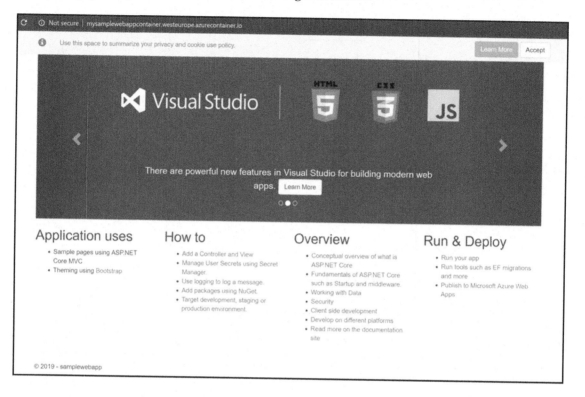

Azure Kubernetes Service

Azure Container Services has been deprecated, and instead, all new additions are happening on Azure Kubernetes Service. Azure Kubernetes Service is one of the leading managed container environments in the world. Before getting into Azure Kubernetes Service, let's understand what Kubernetes is and why it is required.

Kubernetes is a container orchestration engine and service. Orchestration of containers is a must for any enterprise solution deployed on top of containers. Imagine that there are four containers for a solution, which are hosted on four different virtual machines, as shown in the following diagram:

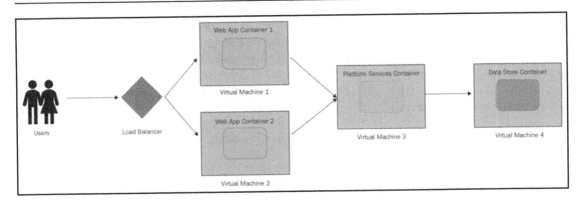

Containers, by their very nature, are quite fleeting. They can be created easily and quite quickly, and can be torn just down as easily. For example, if virtual machine 3 is restarted, the container running on it will also be destroyed. If any container, or any host hosting a container, goes down due to any reason, the whole application and solution also goes down with it. This is because there is no active monitoring of these containers and hosts.

Although traditional monitoring systems can be used to monitor the hosts, there is no single solution that manages and monitors the hosts and containers together. Moreover, the problem is not only related to availability. The health of the hosts and containers can also have a significant impact for the functioning of the application. Even if one container is not able to perform as expected, the entire solution will have downgraded performance.

Container orchestrators solve these aforementioned problems with containers. The orchestrators take away the burden of active monitoring and management from user and automate the entire set of activities and its impact. An orchestrator can identify whether any host or any container is suffering from degraded performance. It can immediately spin up new containers on different hosts. Not only this, but even if one of the containers goes down, a new container instance can be created on another host. This does not stop here. If a complete host goes down, all the containers running on that host can be recreated on a different host. These are all the responsibility of container orchestrators.

A container orchestrator should be told the desired and expected amount of each type of container. For our example, the desired amount of web app containers is two, for platform services it's one, and for the data store it's one. If this information is fed into an orchestrator, it will always try to maintain the environment to have the desired amount of containers. If containers go down in any host, the orchestrator will notice that and create a new container on another host to compensate.

Kubernetes is a container orchestrator and it provides all these features.

Kubernetes can be deployed on virtual machines directly via IaaS deployment, and at the same time it can be provisioned as Azure Kubernetes Service. The difference between the two different deployment paradigms is that IaaS deployment is controlled and managed by the user, while Azure Kubernetes Service is a managed service and all hosts and containers are managed by Azure without any effort from the user deploying it. Managing an IaaS-based Kubernetes deployment is not an easy task. Only people with in-depth knowledge of Kubernetes are able to manage such an environment, and it is not easy to find such professionals. Moreover, the overall deployment of Kubernetes and its management is a complex and cumbersome exercise that few organizations are willing to undertake. For such reasons, Azure Kubernetes Service is popular among organizations that are outsourcing the entire management of Kubernetes to Azure.

Kubernetes, being based on orchestrator engines, works seamlessly with the Docker runtime. It can, however, even work with other container runtimes and network providers.

Kubernetes architecture

Kubernetes comprises a set of servers, and these servers are together called clusters. Kubernetes has two types of nodes:

- Master nodes
- Pod nodes

Master nodes

Master nodes contain all the management components of Kubernetes, such as the API server, scheduler, distributed configuration services such as etcd, and the replication controller, while the pod nodes contain the Kube-Proxy and Kubelet components. The containers are deployed on pod nodes:

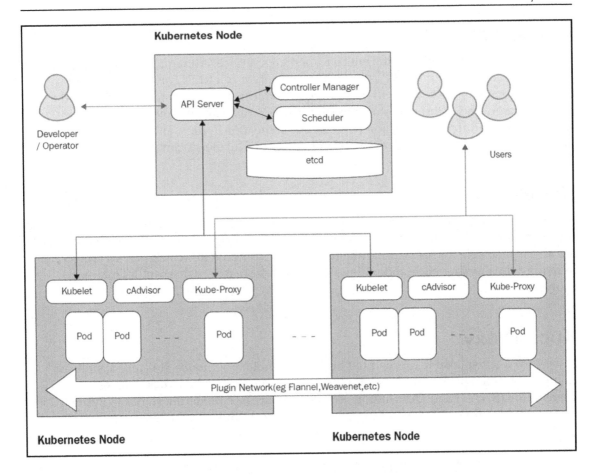

Pods

The first component to understand in Kubernetes is the concept of pods. Pods are collections of containers that are deployed, created, and managed as a single unit. Containers are not the smallest unit of management in Kubernetes; those would be pods.

Pods are created either using Kubernetes-provided CLI tools, such as Kubectl, or using YAML files. These YAML files contain the pod metadata and configuration information. When these YAML files are submitted to Kubernetes, the main Kubernetes engine schedules the creation of pods on pod nodes.

API server

The API server is the brain for the entire Kubernetes service. All requests from users actually get submitted to the API server. The API server is a REST-based endpoint that accepts requests and acts on them. For example, requests to create pods are submitted to the API server. The API server stores this information and informs another component, known as a scheduler, to provision pods based on the YAML files. The health information of the pods and nodes is also sent to the API server by Kubelets from pod nodes.

Kubelets

Kubelets are components that are provisioned on pod nodes. Their job is to monitor the pod nodes and the pods on those nodes and inform the API server about their health. Kubelets are also responsible for configuring the Kube-Proxy component, which plays a crucial role in request flow among pods and nodes arising both from external as well as internal sources.

Kube-Proxy

Kube-Proxy is responsible for maintaining routes on the pod nodes. It is responsible for changing the data packet headers with the appropriate **Source Network Address Translation (SNAT)** and **Destination Network Address Translation (DNAT)** information and enables the flow of traffic among pods and nodes within the cluster.

Replication controller/controller manager

The replication controller is responsible for maintaining the desired number of pod instances. If pods or nodes go down, the Kubelet informs the API server and the API server informs the replication controller. The controller will immediately schedule the creation of new pods on the same or different nodes, based on the current health of the node.

Azure Kubernetes architecture

When we provision Azure Kubernetes Service, we get an environment consisting of an entire Kubernetes cluster comprising both master and pod nodes. These pod nodes already have the Docker runtime and network plugins installed and configured.

The master has all the components installed and configured. The master is managed by Azure Kubernetes Service while the nodes are managed by the customers. This is shown in the following diagram:

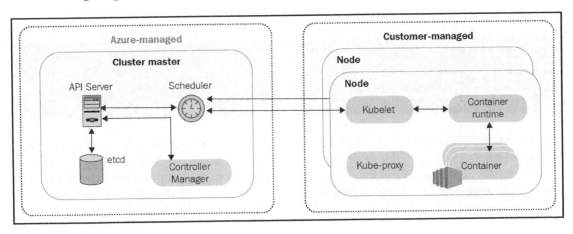

Provisioning Azure Kubernetes Service

In this section, we will provision Azure Kubernetes Service using Azure CLI. Azure Kubernetes Service can also be provisioned from the Azure portal and Azure PowerShell:

1. Log into Azure using the following command:

   ```
   az login
   ```

2. Select an appropriate subscription using the following command:

   ```
   az account set –subscription <<xxxxxxxxxxxxx-xxxx-xxxx-xxxx-
   xxxxxxxx>>
   ```

3. The Azure Kubernetes Service features are available from the `az aks` command.

4. Create a new resource group to host Azure Kubernetes Service using the following command:

   ```
   az group create --name "akdemo" --location "west Europe"
   ```

5. Once the resource group is created, we can create the Kubernetes cluster using the following command:

   ```
   az aks create --resource-group akdemo --name AKSPortalCluster --
   node-count 2 --enable-addons monitoring --generate-ssh-keys
   ```

6. This command takes a while to create the Kubernetes cluster.
7. After the cluster is provisioned, it is possible to download the Kubectl CLI tool using the Azure CLI and configure it to work without the cluster.
8. The command to download the Kubectl tool is `az aks install-cli`:

```
C:\Users\citynextadmin>az aks install-cli
Downloading client to "C:\Users\citynextadmin\.azure-kubectl\kubectl.exe" from "https://storage.googleapis.com/kubernetes-release/release/v1.13.2/bin/w
ndows/amd64/kubectl.exe".
Please add "C:\Users\citynextadmin\.azure-kubectl" to your search PATH so the "kubectl.exe" can be found. 2 options:
    1. Run "set PATH=%PATH%;C:\Users\citynextadmin\.azure-kubectl" or "$env:path += 'C:\Users\citynextadmin\.azure-kubectl'" for PowerShell. This is go
d for the current command session.
    2. Update system PATH environment variable by following "Control Panel->System->Advanced->Environment Variables", and re-open the command window. Y
u only need to do it once
```

It is important to note that the Kubectl tool should be in the search path to execute it on the command line by its name. If it's not in the path, then the entire path of the Kubectl tool should be provided every time it needs to be executed. An ideal approach is to add it to the search path using the following command:

```
set PATH=%PATH%;C:\Users\citynextadmin\.azure-kubectl
```

After executing this command, it is possible to execute the `kubectl` command:

```
C:\Users\citynextadmin>kubectl
kubectl controls the Kubernetes cluster manager.

Find more information at: https://kubernetes.io/docs/reference/kubectl/overview/

Basic Commands (Beginner):
  create      Create a resource from a file or from stdin.
  expose      Take a replication controller, service, deployment or pod and expose it as a new Kubernetes Service
  run         Run a particular image on the cluster
  set         Set specific features on objects

Basic Commands (Intermediate):
  explain     Documentation of resources
  get         Display one or many resources
  edit        Edit a resource on the server
  delete      Delete resources by filenames, stdin, resources and names, or by resources and label selector
```

At this stage, the Kubectl tool is able to be executed but it is still not connected to our recently provisioned cluster. Kubectl needs credentials configured such that it can be authenticated by the cluster. Please note that we did not provide any credential information when creating the cluster and the credentials were generated by Azure Kubernetes Service when provisioning the cluster.

These credentials can be downloaded, and Kubectl can be configured using the command provided by Azure Kubernetes Service on the Azure CLI:

```
C:\Users\citynextadmin>az aks get-credentials --resource-group akdemo --name AKSPortalCluster
Merged "AKSPortalCluster" as current context in C:\Users\citynextadmin\.kube\config
```

The next step is to create pods on the cluster. For this, we will create a new YAML file and submit it to the API server using the commands available in the Kubectl CLI tool.

The YAML file should be saved on a local machine such that it can be referenced from the command line. It is not possible to explain the YAML file in this book, but there are other books that cover YAML and Kubernetes configurations in detail. The sample YAML is listed here:

```
apiVersion: apps/v1
kind: Deployment
metadata:
  name: azure-vote-back
spec:
  replicas: 1
  selector:
    matchLabels:
      app: azure-vote-back
  template:
    metadata:
      labels:
        app: azure-vote-back
    spec:
      containers:
      - name: azure-vote-back
        image: redis
        resources:
          requests:
            cpu: 100m
            memory: 128Mi
          limits:
            cpu: 250m
            memory: 256Mi
        ports:
        - containerPort: 6379
          name: redis
---
apiVersion: v1
kind: Service
metadata:
  name: azure-vote-back
```

```
spec:
  ports:
  - port: 6379
  selector:
    app: azure-vote-back
---
apiVersion: apps/v1
kind: Deployment
metadata:
  name: azure-vote-front
spec:
  replicas: 1
  selector:
    matchLabels:
      app: azure-vote-front
  template:
    metadata:
      labels:
        app: azure-vote-front
    spec:
      containers:
      - name: azure-vote-front
        image: microsoft/azure-vote-front:v1
        resources:
          requests:
            cpu: 100m
            memory: 128Mi
          limits:
            cpu: 250m
            memory: 256Mi
        ports:
        - containerPort: 80
        env:
        - name: REDIS
          value: "azure-vote-back"
---
apiVersion: v1
kind: Service
metadata:
  name: azure-vote-front
spec:
  type: LoadBalancer
  ports:
  - port: 80
  selector:
    app: azure-vote-front
```

The file was saved as `aksdemo.yaml`. This YAML file is responsible for creating two types of pod. Each of these types should be used to create a single instance. It short, there should be two pods created, one for each type. Both the pod specifications are available in the YAML file within the `template` section.

The YAML file can be submitted using the `apply` command:

```
C:\Users\citynextadmin>kubectl apply -f aksdemo.yaml
deployment.apps/azure-vote-back created
service/azure-vote-back created
deployment.apps/azure-vote-front created
service/azure-vote-front created
```

At this stage, nodes can be queried as follows:

```
C:\Users\citynextadmin>kubectl get nodes
NAME                      STATUS   ROLES   AGE   VERSION
aks-nodepool1-39448715-0  Ready    agent   20m   v1.9.11
aks-nodepool1-39448715-1  Ready    agent   20m   v1.9.11
```

Pods can be queried as shown in the following screenshot:

```
C:\Users\citynextadmin>kubectl get pods
NAME                             READY  STATUS            RESTARTS  AGE
azure-vote-back-f7c88f6f5-2zxp7  1/1    Running           0         67s
azure-vote-front-7c79dddc4c-f99hl 0/1   ContainerCreating 0         67s
```

Once the pods are created, they should show a `Running` status. However, its not only the pods that needed to be created. There are more resources to create on the cluster as shown in next screenshot.

This includes two services. One service, of the `ClusterIP` type, is used for internal communication between pods, and the other one, of the `LoadBalancer` type, is used for enabling external requests to reach to the pod. The configuration of services is available in the YAML file as `kind: Service`. There are two deployments as well; deployments are resources that manage the deployment process. The configuration of services is available in the YAML file as `kind: Deployment`.

Two replica sets are also created, one for each pod type. Replica sets were previously known as replication controllers, and they ensure that the desired number of pod instances are always maintained within the cluster. The configuration of services is available in the YAML file as the `spec` element:

```
C:\Users\citynextadmin>kubectl get all
NAME                                         READY   STATUS    RESTARTS   AGE
pod/azure-vote-back-f7c88f6f5-2zxp7          1/1     Running   0          4m11s
pod/azure-vote-front-7c79dddc4c-f99hl        1/1     Running   0          4m11s

NAME                        TYPE           CLUSTER-IP     EXTERNAL-IP      PORT(S)        AGE
service/azure-vote-back     ClusterIP      10.0.180.11    <none>           6379/TCP       4m11s
service/azure-vote-front    LoadBalancer   10.0.56.53     52.236.179.79    80:32110/TCP   4m11s
service/kubernetes          ClusterIP      10.0.0.1       <none>           443/TCP        27m

NAME                                      READY   UP-TO-DATE   AVAILABLE   AGE
deployment.extensions/azure-vote-back     1/1     1            1           4m11s
deployment.extensions/azure-vote-front    1/1     1            1           4m11s

NAME                                              DESIRED   CURRENT   READY   AGE
replicaset.extensions/azure-vote-back-f7c88f6f5   1         1         1       4m11s
replicaset.extensions/azure-vote-front-7c79dddc4c 1         1         1       4m11s
```

App Service containers

Previously, it was not possible to use containers along with Azure App Service. App Service provided the ability to host applications on virtual machines. There is now a new preview feature that has been recently added to Azure App Service. This feature allows you to host containers on App Service and have containers contain the application binaries and dependencies together:

1. To deploy a container on App Service, go to the Azure portal and select **Web App for Containers** and create one:

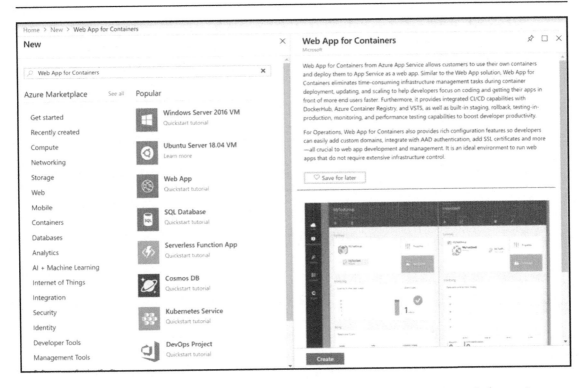

2. Provide a name to it along with subscription and resource group information. Select an appropriate operating system. Both Linux and Windows are available as options.

3. Either create a new App Service plan, as shown in the following screenshot, or use an existing plan:

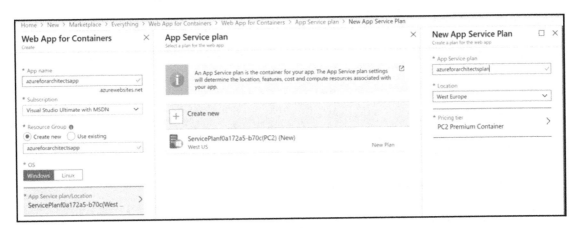

4. Provide the **Configure container** configuration information. Here we already
    have our image on Azure Container Registry, which has been chosen for this
    example. The other choices are Docker Hub and private registries. Provide the
    information about the registry hosting the image. Since we've already uploaded
    an image to Docker Hub, it is possible to use the Docker Hub image instead of
    Azure Container Registry:

5. The complete configuration for Web App for Containers should be similar to that shown in the following screenshot. Creating the App Service will download the image from the container registry and create a new container out of it:

6. It takes a while for the container to be up and running. Meanwhile, if you navigate to the URL generated for App Service, it will show the following page:

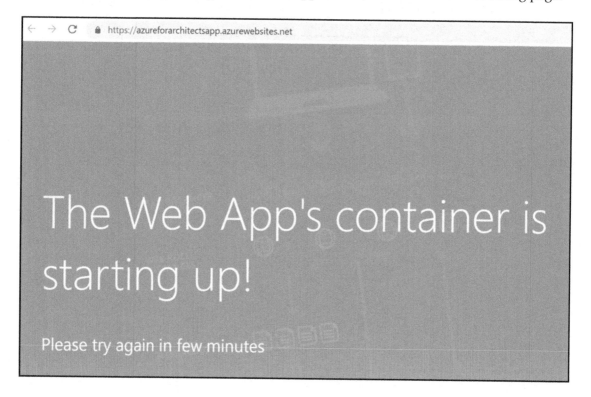

7. If you navigate to the **Container settings** menu on left, it will show the diagnostic logs for the container:

Comparing all container options

It's time to compare all container hosting options in Azure. This is one of the most crucial skills that architects should possess to decide the optimal resource for their requirements. The options for hosting containers are as follows:

- Containers on virtual machines
- Containers on virtual machines with Kubernetes as the orchestrator
- Azure Kubernetes Service
- Containers in Azure App Service
- Containers in Azure Container Instances
- Containers in Azure Functions
- Containers in Service Fabric

Given the large number of options for hosting containers, it is important to understand their nature, including their cost and benefits, before finalizing a resource or group of resources. In this section, we will evaluate and compare resources based on the following:

- Cost
- Complexity
- Control
- Agility and flexibility
- Scalability and availability

Containers on virtual machines

When deploying containers on virtual machines without an orchestrator, the entire burden of ensuring that the containers are running is on the customer. The customer may have to purchase additional monitoring services that can monitor hosts as well as containers. This, however, is also not an ideal situation. This is because while monitoring can generate alerts and inform the administrators, the customer must spend more to create automation on top of those alerts.

This option is also costly compared to others, as the cost will involve the cost of the virtual machines, along with the cost of other Azure resources such as Azure Storage, Load Balancer, and so on.

For production environments and mission-critical application, this option is not advisable.

Containers on virtual machines with Kubernetes as the orchestrator

When deploying containers on virtual machines without an orchestrator, the cost will be higher compared to that without an orchestrator because of the need for additional virtual machines to act as management servers hosting the API server, schedulers, and controllers. If the master is highly available, then additional virtual machines will be required. The benefit of this solution compared to previous one is that the applications will be continually available without downtime as Kubernetes will ensure that if a host or pod goes down, the pods will be created on other hosts.

This option is ideal when an organization wants full control over the environment and solution and has skilled people to manage the environment. The option also helps in rolling upgrades for the application. The scaling of hosts will be a manual activity, which could make operations complex and time consuming unless virtual machine scale sets with scaling rules are used for scaling.

Azure Kubernetes Service

Azure Kubernetes Service is a **Platform-as-a-Service (PaaS)**. This means that when deploying Azure Kubernetes Service, customers do not need access to master and pod nodes. The only access needed by customers is to the Kubectl CLI tool, which interacts with the API server. Customers of Azure Kubernetes Service do not have to manage the nodes, and Azure will ensure that all upgrades, as well as planned and unplanned maintenance, are taken care of automatically. Customers can deploy their pods on the cluster and can rest assured that the desired state of the container environment will be maintained by Azure Kubernetes Service.

This solution is not complex compared to the previous two solutions and does not require highly skilled Kubernetes operators. The solution is highly scalable as Azure Kubernetes Service provides the means with which you can increase the number of nodes on demand. It is also highly available as Azure Kubernetes Service ensures that if a node goes down, another node is made available to the cluster.

The disadvantage of this solution is that customers lose control over the underlying infrastructure. An important thing to note about this solution is that it works great with Linux-based images; however, there are additional tasks that would need to be performed in the case of Windows. Also, the master nodes are always Linux-based. These are limitations that will definitely change in future as Microsoft makes Windows completely native to containers.

This is one of the highly recommended options and solutions out of all available options.

Containers on Azure App Service

This is a relatively new feature provided by Azure and is currently in preview at the time of writing. Azure App Service is another PaaS that provides a managed environment for deploying applications. App Service can be automatically scaled up and out based on rules and conditions, and containers can be created on these new nodes. Web Apps for Containers provides all the benefits of Azure App Service with an additional benefit. When provisioning an App Service, customers are bound by the given platform in terms of .NET version and operating system. Customers cannot control the operating system version or the .NET version. However, when deploying containers on top of App Service, the container images can consist of any .NET runtime, framework, and SDK. Moreover, the container image can be based on any compatible version of the base operating system. In short, containers on App Service provide much more flexibility for provisioning an environment. It is also cost-effective compared to IaaS container options; however, there is reduced control on virtual machines. This option, however, provides key-hole access to the underlying services and servers.

This option necessitates that the images are stored on some registry. It could be Azure Container Registry, Docker Hub, or any private registry. It is not possible to upload a Dockerfile targeting Windows images to App Service; however, this option of using Docker Compose and Kubernetes is available for Linux containers.

The complexity of creating and maintaining applications with Web Apps for Containers is considerably lower compared to other options. It's a great solution for demo and dev/test environments.

Containers in Azure Container Instances

This, again, is a relatively new feature in Azure, and helps in hosting containers. It helps in quickly creating a container and hosting it without the need for any virtual machines. One of the major complexities of this solution is that multi-container solutions need more attention, as this service treats every container as a standalone solution. It can download images from Azure Container Registry.

Containers in Azure Functions

This resource is specific to running Azure Functions within containers. If customers are writing and deploying functions and want to host in any environment that is different than the out-of-the-box environment provided by Azure, then this is a good solution. Microsoft already provided a few images hosted in Docker Hub related to functions. These images already contain the Azure Functions runtime and framework. It is important to note that images not containing the Azure Functions runtime should not be used for hosting containers with Functions.

The benefits and constraints for this solution are similar to those of containers with web apps.

Containers in Service Fabric

Service Fabric is another Azure resource on which containers can be hosted. Service Fabric can be hosted on premises, on Azure virtual machines, and as a managed service by providing a managed platform.

The advantages and disadvantages are similar to those of the IaaS and PaaS solutions mentioned earlier in this chapter.

Summary

This chapter was focused on containers in Azure. Azure provides multiple services that are either native or compatible with containers. These services are relatively new features and newer capabilities are being added to them on an on-going basis. Some of the important Azure services related to containers are Azure Container Registry, Azure Container Instances, Azure Kubernetes Service, and Azure App Service. There are other services, such as Azure Service Fabric, which supports hosting containers, and function app containers, which supports running functions in containers. Containers can be hosted either as IaaS or PaaS. Both have their advantages and disadvantages, and organizations should evaluate their requirements and choose an appropriate service for their containers. It is important to know which container service to use in different scenarios, as that would be a key factor for success for an architect in Azure.

11
Azure DevOps

Software development is a complex undertaking composed of multiple processes and tools, and involves people from different departments. They all need to come together and work in a cohesive manner. With so many variables, the risks are high while delivering to the end customers. One small omission or misconfiguration, and the application might come crashing down. This chapter is about adopting and implementing practices that reduce this risk considerably and ensure that high-quality software can be delivered to the customer again and again.

Before getting into the details of DevOps, let's list the problems faced by software companies that DevOps addresses:

- Organizations are rigid and don't welcome change
- Rigid and time-consuming processes
- Isolated teams working in silos
- Monolithic design and big bang deployments
- Manual execution
- Lack of innovation

In this chapter, we will cover the following topics:

- DevOps
- DevOps practices
- Azure DevOps
- DevOps preparation
- DevOps for PaaS solutions
- DevOps for virtual machine-based (IaaS) solutions
- DevOps for container-based (IaaS) solutions
- Azure DevOps and Jenkins
- Azure Automation
- Azure tools for DevOps

DevOps

There's currently no industry-wide consensus regarding the definition of DevOps. Organizations have formulated their own definition of DevOps and tried to implement it. They have their own perspective and think they've implemented DevOps if they implement automation and configuration management, and use Agile processes.

DevOps is about the delivery mechanism of software systems. It's about bringing people together, making them collaborate and communicate, working together towards a common goal and vision. It's about taking joint responsibility, accountability, and ownership. It's about implementing processes that foster collaboration and a service mindset. It enables delivery mechanisms that bring agility and flexibility to the organization. Contrary to popular belief, DevOps isn't about tools, technology, and automation. These are enablers that help in collaboration and the implementation of Agile processes and faster and better delivery to the customer.

There are multiple definitions available on the internet for DevOps and they aren't wrong. DevOps doesn't provide a framework or methodology. It's a set of principles and practices that, when employed within an organization, engagement, or project, achieve the goal and vision of both DevOps and the organization. These principles and practices don't mandate any specific process, tools and technologies, or environments. DevOps provides guidance that can be implemented through any tool, technology, or process, although some of the technology and processes might be more applicable than others to achieve the vision of DevOps' principles and practices.

Although DevOps practices can be implemented in any organization that provides services and products to customers, going forward in this book, we'll look at DevOps from the perspective of software development and the operations department of any organization.

So, what is DevOps? DevOps is defined as a set of principles and practices bringing both all teams including developers and operations together from the start of the software system for faster, quicker, and efficient end-to-end delivery of value to the end customer, again and again in a consistent and predictable manner reducing time to market, thereby gaining competitive advantage.

Read the preceding definition of DevOps out loud; if you look at it closely, it doesn't indicate or refer to any specific processes, tools, or technology. It doesn't prescribe any methodology or environment.

The goal of implementing DevOps principles and practices in any organization is to ensure that the demands of stakeholders (including customers) and expectations are met efficiently and effectively.

The customer's demands and expectations are met when the following happens:

- The customer gets the features they want.
- The customer gets the feature when they want.
- The customer gets faster updates on features.
- The quality of delivery is high.

When an organization can meet these expectations, customers are happy and remain loyal. This, in turn, increases the market competitiveness of the organization, which results in a bigger brand and market valuation. It has a direct impact on the top and bottom lines of the organization. The organization can invest further in innovation and customer feedback, bringing about continuous changes to its system and services to stay relevant.

The implementation of DevOps principles and practices in any organization is guided by its surrounding ecosystem. This ecosystem is made up of the industry and domains the organization belongs to.

DevOps is based on a set of principles and practices. We'll look into details about these principles and practices later in this chapter. The core principles of DevOps are the following:

- Agility
- Automation
- Collaboration
- Feedback

The core DevOps practices are the following:

- Continuous integration
- Configuration management
- Continuous deployment
- Continuous delivery
- Continuous learning

DevOps is not a new paradigm; however, it's gaining a lot of popularity and traction in recent times. Its adoption is at its highest level and more and more companies are undertaking this journey. I purposely mentioned DevOps as a journey because there are different levels of maturity within DevOps. While successfully implementing continuous deployment and delivery are considered the highest level of maturity in this journey, adopting source code control, Agile software development is considered as first step in the DevOps journey.

One of the first things DevOps talks about is breaking down the barriers between the development and the operations teams. It brings about close collaboration between multiple teams. It's about breaking the mindset that the developer is responsible for writing the code only and passing it on to operations for deployment once it's tested. It's also about breaking the mindset that operations have no role to play in development activities. Operations should influence the planning of the product and should be aware of the features coming up as releases. They should also continually provide feedback to the developers on the operational issues such that they can be fixed in subsequent releases. They should influence the design of the system to improve the operational working of the system. Similarly, the developers should help the operations team to deploy the system and solve incidents when they arise.

The definition of DevOps talks about faster, and more efficient end-to-end delivery of systems to stakeholders. It doesn't talk about how fast, or efficient the delivery should be. It should be fast enough depending on the organization domain, industry, customer segmentation, and needs. For some organizations, quarterly releases are good enough, while for others it could be weekly. Both are valid from a DevOps point of view, and these organizations can deploy relevant processes and technologies to achieve their target release deadlines. DevOps doesn't mandate any specific time frame for CI/CD. Organizations should identify the best implementation of DevOps principles and practices based on their overall project, engagement, and organizational vision.

The definition also talks about end-to-end delivery. This means that everything from the planning and delivery of the system through to the services and operations should be part of the DevOps adoption. The processes should be such that it allows for greater flexibility, modularity, and agility in the application the development life cycle. While organizations are free to use the best fit process—Waterfall, Agile, Scrum, and more. Typically, organizations tend to favor Agile processes with iterations-based delivery. This allows for faster delivery in smaller units, which are far more testable and manageable, compared to a large delivery.

DevOps repeatedly talks about end customers in a consistent and predictable manner. This means that organizations should continually deliver to customers with newer and upgraded features using automation. We can't achieve consistency and predictability without the use of automation. Manual work should be nonexistent to ensure a high level of consistency and predictability. The automation should also be end-to-end, to avoid failures. This also indicates that the system design should be modular, allowing faster delivery on systems that are reliable, available, and scalable. Testing plays a big role in consistent and predictable delivery.

The end result of implementing these practices and principles is that the organization is able to meet the expectations and demands of customers. The organization is able to grow faster than the competition, and further increase the quality and capability of their product and services through continuous innovation and improvement.

DevOps practices

DevOps consists of multiple practices, each providing a distinct functionality to the overall process. The following figure shows the relationship between them. Configuration management, continuous integration, and continuous deployment form the core practices that enable DevOps. When we deliver software services that combine these three services, we achieve continuous delivery. Continuous delivery is a capability and level of maturity of an organization dependent on the maturity of configuration management, continuous integration, and continuous deployment. Continuous feedback at all stages forms the feedback loop that helps to provide superior services to customers. It runs across all DevOps practices. Let's deep dive into each of these capabilities and DevOps practices:

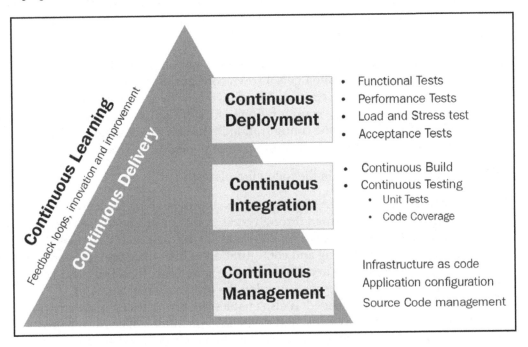

Configuration management

Business applications and services need an environment on which they can be deployed. Typically, the environment is an infrastructure composed of multiple servers, computers, network, storage, containers, and many more services working together such that business applications can be deployed on top of them. Business applications are decomposed into multiple services running on multiple servers, either on-premise or on the cloud, and each service has its own configuration along with requirements related to the infrastructure's configuration. In short, both the infrastructure and the application are needed to deliver systems to customers and both of them have their own configuration. If the configuration drifts, the application might not work as expected, leading to downtime and failure. Moreover, as the ALM process dictates the use of multiple stages and environments, an application would be deployed to multiple environments with different configurations. The application will be deployed to the development environment for developers to see the result of their work. The application will be deployed to multiple test environments with different configurations for functional tests, load and stress tests, performance tests, integration tests, and more; it would also be deployed to the preproduction environment to conduct user-acceptance tests and finally onto the production environment. It's important that an application can be deployed to multiple environments without undertaking any manual changes to its configuration.

Configuration management provides a set of processes and tools and they help to ensure that each environment and application gets its own configuration. Configuration management tracks configuration items, and anything that changes from environment to environment should be treated as a configuration item. Configuration management also defines the relationships between the configuration items and how changes in one configuration item will impact the other configuration items.

Configuration management helps in the following places:

- **Infrastructure as Code**: When the process of provisioning infrastructure and its configuration is represented through code, and the same code goes through the application life cycle process, it's known as Infrastructure as Code. IaC helps to automate the provisioning and configuration of infrastructure. It also represents the entire infrastructure in code that can be stored in a repository and version-controlled. This allows users to employ the previous environment's configurations when needed. It also enables the provisioning of an environment multiple times in a consistent and predictable manner. All environments provisioned in this way are consistent and equal in all ALM stages.

- **Deploying and configuring the application**: The deployment of an application and its configuration is the next step after provisioning the infrastructure. Examples include deploying a webdeploy package on a server, deploying a SQL server schema and data (bacpac) on another server, and changing the SQL connection string on the web server to represent the appropriate SQL server. Configuration management stores values for the application's configuration for each environment on which it is deployed.

The configuration applied should also be monitored. The expected and desired configuration should be consistently maintained. Any drift from this expected and desired configuration would render the application unavailable. Configuration management is also capable of finding the drift and re-configuring the application and environment to its desired state.

With automated configuration management in place, nobody on the team has to deploy and configure the environments and applications on production. The operations team isn't reliant on the development team or long deployment documentation.

Another aspect of configuration management is source code control. Business applications and services comprise code and other artifacts. Multiple team members work on the same files. The source code should always be up to date and should be accessible by only authenticated team members. The code and other artifacts by themselves are configuration items. Source control helps in collaboration and communication within the team since everybody is aware of what everyone else is doing and conflicts are resolved at an early stage.

Configuration management can be broadly divided into two categories:

- Inside the virtual machine
- Outside the virtual machine

The tools available for configuration management inside the virtual machine are discussed next.

Desired State Configuration

Desired State Configuration (**DSC**) is a new configuration-management platform from Microsoft, built as an extension to PowerShell. DSC was originally launched as part of Windows Management Framework (WMF) 4.0. It's available as part of WMF 4.0 and 5.0 for all Windows Server operating systems before Windows 2008 R2. WMF 5.1 is available out of the box on Windows Server 2016 and Windows 10.

Chef, Puppet, and Ansible

Apart from DSC, there's a host of configuration-management tools, such as Chef, Puppet, and Ansible, supported by Azure. Details about these tools aren't covered in this book.

The tools available for configuration management outside of a virtual machine are mentioned next.

ARM Templates

ARM templates are the primary means of provisioning resources in ARM. ARM templates provide a declarative model through which resources, their configuration, scripts, and extensions are specified. ARM templates are based on **JavaScript Object Notation (JSON)** format. It uses the JSON syntax and conventions to declare and configure resources. JSON files are text-based, user-friendly, and easily-readable. They can be stored in a source-code repository and have version control on them. They are also means to represent infrastructure as code that can be used to provision resources in Azure resource groups again and again, predictably, consistently, and uniformly. A template needs a resource group for deployment. It can only be deployed to a resource group and the resource group should exist before executing template deployment. A template isn't capable of creating a resource group.

Templates provide the flexibility to be generic and modular in their design and implementation. Templates give us the ability to accept parameters from users, declare internal variables, help in defining dependencies between resources, link resources within the same or different resource groups, and execute other templates. They also provide scripting language-type expressions and functions that make them dynamic and customizable at runtime.

Continuous integration

Multiple developers write code that's eventually stored in a common repository. The code is normally checked in or pushed to the repository when the developer has finished developing their feature. This can happen in a day or might take days or weeks. Some of the developers might be working on the same feature and they might also follow the same practices of pushing/checking-in code in days or weeks. This can create issues with the quality of the code. One of the tenets of DevOps is to fail fast. Developers should check-in/push their code to the repository often and compile the code to check whether they've introduced bugs, and that the code is compatible with the code written by their colleagues. If the developer doesn't follow this practice, the code on their machine will grow too large and will be difficult to integrate with other code. Moreover, if the compile fails, it's difficult and time-consuming to fix the issues that will arise.

Continuous integration solves these kinds of challenges. Continuous integration helps in compiling and validating the code pushed/checked-in by a developer by taking it through a series of validation steps. Continuous integration creates a process flow that consists of multiple steps. Continuous integration is composed of continuous automated builds and continuous automated tests. Normally, the first step is compiling the code. After the successful compilation, each step is responsible for validating the code from a specific perspective. For example, unit tests can be executed on the compiled code, and then code coverage can be executed to check which code paths are executed by unit tests. These could reveal whether comprehensive unit tests are written or there's scope to add further unit tests. The end result of continuous integration is deployment packages that can be used by continuous deployment to deploy them to multiple environments.

Developers are encouraged to check-in their code multiple times a day, instead of doing so after days or weeks. Continuous integration initiates the execution of the entire pipeline as soon as the code is checked-in or pushed. If compilation succeeds, code tests, and other activities that are part of the pipeline, are executed without error; the code is deployed to a test environment and integration tests are executed on it. Although every system demands its own configuration of continuous integration, a minimal sample continuous integration is shown in the following diagram.

Continuous integration increases developer productivity. They don't have to manually compile their code, run multiple types of tests one after another, and then create packages out of it. It also reduces the risk of getting bugs introduced in the code and the code doesn't get stale. It provides early feedback to the developers about the quality of their code. Overall, the quality of deliverables is high and they are delivered faster by adopting continuous integration practices. A sample continuous integration pipeline is shown next:

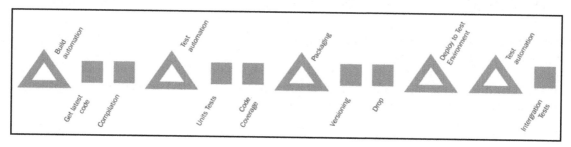

Build automation

Build automation consists of multiple tasks executing in sequence. Generally, the first task is responsible for fetching the latest source code from the repository. The source code might comprise multiple projects and files. They are compiled to generate artifacts, such as executables, dynamic link libraries, and assemblies. Successful build automation reflects that there are no compile-time errors in the code.

There could be more steps in build automation, depending on the nature and type of the project.

Test automation

Test automation consists of tasks that are responsible for validating different aspects of code. These tasks are related to testing code from a different perspective and are executed in sequence. Generally, the first step is to run a series of unit tests on the code. Unit testing refers to the process of testing the smallest denomination of a feature by validating its behavior in isolation from other features. It can be automated or manual, however, the preference is toward automated unit testing.

Code coverage is another type of automated testing that can be executed on the code to find out how much of the code is executed when running the unit tests. It's generally represented as a percentage and refers to how much code is testable through unit testing. If the code coverage isn't close to 100%, it's either because the developer hasn't written unit tests for that behavior or the uncovered code isn't required at all.

The successful execution of the test automation, resulting in no significant code failure, should start executing the packaging tasks. There could be more steps in the test automation depending on the nature and type of the project.

Packaging

Packaging refers to the process of generating deployable artifacts, such as MSI, NuGet and webdeploy packages, and database packages, versioning them, and then storing them at a location such that they can be consumed by other pipelines and processes.

Continuous deployment

By the time the process reaches continuous deployment, continuous integration has ensured that we have fully-working bits of an application that can now be taken through different continuous-deployment activities. Continuous deployment refers to the capability of deploying business applications and services to preproduction and production environments through automation. For example, continuous deployment could provision and configure the preproduction environment, deploy applications to it, and configure the applications. After conducting multiple validations, such as functional tests and performance tests on the preproduction environment, the production environment is provisioned, configured, and the application is deployed through automation. There are no manual steps in the deployment process. Every deployment task is automated. Continuous deployment can provision the environment and deploy the application from scratch while it can just deploy the delta changes to existing environment if the environment already exists.

All the environments are provisioned through automation using Infrastructure as Code. This ensures that all environments, whether development, test, preproduction, or production are the same. Similarly, the application is deployed through automation, ensuring that it's also deployed uniformly across all environments. The configuration across these environments could be different for the application.

Continuous deployment is generally integrated with continuous integration. When continuous integration has done its work, by generating the final deployable packages, continuous deployment kicks in and starts its own pipeline. This pipeline is called the release pipeline. The release pipeline consists of multiple environments, with each environment consisting of tasks responsible for provisioning the environment, configuring the environment, deploying applications, configuring applications, executing operational validation on environments, and testing the application on multiple environments.

Employing continuous deployment provides immense benefits. There is a high level of confidence in the overall deployment process, which helps with faster and risk-free releases on production. The chances of anything going wrong decreases drastically. The team will be less stressed, and rollback to the previous working environment is possible if there are issues with the current release:

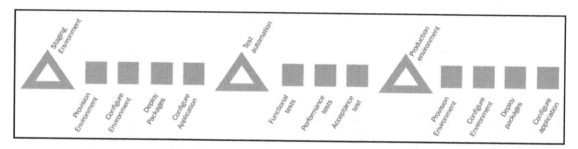

Although every system demands its own configuration of the release pipeline, a small sample of continuous deployment is shown in the preceding diagram. It's important to note that, generally, provisioning and configuring multiple environments is part of the release pipeline, and approvals should be sought before moving to the next environment. The approval process might be manual or automated, depending on the maturity of the organization.

Test environment deployment

The release pipeline starts once the drop is available from continuous integration and the first step it should take is to get all the artifacts from the drop. After which, it might create a completely new bare-metal test environment or reuse an existing one. This is again dependent on the type of project and the nature of the testing planned to be executed on this environment. The environment is provisioned and configured. The application artifacts are deployed and configured.

Test automation

After deploying an application, a series of tests can be performed on the environment. One of the tests executed here is a functional test. Functional tests are primarily aimed at validating the feature completeness and functionality of the application. These tests are written from requirements gathered from the customer. Another set of tests that can be executed is related to the scalability and availability of the application. This typically includes load tests, stress tests, and performance tests. It should also include an operational validation of the infrastructure environment.

Staging environment deployment

This is very similar to the test environment deployment, the only difference being that the configuration values for the environment and application would be different.

Acceptance tests

Acceptance tests are generally conducted by application stakeholders, and this can be manual or automated. This step is a validation from the customer's point of view about the correctness and completeness of the application's functionality.

Deployment to production

Once the customer gives their approval, the same steps as that of the test and staging environment deployment are executed, the only difference being that the configuration values for the environment and application are specific to the production environment. A validation is conducted after deployment to ensure that the application is running according to expectations.

Continuous delivery

Continuous delivery and continuous deployment might sound similar to you, however, they aren't the same. While continuous deployment talks about deployment to multiple environments and finally to the production environment through automation, continuous delivery is the ability to generate application packages that are readily deployable in any environment. For generating artifacts that are readily deployable, continuous integration should be used to generate the application artifacts, a new or existing environment should be used to deploy these artifacts, and conduct functional tests, performance tests, and user-acceptance tests through automation. Once these activities are successfully executed without any errors, the application package is considered readily deployable. Continuous delivery includes continuous integration and deployment to an environment for final validations. It helps in getting feedback faster from both the operations as well as the end user. This feedback can then be used to implement subsequent iterations.

Continuous learning

With all the before-mentioned DevOps practices, it's possible to create great business applications and deploy them automatically to the production environment; however, the benefits of DevOps won't last for long if continuous improvement and feedback principles are not in place. It's of the utmost importance that real-time feedback about the application behavior is passed on as feedback to the development team from both end users and the operations team.

Feedback should be passed to the teams, providing relevant information about what's going well and what isn't.

An application's architecture and design should be built with monitoring, auditing, and telemetry in mind. The operations team should collect telemetry information from the production environment, capture any bugs and issues, and pass it on the development team so that it can be fixed for subsequent releases.

Continuous learning helps to make the application robust and resilient to failure. It helps in making sure that the application is meeting consumer requirements. The following diagram shows the feedback loop that should be implemented between different teams:

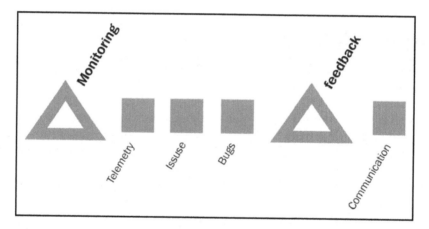

Azure DevOps

Now, it's time to focus on another revolutionary online service that enables continuous integration, continuous deployment, and continuous delivery seamlessly: Azure DevOps. In fact, it would be more appropriate to call it a suite of services available under a single name. Azure DevOps is a PaaS provided by Microsoft and hosted on the cloud. The same service is available as **Team Foundation Services (TFS)** on-premise. All examples shown in this book use Azure DevOps.

According to Microsoft, Azure DevOps is a cloud-based collaboration platform that helps teams to share code, track work, and ship software. Azure DevOps is a new name; earlier, it was known as **Visual Studio Team Services (VSTS)**. Azure DevOps is an enterprise software-development tool and service that enables organizations to provide automation facilities to their end-to-end application life cycle management process, from planning to deploying applications, and getting real-time feedback from software systems. This increases the maturity and capability of an organization to deliver high-quality software systems to their customers.

Successful software delivery involves efficiently bringing numerous processes and activities together. These include executing and implementing various Agile processes, increasing collaboration among teams, the seamless and automatic transition of artifacts from one phase of the ALM to another phase, and deployments to multiple environments. It's important to track and report on these activities to measure and improve delivery processes. Azure DevOps makes this simple and easy. It provides a whole suite of services that enables the following:

- Collaboration among every team member by providing a single interface for the entire application life cycle management.
- Collaboration among development teams using source-code-management services.
- Collaboration among test teams using test-management services.
- Automatic validation of code and packaging through continuous integration using build-management services.
- Automatic validation of application functionality, deployment, and configuration of multiple environments through continuous deployment and delivery using release-management services.
- Tracking and work-item management using work-management services.

The following screenshot shows all the services available to a project from the **Azure DevOps** left navigation bar:

An organization in Azure DevOps is a security boundary and logical container that provides all the services that are needed to implement a DevOps strategy. Azure DevOps allows for the creation of multiple projects within a single organization. By default, a repository is created with the creation of a project; however, Azure DevOps allows for the creation of additional repositories within a single project. The relationship between the **Azure DevOps Organization**, **Projects**, and **Repository** is shown in the following diagram:

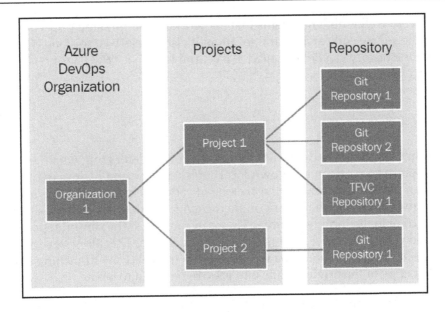

Azure DevOps provides two types of repositories:

- Git
- **Team Foundation Version Control (TFVC)**

It also provides the flexibility to choose between the Git or TFVC source-control repository. There can be a combination of TFS and TFVC repositories available within a single project.

Team Foundation Version Control

TFVC is the traditional and centralized way of implementing version control, where there's a central repository and developers work on it directly in connected mode to check-in their changes. If the central repository is offline or unavailable, developers can't check-in their code and have to wait for it to be online and available. Other developers can see only the checked-in code. Developers can group multiple changes into a single change set for checking-in code changes that are logically grouped to form a single change. TFVC locks the code files that are undergoing edits. Other developers can read the locked-up file, but they can't edit it. They must wait for the prior edit to complete and release the lock before they can edit. The history of check-ins and changes is maintained on the central repository, while the developers have the working copy of the files but not the history.

TFVC works very well with large teams that are working on the same projects. This enables control over the source code at a central location. It also works best for long duration projects since the history can be managed at a central location. TFVC has no issues working with large and binary files.

Git

Git, on the other hand, is a modern, distributed way of implementing version control, where developers can work on their own local copies of code and history in offline mode. Developers can work offline on their local clone of code. Each developer has a local copy of code and entire history, and they work on their changes with this local repository. They can commit their code to the local repository. They can connect to the central repository for synchronization of their local repository on a per-need basis. This allows every developer to work on any file, since they would be working on their local copy. Branching in Git doesn't create another copy of the original code and is extremely fast to create.

Git works well with a smaller team. With larger teams, there's a substantial overhead to manage multiple pull requests to merge the code onto a central repository. It also works best for short-term projects, as this way, the history wouldn't get too large to be downloaded and manageable on every developer's local repository. Branching and merging is a breeze with advance options.

Git is the recommended way of using source control because of the rich functionality it provides. We'll use Git as the repository for our sample application in this book.

Preparing for DevOps

Going forward, our focus will be on process and deployment automation using different patterns in Azure. These include the following:

- DevOps for IaaS solutions
- DevOps for PaaS solutions
- DevOps for container-based solutions

Generally, there are shared services that aren't unique to any one application. Their services are consumed by multiple applications from different environments, such as development, testing, and production. The life cycle of these shared services is different for each application. Therefore, they have different version-control repositories, a different code base, and build and release management. They have their own cycle of plan, design, build, test, and release.

The resources that are part of this group are provisioned using ARM templates, PowerShell, and DSC configurations.

The overall flow for building these common components is shown here:

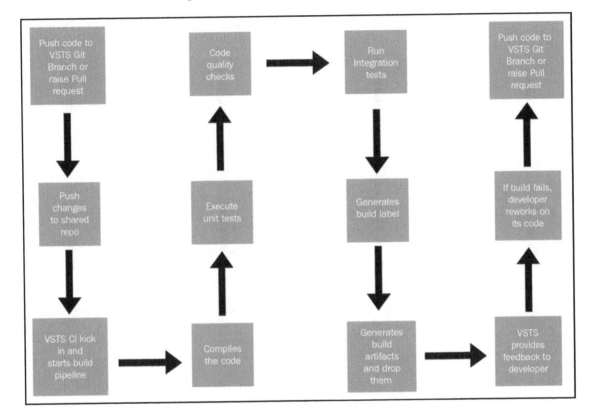

The release process is shown in the following diagram:

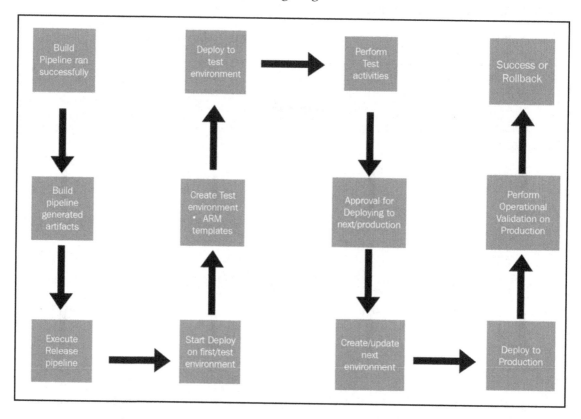

On the DevOps journey, it's important to understand and provision the common components and services before starting any software engagement, product, or service.

Provisioning Azure DevOps organization

A version-control system is needed to collaborate at code level. Azure DevOps helps in providing both centralized and decentralized versions of control systems. Azure DevOps also provides orchestration services for building and executing build and release pipelines. It's a mature platform to organize all DevOps-related version control, and to build and release work-item-related artifacts. After an organization is provisioned in Azure DevOps, an Azure DevOps project should be created to hold all project-related artifacts.

An Azure DevOps organization can be provisioned by visiting `https://dev.azure.com`.

Provisioning the Azure Key Vault

It isn't advisable to store secrets, certificates, credentials, or other sensitive information in code configuration files, databases, or any other general storage system. It's advised to store this important data in a vault that's specifically designed for storing secrets and credentials. The Azure Key Vault provides such a service. The Azure Key Vault is available as a resource and service from Azure.

Provisioning a configuration-management server/service

A configuration-management server/service that provides storage for configurations and applyies those configurations to different environments is always a good strategy for automating deployments. DSC on custom virtual machines, DSC from Azure Automation, Chef, Puppet, and Ansible are some options, and can be used on Azure seamlessly for both Windows as well as Linux environments. This book uses DSC as a configuration-management tool for all purposes, and it provides a pull server that holds all configuration documents (MOF files) for the sample application. It also maintains the database of all virtual machines and containers that are configured and registered with the pull server to pull configuration documents from it. The local configuration manager on these target virtual machines and containers periodically checks the availability of new configurations as well as drifts in current configuration and reports it back to the pull server. It also has built-in reporting capabilities that provide information about nodes that are compliant, as well as those that are non-compliant, within a virtual machine. A pull server is a general web application that hosts the DSC pull server endpoint.

Provisioning log analytics

Log analytics is an audit and monitoring service provided by Azure to get real-time information about all changes, drifts, and events occurring within virtual machines and containers. It provides a centralized workspace and dashboard for IT administrators for viewing, searching, and conducting drill-down searches on all changes, drifts, and events that occur on these virtual machines. It also provides agents that are deployed on target virtual machines and containers. Once deployed, these agents start sending all changes, events, and drifts to the centralized workspace.

Azure Storage account

Azure Storage is a service provided by Azure to store files as blobs. All scripts and code for automating the provisioning, deployment, and configuration of the infrastructure and sample application are stored in the Azure DevOps Git repository, and are packaged and deployed in an Azure Storage account. Azure provides PowerShell script-extension resources that can automatically download DSC and PowerShell scripts and execute them on virtual machines during the execution of Azure resource-manager templates. This storage acts as a common storage across all deployments for multiple applications.

Source images

Both virtual machine and container images should be built as part of the common services build-and-release pipeline. Tools such as Packer and Docker Build can be used to generate these images.

Monitoring tools

All monitoring tools, such as Azure Monitor, Application Insights, Log Analytics, OMS, and the System Center Operations Manager should be provisioned and configured during the release pipeline of common services.

Management tools

All management tools, such as Kubernetes, DC/OS, Docker Swarm, and ITIL tools, should be provisioned at this stage.

DevOps for PaaS solutions

The typical architecture for Azure PaaS app services is based on the following diagram:

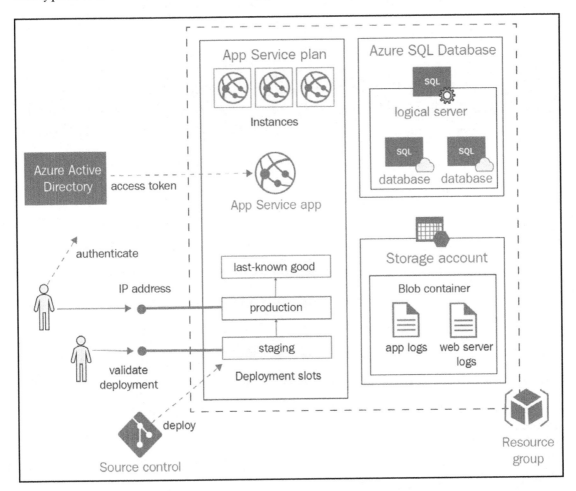

The architecture shows some of the important components, such as Azure SQL, storage accounts, the version-control system, that participate in the Azure App Services-based cloud solution architecture. These artifacts should be created using Azure resource-manager templates. These ARM templates should be part of the overall configuration-management strategy. It can have its own build and release management pipelines, similar to the one shown in the following diagram:

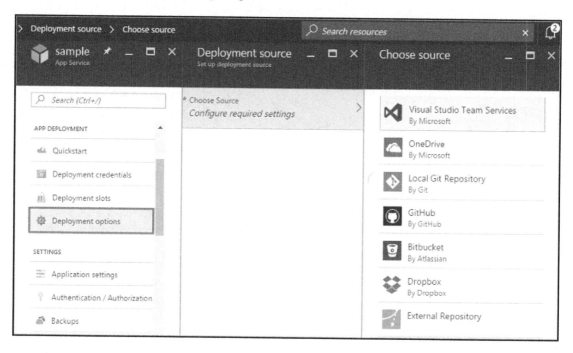

The template should also configure continuous deployment by configuring **Deployment options**.

Azure App Services

Azure App Services provides managed hosting services for cloud solutions. It's a fully-managed platform that provisions and deploys cloud solutions. App Services takes away the burden of creating and managing infrastructure and provides minimum **service-level agreements (SLA)** for hosting your cloud solutions.

They are open; they let users decide on the language they want to use to build their cloud solutions, and flexible enough to host the cloud solution on either the Windows or Linux operating system. Creating an app service internally provisions virtual machines behind the scene that are completely managed by Azure, and users don't see them at all. Multiple types of cloud solutions, such as web applications, mobile backend APIs, API endpoints, and containers can be hosted seamlessly on Azure App Services.

Deployment slots

Azure App Services provides deployment slots that make deployment to them seamless and easy. There are multiple slots and swapping between slots is at DNS level. It means anything on production slot can be swapped with a staging slot by just swapping the DNS entries. This helps in deploying the custom cloud solution to staging and, after all checks and tests, they can be swapped to production if found satisfactory. However, in case of any issue in production after swapping, the previous good values from the production environment can be reinstated by swapping again.

Azure SQL

Azure SQL is a SQL PaaS service provided by Azure to host databases. Azure provides a secure platform to host databases and takes complete ownership to manage the availability, reliability, and scalability of the service. With Azure SQL, there's no need to provision custom virtual machines, deploy a SQL server, and configure it. Instead, the Azure team does this behind the scenes and manages it on our behalf. It also provides a firewall service that enables security; only an IP address allowed by the firewall can connect the server and access the database. The virtual machines provisioned to host web applications have distinct public IP addresses assigned to them and they're added to Azure SQL firewall rules dynamically. Azure SQL Server and its database is created upon executing the Azure resource-manager template.

The build-and-release pipeline

In this section, a new build pipeline is created that compiles and validates an ASP.NET MVC application, and then generates packages for deployment. After package-generation, a release definition ensures that deployment to the first environment happens in an app service and Azure SQL as part of continuous deployment.

The project structure of the sample application is shown in the following screenshot:

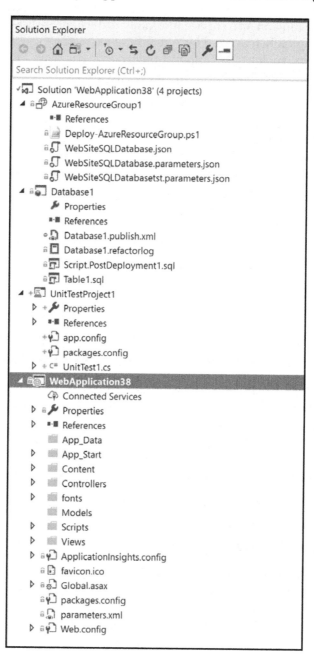

In this project, there's an ASP.NET MVC application – the main application, which consists of application pages. Webdeploy packages will be generated out of this project from build pipelines and they will eventually be on Azure Web Apps.

- **Unit test project**: Code for unit-testing the ASP.NET MVC application. Assemblies from this project will be generated and executed in build execution.
- **SQL Database project**: Consisting of code related to the SQL database schema, structure, and master data. DacPac files will be generated out of this project using the build definition.
- **Azure Resource group project**: Consisting of ARM templates and parameters code to provision the entire Azure environment on which the ASP.NET MVC application and the SQL tables are created.

The build pipeline is shown in the following screenshot:

The configuration of each task is shown in the following table:

Task name	Task configuration
Use NuGet 4.4.1	NuGet Tool Installer ⓘ ⟳ Link settings 📄 View YAML ✕ Remove Version 0.* ⌄ Display name * Use NuGet 4.4.1 Version of NuGet.exe to install * ⓘ 4.4.1 ☐ Always download the latest matching version ⓘ Control Options ⌄ Output Variables ⌄
NuGet restore	NuGet ⓘ ⟳ Link settings 📄 View YAML ✕ Remove Version 2.* ⌄ Display name * NuGet restore Command * ⓘ restore ⌄ Path to solution, packages.config, or project.json * ***.sln
Build solution	Visual Studio Build ⓘ ⟳ Link settings 📄 View YAML ✕ Remove Version 1.* ⌄ Display name * Build solution Solution * ⓘ WebApplication38/WebApplication38.csproj ... Visual Studio Version ⓘ Latest ⌄ MSBuild Arguments ⓘ /p:DeployOnBuild=true /p:WebPublishMethod=Package /p:PackageAsSingleFile=true /p:SkipInvalidConfigurations=true /p:PackageLocation='$(build.artifacts tagingdirectory)\\' Platform ⓘ $(BuildPlatform) Configuration ⓘ $(BuildConfiguration)

Test Assemblies	Visual Studio Test ⓘ 🔗 Link settings 📄 View YAML ✕ Remove Version 2.* ∨ Display name * Test Assemblies Test selection ∧ Select tests using * ⓘ Test assemblies ∨ Test files * ⓘ **\$(BuildConfiguration)*test*.dll !**\obj** Search folder * ⓘ $(System.DefaultWorkingDirectory)
Publish symbols path	Index Sources & Publish Symbols ⓘ 🔗 Link settings 📄 View YAML ✕ Remove Version 2.* ∨ Display name * Publish symbols path Path to symbols folder ⓘ $(Build.SourcesDirectory) Search pattern * ⓘ **\bin***.pdb ☑ Index sources ⓘ ☐ Publish symbols ⓘ
Publish Artifact – MVC application	Publish Build Artifacts ⓘ 🔗 Link settings 📄 View YAML ✕ Remove Version 1.* ∨ Display name * Publish Artifact - MVC application Path to publish * ⓘ $(build.artifactstagingdirectory) ... Artifact name * drop
Publish Artifact – IaaS code (ARM templates)	Publish Build Artifacts ⓘ 🔗 Link settings 📄 View YAML ✕ Remove Version 1.* ∨ Display name * Publish Artifact - IaaS code (ARM templates) Path to publish * ⓘ AzureResourceGroup1 ... Artifact name * ⓘ drop1 Artifact publish location * ⓘ Azure Pipelines/TFS ∨

Build solution Database1/Database1.sqlproj	**MSBuild** ⓘ 🔗 Link settings 📄 View YAML ✕ Remove Version 1.* ⌄ Display name * Build solution Database1/Database1.sqlproj Project * ⓘ Database1/Database1.sqlproj ... MSBuild ⓘ ⦿ Version ◯ Specify Location MSBuild Version ⓘ Latest ⌄ MSBuild Architecture ⓘ MSBuild x64 ⌄ Platform ⓘ Configuration ⓘ MSBuild Arguments ⓘ /t:build /p:CmdLineInMemoryStorage=True
Copy Files to: $(build.artifactstagingdirectory)	**Copy Files** ⓘ 🔗 Link settings 📄 View YAML ✕ Remove Version 2.* ⌄ Display name * Copy Files to: $(build.artifactstagingdirectory) Source Folder ⓘ ... Contents * ⓘ ***.dacpac Target Folder * ⓘ $(build.artifactstagingdirectory)

The build pipeline is configured to execute automatically as part of continuous integration, as shown in the following screenshot:

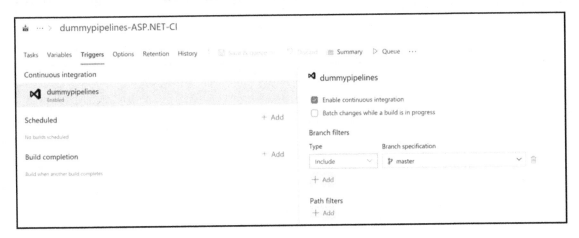

The release definition consists of multiple environments, such as development, testing, SIT, UAT, preproduction, and production. The tasks are pretty similar in each environment, with the addition of tasks specific to that environment. For example, a test environment has additional tasks related to UI, functional, and integration testing, compared to a development environment.

The release definition for this application are shown in following screenshot:

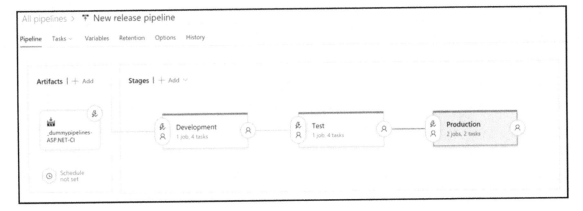

The release tasks for a single environment is shown in the following screenshot:

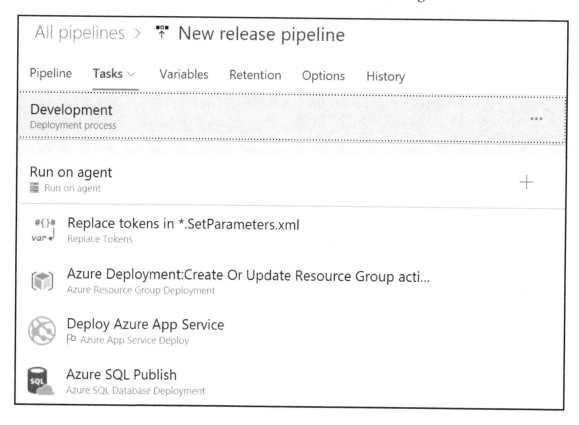

The configure for each of the tasks is listed here:

Task name	Task configuration
Replace tokens in `*.SetParameters.xml` **(This is a task installed from MarketPlace)**	Version 3.* ∨ Display name * Replace tokens in *.SetParameters.xml Root directory ⓘ $(System.DefaultWorkingDirectory)/_dummypipelines-ASP.NET-CI/drop ··· Target files * ⓘ *.SetParameters.xml Files encoding * ⓘ auto ∨ ☑ Write unicode BOM ⓘ Missing variables ∧ Action * ⓘ log warning ∨ ☑ Keep token ⓘ Advanced ∧ Token prefix * ⓘ __ Token suffix * ⓘ __ Empty value ⓘ (empty) Escape values type ⓘ no escaping ∨

Azure Deployment:Create Or Update Resource Group action on devRG	Azure Resource Group Deployment ⓘ ✕ Remove
	Version 2.* ⌄
	Display name *
	Azure Deployment:Create Or Update Resource Group action on devRG
	Azure Details ⌃
	Azure subscription * ⓘ | Manage ↗
	myconnection ⌄ ↻
	⊘ Scoped to subscription Visual Studio Enterprise
	Action * ⓘ
	Create or update resource group ⌄
	Resource group * ⓘ
	devRG ⌄ ↻
	Location * ⓘ
	West Europe ⌄ ↻
	Template ⌃
	Template location *
	Linked artifact ⌄
	Template * ⓘ
	$(System.DefaultWorkingDirectory)/_dummypipelines-ASP.NET-CI/drop1/WebSiteSQLDatabase.json ...
	Template parameters ⓘ
	$(System.DefaultWorkingDirectory)/_dummypipelines-ASP.NET-CI/drop1/WebSiteSQLDatabase.parameters.json ...
	Override template parameters ⓘ
	-sqlserverName $(SQLServerName) -hostingPlanName $(AppServiceName) ...
	Deployment mode * ⓘ
	Incremental ⌄

Deploy Azure App Service	Azure App Service Deploy ⓘ ✕ Remove
	▷ Version 3.* ⌄
	Display name *
	Deploy Azure App Service
	Azure subscription * ⓘ | Manage ↗
	myconnection ⌄ ↻
	ⓘ Scoped to subscription 'Visual Studio Enterprise'
	App type * ⓘ
	webApp ⌄
	App Service name * ⓘ
	$(AppServiceName) ⌄ ↻
	☐ Deploy to slot ⓘ
	Virtual application ⓘ
	Package or folder * ⓘ
	$(System.DefaultWorkingDirectory)/_dummypipelines-ASP.NET-CI/drop/WebApplication38.zip ...
Azure SQL Publish	Azure SQL Database Deployment ⓘ ✕ Remove
	Version 1.* ⌄
	Display name *
	Azure SQL Publish
	Azure Service Connection Type
	Azure Resource Manager ⌄
	Azure Subscription * ⓘ | Manage ↗
	myconnection ⌄ ↻
	ⓘ Scoped to subscription 'Visual Studio Enterprise'
	SQL DB Details ⌃
	Azure SQL Server Name * ⓘ
	mdemoclasssql.database.windows.net
	Database Name * ⓘ
	myecommerce
	Server Admin Login * ⓘ
	citynextadmin
	Password * ⓘ
	citynext!1234
	Deployment Package ⌃
	Action * ⓘ
	Publish ⌄
	Type
	SQL DACPAC File ⌄
	DACPAC File * ⓘ
	$(System.DefaultWorkingDirectory)/_dummypipelines-ASP.NET-CI/drop2/Database1/bin/Debug/Database1.dacpac ...

DevOps for virtual machine (IaaS)-based solutions

The typical architecture for an IaaS virtual machine-based solution is shown here:

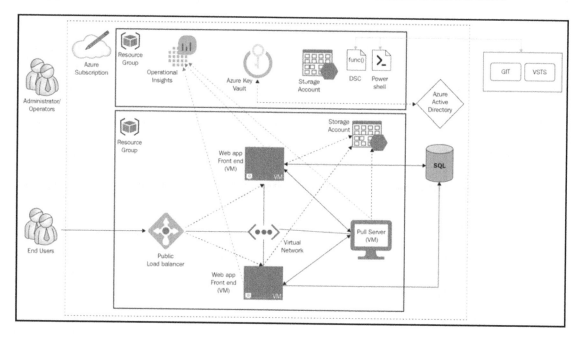

Azure Virtual Machines (VM)

Azure Virtual Machines that host web applications, application servers, database, and other services are provisioned using ARM templates. Each virtual machine has a single network card with a public IP assigned to it. They're attached to a virtual network and have a private IP address from the same network. The public IP for virtual machines is optional since they're attached to a public load balancer. These virtual machines are based on a Windows 2016 server image. Operational insight agents are installed on virtual machines to monitor the virtual machines. PowerShell scripts are also executed on these virtual machines, downloaded from a storage account available in another resource group to open relevant firewall ports, download appropriate packages, and install local certificates to secure access through PowerShell. The web application is configured to run on the provided port on these virtual machines. The port number for the web application and all its configuration is pulled from the DSC pull server and dynamically assigned.

Azure public load balancers

A public load balancer is attached to some of the virtual machines for sending requests to them in a round-robin fashion. This is generally needed for frontend web applications and APIs. A public IP address and DNS name can be assigned to a load balancer such that it can serve internet requests. It accepts HTTP web requests on different port, and routes them to the virtual machines. It also probes certain ports on HTTP protocols with some provided application paths. **Network Address Translation (NAT)** rules can also be applied such that they can be used to log into the virtual machines using remote desktops.

An alternative resource to the Azure public load balancer is the Azure application gateway. Application gateways are layer-7 load balancers and provide features such as SSL termination, session affinity, and URL-based routing.

The build pipeline

A typical build pipeline for an IaaS virtual machine-based solution is shown next. A release pipeline starts when a developer pushes their code to the repository. The build pipeline starts automatically as part of continuous integration. It compiles and builds the code, executes unit tests on it, checks code quality and generates documentation from code comments. It deploys the new binaries into the development environment (note that development environment is not newly created), changes configuration, executes integration tests, and generates build labels for easy identification. It then drops the generated artifacts into a location accessible by the release pipeline. In case there are issues during the execution of any step in this pipeline, this is communicated to the developer as part of the build pipeline feedback so that they can re-work and resubmit their changes. The build pipeline should fail or pass based on the severity of issues found, and that varies from organization to organization. A typical build pipeline is shown in the following diagram:

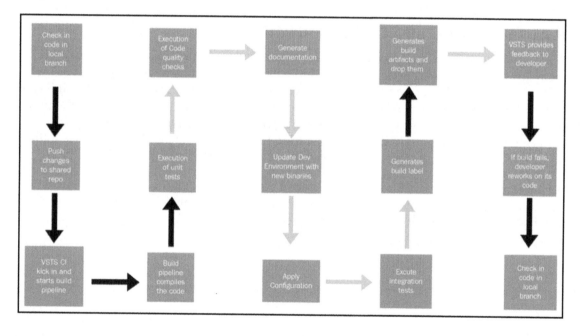

The release pipeline

A typical release pipeline for an IaaS virtual machine-based deployment is shown next. A release pipeline starts after the completion of the build pipeline. The first step for the release pipeline is to gather the artifacts generated by the build pipeline. They are generally deployable assemblies, binaries, and configuration documents. The release pipeline executes and creates or updates the first environment, which generally is a test environment. It uses ARM templates to provision all IaaS and PaaS services and resources on Azure, and configures them as well. They also help in executing scripts and DSC configuration after virtual machines are created as post-creation steps. This helps to configure the environment within the virtual machine and the operating system. At this stage, application binaries from the build pipeline are deployed and configured. Different automated tests are performed to check the solution and, if found satisfactory, the pipeline moves deployment to the next environment after obtaining the necessary approvals. The same steps are executed on the next environment, including the production environment. Finally, the operational validation tests are executed on production to ensure that the application is working as expected and there are no deviations.

At this stage, if there are any issues or bugs, they should be rectified and the entire cycle should be repeated; however, if this doesn't happen within a stipulated time frame, the last-known snapshot should be restored on the production environment to minimize downtime. A typical release pipeline is shown in the following diagram:

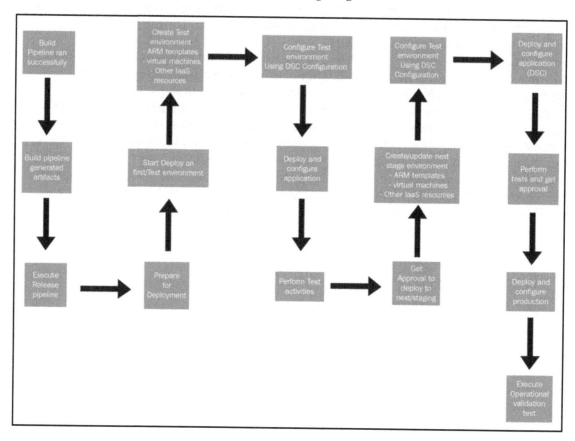

DevOps for container-based (IaaS) solutions

The typical architecture for IaaS container-based solutions is shown here:

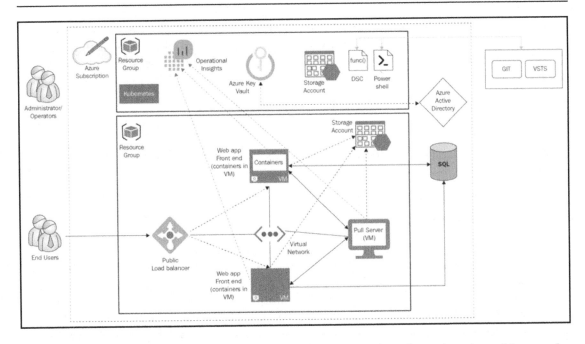

In the architecture shown before, container runtime are deployed on virtual machines and containers are run within them. These containers are managed by container orchestrators like Kubernetes. Monitoring services are provided by Log Analytics and all secrets and keys are stored in Azure Key Vault. There is also a pull server that could be on a virtual machines or Azure Automation providing configuration information to the virtual machines.

Containers

Containers are a virtualization technology; however, they don't virtualize physical servers. Instead, containers are an operating-system-level virtualization. This means that containers share the operating system kernel provided by their host among themselves and with the host. Running multiple containers on a host (physical or virtual) shares the host operating system kernel. There's a single operating-system kernel provided by the host and used by all containers running on top of it.

Containers are also completely isolated from their host and other containers, much like a virtual machine. Containers uses Windows storage filter drivers and session isolation to isolate operating system services, such as filesystems, registry, processes, and networks. Each container gets its own copy of the operating system resources.

Docker

Docker provides management features to Windows containers. It comprises two executables:

- Docker daemon
- Docker client

Docker daemon is the workhorse for managing containers. It's a Windows service responsible for managing all activities on the host related to containers. Docker client interacts with Docker daemon and is responsible for capturing input and sending them to Docker daemon. Docker daemon provides the runtime, libraries, graph drivers, engines to create, manage and monitor containers, and images on the host server. It also provides capabilities to create custom images that are used for building and shipping applications to multiple environments.

Dockerfile

Dockerfile is the primary building block for creating Windows container images. It's a simple text-based human-readable file without an extension and is named Dockerfile. Although there's a mechanism to name it differently, generally it's named Dockerfile. Dockerfile contains instructions to create a custom container image from a base image. These instructions are executed sequentially from top to bottom by the Docker daemon, the engine behind all activities related to Windows containers. The instructions refer to the command and their parameters as understood by Docker daemon. Dockerfile enables Infrastructure as Code practices by converting the application deployment and configuration into instructions that can be versioned and stored in a source-code repository.

The build pipeline

There's no difference, from the build perspective, between the container and a virtual-machine-based solution. The build step remains the same. Please refer to the earlier section, *DevOps for virtual machine (IaaS) based solutions*, for build pipeline details.

The release pipeline

A typical release pipeline for an IaaS container-based deployment is shown next. The only difference between this and the release pipeline is the container-image management and the creation of containers using Dockerfile and Docker Compose. Advanced container-management utilities, such as Docker Swarm, DC/OS, and Kubernetes, can also be deployed and configured as part of the release management. However, note that these container management tools should be part of the shared services release pipeline, as discussed earlier. The following diagram shows a typical release pipeline for a container based solution:

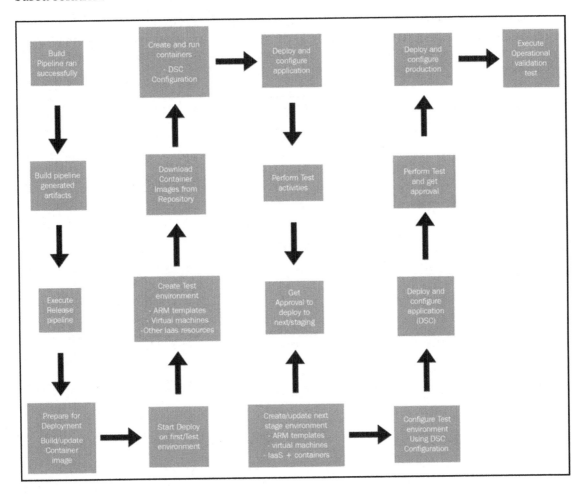

Azure DevOps and Jenkins

Azure DevOps is an open platform orchestrator that integrates with other orchestrator tools seamlessly. It provides all the necessary infrastructure and features that integrate well with Jenkins, as well. Organizations with well-established CI/CD pipelines built on Jenkins can reuse them with the advanced but simple features of Azure DevOps to orchestrate them.

Jenkins can be used as a repository and can execute CI/CD pipelines in Azure DevOps, while it's also possible to have a repo in Azure DevOps and execute CI/CD pipelines in Jenkins.

The Jenkins configuration can be added in Azure DevOps as service hooks, and whenever any code change is committed to the Azure DevOps repository, it can trigger pipelines in Jenkins. The next screenshot shows configuration of Jenkins from the Azure DevOps service hook configuration section:

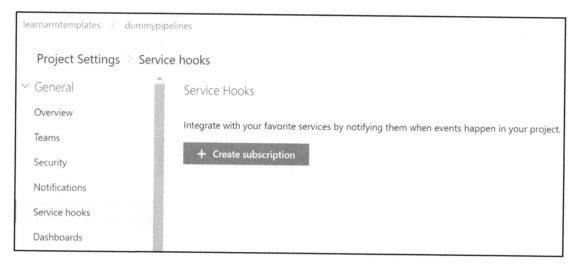

There are multiple triggers that execute the pipelines in Jenkins; one of them is **Code pushed**, as shown in the following screenshot:

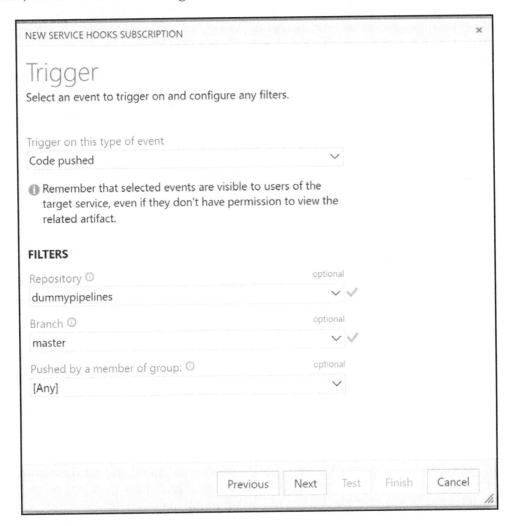

It's also possible to deploy to Azure VM and execute Azure DevOps release pipelines, as depicted here: `https://docs.microsoft.com/en-us/azure/virtual-machines/linux/tutorial-build-deploy-jenkins`.

Jenkins should already be deployed before using it in any scenario. The deployment process on Linux can be found at `https://docs.microsoft.com/en-us/azure/virtual-machines/linux/tutorial-jenkins-github-docker-cicd`.

Azure Automation

Azure Automation is Microsoft's platform for all automation implementation with regard to cloud, on-premise, and hybrid deployments. Azure Automation is a mature automation platform that provides rich capabilities in terms of the following:

- Defining assets, such as variables, connections, credentials, certificates, and modules
- Implementing runbooks using Python, PowerShell scripts, and PowerShell workflows
- Providing user interfaces to create runbooks
- Managing the full runbook life cycle, including building, testing, and publishing
- Scheduling runbooks
- The ability to run runbooks anywhere—on cloud or on-premise
- DSC as a configuration-management platform
- Managing and configuring environments—Windows and Linux, applications, and deployment
- The ability to extend Azure Automation by importing custom modules

Azure Automation provides a DSC pull server that helps to create a centralized configuration-management server that consists of configurations for nodes/virtual machines and their constituents.

It implements the hub and spoke pattern wherein nodes can connect to the DSC pull server and download configurations assigned to them, and reconfigure themselves to reflect their desired state. Any changes or deviations within these nodes are auto-corrected by DSC agents the next time they run. This ensures that administrators don't need to actively monitor the environment to find any deviations.

DSC provides a declarative language in which you define the intent and configuration, but not how to run and apply those configurations. These configurations are based on the PowerShell language and ease the process of configuration management.

In this section, we'll look into a simple implementation of using Azure Automation DSC to configure a virtual machine to install and configure the web server (IIS) and create an index.htm file that informs users that the website is under maintenance.

Provisioning the Azure Automation account

Create a new Azure Automation account from the Azure portal or PowerShell within an existing or new resource group. Astute readers will find in the following diagram that Azure Automation provides menu items for DSC. It provides the following:

- **DSC nodes**: It lists all the virtual machines and containers that are enlisted with the current Azure Automation DSC pull server. These virtual machines and containers are managed using configurations from the current DSC pull server.
- **DSC configurations**: It lists all the raw PowerShell configurations imported and uploaded to the DSC pull server. They are in human-readable format and aren't in a compiled state.
- **DSC node configurations**: It lists all compiles of DSC configurations available on the pull server to be assigned to nodes—virtual machines and containers. A DSC configuration produces MOF files after compilations and they're eventually used to configure nodes. The next screenshot shows an Azure Automation account after getting provisioned:

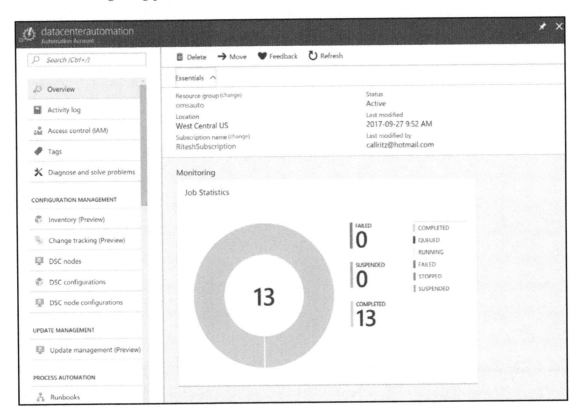

Creating DSC configuration

The next step is to write a DSC configuration using any PowerShell editor to reflect the intent of the configuration. For this sample, a single configuration, ConfigureSiteOnIIS, is created. It imports the base DSC module, PSDesiredStateConfiguration, which consists of resources used within the configuration. It also declares a node web server. When this configuration is uploaded and compiled, it will generate a DSCConfigurationNodes named ConfigureSiteOnIISwebserver. This configuration can then be applied to nodes.

The configuration consists of a few resources. These resources configure the target node. The resources install a web server, ASP.NET, and framework, and create an index.htm file within the inetpub\wwwroot directory with content to show that the site is under maintenance. For more information about writing DSC configuration, refer to https://docs.microsoft.com/en-us/PowerShell/dsc/configurations.

```
Configuration ConfigureSiteOnIIS {
    Import-DscResource -ModuleName 'PSDesiredStateConfiguration'
    Node WebServer {
      WindowsFeature IIS
        {
            Name = "Web-Server"
            Ensure = "Present"
        }
      WindowsFeature AspDotNet
        {
            Name = "net-framework-45-Core"
            Ensure = "Present"
            DependsOn = "[WindowsFeature]IIS"
        }
      WindowsFeature AspNet45
        {
            Ensure       = "Present"
            Name         = "Web-Asp-Net45"
            DependsOn = "[WindowsFeature]AspDotNet"
        }
      File IndexFile
        {
            DestinationPath = "C:\inetpub\wwwroot\index.htm"
            Ensure = "Present"
            Type = "File"
            Force = $true
            Contents = "<HTML><HEAD><Title> Website under
construction.</Title></HEAD><BODY> `
            <h1>If you are seeing this page, it means the website is under
maintenance and DSC Rocks !!!!!</h1></BODY></HTML>"
```

```
            }
        }
    }
```

Importing the DSC configuration

The DSC configuration still isn't known to Azure Automation. It's available on some local machines. It should be uploaded to Azure Automation DSC Configurations. Azure Automation provides the `Import-AzureRMAutomationDscConfiguration` cmdlet to import the configuration to Azure Automation:

```
Import-AzureRmAutomationDscConfiguration -SourcePath
"C:\DSC\AA\DSCfiles\ConfigureSiteOnIIS.ps1" -ResourceGroupName "omsauto" -
AutomationAccountName "datacenterautomation" -Published -Verbose
```

The DSC configuration on Azure after applying the configuration to the node should appear as follows:

Compiling the DSC configuration

After the DSC configuration is available in Azure Automation, it can be asked to compile. Azure Automation provides another cmdlet for this. Use the `Start-AzureRmAutomationDscCompilationJob` cmdlet to compile the imported configuration. The configuration name should match the name of the uploaded configuration. Compilation creates an MOF file named after the configuration and node name together, which in this case is the `ConfigureSiteOnIIS` web server. The execution of command is shown here:

```
Start-AzureRmAutomationDscCompilationJob -ConfigurationName
ConfigureSiteOnIIS -ResourceGroupName "omsauto" -AutomationAccountName
"datacenterautomation" -Verbose
```

The DSC node's configuration on Azure after applying the configuration should appear as follows:

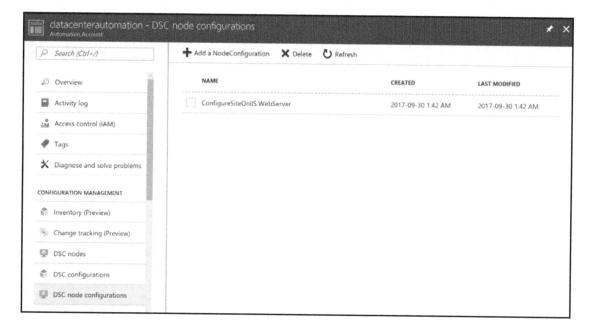

Assigning configurations to nodes

The compiled DSC configurations can be applied to nodes. Use `Register-AzureRmAutomationDscNode` to assign the configuration to a node. The `NodeConfigurationName` parameter identifies the configuration name that should be applied to the node. This is a powerful cmdlet that can also configure the DSC agent, that is `localconfigurationmanager`, on nodes before they can download configurations and apply them. There are multiple `localconfigurationmanager` parameters that can be configured—details are available at `https://docs.microsoft.com/en-us/PowerShell/dsc/metaconfig`.

```
Register-AzureRmAutomationDscNode -ResourceGroupName "omsauto" -
AutomationAccountName "datacenterautomation" -AzureVMName testtwo -
ConfigurationMode ApplyAndAutocorrect -ActionAfterReboot
ContinueConfiguration -AllowModuleOverwrite $true -AzureVMResourceGroup
testone -AzureVMLocation "West Central US" -NodeConfigurationName
"ConfigureSiteOnIIS.WebServer" -Verbose
```

After applying the configuration, the DSC nodes on Azure should appear as follows:

Browsing the server

If appropriate, Network security groups and firewalls are opened and enabled for port 80, and a public IP is assigned to the virtual machine; the default website can be browsed using the IP address. Otherwise, log into the virtual machine that's used to apply the DSC configuration and navigate to `http://localhost`.

It should show the following page:

This is the power of configuration management: without writing any significant code, authoring a configuration once can be applied multiple times to the same and multiple servers, and you can be assured that they will be running in the desired state without any manual intervention.

Azure for DevOps

As mentioned before, Azure is a rich and mature platform that provides the following:

- Multiple choices of languages
- Multiple choices of operating systems
- Multiple choices of tools and utilities
- Multiple patterns for deploying solutions (virtual machines, app services, containers, micro-services)

With so many options and choices, Azure offers the following:

- **Open cloud**: It is open for open source, Microsoft, and non-Microsoft products, tools, and services.
- **Flexible cloud**: It is easy enough for both business users and developers to use it with their existing skills and knowledge.
- **Unified management**: It provides seamless monitoring and management features.

All the features mentioned here are important for the successful implementation of DevOps. The next diagram shows the open source tools and utilities that can be used for different phases in managing the application life cycle and DevOps in general. This is just a small representation of all the tools and utilities – there are many more options available, as follows:

- The Jenkins, Hudson, Grunt, and Gradle tools for constructing the build pipeline
- Selenium for testing
- Chef, Puppet, Jenkins, Hudson, Grunt, and Gradle for deployment or configuration management
- Nagios for alerting and Monitoring
- Jira and Redmine for managing processes

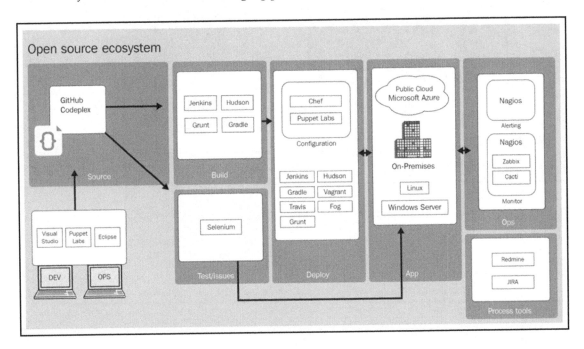

The following diagram shows the Microsoft tools and utilities that can be used for different phases in managing the application life cycle and DevOps in general. Again, this is just a small representation of all the tools and utilities – there are many more options available, such as the following:

- Azure DevOps build orchestration for constructing a build pipeline
- Microsoft Test Manager and Pester for testing
- Desired State Configuration, PowerShell, and ARM templates for deployment or configuration management
- Log Analytics, Application Insights, and **System Center Operations Manager (SCOM)** for alerting and monitoring
- Azure DevOps and System Center Service Manager for managing processes

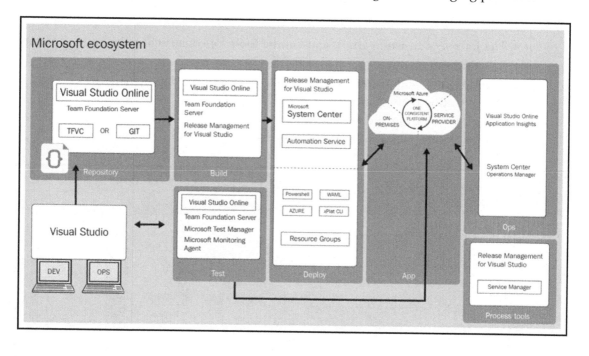

Summary

DevOps is gaining a lot of traction and momentum in the industry. Most organizations have realized its benefits and are looking to implement DevOps. This is happening while most of them are moving to the cloud. Azure, as a cloud model, provides rich and mature DevOps services, making it easy for organizations to implement DevOps. In this chapter, we discussed DevOps along with its core practices, such as configuration management, continuous integration, continuous delivery, and deployment. We also discussed different cloud solutions based on PaaS, a virtual machine IaaS, and a container IaaS, along with their respective Azure resources, the build and release pipelines. Configuration management was the core part of this chapter, and we discussed DSC services from Azure Automation and using pull servers to configure virtual machines automatically. Finally, we covered Azure's openness and flexibility regarding the choice of languages, tools, and operating systems.

12
Azure OLTP Solutions Using Azure SQL Sharding, Pools, and Hybrid

Azure provides both **Infrastructure as a Service (IaaS)** and **Platform as a Service (PaaS)** services. Both these types of services provide organizations with different levels and controls over storage, compute, and networks. Storage is the resource used when working with the storing and transmission of data. Azure provides lots of options for storing data, such as Azure storage blobs, tables, Cosmos DB, Azure SQL, Azure Data Lake, and more. While some of them are meant for big data storage, analytics, and presentation, there are others that are meant for applications that process transactions. Azure SQL is the primary resource in Azure that works with transaction data.

This chapter will focus on various aspects of using transaction data stores, such as Azure SQL and other open source databases, typically used in **Online Transaction Processing (OLTP)** systems, and will cover the following topics:

- OLTP applications
- Relational databases
- Deployment models
- Azure SQL Database
- Elastic pools
- Managed instances
- SQL database pricing

Azure cloud services

A search for `sql` in the Azure portal provides multiple results. I have marked some of them to show the resources that can be used directly for OLTP applications:

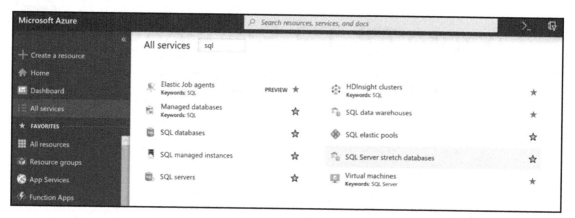

The previous screenshot shows the varied features and options available for creating SQL Server-based databases on Azure.

Again, a quick search for `database` on the Azure portal provides multiple resources, and the marked ones can be used for OLTP applications:

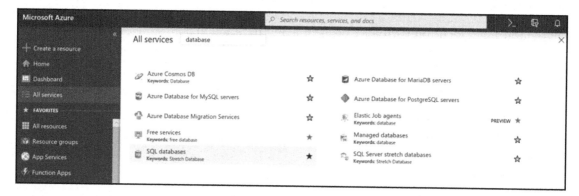

The previous screenshot shows resources provided by Azure that can host data in a variety of databases, including the following:

- MySQL databases
- MariaDB databases

- PostgreSQL databases
- Cosmos DB

OLTP applications

OLTP applications are applications that help in the processing and management of transactions. These applications perform data capture, data processing, retrieval, modification, and storage. However, it does not stop here. OLTP applications treat these data tasks as transactions. Transactions have a few important properties and OLTP applications adhere to these properties. These properties are grouped under the acronym **ACID**. Let's discuss these properties:

- **Atomicity**: This property states that a transaction must consist of statements and either all statements should complete successfully or no statement should be executed. If multiple statements are grouped together, these statements together form the transaction. Atomicity means each transaction is treated as the lowest single unit of execution that either completes successfully or fails.
- **Consistency**: This property focuses on the state of data in a database. It dictates that any change in state should be complete and based on the rules and constraints of the database, and that partial updates should not be allowed.
- **Isolation**: This property states that there can be multiple concurrent transactions executed on the system and each transaction should be treated in isolation. One transaction should not know about or interfere with any other transaction. If the transactions were to be executed in sequence, by the end, the state of data should be the same as before.
- **Durability**: This property states that the data should be persisted and available, even after failure, once it is committed to the database. A committed transaction becomes a fact.

Relational databases

OLTP applications have generally been relying on relational databases for their transaction management and processing. Relational databases typically come in a tabular format consisting of rows and columns. The data model is converted into multiple tables where each table is connected to another table (based on rules) using relationships. This process is also known as normalization.

As mentioned before, Azure provides multiple relational databases, such as SQL Server, MySQL, and PostgreSQL.

Deployment models

There are two deployment models for deploying databases on Azure:

- Databases on Azure virtual machines (IaaS)
- Databases hosted as managed services (PaaS)

Databases on Azure virtual machines

Azure provides multiple SKUs for virtual machines. There are high-compute, high-throughput (IOPS) machines that are also available along with general-usage virtual machines. Instead of hosting a SQL Server, MySQL or any other database on on-premises servers, it is possible to deploy these databases on these virtual machines. The deployment and configuration of these databases is no different than that done for on-premises deployments. The only difference is that the database is hosted on the cloud instead of on on-premises servers. Administrators must perform the same activities and steps that they normally would for on-premises deployment. Although this option is great when customers want full control over their deployment, there are models that can be more cost effective, scalable, and highly available compared to this option.

The steps to deploy any database on Azure virtual machines are as follows:

1. Create a virtual machine with a size that caters to the performance requirements of the application
2. Deploy database on top of it
3. Configure the virtual machine and database configuration

This option does not provide any out-of-the-box high availability unless multiple servers are provisioned, and SQL Server is configured with an **AlwaysOn** configuration. It also does not provide any features for automatic scaling unless custom automation supports it.

Disaster recovery is also the responsibility of the customer, and they should deploy servers on multiple regions connected using global peering or network VPN gateways. It is possible for these virtual machines to be connected to an on-premises data center through site-to-site VPNs or ExpressRoute without having any exposure to the outside world.

These databases are also known as **unmanaged databases**.

Databases hosted as managed services

Databases hosted with Azure other than virtual machines are managed by Azure and are known as **managed services**. Managed services means that Azure provides management services for the databases. These managed services include the hosting of the database, ensuring that the host is highly available, ensuring that the data is replicated internally for availability during disaster recovery, ensuring scalability within the constraint of a chosen SKU, monitoring the hosts and databases and generating alerts for notifications or executing actions, providing log and auditing services for troubleshooting, and taking care of performance management and security alerts.

In short, there are a lot of services that customers get out of the box when using managed services from Azure, and they do not need to perform active management on these databases. In this chapter, we will look at Azure SQL in depth and provide information on other databases such as Cosmos DB, MySQL, and Postgre.

Azure SQL Database

Azure SQL provides a relational database hosted as a PaaS. Customers can provision this service, bring their own database schema and data, and connect their applications to it. It provides all the features of SQL Server that you get when deploying on a virtual machine. These services do not provide a user interface to create tables and its schema, nor do they provide any querying capabilities directly. You should be using SQL Server Management Studio and the SQL CLI tools to connect to these services and directly work with them.

Azure SQL Database comes with three distinct deployment models:

- **Single instance**: In this deployment model, a single database is deployed on a logical server. This involves the creation of two resources on Azure:
  - SQL logical server
  - SQL database
- **Elastic pool**: In this deployment mode, multiple databases are deployed on a logical server. Again, this involves the creation of two resources on Azure:
  - SQL logical server
  - SQL elastic database pool – this consists of all the databases

- **Managed instance**: This is a relatively new deployment model from the Azure SQL team. This deployment reflects a collection of databases on a logical server providing complete control over the resources in terms of system databases. Generally, system databases are not visible in other deployment models, but they are available in the model. This model comes very close to the deployment of SQL Server on premises:

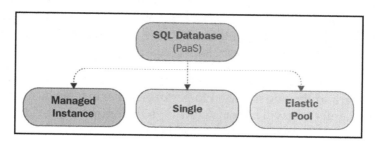

Application features

Azure SQL provides multiple application-specific features that cater to the different requirements of OLTP systems:

- **Columnar store**: This feature allows the storage of data in a columnar format rather than in a row format.
- **In-memory OLTP**: Generally, the data is stored in backend files in SQL and data is pulled from them whenever it is needed by the application. Contrary to this, in-memory OLTP puts all data in memory and there is no latency in reading the storage for data. Storing in-memory OLTP data on SSD provides the best possible performance for Azure SQL.
- All features of on-premises SQL Server.

Single instance

Single-instance databases are hosted as a single database on a single logical server. These databases do not have access to the complete features provided by SQL Server.

High availability

Azure SQL, by default, is 99.99% highly available. It has two different architectures for maintaining high availability based on the SKUs. For the Basic, Standard, and General SKUs, the entire architecture is broken down into the following two layers. There is redundancy built in for both of these layers to provide high availability:

- Compute layer
- Storage layer:

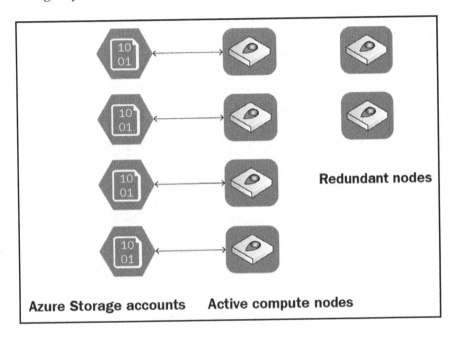

For the Premium and business-critical SKUs, both compute and storage are on the same layer. High availability is achieved by replication of compute and storage deployed in a four-node cluster, using technology similar to SQL Server AlwaysOn Availability Groups:

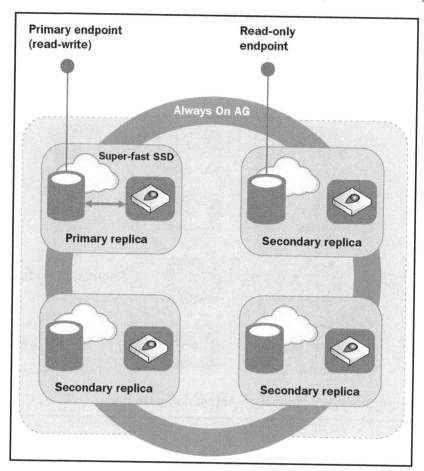

Backups

Azure SQL also provides features to automatically back up databases and store them on storage accounts. This feature is important especially in cases where a database becomes corrupt or a user accidentally deletes a table. This feature is available at the server level, as shown in the following screenshot:

Architects should prepare a backup strategy such that backups can be used in times of need. They should not be very old nor should they be configured for very frequent backups. Based on business needs, a weekly backup or even a daily backup should be configured, or even more frequently than that, if required. These backups can be used for restoration purposes.

Geo-replication

Azure SQL also provides the benefit of being able to replicate the database to a different region, also known as a secondary region. The database at the secondary region can be read by applications. It allows for readable secondary databases. This is a great business continuity solution as the readable database is available at any point in time. With geo-replication, it is possible to have up to four secondaries of a database on different regions or the same region. These are readable databases. With geo-replication, it is also possible to failover to a secondary database in the case of a disaster. Geo-replication is configured at the database level, as shown in the following screenshot:

If you scroll down on this screen, the regions that can act as secondaries are listed, as shown in the following screenshot:

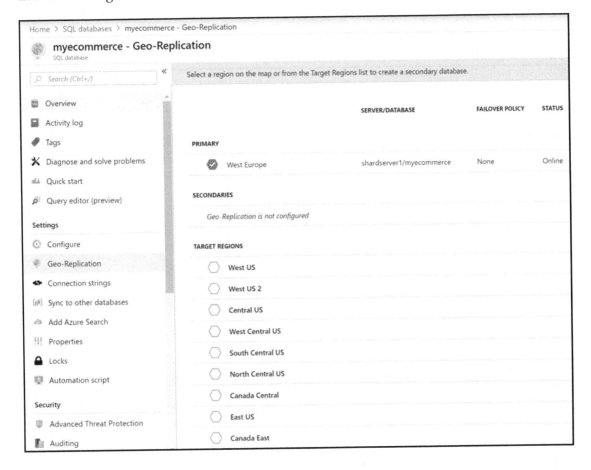

Scalability

Azure SQL provides vertical scalability by adding more resources (such as compute, memory, and IOPS). This can be done by increasing the number of DTUs provisioned for it. The single-instance SQL provides features for manual scaling only:

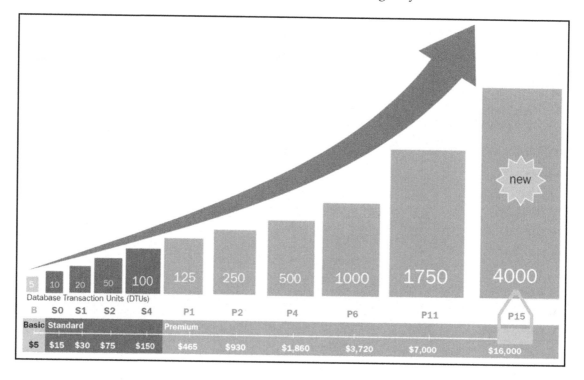

Security

Security is an important factor for any database solution and service. Azure SQL provides enterprise-grade security for Azure SQL, and this section will list some of the important security features in Azure SQL.

Firewall

Azure SQL, by default, does not provide access to any requests. Source IP addresses should be explicitly whitelisted for access to SQL Server. There is an option to allow all Azure-based services access to the SQL database as well. This option includes virtual machines hosted on Azure.

The firewall can be configured at the server level instead of the database level. The **Allow access to Azure services** option allows all services, including virtual machines, to access the database hosted on the logical server:

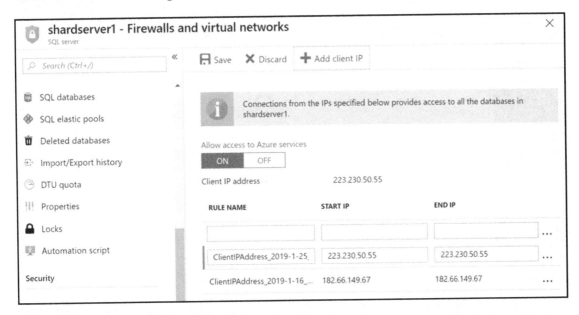

Azure SQL Server on dedicated networks

It is also possible to host the server on a pre-defined virtual network. This is a relatively new feature in Azure. This helps in accessing data within SQL Server from application on another server of the virtual network without the request going through the internet.

For this, a service endpoint of the `Microsoft.Sql` type should be added within the virtual network, and the virtual network should be in the same region as that of Azure SQL:

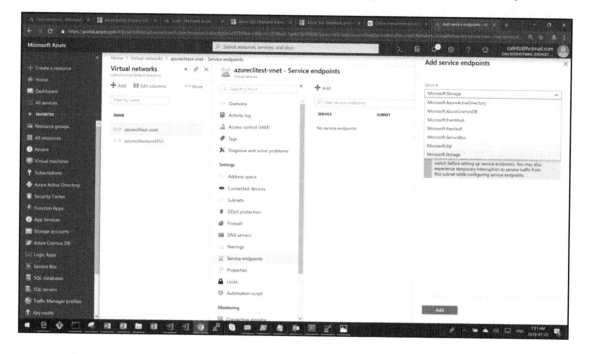

An appropriate subnet within the virtual networks should be chosen:

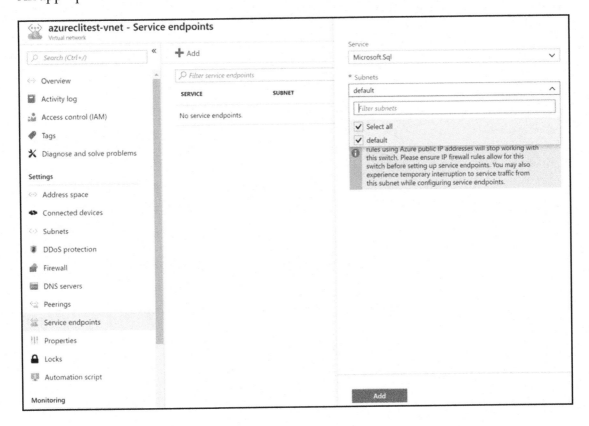

Finally, from the Azure SQL Server configuration blade, an existing virtual network should be added that has a **Microsoft.Sql** service endpoint enabled:

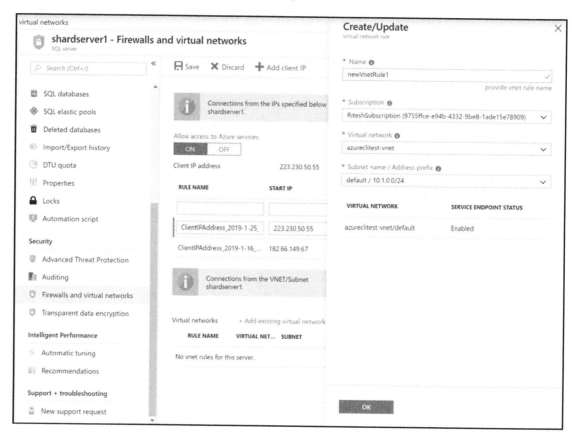

Encrypted databases at rest

The databases should be in an encrypted form when at rest. **Rest** here means the location the database is stored at. Although you might not have access to SQL Server and its database, someone might be trying to get access to the LDF and MDF files in which the data is stored. It is always advised to encrypt these files at rest.

Databases on the filesystem can be encrypted using keys. These keys must be stored in Azure Key Vault and the vault must be available in the same region as that of Azure SQL Server. The filesystem can be encrypted by using the **Transparent data encryption** menu item of the SQL Server configuration blade and selecting **Yes** for **Use your own key**. The key is an RSA 2048 key and must exist within the vault. SQL Server will decrypt the data at the page level when it wants to read it and send it to the caller, then it will encrypt it after writing to the database. This requires no changes to the applications and is completely transparent to them:

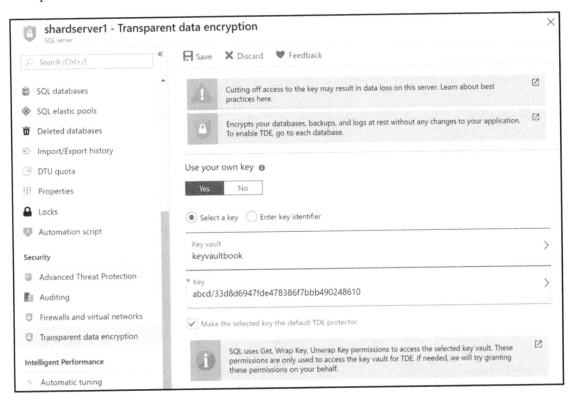

Dynamic Data Masking

SQL Server also provides the feature of masking individual columns that contain sensitive data such that no one apart from privileged users can view the actual data by querying it in SQL Server Management Studio. The data will remain masked and will only be unmasked when an authorized application or user queries the table. Architects should ensure that sensitive data such as credit card details, social security numbers, phone numbers, email addresses, and other financial details should be masked.

Azure Active Directory integration

Another important security feature of Azure SQL is that it can be integrated with Azure **Active Directory (AD)** for authentication purposes. Without integrating with Azure AD, the only authentication mechanism available to SQL Server is via username and password authentication; that is, SQL authentication. It is not possible to use integrated Windows authentication. The connection string for SQL authentication consists of both the username and password in plaintext, which is not secure. Integrating with Azure AD, enabled authenticating application with Windows authentication, service principal name or token based. It is a good practice to used Azure SQL integrated with Azure AD.

There are other security features such as advanced threat protection, auditing of the environment, and monitoring that should be enabled on any enterprise-level Azure SQL deployments:

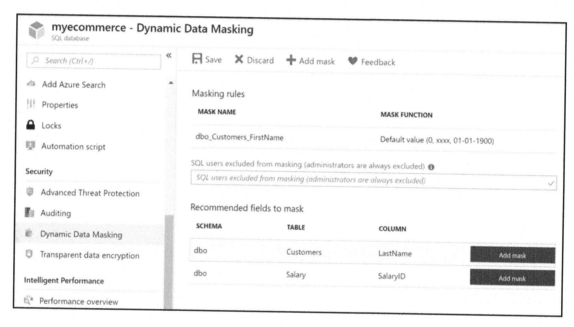

Elastic pools

An elastic pool is a logical container that can host multiple databases in a single logical server. The SKUs available for elastic pools are as follows:

- Basic
- Standard
- Premium

The following screenshot shows the maximum amount of DTUs that can be provisioned for each SKU:

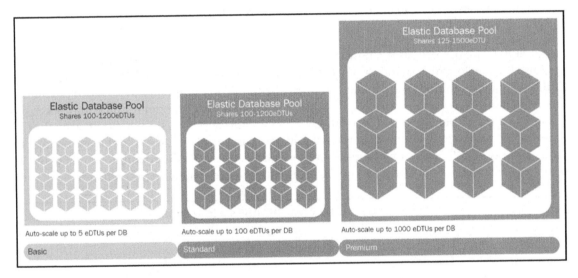

All the features discussed for Azure SQL single instances are available to elastic pools as well; however, horizontal scalability is an additional feature it provides with the help of shading. Shading refers to the vertical or horizontal partitioning of data and the storing of it into separate databases. It is also possible to have auto-scaling of individual databases in an elastic pool by consuming more DTUs than are actually allocated to that database.

Elastic pools also provide another advantage in terms of cost. We will see in a later section that Azure SQL is priced using the concept of DTUs, and DTUs are provisioned as soon as the SQL Server service is provisioned. DTUs are charged for irrespective of whether those DTUs are consumed. If there are multiple databases, then it is possible to put these databases into elastic pools and they can share the DTUs among them.

All information for implementing sharding with Azure SQL elastic pools has been provided at https://docs.microsoft.com/en-us/azure/sql-database/sql-database-elastic-scale-introduction.

Managed Instance

Managed Instance is a unique service that provides a managed SQL server similar to what's available on on-premises servers. Users have access to master, model, and other system databases. Use of Managed Instance is suitable when there are multiple databases and customers migrating their instances to Azure. Managed Instance consists of multiple databases.

Azure SQL Database provides a new deployment model known as Azure SQL Database Managed Instance that provides almost 100% compatibility with the SQL Server Enterprise Edition Database Engine. This model provides a native VNet implementation addressing the usual security issues and is a highly recommended business model for on-premises SQL Server customers. Managed Instance allows existing SQL Server customers to lift and shift their on-premises applications to the cloud with minimal application and database changes, while preserving all PaaS capabilities at the same time. These PaaS capabilities drastically reduce the management overhead and TCO, as shown in the following screenshot:

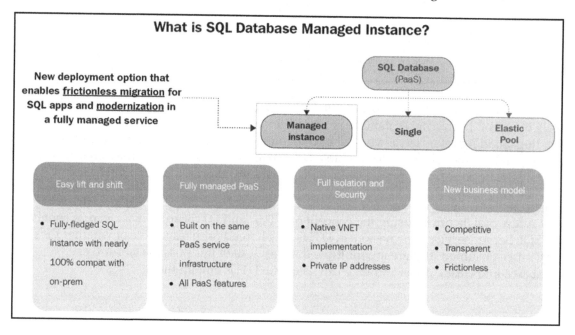

The key features of Managed Instance are shown in the following screenshot:

The key features of Managed Instance are shown in the following table:

Feature	Description
SQL Server version / build	SQL Server Database Engine (latest stable)
Managed automated backups	Yes
Built-in instance and database monitoring and metrics	Yes
Automatic software patching	Yes
The latest Database Engine features	Yes
Number of data files (ROWS) per the database	Multiple
Number of log files (LOG) per database	1
VNet - Azure Resource Manager deployment	Yes
VNet - Classic deployment model	No
Portal support	Yes
Built-in Integration Service (SSIS)	No - SSIS is a part of Azure Data Factory PaaS
Built-in Analysis Service (SSAS)	No - SSAS is separate PaaS
Built-in Reporting Service (SSRS)	No - use Power BI or SSRS IaaS

SQL database pricing

Azure SQL previously had just one pricing model – a model based on **Database Throughput Units (DTUs)** and a more recent alternative pricing model based on vCPUs have also been launched.

DTU-based pricing

The DTU is the smallest unit of performance measure for Azure SQL. Each DTU corresponds to a certain amount of resources. These resources include storage, CPU cycles, IOPS, and network bandwidth. For example, a single DTU might provide three IOPS, a few CPU cycles, and an IO latency of 5 ms for read operations and 10 ms for write operations.

Azure SQL provides multiple SKUs for creating databases, and each of these SKUs has defined constraints for the maximum amount of DTUs. For example, the Basic SKU provides just 5 DTUs with a maximum 2 GB of data, as shown in the following screenshot:

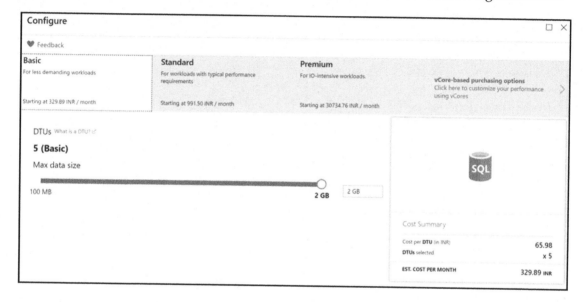

On the other hand, the standard SKU provides anything between 10 DTUs and 300 DTUs with a maximum of 250 GB of data. As you can see here, each DTU costs around 999 rupees or around $1.40:

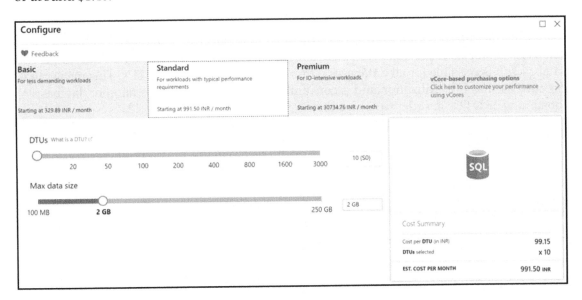

A comparison between these SKUs in terms of performance and resources is provided by Microsoft, as shown in the following screenshot:

	Basic	Standard	Premium
Target workload	Development and production	Development and production	Development and production
Uptime SLA	99.99%	99.99%	99.99%
Backup retention	7 days	35 days	35 days
CPU	Low	Low, Medium, High	Medium, High
IO throughput (approximate)	2.5 IOPS per DTU	2.5 IOPS per DTU	48 IOPS per DTU
IO latency (approximate)	5 ms (read), 10 ms (write)	5 ms (read), 10 ms (write)	2 ms (read/write)
Columnstore indexing	N/A	S3 and above	Supported
In-memory OLTP	N/A	N/A	Supported

Once you provision a certain number of DTUs, the backend resources (CPU, IOPS, and memory) are allocated and are charged for whether they are consumed or not. If more DTUs are procured than are actually needed, it leads to wastage, while there would be performance bottlenecks if not enough DTUs are provisioned.

Azure provides elastic pools for this purpose as well. As we know, there are multiple databases in an elastic pool and DTUs are assigned to elastic pools instead of individual databases. It is possible for all databases within the pool to share the DTUs. This means that if a database has low utilization and is consuming 5 DTUs, there will be another database consuming 25 DTUs in order to compensate.

It is important to note that, collectively, DTU consumption cannot exceed the amount of DTUs provisioned for the elastic pool. Moreover, there is a minimum amount of DTUs that should be assigned to each database within the elastic pool, and this minimum DTU count is pre-allocated for the database.

An elastic pool comes with its own SKUs:

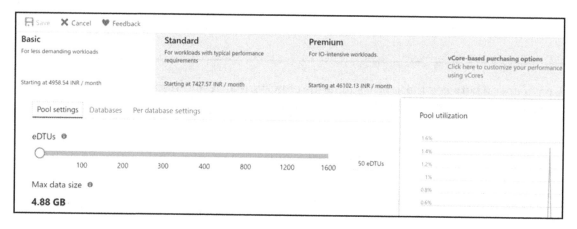

Also, there is a limitation on the maximum amount of databases that can be created within a single elastic pool.

vCPU based pricing

This is the new pricing model for Azure SQL. In this pricing model, instead of identifying the amount of DTUs required for an application, it provides options to procure the number of **virtual CPUs (vCPUs)** allocated for the server. A vCPU is a logical CPU with attached hardware such as storage, memory, and CPU cores.

In this model, there are three SKUs, General Purpose, Hyperscale, and Business Critical, with a varied number of vCPUs and resources available. This pricing is available for all SQL deployment models:

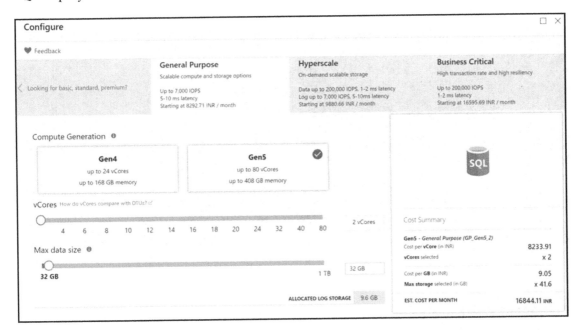

How to choose the appropriate pricing model

Architects should be able to choose an appropriate pricing model for Azure SQL. DTUs are a great mechanism for pricing where there is a usage pattern applicable and available for the database. Since resource availability in the DTU scheme of things is linear, as shown in the next diagram, it is quite possible for the usage to be more memory intensive than CPU intensive. In such cases, it is possible to choose different levels of CPU, memory, and storage for a database. In DTUs, resources come packaged, and it is not possible to configure these resources at a granular level. With a vCPU model, it is possible to choose different levels of memory and CPU for different databases. If the usage pattern for an application is known, using the vCPU pricing model could be a better option compared to the DTU model. In fact, the vCPU model also provides the benefit of hybrid licenses if an organization already has on-premises SQL Server licenses. There is a discount of up to 30% provided to these SQL Server instances.

In the following screenshot, you can see from the left-hand graph that as the amount of DTUs increases, resource availability also grows linearly; however, with vCPU pricing (in the right-hand graph), it is possible to choose independent configurations for each database:

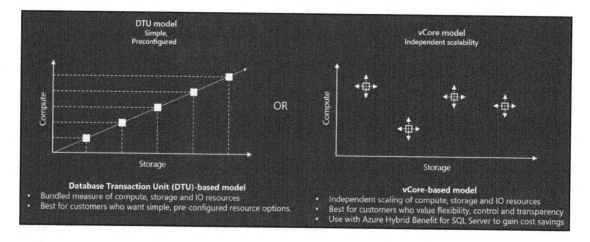

Summary

Azure SQL is one the flagship services of Azure. Millions of customers are using this service today and it provides all the enterprise capabilities that are needed for a mission-critical database management system. There are multiple deployment types for Azure SQL, such as single instance, Managed Instance, and elastic pools. Architects should do a complete assessment of their requirements and choose the appropriate deployment model. After they choose a deployment model, they should choose a pricing strategy between DTUs and vCPUs. They should also configure all the security, availability, disaster recovery, monitoring, performance, and scalability requirements in Azure SQL with regard to data.

13

Azure Big Data Solutions Using Azure Data Lake Storage and Data Factory

Big data has gaining significant traction in last few years. Specialized tools, software and storage are required to handle them. These tools, platforms and storage were not available as a service few years back. However, with new cloud technology, Azure is providing numerous tools, platform and resources to create big data solution easily.

The following topics will be covered in this chapter:

- Data integration
- **Extract-Transform-Load** (ETL)
- Data Factory
- Data Lake Storage
- Migrating data from Azure Storage to Data Lake Storage

Data integration

We are all well aware of how integration patterns are used for applications: applications composed of multiple services are integrated together using a variety of patterns. However, there is another paradigm that is a requirement for many organizations, known as data integration. This has happened especially during the last decade, when the generation and availability of data has been incredibly high. The velocity, variety, and volume of data being generated has increased drastically, and there is data almost everywhere.

Every organization has many different types of applications, and they all generate data in their own proprietary format. Often, data is also purchased from the marketplace. Even during mergers and amalgamations of organizations, data needs to be migrated and combined.

Data integration refers to the process of bringing data from multiple sources and generating new output that has more meaning and usability.

There is a need for data integration in the following scenarios:

- For migrating data from a source or group of sources to target destinations. There are a variety of reasons for doing so.
- With the rapid availability of data, organizations want insights and to create data warehouses. To build these data warehouses, data should be in a format that is consumable by data warehousing tools.
- For generating real-time dashboards and reports.
- For creating analytics solutions.

Application integration has a runtime behavior when users are consuming the application; for example, in the case of credit card validation and integration. On the other hand, data integration happens as a backend exercise and is not directly linked to user activity.

ETL

A very popular process known as ETL helps in building a target data source to house data that is consumable by applications. Generally, the data is in a raw format, and to make it consumable, the data should go through the following three distinct phases:

- **Extract**: During this phase, data is extracted from multiple places. There could be multiple sources and they all need to be connected to in order to retrieve the data. Extract phases typically use data connectors consisting of connection information related to the target data source. They might also have temporary storage to bring the data from the data source and store it for faster retrieval. This phase is responsible for the ingestion of data.
- **Transform**: The data that is available after the extract phase might not be consumable directly by applications. This could be for a variety of reasons. The data might have irregularities, or there might be missing data or erroneous data. There might be data that is not needed at all.

The format of the data might not be conducive for consumption by target applications. In all such cases, transformation has to be applied to the data such that it can be consumed by applications.

- **Load**: After transformation, data should be loaded to the target data source in a format and schema that enables faster, easier, and performance-centric availability to applications. This again typically consists of data connectors for destination data sources and loading data into them.

A primer on Data Factory

Data Factory is a fully managed, highly available, highly scalable, and easy-to-use tool for creating integration solutions and implementing ETL phases. Data Factory helps create new pipelines in a drag and drop fashion using a user interface without writing any code; however, it still provides features to write code in your preferred language.

There are a few important concepts to learn about before using the Data Factory service, which we will be looking into in the following sections:

- **Activities**: Activities are individual tasks that enable the execution and processing of logic within a Data Factory pipeline. There are multiple types of activities. There are activities related to data movement, data transformation, and control activities. Each activity has a policy through which it can decide the retry mechanism and retry interval.
- **Pipelines**: Pipelines in Data Factory are composed of groups of activities and are responsible for bringing activities together. Pipelines are the workflows and orchestrators that enable the execution of the ETL phases. Pipelines allow the weaving together of activities and allow the declaration of dependencies between them. Using dependencies, it is possible to execute some tasks in parallel and other tasks in sequence.
- **Datasets**: Datasets are the sources and destinations of data. These could be Azure Storage accounts, Data Lake Storage, or a host of other sources.
- **Linked services**: These are services that contain the connection and connectivity information for datasets and are utilized by individual tasks for connecting to them. They are similar to connection strings, which you might have been using to connect to data stores with an additional responsibility of connecting to those data stores.

- **Integration runtime**: The main engine that is responsible for the execution of Data Factory is called the integration runtime. The integration runtime is available on the following three configurations:
    - **Azure:** In this configuration, the data factory executes on compute resources provided by Azure.
    - **Self-hosted**: The data factory in this configuration executes on bringing your own compute resources. This could be on-premises or cloud-based virtual machine servers.
    - **Azure SQL Server Integration Services (SSIS)**: This configuration allows for the execution of traditional SSIS packages written using SQL Server.
- **Versions:** Data Factory comes with two different versions. It is important to understand that all new developments will happen on V2, and that V1 will stay as is or fade out at some point. V2 is preferred because of the following reasons:
    - It provides the capability to execute SQL Server integration packages.
    - It has enhanced functionalities compared to V1.
    - It comes with enhanced monitoring, which is missing in V1.

A primer on Data Lake Storage

Azure Data Lake Storage provides storage for big data solutions. It is especially designed for storing the large amounts of data that are typically needed in big data solutions. It is an Azure-provided managed service and is therefore completely managed by Azure. Customers need only bring their data and store it in a Data Lake.

There are two versions: version 1 (Gen1) and the current version, version 2 (Gen2). Gen2 has all the functionality of Gen1, with the difference that it is built on top of Azure Blob Storage.

As Azure Blob Storage is highly available, can be replicated multiple times, is disaster ready, and is low in cost, these benefits are transferred to Gen2 Data Lake. Data Lake can store any kind of data, including relational, non-relational, filesystem-based, and hierarchical data.

Creating a Data Lake Gen2 instance is as simple as creating a new Storage account. The only change that needs to be done is to enable the hierarchical namespace from the **Advanced** tab of your Storage account.

Understanding big data processing

There are four distinct phases in big data processing:

- Ingestion of big data
- Processing of big data
- Storing the resultant data in a data store
- Presentation of insights and data

These four stages are summarized in the following diagram. We will be looking into each of these phases in the next sections:

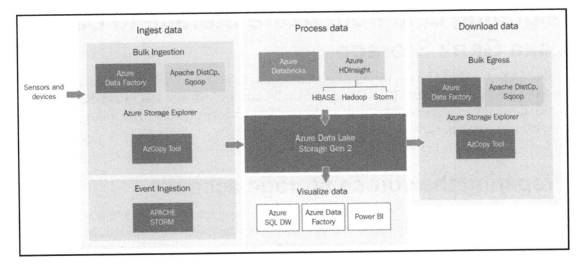

Ingestion

The data ingestion phase brings data into the Data Lake. This data can be streamed in real time using tools such as Azure HDInsight Storm.

On-premises data can be also migrated to the Data Lake.

Processing

The data in the Data Lake can be processed and transformed using tools such as Azure Databricks and HDInsight, and any output that is typically demanded by applications can be generated.

Storage for consumption

In this stage, the transformed data is moved to data stores such as data warehouses, Cosmos DB, and Azure SQL such that it can be consumed by applications directly.

Presentation of data

The insights and wisdom generated can be used for visualization, real-time dashboards, reports, and notifications.

Migrating data from Azure Storage to Data Lake Gen2 Storage

In this section, we will be migrating data from Azure Blob Storage to another Azure container of the same Azure Blob Storage instance, and we will also migrate data to an Azure Gen2 Data Lake instance using an Azure Data Factory pipeline. The following are the steps for creating such an end-to-end solution.

Preparing the source storage account

Before we can create Azure Data Factory pipelines and use them for migration, we need to create a new storage account, consisting of a couple of containers, and upload the data files. In the real world, these files and the storage connection would already be prepared.

Provisioning a new resource group

1. Navigate to the Azure portal, log in, and click on **+ Create a resource**, then search for Resource group.
2. Select **Resource group** from the search results and create a new resource group. Provide a name and choose an appropriate location. Note that all resources should be hosted in the same resource group and location so that it is easy to delete them.

Provisioning a storage account

1. Click on **+ Create a resource** and search for `Storage Account`. Select **Storage Account** from the search results and create a new storage account.

2. Provide a name and location, then select a subscription based on the resource group created earlier.

3. Select **StorageV2 (general purpose v2)** for **Account kind**, **Standard** for **Performance**, and **Locally-redundant storage (LRS)** for **Replication**:

Create storage account

Azure Storage is a Microsoft-managed service providing cloud storage that is highly available, secure, durable, scalable, and redundant. Azure Storage includes Azure Blobs (objects), Azure Data Lake Storage Gen2, Azure Files, Azure Queues, and Azure Tables. The cost of your storage account depends on the usage and the options you choose below. Learn more

PROJECT DETAILS

Select the subscription to manage deployed resources and costs. Use resource groups like folders to organize and manage all your resources.

* Subscription	RiteshSubscription ⌄
* Resource group	BigDataSolutions ⌄
	Create new

INSTANCE DETAILS

The default deployment model is Resource Manager, which supports the latest Azure features. You may choose to deploy using the classic deployment model instead. Choose classic deployment model

* Storage account name ❶	adfsamplesourcedata ✓
* Location	East US ⌄
Performance ❶	◉ Standard ◯ Premium
Account kind ❶	StorageV2 (general purpose v2) ⌄
Replication ❶	Locally-redundant storage (LRS) ⌄
Access tier (default) ❶	◯ Cool ◉ Hot

---

4. Create a couple of containers within the storage account. **rawdata** contains the files that would be extracted by the Data Factory pipeline and will act as the source dataset, and **finaldata** will contain files that the Data Factory pipelines will write data to and will act as the destination dataset:

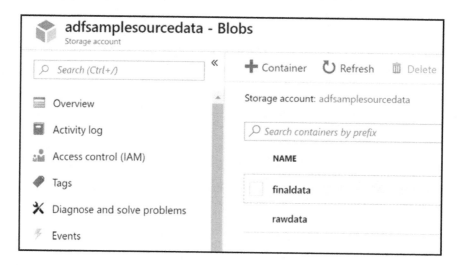

5. Upload a data file (this file is available with the source code) to the **rawdata** container:

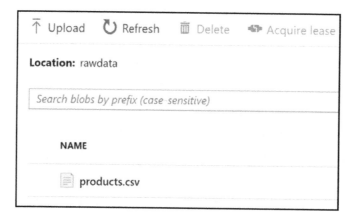

Creating a new Data Lake Gen2 service

As we know, the Data Lake Gen3 service is built on top of the Azure Storage account. As such, we will be creating a new Storage account in the same way we did earlier, with the only difference being the selection of **Enabled** for **Hierarchical namespace** in the **Advanced** tab of the new Azure Storage account. This will create the new Data Lake Gen2 service:

Create storage account

Basics   Advanced   Tags   Review + create

SECURITY

Secure transfer required ⓘ   ◯ Disabled   ⦿ Enabled

VIRTUAL NETWORKS

Allow access from   ⦿ All networks   ◯ Selected network

ⓘ All networks will be able to access this storage account. Learn more

DATA LAKE STORAGE GEN2 (PREVIEW)

Hierarchical namespace ⓘ   ◯ Disabled   ⦿ Enabled

Creating a new Data Factory pipeline

1. Create a new Data Factory pipeline by selecting **V2** and by providing a name and location along with a resource group and subscription selection, as shown:

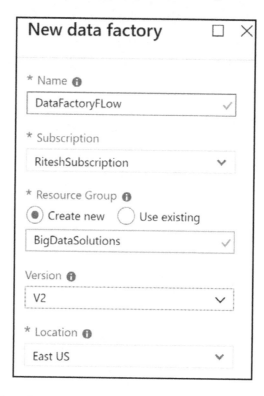

2. Data Factory has three different versions, as shown in the following screenshot. We've already discussed V1 and V2. V2 with data flow is in preview, and you need to get your subscription whitelisted before using it:

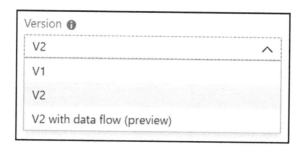

3. Once the Data Factory resource is created, click on the **Author & Monitor** link from the central page:

4. This will open another window, consisting of the Data Factory designer for pipelines:

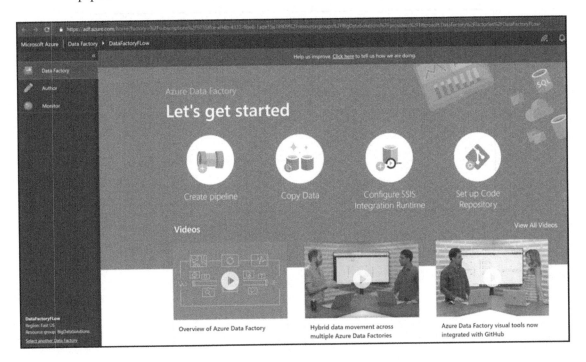

Repository settings

Before creating any Data Factory artifacts, such as datasets and pipelines, it is a good idea to set up the code repository for hosting files related to Data Factory:

1. Click on the **Data Factory** dropdown from the top menu:

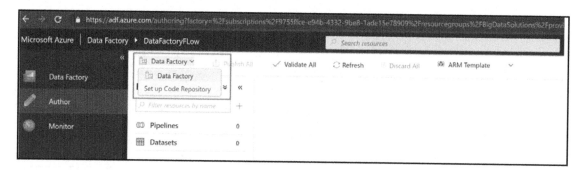

2. From the resultant blade, select any one of the repositories that you would like to store Data Factory code files in. In this case, **GitHub** is selected:

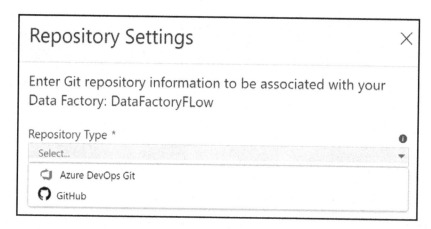

3. It will ask for authorization to the GitHub account.

4. Log into GitHub with your credentials and provide permissions to the Azure Data Factory service:

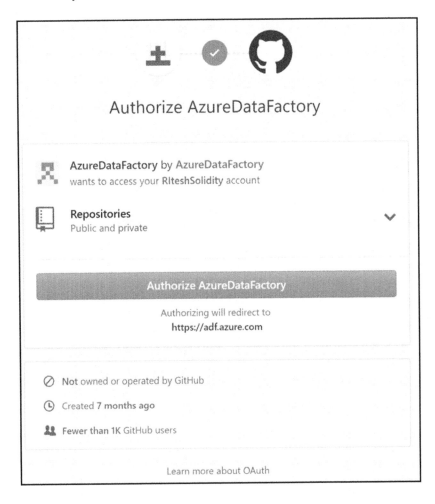

5. Create or reuse an existing repository from GitHub. In our case, we are creating a new repository named ADF. If you are creating a new repository, ensure that it is already initialized, otherwise the Data Factory repository setting will complain:

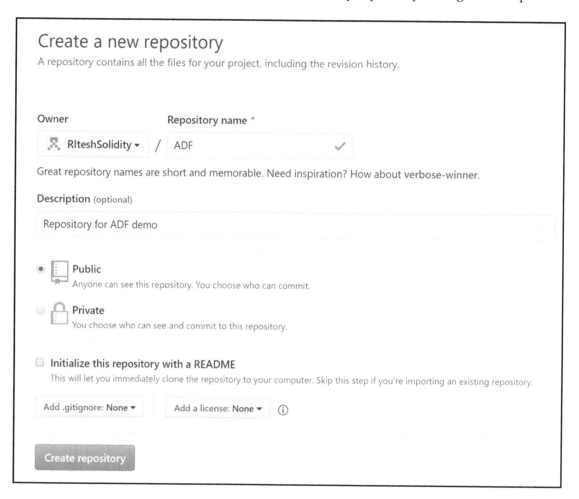

6. Now we can move back to the Data Factory pipeline window and ensure that the repository settings are appropriate, including the repository name, collaboration branch, root folder, and branch, which will act as the main branch:

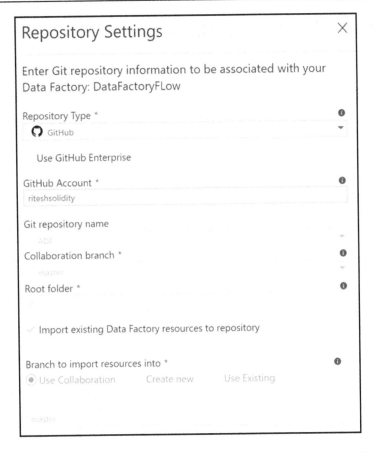

7. On the next screen, create a new branch on which developers will be working. In our case, a new **development** branch is created:

Creating the first dataset

Now back to the Data Factory pipeline: create a new dataset that will act as the source dataset. It will be the first storage account that we created and uploaded the sample `products.csv` file to:

1. Click on **+ Dataset** from the top menu and select **Azure Blob Storage**:

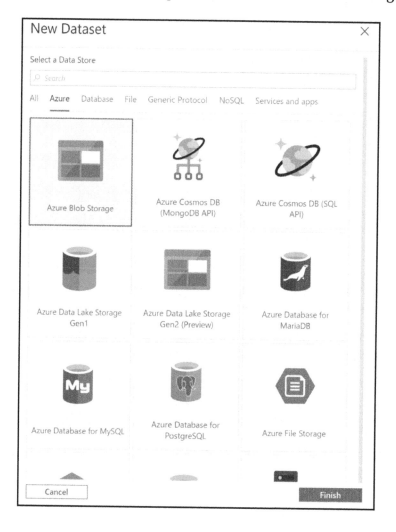

2. On the resultant lower pane, in the **General** tab, provide a name to the dataset:

3. From the **Connection** tab, create a new linked service according to the configuration shown here:

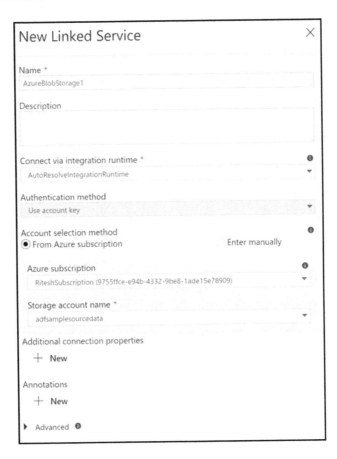

4. Linked services provide multiple authentication methods, and we are using the **shared access signature (SAS) uniform resource locator (URI)** method. It is also possible to use an account key, service principal, and managed identity as authentication methods:

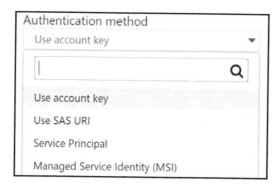

5. The **Connection** tab after configuration should look as shown in the following screenshot. Notice the path includes the name of the container and the name of the file:

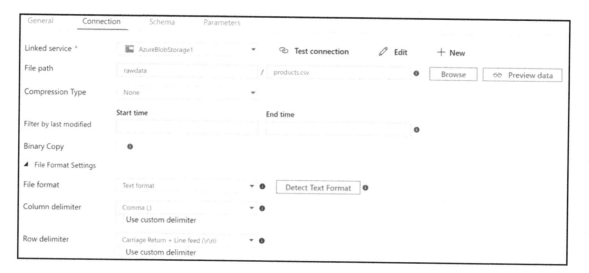

6. At this point, if you click on the **Preview data** button, it shows preview data from the `products.csv` file. On the **Schema** tab, add two columns and name them `ProductID` and `ProductPrice`. The schema helps in providing an identifier to the columns and helps in mapping the source columns in the source dataset to the target columns in the target dataset when the names are not the same:

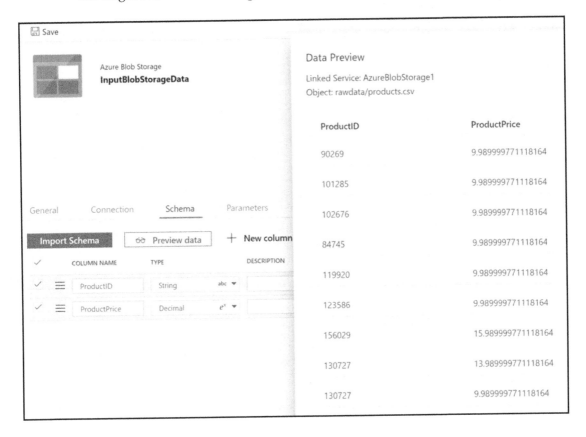

Creating the second dataset

Create a new dataset and linked service for the destination Blob Storage account as you did before. Note that the Storage account is the same as source but the container is different. Ensure that the incoming data have schema information associated with them as well, as shown in the following screenshot:

Creating a third dataset

Create a new dataset for the Data Lake Gen2 storage instance as the target dataset. Select the new dataset and select **Azure Data Lake Storage Gen2 (Preview)**:

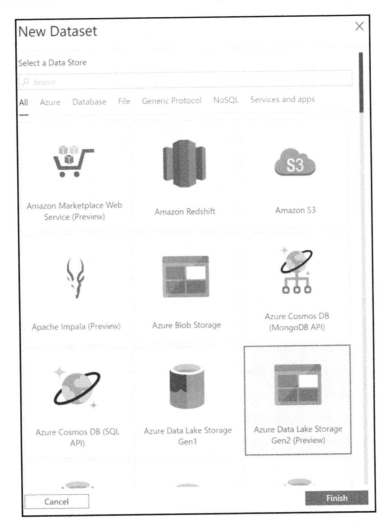

Give the new dataset a name and create a new linked service from the **Connection** tab. Choose **Use account key** as the authentication method and the rest of the configuration will be auto-filled after selecting the Storage account name. Test the connection by clicking on the **Test connection** button. Keep the default configuration for the rest of the tabs:

Creating a pipeline

1. Now click on the **+ Pipeline** menu from the top menu to create a new pipeline. Drag and drop the **Copy Data** activity from the **Move & Transform** menu:

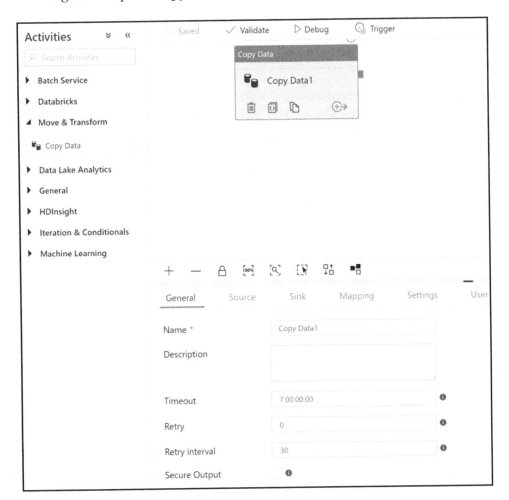

2. The resultant **General** tab can be left as is, and the **Source** tab should be configured to use the source dataset configured earlier:

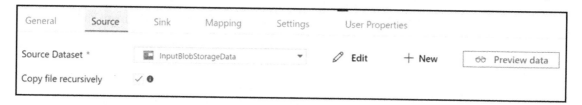

3. The **Sink** tab is for configuring the destination data store and dataset, and it should be configured to use the target dataset configured earlier:

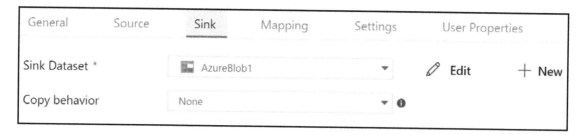

4. On the **Mapping** tab, map the columns from the source to the destination dataset columns:

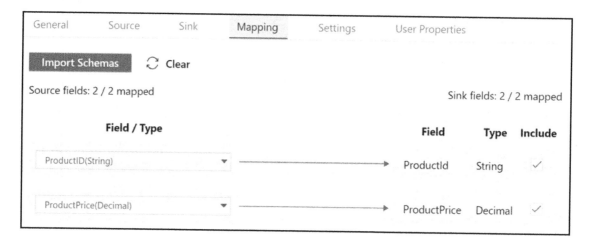

Add one more copy data activity

1. Add another **Copy Data** activity from the left activity menu for migrating data to Data Lake Storage. Both the copy tasks will execute in parallel:

2. The configuration for the source is the Azure Blob Storage account containing the `products.csv` file.
3. The sink configuration will target the Data Lake Gen2 storage account.
4. The rest of the configuration can be left as default for the second copy data activity.

Publishing

1. Now you can run the pipeline in debug mode. After running, we will publish the pipeline. However, before we can publish the pipeline, we should merge the code from development branch to the master branch and, optionally, delete the development branch:

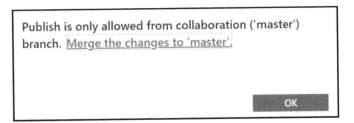

2. Go to the GitHub account and raise a new pull request for merging the code from the development branch to the master branch. This is because the entire code of the pipelines, datasets, linked services, and ARM templates is in the development branch:

3. After the pull request is raised, accept the pull request and merge the code from the development branch to the master branch:

4. Back in the Data Factory designer, select the master branch from the top menu and publish the code:

5. Click on the resultant blade:

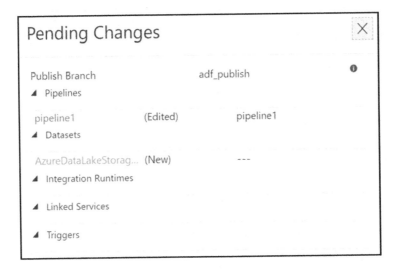

6. Finally, the GitHub repository should look as in the following screenshot:

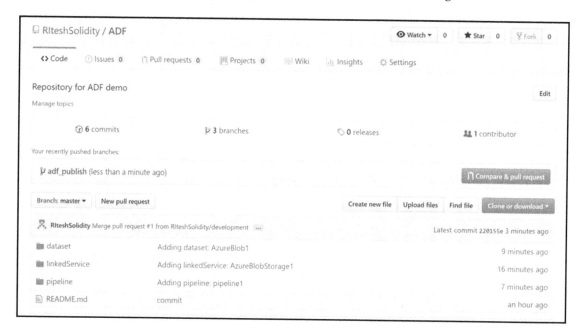

7. Trigger the pipeline by clicking on the **Trigger Now** button from the top menu once the publishing is complete:

Triggering a data factory will push the code to the repository, generate the ARM templates, and execute the pipeline.

Final result

If we navigate to the Storage account containing both the source and destination containers, we should be able to see our new file as `processedproducts.csv`:

We cannot see the files for Data Lake Storage. We have to download the Storage Explorer tool to view files in the Data Lake Storage account:

The tool should be of minimum version 1.6.2 and can be downloaded from `https://aka.ms/portalfx/downloadstorageexplorer`.

Summary

This was another chapter on handling big data. This chapter dealt with the Azure Data Factory service, which is responsible for providing ETL services on Azure. Since it is a PaaS, it provides unlimited scalability, high availability, and easy-to-configure pipelines. Its integration with Azure DevOps and GitHub is also seamless. We also saw the features and benefits of using Azure Data Lake Gen2 storage for storing any kind of big data. It is a cost-effective, highly scalable, hierarchical data store for handling big data, with compatibility with Azure HDInsight, Databricks, and the Hadoop ecosystem.

14

Azure Stream Analytics and Event Hubs

Events are everywhere! Any activity or task that changes the current state generates an event. Events were not that popular a few years back. A few years back, there was no cloud, and not much traction for the **Internet of Things (IoT)** and devices/sensors. Organizations were using hosted environments from ISPs that just had monitoring systems on top of them. These monitoring systems raised events that were few and far between.

However, with the advent of the cloud, things changed rapidly. With increased deployments on the cloud, especially of **Platform as a Service (PaaS)** services, organizations do not need so much control over the hardware and the platform, and now every time there is change in an environment, an event is raised. With the emergence of cloud events, IoT gained a lot of prominence and events started taking center stage.

Another phenomenon during this time was the rapid burst of growth in the availability of data. The velocity, variety, and volume of data spiked, and so did the need for solutions to its storage and processing. Multiple solutions and platforms emerged, such as Hadoop, data lakes for storage, data lakes for analytics, and machine learning services for analytics.

Apart from storage and analytics, there is also a need for services that are capable of ingesting millions upon millions of events and messages from various sources. There is also a need for services that can work on temporal data rather than working on the entire snapshot of data.

In this chapter, we will go through a couple of pertinent services in Azure:

- Azure Event Hubs
- Azure Stream Analytics

A primer on Event Hubs

The first resource in this chapter that we will look at is Event Hubs. Events Hubs can be used in any solution that wants to store millions of events on Azure. However, it is important to first understand the basics of events.

Events

Events help change the current state to the target state. Events are different to messages. Messages are related to business functionality, such as sending order details to another system; events are different. For instance, a virtual machine being stopped is an event.

An event, along with the current state, helps in transitioning from current state to target state, and this transition is shown in the following diagram:

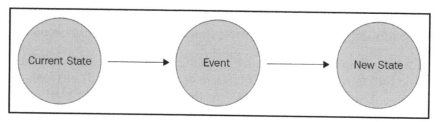

Event streaming

If there are only a few events, there is not much of a need for event streaming, as event streaming provides real value with big data processes, where data comes in high volumes and in many different formats.

Event streaming refers to services that can accept data as and when it arises rather than accepting it periodically. For example, event streams should be capable of accepting temperature information from devices as and when they send it, rather than making the data wait in a queue or a staging environment.

Event streaming has the capability to query data while in transit. This is temporal data that is not stored, and the queries happen on the moving data. The data is not stationary. This capability is not available in other data platforms, which can query only stored data, not temporal data that has just been ingested.

Event streaming services should be able to scale easily to accept millions or even billions of events. They should be highly available such that sources can send events and data to them any time. Real-time data ingestion and being able to work on that data rather than data stored in a different location is the key to event streaming.

It should occur to the curious mind that when we already have so many data platforms with advanced query execution capabilities, why do we need event steaming? Let me provide you with some scenarios in which working on incoming data is quite important. These scenarios cannot be effectively and efficiently solved by existing data platforms:

- **Credit card fraud detection**: This should happen as and when a fraudulent transaction is happening.
- **Telemetry information from sensors**: In the case of IoT devices sending vital information about their environments, the user should be notified as and when an anomaly is detected.
- **Live dashboards**: Event streaming is needed to create dashboards that show live information.
- **Data center environment telemetry**: This will let the user know about any intrusions, security breaches, failures of components, and more.

There are many possibilities for applying event streaming within an enterprise, and its importance cannot be stressed enough.

Event Hubs

Event Hubs is the service in Azure that provides capability related to the ingestion and storage of events that are needed for streaming.

It can ingest data from a variety of sources. The sources could be IoT sensors or any applications using the Event Hubs SDK to send data. It supports multiple protocols for ingesting and receiving data. These protocols are industry standards, and they include the following:

- **HTTP**: This is a stateless option and does not require an active session
- **Advanced Messaging Queuing Protocol (AMQP)**: This requires an active session (established connection using sockets) and works with TLS and SSL
- **Apache Kafka**: This is a distributed streaming platform similar to Stream Analytics

Event Hubs is an event ingestion service. It does not have the capability to query and output query results to another location. That is the responsibility of Stream Analytics, which is covered in the next section.

Event Hubs, being a PaaS on Azure, is highly distributed, highly available, and highly scalable.

Event Hubs comes with the following two SKUs or pricing tiers:

- **Basic**: This comes with one consumer group and can retain messages for 1 day. It can have a maximum of 100 brokered connections.
- **Standard**: This comes with a maximum of 20 consumer groups and can retain messages for 1 day with additional storage for 7 days. It can have a maximum of 1,000 brokered connections. It is also possible to define policies in this SKU.

The next screenshot shows the form for creating a new Event Hubs Namespace. It provides an option to choose an appropriate pricing tier along with other important details:

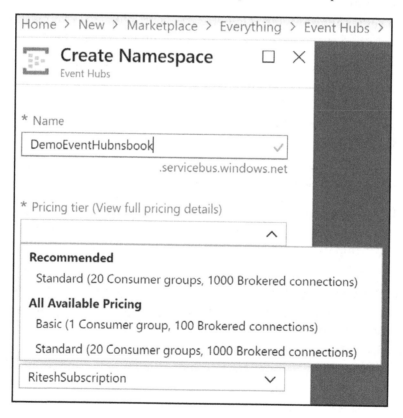

It is important to note that the SKU cannot be changed after provisioning an Event Hubs namespace. Due consideration and planning should be taken before selecting an SKU. The planning should include planning the number of consumer groups required and the number of applications interested in reading events from the event hub.

Architecture of Event Hubs

There are three main components of the Event Hubs architecture: the **Event Producers**, the **Event Hub**, and the **Event Consumer**, as shown in the following diagram:

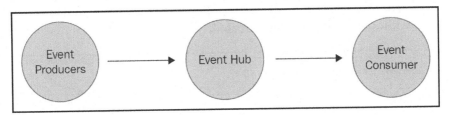

Event Producers generate events and send them to the **Event Hub**. The **Event Hub** stores the ingested events and provides that data to the **Event Consumer**. The **Event Consumer** is whatever is interested in those events, and they connect to the **Event Hub** to fetch the data.

Event hubs cannot be created without an Event Hubs namespace. The Event Hubs namespace acts as a container and can host multiple event hubs. Each Event Hubs namespace provides a unique REST-based endpoint that is consumed by clients to send data to Event Hubs. This namespace is the same namespace as is needed for Service Bus artifacts, such as topics and queues.

The connection string of an Event Hubs namespace is composed of its URL, policy name, and the key. A sample connection string is shown next:

```
Endpoint=sb://demoeventhubnsbook.servicebus.windows.net/;SharedAccessKeyNam
e=RootManageSharedAccessKey;SharedAccessKey=M/E4eeBsr7DAlXcvw6ziFqlSDNbFX6E
49Jfti8CRkbA=
```

This can be found in the **Shared Access Signature (SAS)** menu item of the namespace. There can be multiple policies defined for a namespace, with each having different levels of access to the namespace. The three levels of access are as follows:

- **Manage**: This can manage the event hub from an administrative perspective. It also has rights for sending and listening to events.
- **Send**: This can write events to Event Hubs.
- **Listen**: This can read events from Event Hubs.

By default, the `RootManageSharedAccessKey` policy is created when creating an event hub, as shown in the following screenshot. Policies help in creating granular access control on Event Hubs. The key associated with each policy is used by consumers to determine their identity. Additional policies can be created:

Event hubs can be created from the Event Hubs namespace service by clicking on **Event Hubs** in the left-hand menu and clicking on **+ Event Hub** in the resultant screen:

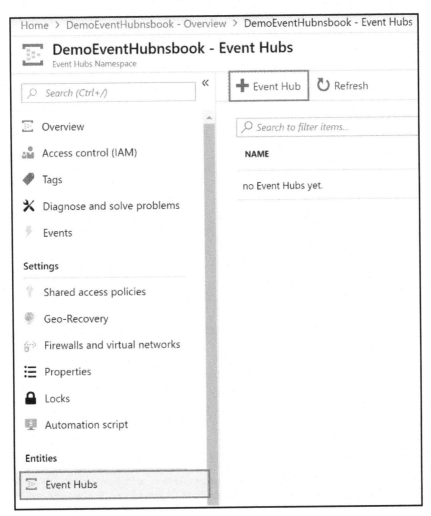

Provide information about the **Partition Count** and **Message Retention** values, along with the name to create the event hub with. Select **Off** for **Capture**:

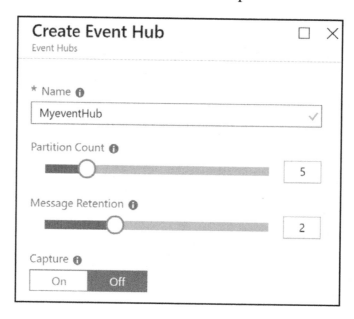

Separate policies can be assigned to event hubs by adding a new policy at the event hub level.

After creating the policy, the connection string is available from the **Secure Access Signature** left-menu item on the Azure portal.

Since a namespace can consist of multiple event hubs, the connection string for an individual event hub would be similar to what's shown next. The difference is in the key value and the addition of `EntityPath` with the name of the event hub:

```
Endpoint=sb://azuretwittereventdata.servicebus.windows.net/;SharedAccessKey
Name=EventhubPolicy;SharedAccessKey=rxEu5K4Y2qsi5wEeOKuOvRnhtgW8xW35UBex4Vl
IKqg=;EntityPath=myeventhub
```

We had to keep the **Capture** option **Off** while creating the event hub. It can be switched on after creating the event hub. It helps to save events to Azure Blob Storage or an Azure Data Lake Storage account automatically, along with the configuration for the size and time interval:

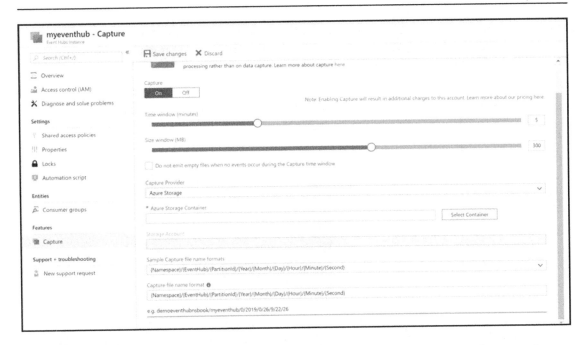

We did not cover the concepts of partitions and message retention options when creating an event hub.

Partition is an important concept related to the scalability of any data store. Events are retained within event hubs for a specific period of time. If all the events are stored within the same data store, then it becomes extremely difficult to scale that data store. Every event producer will connect to the same data store and send their events to it. Compare this with a data store that can partition the same data into multiple smaller data stores, each uniquely identified with a value. The smaller data store is called a **partition**, and the value that defines the partition is known as the **partition key**. The partition key is part of the event data.

Now, the event producers can connect to the event hub, and based on the value of the partition key, the event hub will store the data in an appropriate partition. This will allow the event hub to ingest multiple events at the same time in parallel.

Deciding on the number of partitions is a crucial aspect for the scalability of an event hub. The diagram shows that ingested data is stored in the appropriate partition internally by Event Hubs using the partition key:

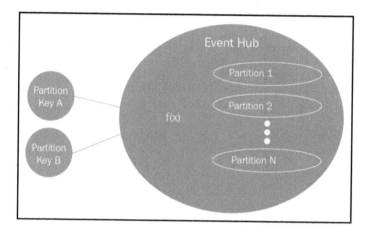

It is important to understand that the same partition might have multiple keys. The user decides how many partitions are required, and the event hub internally decides the best way to allocate partition keys between them. Each partition stores data in an orderly way using a timestamp, and newer events are appended toward the end of the partition.

It is important to note that it is not possible to even change the number of partitions once the event hub is created.

It is also important to remember that partitions also help in bringing parallelism and concurrency for applications reading the events. If there are 10 partitions, 10 parallel readers can read the events without any degradation in performance.

Consumer groups

Consumers are applications that read events from an event hub. Consumer groups are created for consumers to connect to it for reading the events. There can be multiple consumer groups for an event hub, and each consumer group has access to all partitions within an event hub. Each consumer group forms a query on the events in events hubs. Applications can use consumer groups and each application will get a different view of the event hub events. A default $default consumer group is created when creating an event hub. It is a good practice for one consumer to be associated with one consumer group for optimal performance. However, it is possible to have five readers on each partition in a consumer group:

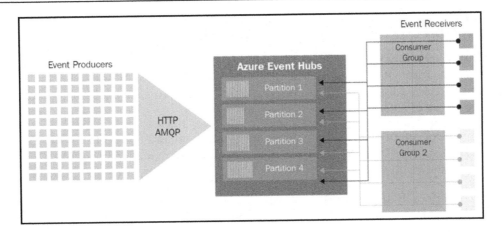

Throughput

Partitions help in scalability and throughput helps in capacity per second. What is capacity for Event Hubs? It is the amount of data that can be handled per second.

In Event Hubs, a single throughput unit allows the following:

- 1 MB of ingestion data per second, or 1,000 events per second, whichever happens first
- 2 MB of egress data per second, or 4,096 events per second, whichever happens first

Auto-inflate helps in increasing the throughput automatically in the case of the number of incoming/outgoing events or the incoming/outgoing total size crossing a threshold. Instead of throttling, the throughput will scale up and down. The configuration of throughput at the time of the creation of the namespace is shown in the following screenshot. Again, careful thought should go into deciding the throughput units:

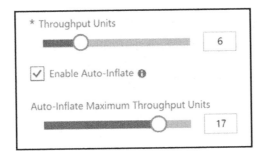

A primer on Stream Analytics

Event Hubs is only an event ingestion platform, so we need another service that can process these events as a stream rather than just as stored data. Stream Analytics helps in processing and examining a stream of big data, and Stream Analytics jobs help to execute the processing of events.

Stream Analytics can process millions of events per second and it is quite easy to get started with it. Azure Stream Analytics is a PaaS that is completely managed by Azure. Customers of Stream Analytics do not have to manage the underlying hardware and platform.

Each job comprises multiple inputs, outputs, and a query, which does the transformation of incoming data into new output. The whole architecture of Stream Analytics is shown in the following diagram:

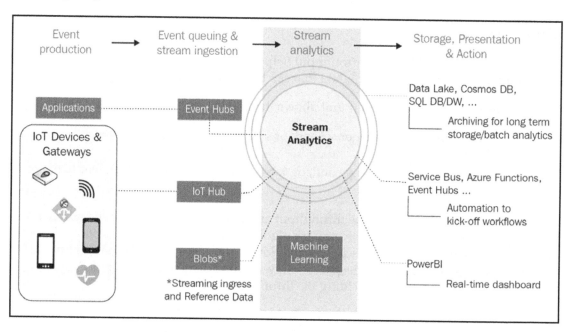

In the diagram, on the extreme left are the event sources. These are the sources that produce the events. They could be IoT devices, custom applications written in any programming language, or events coming from other Azure platforms such as Log Analytics or Application Insights.

These events must first be ingested into the system, and there are numerous Azure services that can help ingest this data. We've already looked event hubs and how they help in ingesting data. There are other services, such as IoT Hub, that also help in ingesting device- and sensor-specific data. IoT Hub and ingestion is covered in detail in the chapter related to IoT Hub. This ingested data undergoes processing as it arrives in a stream, and this processing is done using Stream Analytics. The output from Stream Analytics could be a presentation platform such as Power BI, showing real-time data to stakeholders, or a storage platform such as Cosmos DB, Data Lake Storage, or Azure Storage, from which the data can be read and actioned later by Azure Functions and Service Bus queues, for instance.

Stream Analytics is capable of ingesting millions of events per second and has the capability to execute queries on top on them. At the time of writing, Stream Analytics supports the three sources of events listed here:

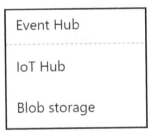

Input data is supported in any of the three following formats:

- **JavaScript Object Notation (JSON)**: This is a lightweight, plaintext-based format that is human readable. It consists of name-value pairs. A sample JSON event is shown here:

```
{
 "SensorId" : 2,
 "humidity" : 60,
 "temperature" : 26C
}
```

- **Comma-Separated Values (CSV)**: These are also plaintext values, separated by commas. Some sample CSV is shown here:
    - SensorIdentifier, humidity, temperature
    - 2,60,26C
    - 3,65,31C

- **Avro**: This format is similar to JSON; however, it is stored in binary format rather than text format.

Not only can Stream Analytics receive events, but it also provides advanced query capability for the data that it receives. The queries can extract important insights from the temporal data streams and output them. As shown in the following screenshot, there is an input and an output.

The query moves events from input to output. The INTO clause refers to the output location, and the FROM clause refers to the input location. The queries are very similar to SQL queries, so the learning curve is not steep for SQL programmers:

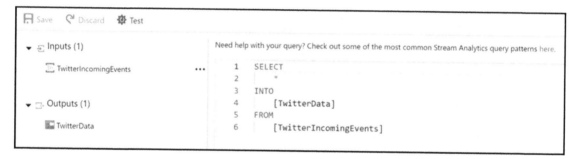

Event Hubs also provides mechanisms for sending outputs from queries to target destinations. At the time of writing, Stream Analytics supports multiple destinations for events and query outputs. These destinations are shown in the next screenshot:

```
Event Hub

SQL Database

Blob storage

Table storage

Service Bus topic

Service Bus queue

Cosmos DB

Power BI

Data Lake Storage Gen1
Azure function
```

It is also possible to define custom functions that can be reused within queries. There are three options provided to define custom functions:

```
Javascript UDF

Azure ML

Javascript UDA
```

Hosting environment

Stream Analytics jobs can run on hosts running on the cloud or they can run on IoT edge devices. IoT edge devices are devices that are near to IoT sensors rather than on the cloud. The following screenshot shows the **New Stream Analytics job** blade:

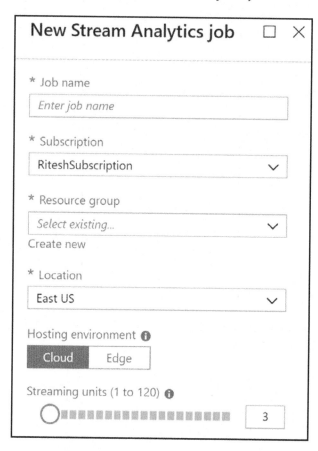

Streaming units

From the previous screenshot, we can see that the only configuration that is unique to Stream Analytics is **Streaming units**. **Streaming units** refers to the resources (CPU and memory) assigned for running a Stream Analytics job. The minimum and maximum streaming units are 1 and 120, respectively.

Depending on the amount of data and the queries executed on that data, streaming units must be pre-allocated; otherwise, the job will fail.

It is possible to scale the streaming units up and down from the Azure portal.

A sample application using Event Hubs and Stream Analytics

In this section, we will be creating a sample application comprising multiple Azure services, including Azure Logic Apps, Azure Event Hubs, Azure Storage, and Azure Stream Analytics.

In this sample application, we will be reading all tweets containing the word "Azure" in it and storing them in an Azure Storage account.

To create this solution, we first need to provision all the necessary resources.

Provisioning a new resource group

Navigate to the Azure portal, log in using valid credentials, click on **+ Create a resource**, and search for `Resource group`. Select **Resource group** from the search results and create a new resource group. Provide a name and choose an appropriate location. Note that all resources should be hosted in the same resource group and location so that it is easy to delete them:

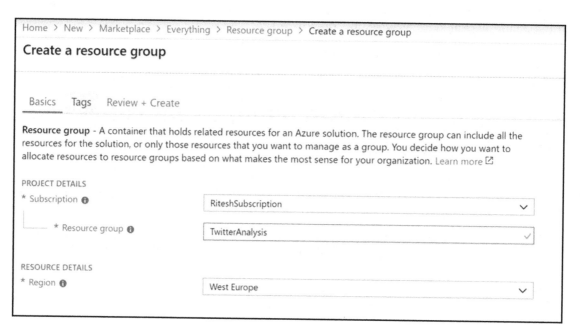

Creating an Event Hubs namespace

Click on **+ Create a resource** and search for `Event hubs`. Select **Event hubs** from the search results and create a new event hub. Provide a name and location, and select a subscription based on the resource group created earlier. Select **Standard** as the pricing tier and also select **Enable Auto-inflate**:

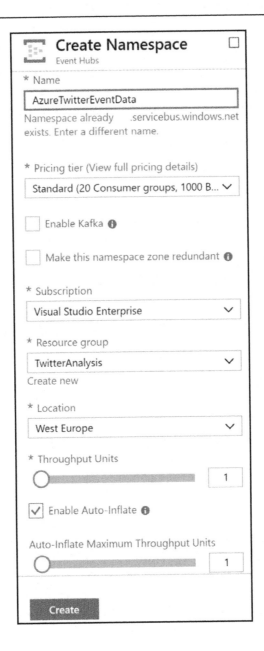

Creating an event hub

From the Event Hubs namespace service, click on **Events hubs** in the left menu and click on **+ Event hubs** to create a new event hub. Name it `azuretwitterdata` and provide an optimal number of partitions and a **Message Retention** value:

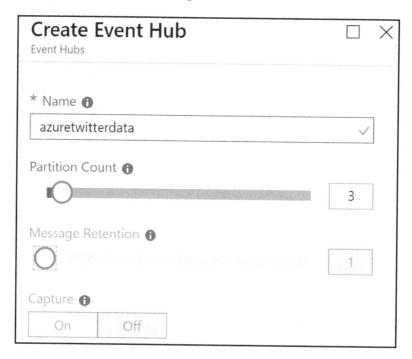

Provisioning logic apps

After the resource group is provisioned, click on **+ Create a resource** and search for `Logic Apps`. Select **Logic Apps** from the search results and create a new logic app. Provide a name and location, and select a subscription based on the resource group created earlier. It is a good practice to enable **Log Analytics**. Logic Apps is covered in detail in the `Chapter 7, Azure Integration Solutions`. The logic app is responsible for connecting to Twitter using an account and fetching all tweets with `Azure` in them:

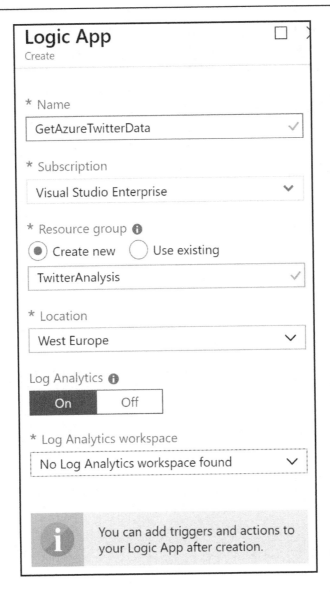

After the logic app is created, configure it as shown here from the Logic App designer.

Select the **When a new tweet is posted** trigger on the design surface, sign in, and configure it as shown in the following screenshot. You will need a valid Twitter account before configuring this trigger:

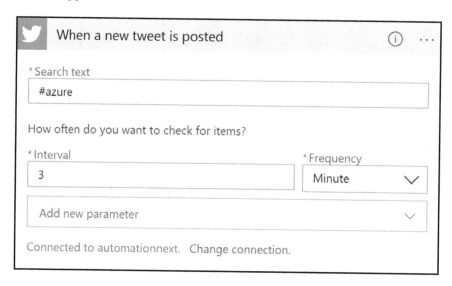

Drop a **Send event** action on the designer surface. This action is responsible for sending tweets to the event hub:

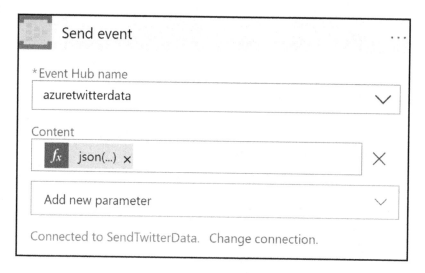

Select the event hub name that was created in an earlier step.

The value specified in the content text box is an expression dynamically composed using Logic Apps-provided functions and Twitter data. Clicking on **Add dynamic content** provides a dialog through which the expression can be composed:

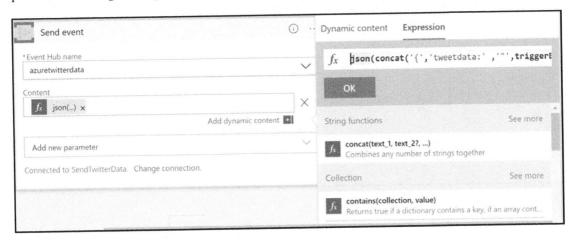

The value of the expression is as follows:

```
json(concat('{','tweetdata:' ,'"',triggerBody()?['TweetText'],'"', '}'))
```

Provisioning the Storage account

Click on **+ Create a resource** and search for `Storage Account`. Select **Storage Account** from the search results and create a new Storage account. Provide a name and location, and select a subscription based on the resource group created earlier. Select **StorageV2** for **Account Kind**, **Standard** for **Performance**, and **Locally-redundant storage (LRS)** for the **Replication** field.

Creating a storage container

Stream Analytics will output the data as files that will be stored within a Blob Storage container. A container named **twitter** is created within Blob Storage:

Creating Stream Analytics jobs

Create a new Stream Analytics job with a hosting environment on the cloud and set the streaming units to the default. The input for this Stream Analytics job comes from the event hub, and so we need to configure this from the inputs menu:

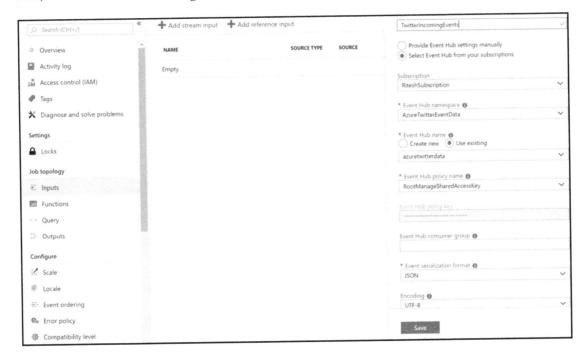

The output for the Stream Analytics job is a Blob Storage account, so we need to configure the output accordingly. Provide a path pattern that is suitable for this exercise. For example, {datetime:ss} is the path pattern used for this exercise:

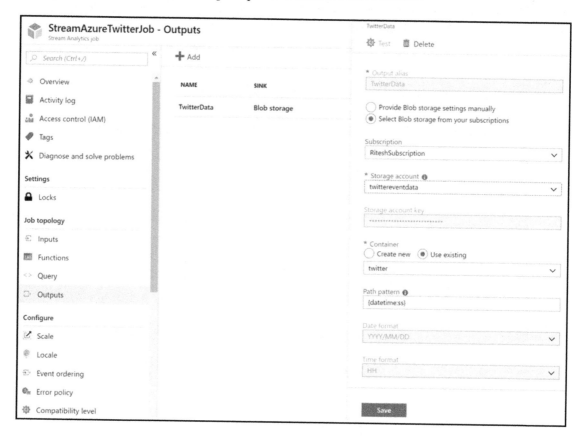

The query is quite simple. We are just copying the date from input to output:

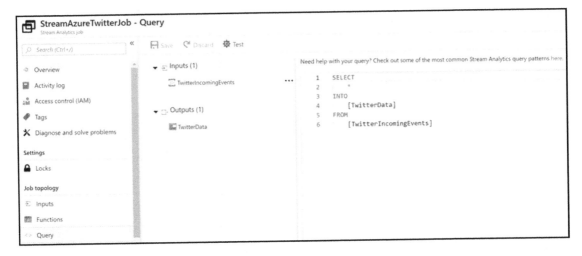

Running the application

The logic app should be enabled and Stream Analytics should be running. Execute the logic app. It should have jobs created as shown in the following screenshot:

The Storage account container should get data as shown here:

As an exercise, you can extend this sample solution and evaluate the sentiment of the tweets every 3 minutes. The Logic Apps workflow for such an exercise would look as follows:

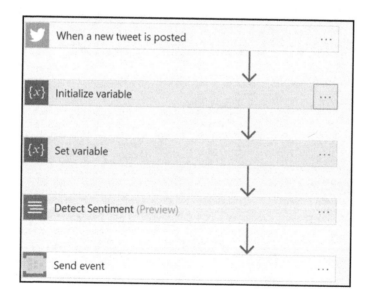

Detecting sentiment uses the Text Analytics API, which should be configured before being used in Logic Apps.

Summary

This chapter focused on topics related to streamed and temporal events. Events are raised from multiple sources, and to get insights in real time about activities and their related events, services such as Event Hubs and Stream Analytics play a significant role. Event Hubs is a service that helps in ingesting millions of events per second and temporally storing them. This data can be sent to Stream Analytics for processing. During processing, additional insights can be fetched using custom queries, and these insights then can be sent as outputs to multiple destinations. These services work on real-time data that isn't stored in any permanent storage.

In the next chapter, we will go through creating an IoT solution using Azure IoT Hub and explore its various features.

15
Designing IoT Solutions

So far, we have been dealing with architectural concerns and their solutions on Azure in general. This chapter is not based on generalized architecture. This chapter is about one of the most disruptive technologies of this century. This chapter will get into the details of the **Internet of Things (IoT)** architecture and Azure.

This chapter will specifically cover the following topics:

- Azure and IoT
- Azure IoT overview
- Device management:
    - Registering devices
    - Device-to-IoT-hub communication
- Scaling IoT solutions
- High availability of IoT solutions
- IoT protocols
- Using message properties for routing messages

IoT

To understand what IoT is better, let's go back a few years.

In the nineties, the internet was invented and became generally available. During this time, almost everyone moved toward having a presence on the internet and started creating static web pages. Eventually, the static content became dynamic and content was generated on the fly, based on context. In almost all cases, a browser was needed to access the internet. There was a plethora of browsers; without them, using the internet was a challenge.

During the first decade of this century, there was an interesting development growing – the rise of hand-held devices, such as mobile phones and tablets. Mobile phones started becoming cheaper by the day and available ubiquitously. The hardware and software capabilities of these handheld devices were improving considerably; so much so that people started using browsers on mobile devices rather than desktops. But one particularly distinct change was the rise of mobile apps. Mobile apps are downloaded from some store and connected to the internet to talk to backend systems. Toward the end of the last decade, there were millions of apps available with almost every conceivable functionality built into them. The backend system for these apps was built on the cloud so that they could be scaled rapidly. This was the age of connecting applications and servers.

But, was this the pinnacle of innovation? What was the next evolution of the internet? Another paradigm has been taking center-stage: **IoT**. Instead of just mobile and tablet devices connecting to the internet, why can't other devices connect to the internet? Previously, such devices were available only in select markets, were costly, were not available to the masses, and had limited hardware and software capabilities. However, during the first part of the current decade, the commercialization of these devices started on a grand scale. These devices have been becoming smaller and smaller, more capable in terms of hardware and software, have more storage and compute power, can connect to the internet on various protocols, and can be attached to almost anything. This is the age of connecting devices to servers, applications, and other devices.

This led to the formulation of the idea that IoT applications could change the way industries were operating. Newer solutions that were unheard of before started being realized. Now these devices can be attached to anything; they can get information and send it to a backend system that can assimilate information from all the devices and either take action on or report incidents.

Examples of IoT applications include vehicle tracking systems, which can track all the vital parameters of a vehicle and send details to a centralized data store for analysis; smart city services, such as tracking pollution levels, temperature, street congestion, and so on; and agriculture-related activities, such as measuring soil fertility, humidity, and so on.

IoT architecture

Before getting into Azure and its features and services with regards to IoT, it is important to understand the various components needed to create end-to-end IoT solutions.

Imagine that IoT devices across the globe are sending millions of messages every second to a centralized database. Why is this data being collected? To extract rich information about events, anomalies, and outliers to do with whatever those devices are monitoring.

Let's understand this in more detail.

IoT architecture can be divided into distinct phases:

- Connectivity
- Identity
- Capture
- Ingestion
- Storage
- Transform
- Analytics
- Presentation

The following diagram shows a generic IoT-based architecture. Data is generated or collected by devices and sent over to cloud gateways. The cloud gateway, in turn, sends the data to multiple backend services for processing. Cloud gateways are optional components. They should be used when the devices themselves are not capable of sending requests to backend services, either because of their resource constraints or the lack of a reliable network. These cloud gateways can collate date from multiple devices and send it to backend services. The data can then be processed by backend services and shown as insights or dashboards to users:

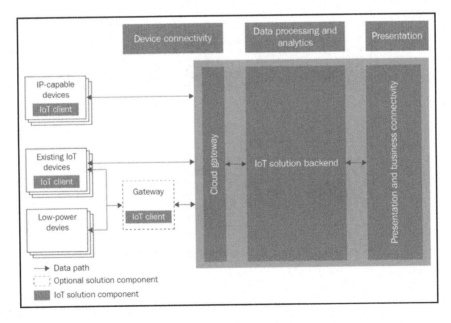

Connectivity

IoT devices need to communicate. There are various connectivity types. Connectivity could exist between devices in a region, between devices and a centralized gateway, between devices and an IoT platform, and more.

In all such cases, IoT devices need connectivity capability. This capability could be in the form of internet connectivity, Bluetooth, infrared, or any other near-device communication.

Some devices might not have the capability to connect to the internet. In those cases, they can connect through other means to a gateway, which in turn has connectivity to the internet.

IoT devices use protocols to send messages. The major protocols among these are the **Advanced Message Queuing Protocol (AMQP)** and the **Message Queue Telemetry Transport (MQTT)** protocol.

Device data should be sent to an IT infrastructure. The MQTT protocol is a device-to-server protocol that devices can use to send telemetry data and other information to servers. Once the server receives a message through the MQTT protocol, it needs to transport the message to other servers using a reliable technology based on messages and queues. AMQP is the preferred protocol for moving messages between servers in the IT infrastructure in a reliable and predictable manner:

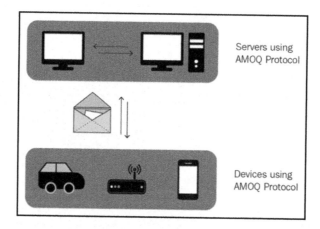

Servers receiving initial messages from IoT devices should send those messages to other servers for whatever processing is necessary, such as saving to logs, evaluation, analytics, and presentation.

Some devices do not have the capability to connect to the internet or do not support protocols understood by an IT infrastructure. To enable these devices to work with an IoT platform and the cloud, intermediate gateways can be used. Gateways help in on-boarding devices whose connectivity and networking capability is slow and not consistent; such devices may use protocols that are not standard, or their capabilities may be limited in terms of resources and power.

In such circumstances, when devices need additional infrastructure to connect to backend services, client gateways can be deployed. These gateways receive messages from near devices and forward and push them to IT infrastructure and the IoT platform for further consumption. These gateways are capable of protocol translation if required.

Identity

IoT devices should be registered with the cloud platform. Not every device should be allowed to connect to a cloud platform. The devices should be registered and be assigned an identity. A device should send its identity information when connecting to the cloud. If the device fails to send this identity information, the connectivity should fail. We will see later in this chapter how to generate an identity for a device using a simulated application.

Capture

IoT devices should be able to capture information. It should have the capability, for example, to read the moisture content in the air or in the soil. The information can be captured based on frequency—maybe even once per second. Once the information is captured, the device should be able to send it across to the IoT platform for processing. If a device does not have the capability to connect to the IoT platform directly, it can connect to an intermediary cloud gateway and have that push the captured information. The size of captured data and the frequency of capture are the most important aspects for the device. Whether a device should have local storage to be able to temporarily store captured data is another important aspect that should be considered. A device can work in offline mode if there is enough local storage available. Even mobile devices sometimes act as IoT devices connected to various instruments, and have the capability to store data.

Ingestion

Data captured and generated by devices should be sent to an IoT platform that is capable of ingesting and consuming that data to extract meaningful information and insights out of it. The ingestion service is a crucial service because its availability and scalability affects the throughput of incoming data. If data starts getting throttled due to scalability issues or data is not able to be ingested due to availability issues, data would be lost and the dataset might get biased or skewed.

Storage

IoT solutions generally deal with millions or even billions of records, spanning terabytes or even petabytes of data. This is valuable data that can provide insights on operations and their health. This data needs to be stored such that analytics can be performed on it. Storage should be readily available for analytics applications and services to consume it. Storage solutions should provide adequate throughput and latency from a performance perspective, and be highly available, scalable, and secure.

Transform

IoT solutions are generally data-driven and have considerably high volumes of data to deal with. Imagine each car having a device and each one is sending messages every five seconds. If there were a million cars sending messages, that would be equal to 288 million messages per day and 8 billion messages per month. Together, this data has lots of hidden information and insights; however, making sense of this kind of data just by looking at it is difficult. The data that is captured and stored by IoT devices can be consumed for solving business problems, but not all data that is captured is of importance. Just a subset of data might be needed to solve a problem. The data that the IoT devices gather might not be consistent, as well. To ensure that the data is consistent and not biased or skewed, appropriate transformations should be executed upon it to make it ready for analysis. During transformation, data is filtered, sorted, removed, enriched, and transformed to a structure, such that the data can be consumed by components and applications further downstream.

Analytics

The data transformed in the previous step becomes the input for the analytics step. Depending on the problem at hand, there are different types of analytics that can be performed on transformed data.

The following are the different types of analytics that can be performed:

- **Descriptive Analytics**: This type of analytics helps in finding patterns and details about the statuses of IoT devices and their overall health. This stage identifies and summarizes the data for further consumption by more advanced stages of analytics. It will help in summarization, finding statistics related to probability, identifying deviation, and other statistical tasks.
- **Diagnostic Analytics**: This type of analytics is more advanced than descriptive analytics. It builds on top of descriptive analytics and tries to answer queries about why things happened. It tries to find the root causes of events. It tries to find answers using advanced concepts, such as hypothesis and correlation.
- **Predictive Analytics**: This type of analytics tries to predict things that have a high probability of happening in future. It's about prediction based on past data. Regression is one of the examples based on past data. Predictive analytics could, for example, predict the price of a car, behavior of a stock in the stock market, when a car tire will burst, and so on.
- **Prescriptive Analytics**: This type of analytics is the most advanced. This stage helps in identifying the action that should be executed to ensure that the health of devices and solutions do not degrade, and identifying proactive measures to undertake. The results of this stage of analytics help in avoiding future issues and eliminating the problems at their root causes.

Presentation

Analytics help in identifying answers, patterns, and insights based on data. These insights also need to be available to all stakeholders in formats they can understand. To this end, dashboards and reports can be generated, statistically or dynamically, and then be presented to stakeholders. Stakeholders can consume these reports for further action and improve continuously on their solutions.

Azure IoT

Now we've learned about the various stages of end-to-end IoT solutions. Each of these stages are crucial and their proper implementation is a must for any solution's success. Azure provides lots of services for each of these stages. Apart from these services, Azure provides IoT Hub, Azure's core IoT service and platform, which is capable of hosting complex, highly available, and scalable IoT solutions. We will dive deep into IoT Hub after going through some other services:

Devices	Device Connectivity	Storage	Analytics	Presentation & Action
	Event Hubs	SQL Database	Machine Learning	App Service
	Service Bus	Table/Blob Storage	Stream Analytics	Power BI
	External Data Sources	DocumentDB	HDInsight	Notification Hubs
		External Data Sources	Data Factory	Mobile Services
				BizTalk Services

Identity

Azure IoT Hub also provide services for authenticating devices. IoT Hub provides an interface for generating unique identity hashes for each device. When devices send their messages containing this hash, an IoT Hub can authenticate them, after verification of its own database for existence of such hashes.

Capture

Azure provides IoT gateways that enable devices that do not comply with IoT Hub to be adapted and push data. Local or intermediary gateways can be deployed near devices such that multiple devices can connect to a single gateway to send their information. Similarly, multiple clusters of devices with local gateways can be deployed. There can be a cloud gateway deployed on the cloud itself, capable of accepting data from multiple sources and ingesting it for IoT Hubs.

Ingestion

An IoT Hub can be a single point of contact for devices and other applications. In other words, the ingestion of IoT messages is the responsibility of the IoT Hub service. There are other services, such as Event Hubs and the Service Bus messaging infrastructure, that can ingest incoming messages; however, the benefits and advantages of using IoT Hub for ingesting IoT data far outweigh those of using event hubs and Service Bus messaging. In fact, IoT Hubs have been made specifically for the purpose of ingesting IoT messages within the Azure ecosystem such that other services and components can act on them.

Storage

Azure provides multiple ways of storing messages from IoT devices. These storage accounts include storing relational data, schema-less NoSQL data, and blobs:

- **SQL database**: SQL database provides storing relational data, JSON, and XML documents. It provides a rich SQL query language and it uses a full-blown SQL server as a service. Data from devices can be stored in SQL databases if data is well defined and the schema will not undergo changes frequently.
- **Azure Storage**: Azure Storage provides table and blob storage. Table storage helps in storing data as entities, where schema is not important. Blobs help in storing files in containers as blobs.
- **CosmosDB/DocumentDB**: DocumentDB is a full-blown enterprise-scale NoSQL database, available as a service capable of storing schema-less data. It is a truly distributed database that can span continents, providing high availability and scalability of data.
- **External data sources:** Apart from Azure services, customers can bring their own data stores, such as a SQL server on Azure virtual machines, and can use them for storing data in relational format.

Transform and analytics

Azure provides multiple resources to execute jobs and activities on ingested data. Some of them are mentioned here.

- **Data Factory**: Azure Data Factory is a cloud-based data integration service that allows us to create data-driven workflows in the cloud for orchestrating and automating data movement and data transformation. Azure Data Factory helps to create and schedule data-driven workflows (called pipelines) that can ingest data from disparate data stores; process/transform data by using compute services such as **Azure HDInsight, Hadoop, Spark, Azure Data Lake Analytics**, and **Azure Machine Learning**; and publish output data to ata Warehouse for **Business Intelligence (BI)** applications than a traditional **Extract-Transform-and-Load (ETL)** platform.

- **Azure HDInsight**: Microsoft and Hortonworks have come together to help companies by offering a big data analytics platform with Azure. HDInsight is a high-powered, fully managed cloud service environment powered by Apache Hadoop and Apache Spark using Microsoft Azure HDInsight. It helps in accelerating workloads seamlessly with Microsoft and Hortonworks' industry-leading big data cloud service.

- **Azure stream analytics**: This is a fully managed real-time data analytics service that helps in performing computation and transformation on streaming data. Stream analytics can examine high volumes of data flowing from devices or processes, extract information from the data stream, and look for patterns, trends, and relationships.

- **Machine learning**: Machine learning is a data science technique that allows computers to use existing data to forecast future behaviors, outcomes, and trends. Using machine learning, computers learn without being explicitly programmed. Azure Machine Learning is a cloud-based predictive analytics service that makes it possible to quickly create and deploy predictive models as analytics solutions. It provides a ready-to-use library of algorithms to create models on an internet-connected PC, and deploy predictive solutions quickly.

Presentation

After appropriate analytics have been conducted on data, the data should be presented to stakeholders in a format that is consumable by them. There are numerous ways in which insights from data can be presented. This includes presenting data using web applications deployed using Azure App Service, sending data to notification hubs that can then notify mobile applications, and more. However, the ideal approach for presenting and consuming insights is by way of using **Power BI** reports and dashboards. Power BI is a Microsoft visualization tool for rendering dynamic reports and dashboards on the internet.

IoT Hubs

IoT projects are generally complex in nature. The complexity arises because of the high volume of devices and data. Devices are embedded across the world; monitoring and auditing devices, storing data, transforming and analyzing petabytes of data, and finally taking action based on insights. Moreover, these projects have long gestation periods, and their requirements keep changing because of timelines.

If an enterprise wants to embark on a journey with an IoT project, sooner than later, it would be realized that the problems we just mentioned are not easily solved. These projects need enough hardware in terms of compute and storage to cope, for instance, and services that can work with such high volumes of data.

IoT Hub is a platform that is built to help ease and enable IoT projects for faster, better, and easier delivery. It provides all the necessary features and services for the following:

- Device registration
- Device connectivity
- Field gateways
- Cloud gateways
- Implementation of industry protocols, such as AMQP and the MQTT protocol
- Hub for storing incoming messages
- Routing of messages based on message properties and content
- Multiple endpoints for different types of processing
- Connectivity to other services on Azure for real-time analytics and more

Protocols

Azure IoT Hub natively supports communication over the MQTT, AMQP, and HTTP protocols. In some cases, devices or field gateways might not be able to use one of these standard protocols and will require protocol adaptation. In such cases, custom gateways can be deployed. A custom gateway can enable protocol adaptation for IoT Hub endpoints by bridging the traffic to and from the IoT Hub.

Device registration

Devices should be registered before they can send messages to an IoT Hub. Registration of devices can be done manually using the Azure portal or can be automated using the IoT Hub SDK. Azure provides sample simulation applications, with the help of which it becomes easy to register virtual devices for development and testing purposes. There is also a Raspberry Pi online simulator that can be used as a virtual device, and then, obviously, there are other physical devices that can be configured to connect to the IoT Hub.

If readers want to simulate a device from a local PC generally used for development and testing purposes, there are tutorials available in the Azure documentation in multiple languages. They are available at https://docs.microsoft.com/en-us/azure/iot-hub/iot-hub-get-started-simulated.

 The Raspberry Pi online simulator is available at https://docs.microsoft.com/en-us/azure/iot-hub/iot-hub-raspberry-pi-web-simulator-get-started, and for using physical devices to be registered with IoT Hub, the steps mentioned at https://docs.microsoft.com/en-us/azure/iot-hub/iot-hub-get-started-physical should be used.

For manually adding a device using the Azure portal, IoT Hub provides a **Device Explorer** menu, which can be used for configuring a new device:

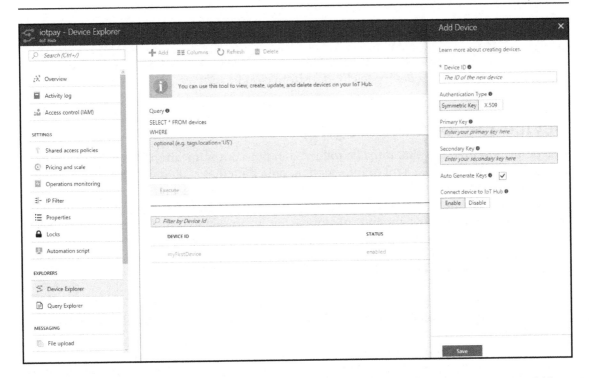

After the device identity is created, a primary key connection string for IoT Hub should be used in each device to connect to it:

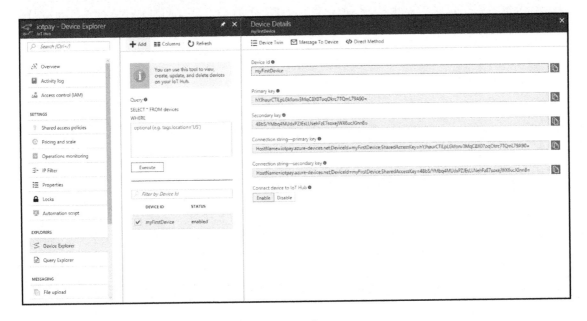

Message management

After devices are registered with the IoT Hub, they can start interacting with it. The interaction could be from device to cloud or from cloud to device.

Device-to-cloud messaging

One of the best practices that must be followed in this communication is that although the device might be capturing a lot of information, only data that is of any importance should be transmitted to the cloud. The size of the message is very important in IoT solutions because of the fact that IoT solutions generally have very high volumes of data. Even 1 KB of extra data can result in a gigabyte of storage and processing wasted. Each message has properties and payloads. Properties define the metadata for the message. This metadata contains data about the device, identification, tags, and other properties that are helpful in routing and identifying messages.

Devices or cloud gateways should connect to IoT Hubs to transfer data. IoT Hubs provide public endpoints that can be utilized by devices to connect and send data. IoT Hub should be considered as the first point of contact for backend processing. IoT Hub is capable of further transmission and routing of these messages to multiple services. By default, the messages are stored in event hubs. Multiple event hubs can be created for different kinds of messages:

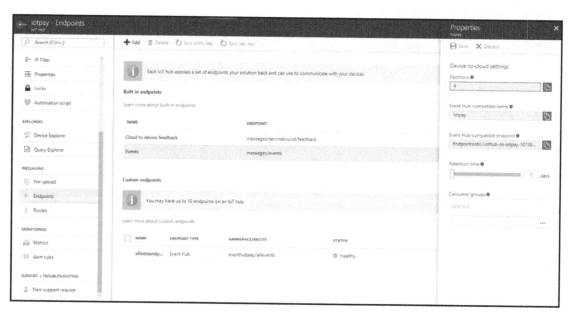

Messages can be routed to different endpoints based on the message header and body properties, as shown:

Messages in an IoT Hub stay there for seven days by default. Their size can go up to 256 KB.

There is a sample simulator provided by Microsoft for simulating sending messages to cloud. It is available in multiple languages and the C# version is at `https://docs.microsoft.com/en-us/azure/iot-hub/iot-hub-csharp-csharp-c2d`.

Cloud-to-device messaging

Azure IoT Hub is a managed service providing bi-directional messaging infrastructure. Messages can be sent from the cloud to devices, and based on the message, the devices can act on them.

There are three types of cloud-to-device messaging patterns:

- Direct methods require immediate confirmation of results. Direct methods are often used for interactive control of devices, such as opening and closing garage shutters. They follow the request-response pattern.

- Setting up device properties using Azure IoT provided **device twin** properties. For example, set the telemetry send interval to 30 minutes. Device twins are JSON documents that store device state information (metadata, configurations, and conditions). An IoT Hub persists a device twin for each device in the IoT Hub.
- Cloud-to-device messages for one-way notifications to the device app. This follow the fire-and-forget pattern.

Security

Security is an important aspect in IoT-based applications. IoT-based applications comprise devices that use the public internet for connectivity to backend applications. Securing devices, backend applications, and connectivity from malicious users and hackers should be considered a top priority for the success of these applications.

Security in IoT

IoT applications are primarily built around the internet, and security should play a major role in ensuring that the solution is not compromised. Some of the most important security decisions affecting IoT architecture are the following:

- Devices using HTTP versus HTTPS REST endpoints – REST endpoints secured by certificates ensure that messages transferred from a device to the cloud and vice versa are well encrypted and signed. The messages should make no sense to an intruder and should be extremely difficult to crack.
- If devices are connected to a local gateway, the local gateway should connect to the cloud using a secure HTTP protocol.
- Devices should be registered to IoT Hubs before they can send any messages.
- The information passed to the cloud should be persisted into storage that is well protected and secure. Appropriate SAS tokens or connection strings that are stored in Azure Key Vault should be used for connection.
- Azure Key Vault should be used to store all secrets, passwords, and credentials, including certificates.

Scalability

Scalability for IoT Hub is a bit different than for other services. In IoT Hub, there are two types of messaging:

- **Incoming**: Device-to-cloud messages
- **Outgoing**: Cloud-to-device messages

Both need to be accounted for in terms of scalability.

IoT Hub provides a couple of configuration options during provision time to configure scalability. These options are also available post-provisioning and can be updated to better suit the solution requirements in terms of scalability.

The scalability options available for IoT Hub are as follows:

- The SKU edition, which is the size of the IoT Hub
- Number of units

SKU edition

The SKU in IoT Hub determines the number of messages a hub can handle per unit per day, and this includes both incoming as well as outgoing messages. There are four tiers. They are as follows:

- **Free**: This allows for 8,000 messages per unit per day and allows both incoming and outgoing messages. A maximum of 1 unit can be provisioned. This edition is suitable for gaining familiarity and testing out the capabilities of the IoT Hub service.
- **Standard (S1)**: This allows for 400,000 messages per unit per day and allows both incoming and outgoing messages. A maximum of 200 units can be provisioned. This edition is suitable for a small number of messages.
- **Standard (S2)**: This allows for six million messages per unit per day and allows both incoming and outgoing messages. A maximum of 200 units can be provisioned. This edition is suitable for a large number of messages.

- **Standard (S3)**: This allows for 300 million messages per unit per day and allows both incoming and outgoing messages. A maximum of 10 units can be provisioned. This edition is suitable for a very large amount of messages:

An astute reader would have noticed that the Standard S3 tier allows for a maximum of only 10 units, compared to other standard units that allow for 200 units. This is directly related to the size of the compute resources that are provisioned to run IoT services. The size and capability of virtual machines for Standard S3 is significantly higher compared to other tiers where the size remains the same.

Units

Units define the number of instances of each SKU running behind the service. For example, 2 units of the Standard S1 SKU tier will mean that the IoT Hub is capable of handling *400K * 2 = 800K* messages per day.

More units increases the scalability of the application:

High availability

IoT Hub is a PaaS platform from Azure. Customers and users do not directly interact with the underlying number and size of virtual machines on which the IoT Hub service is running. Users decide on the region, the SKU of the IoT Hub, and the number of units for their application. The rest of the configuration is determined and executed by Azure behind the scenes. Azure ensures that every PaaS service is highly available by default. It does so by ensuring that multiple virtual machines provisioned behind the service are on separate racks in the data center. It does this by placing those virtual machines on an availability set and on a separate fault and update domain. This helps in high availability for both planned as well as unplanned maintenance. Availability sets take care of high availability at data center level.

To achieve high availability across multiple data centers in a region or across regions, customers should take additional action to provision additional IoT Hub services in different regions, ensure that devices are registered at all IoT Hub services, and ensure that each have the same identifier. The best way to do this is to create a separate monitoring application (such as a web application), all tied up using Traffic Manager, and continually monitor the Traffic Manager endpoint for current location unavailability, such that traffic can be redirected to other IoT Hubs if needs be. For this to happen, you'd need to write logic to route the device messages to the new IoT Hub.

Summary

IoT is one of the biggest upcoming technologies of this decade and is already disrupting industries. Things that sounded impossible are suddenly possible. IoT Hub is a platform that eases the creation and delivery of IoT solutions to the customer in a faster, better, and cheaper way. It provides implementations of all industry protocols, such as the MQTT protocol and AMQP, along with field gateways that can adapt non-standard devices. It provides high availability, scalability, and security features to both messages and the overall solution. It provides connectivity to a large number of Azure services and helps in routing messages to multiple different endpoints, each capable of processing messages. IoT can fast-track the entire development life cycle and help expedite time-to-market for companies.

Azure provides numerous data storage options and services. This is the last chapter of the book, and I hope readers really enjoyed reading all the chapters and are ready to architect solutions on Azure.

Cheers!

Other Books You May Enjoy

If you enjoyed this book, you may be interested in these other books by Packt:

Hands-On Azure for Developers

Kamil Mrzygłód

ISBN: 978-1-78934-062-4

- Implement serverless components such as Azure functions and logic apps
- Integrate applications with available storages and containers
- Understand messaging components, including Azure Event Hubs and Azure Queue Storage
- Gain an understanding of Application Insights and other proper monitoring solutions
- Store your data with services such as Azure SQL and Azure Data Lake Storage
- Develop fast and scalable cloud applications

Hands-On Linux Administration on Azure
Frederik Vos

ISBN: 978-1-78913-096-6

- Understand why Azure is the ideal solution for your open source workloads
- Master essential Linux skills and learn to find your way around the Linux environment
- Deploy Linux in an Azure environment
- Use configuration management to manage Linux in Azure
- Manage containers in an Azure environment
- Enhance Linux security and use Azure's identity management systems
- Automate deployment with Azure Resource Manager (ARM) and Powershell
- Employ Ansible to manage Linux instances in an Azure cloud environment

Leave a review - let other readers know what you think

Please share your thoughts on this book with others by leaving a review on the site that you bought it from. If you purchased the book from Amazon, please leave us an honest review on this book's Amazon page. This is vital so that other potential readers can see and use your unbiased opinion to make purchasing decisions, we can understand what our customers think about our products, and our authors can see your feedback on the title that they have worked with Packt to create. It will only take a few minutes of your time, but is valuable to other potential customers, our authors, and Packt. Thank you!

Index

D